THE PRINCE OF TENNIS
VOL. 2
The SHONEN JUMP Graphic Novel Edition

STORY AND ART BY
TAKESHI KONOMI

English Adaptation/Gerard Jones
Translation/Joe Yamazaki
Touch-up & Lettering/Andy Ristaino
Graphics & Cover Design/Sean Lee
Editor/Michelle Pangilinan

Managing Editor/Frances E. Wall
Editorial Director/Elizabeth Kawasaki
VP & Editor in Chief/Yumi Hoashi
Sr. Director of Acquisitions/Rika Inouye
Sr. VP of Marketing/Liza Coppola
Exec. VP of Sales & Marketing/John Easum
Publisher/Hyoe Narita

Published by VIZ Media, LLC
P.O. Box 77064
San Francisco, CA 94107

Shonen Jump Edition
10 9 8 7 6 5 4 3
First printing, June 2004
Second printing, August 2005
Third printing, August 2006

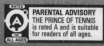

PARENTAL ADVISORY
THE PRINCE OF TENNIS
is rated A and is suitable
for readers of all ages.

THE WORLD'S
MOST POPULAR MANGA

www.viz.com

www.shonenjump.com

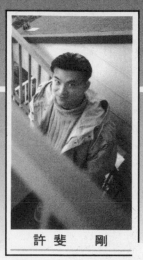

許斐 剛

The weather's good, so I want to go outside.
I have no plans, so I want to go outside.
But even with the clear weather recently, I can't go out at all.
Well, at least I get lots of sunlight from my window.
Everyone seems to be exercising their bodies outside.
Of course, it's because they're reading Prince of Tennis!

Takeshi Konomi 2000

About Takeshi Konomi

Takeshi Konomi exploded onto the manga scene with the incredible manga **The Prince of Tennis**. His refined art style and sleek character designs proved popular with **Weekly Shonen Jump** readers and **The Prince of Tennis** became the No. 1 sports manga in Japan almost overnight. Its cast of cool tennis players enticed legions of female readers, although it was originally intended to be a boy's comic. The manga continues to be a success and is now on its 20th graphic novel. A hit anime series was created as well as several video games and mountains of merchandise.

Shonen Jump Graphic Novel

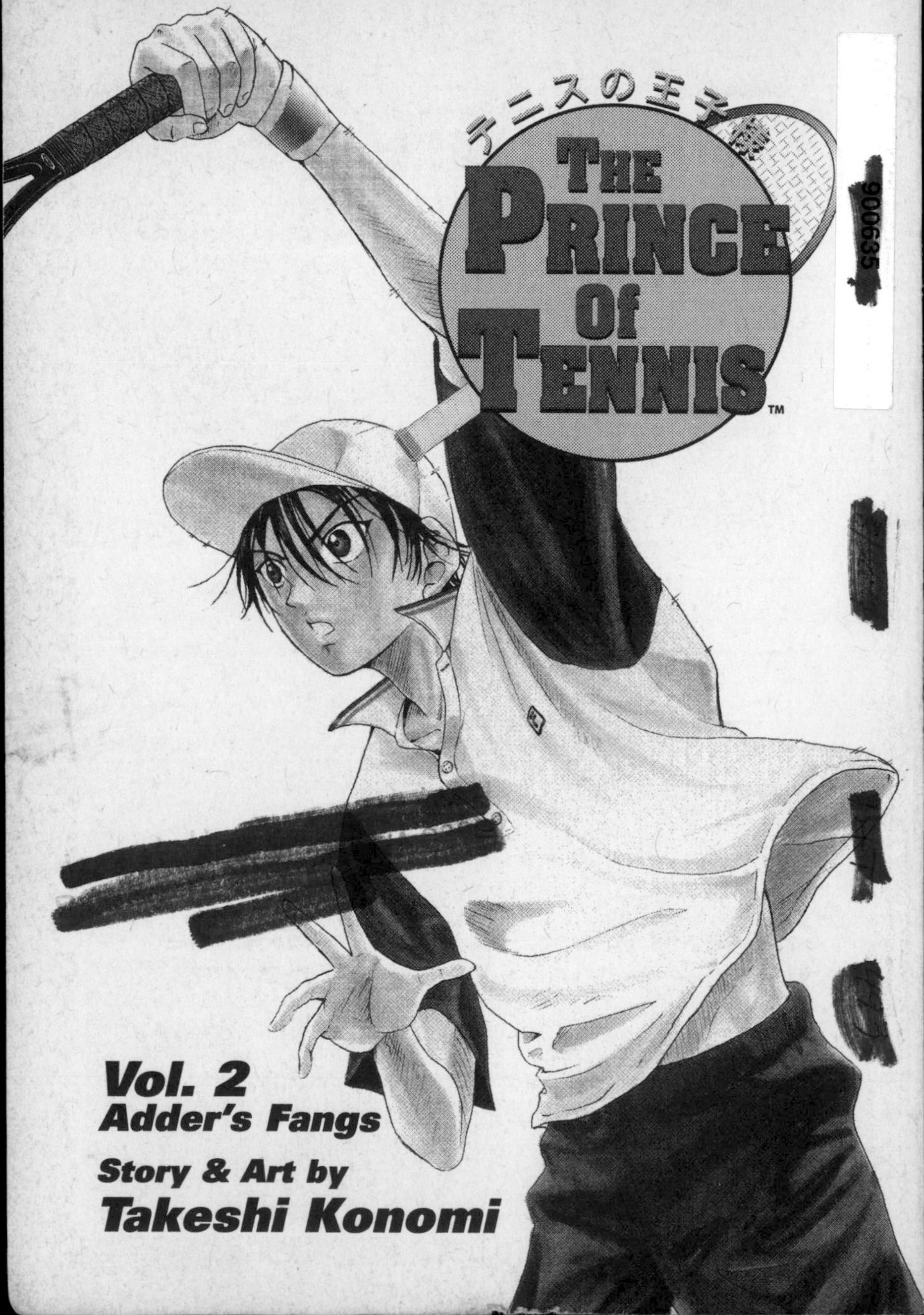
テニスの王子様
THE PRINCE OF TENNIS™

Vol. 2

Adder's Fangs

Story & Art by

Takeshi Konomi

THE PRINCE OF TENNIS

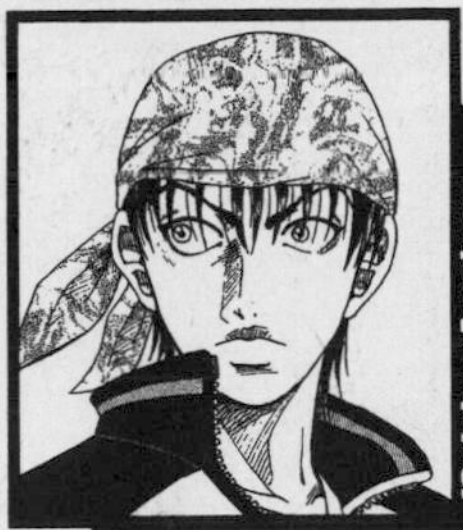
Kaoru Kaido
(Seishun Academy Tennis Team, 8th Grade)

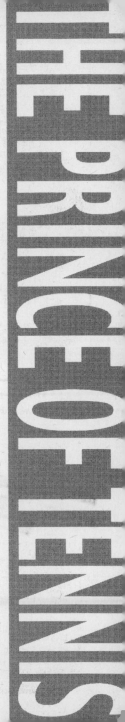

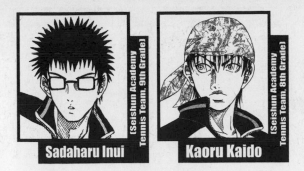

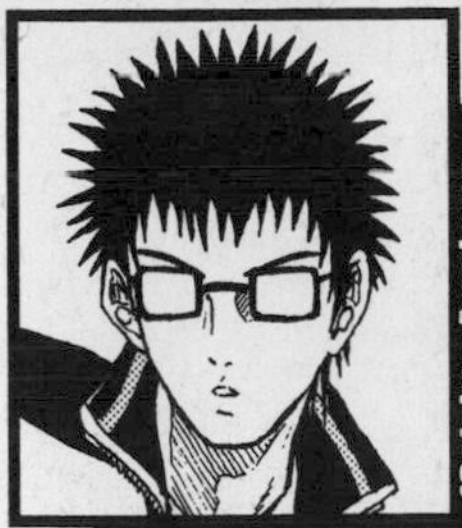
Sadaharu Inui
(Seishun Academy Tennis Team, 9th Grade)

STORY & CHARACTERS

VOLUME 1 ▶ 2

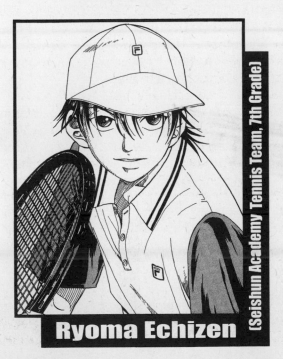

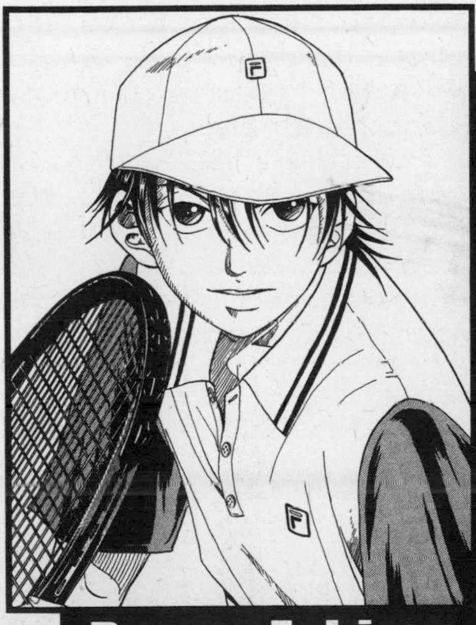
Ryoma Echizen
(Seishun Academy Tennis Team, 7th Grade)

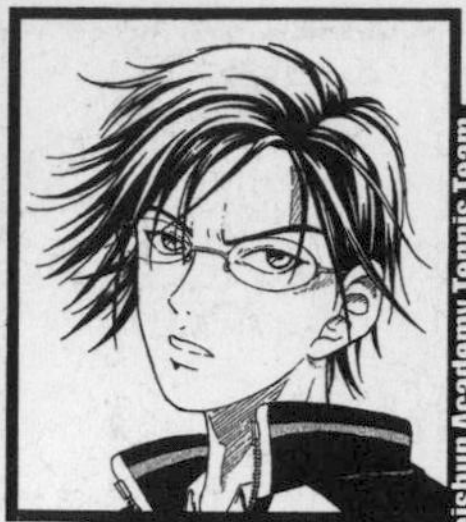

Kunimitsu Tezuka (Seishun Academy Tennis Team Captain, 9th Grade)

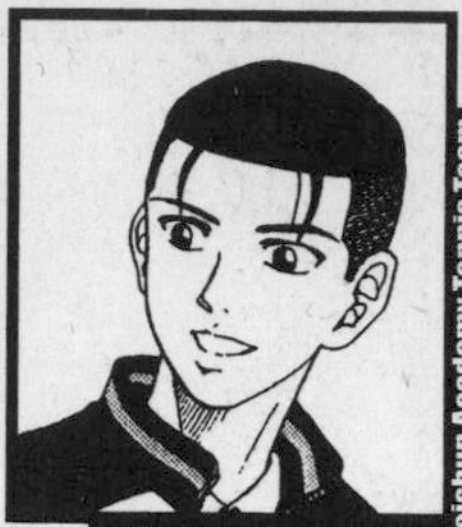

Shuichiro Oishi (Seishun Academy Tennis Team Alternate Captain, 9th Grade)

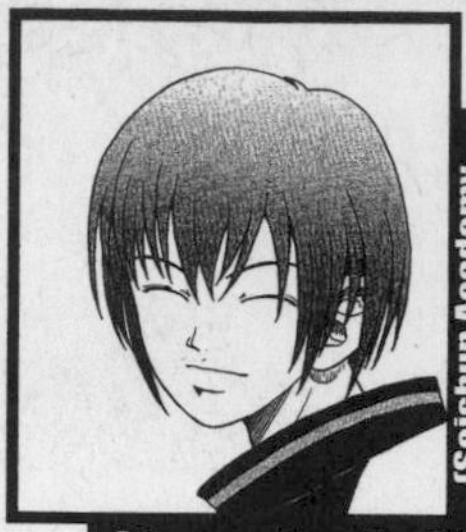

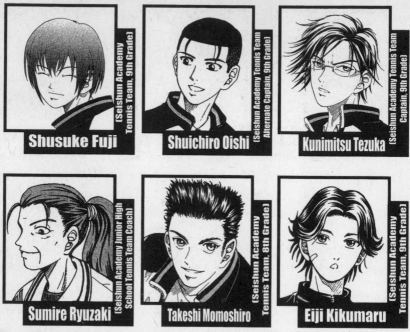

Shusuke Fuji (Seishun Academy Tennis Team, 9th Grade)

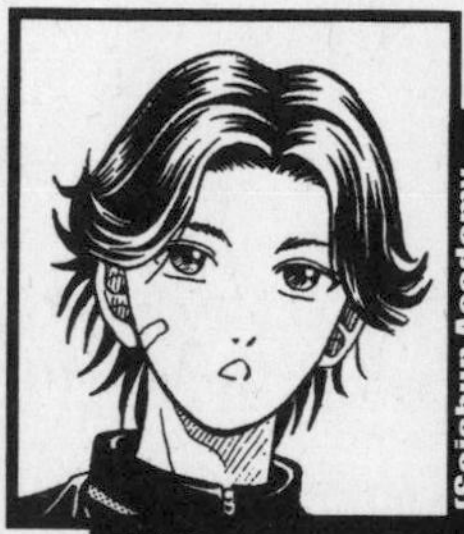

Eiji Kikumaru (Seishun Academy Tennis Team, 9th Grade)

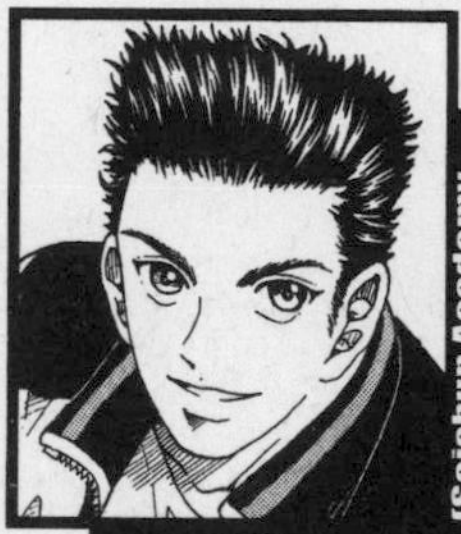

Takeshi Momoshiro (Seishun Academy Tennis Team, 8th Grade)

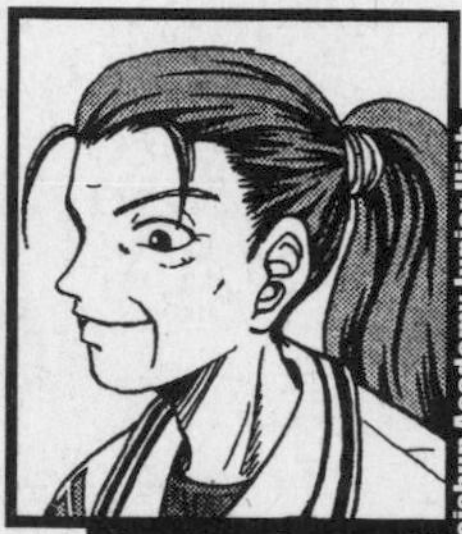

Sumire Ryuzaki (Seishun Academy Junior High School Tennis Team Coach)

Ryoma Echizen, who's just enrolled at Seishun Academy after years in America, is a tennis prodigy: winner of 4 consecutive US Junior Tournaments. His cool confidence raises the hackles of a few older students on the tennis team, and they challenge him to a game—

but none of them even comes close to his skill and knowledge of the game. Now intramural matches to determine the starting members of the team for the upcoming city tournament are about to begin, and although the rules don't allow 7th graders to play in tournaments, the captain has arranged for Ryoma to enter the ranking matches.

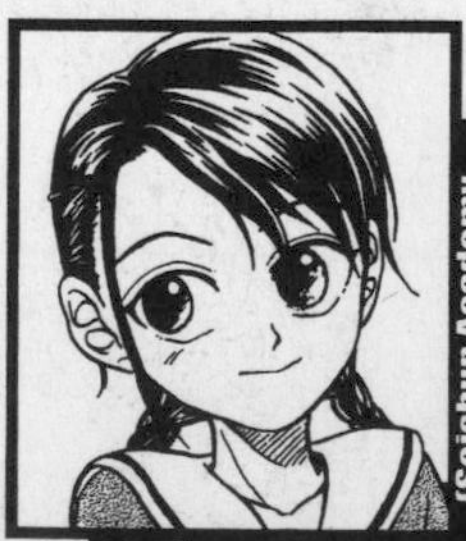

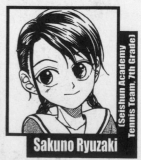

Sakuno Ryuzaki (Seishun Academy Tennis Team, 7th Grade)

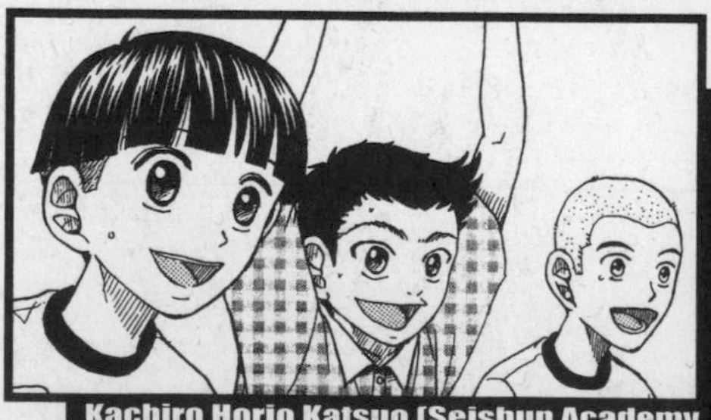

Kachiro, Horio, Katsuo (Seishun Academy Tennis Team, 7th Grade)

CONTENTS

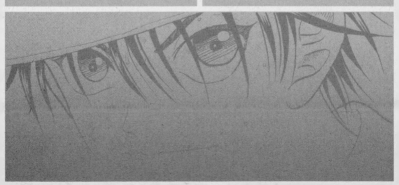

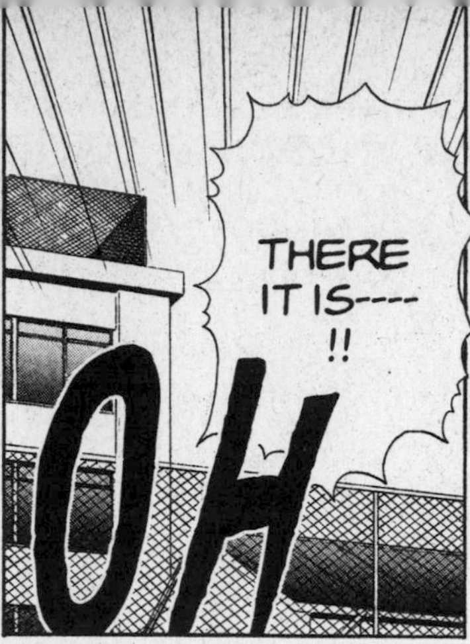
THERE IT IS---- !!
OH

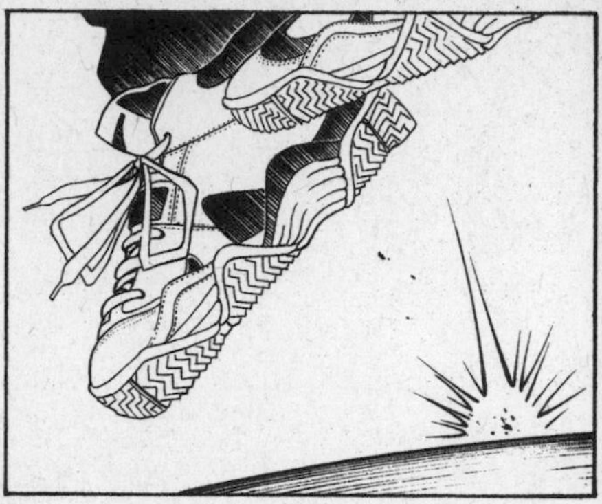

GENIUS 8

ADDER'S FANGS

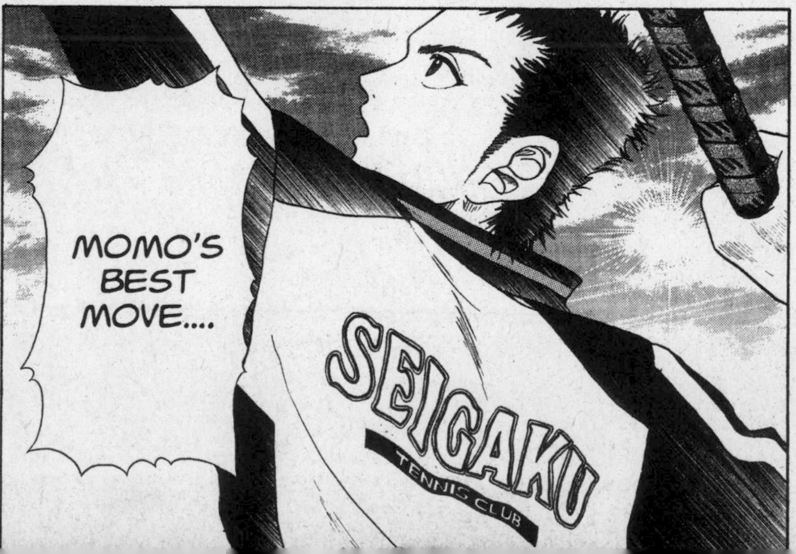
MOMO'S BEST MOVE....
SEIGAKU
TENNIS CLUB

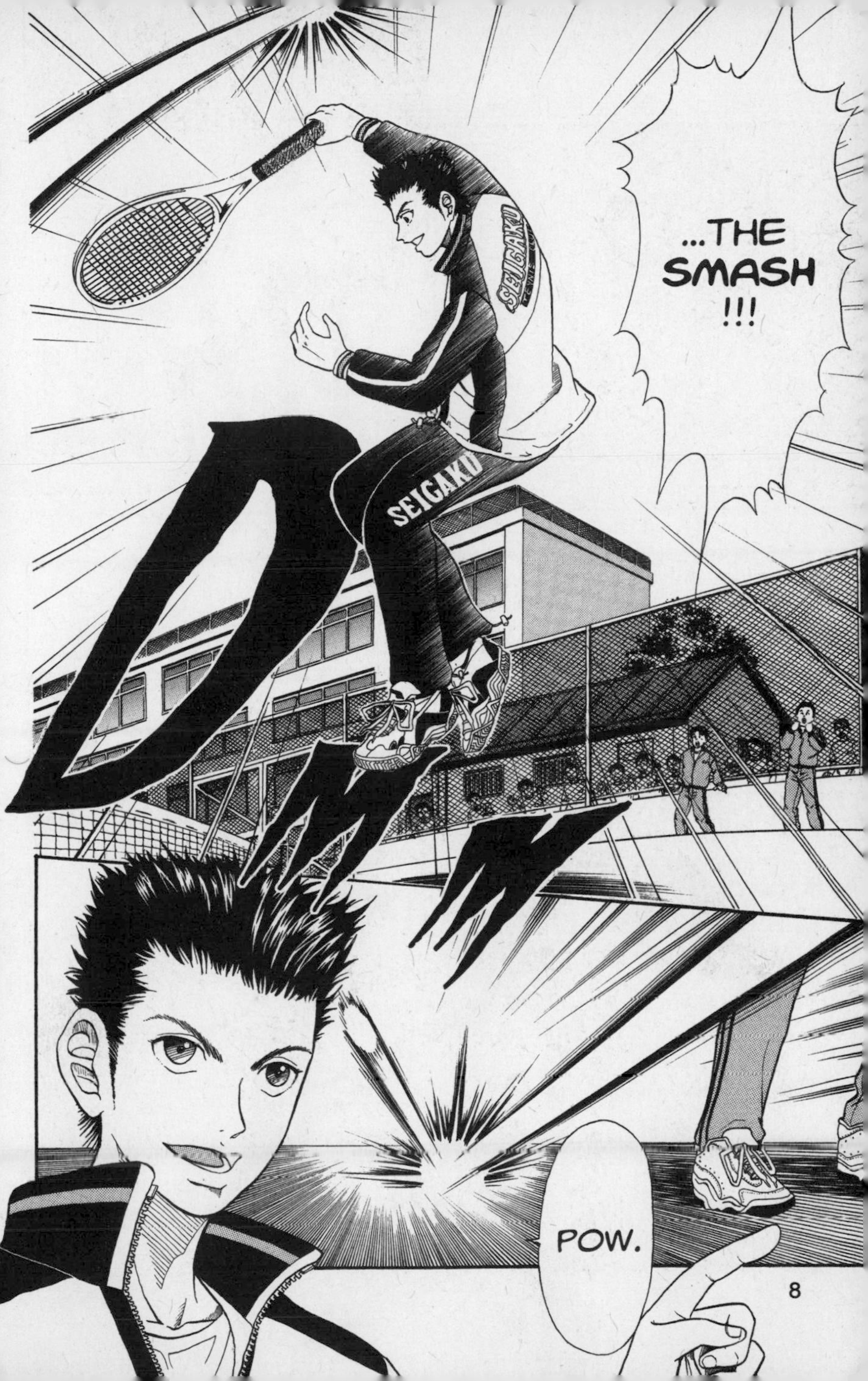
...THE SMASH !!!
POW.

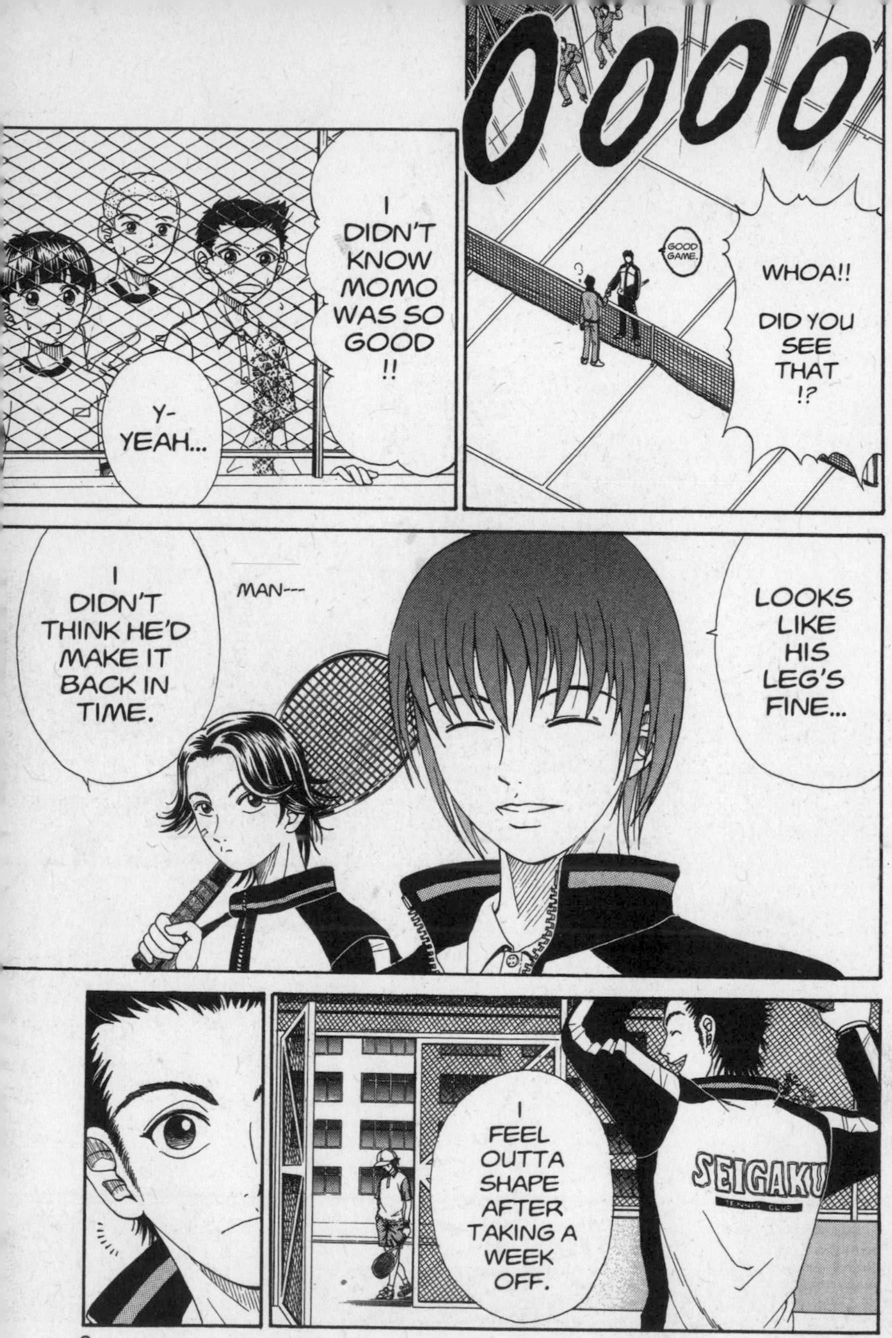
OOOO
WHOA!! DID YOU SEE THAT!?
GOOD GAME.
I DIDN'T KNOW MOMO WAS SO GOOD!!
Y-YEAH...
LOOKS LIKE HIS LEG'S FINE...
MAN---
I DIDN'T THINK HE'D MAKE IT BACK IN TIME.
I FEEL OUTTA SHAPE AFTER TAKING A WEEK OFF.
SEIGAKU
TENNIS CLUB

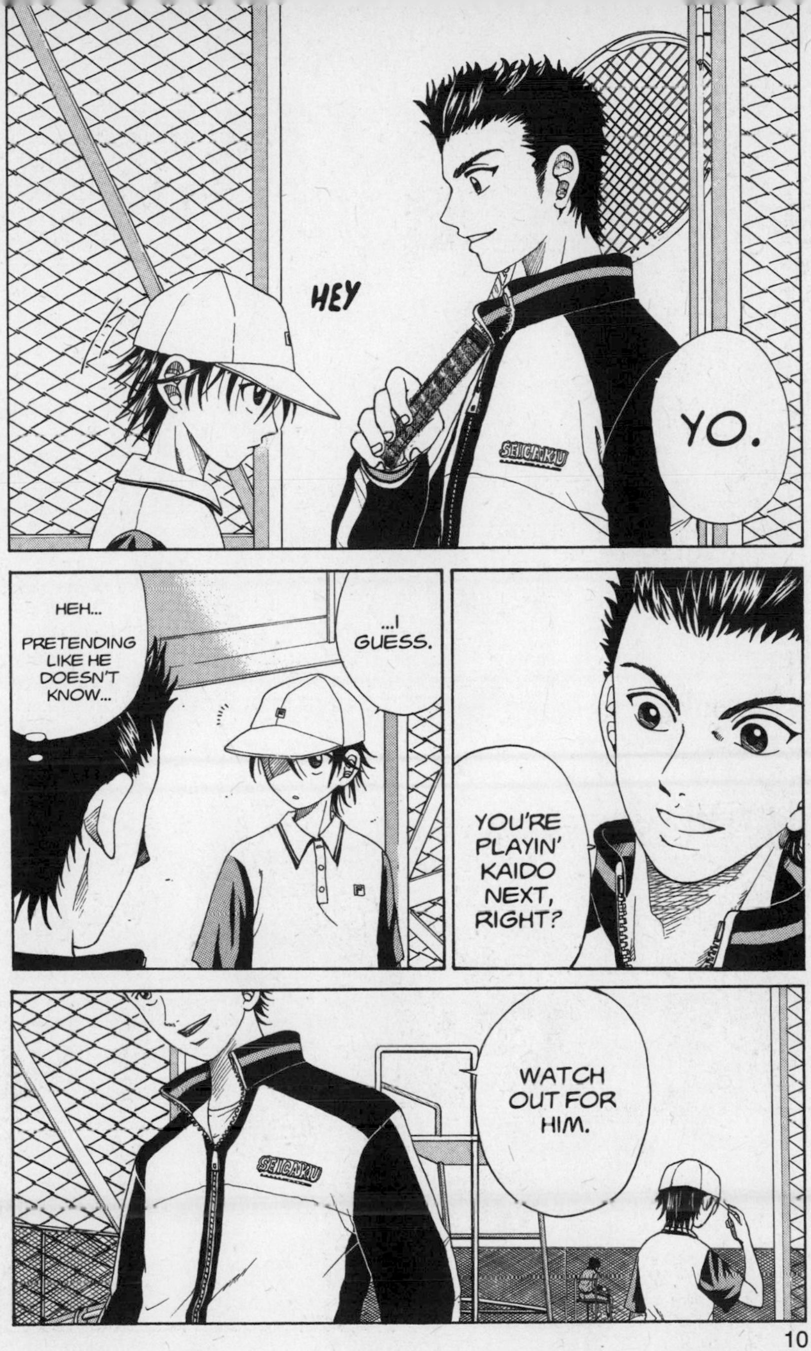
HEY
YO.
YOU'RE PLAYIN' KAIDO NEXT, RIGHT?
...I GUESS.
HEH... PRETENDING LIKE HE DOESN'T KNOW...
WATCH OUT FOR HIM.
SEIGAKU
SEIGAKU

READ THIS WAY

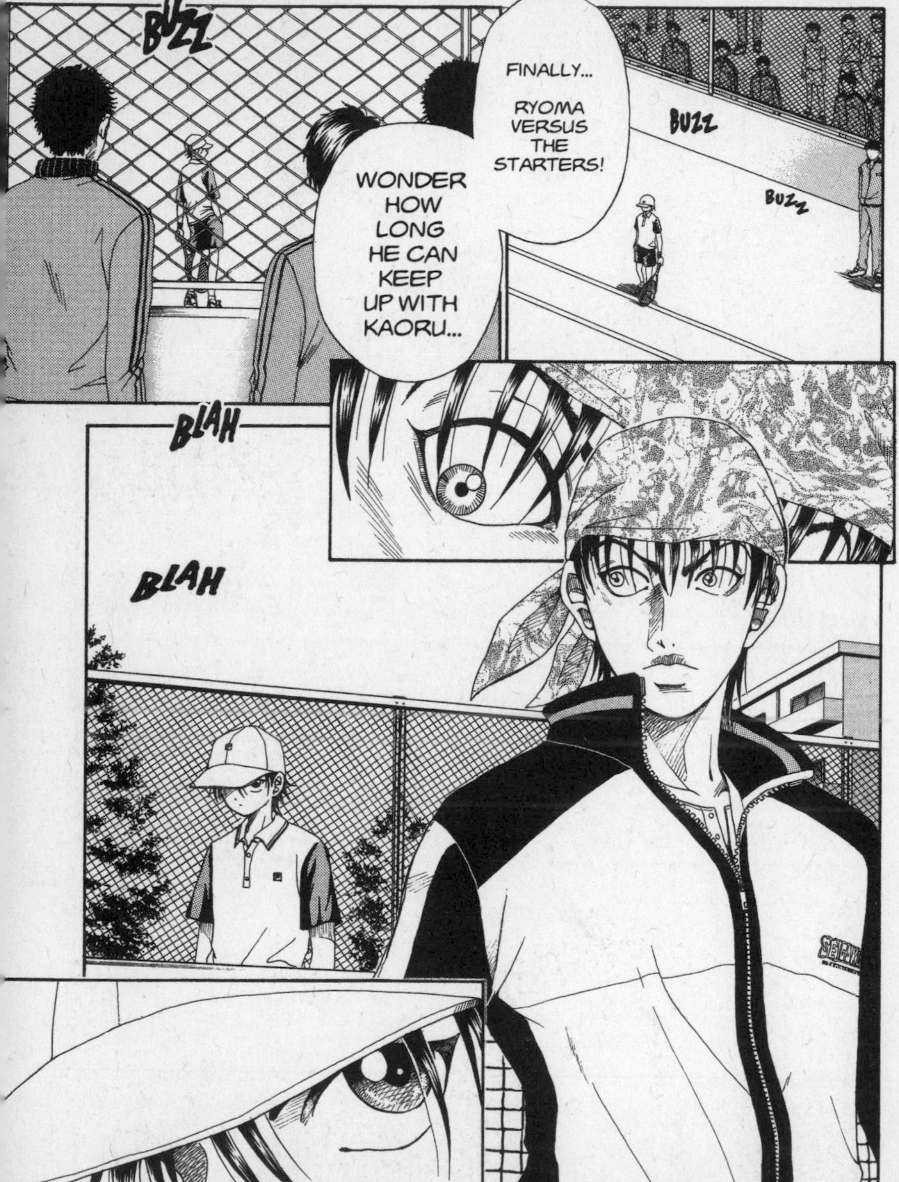
FINALLY... RYOMA VERSUS THE STARTERS!
BUZZ
BUZZ
BUZZ
WONDER HOW LONG HE CAN KEEP UP WITH KAORU...
BLAH
BLAH

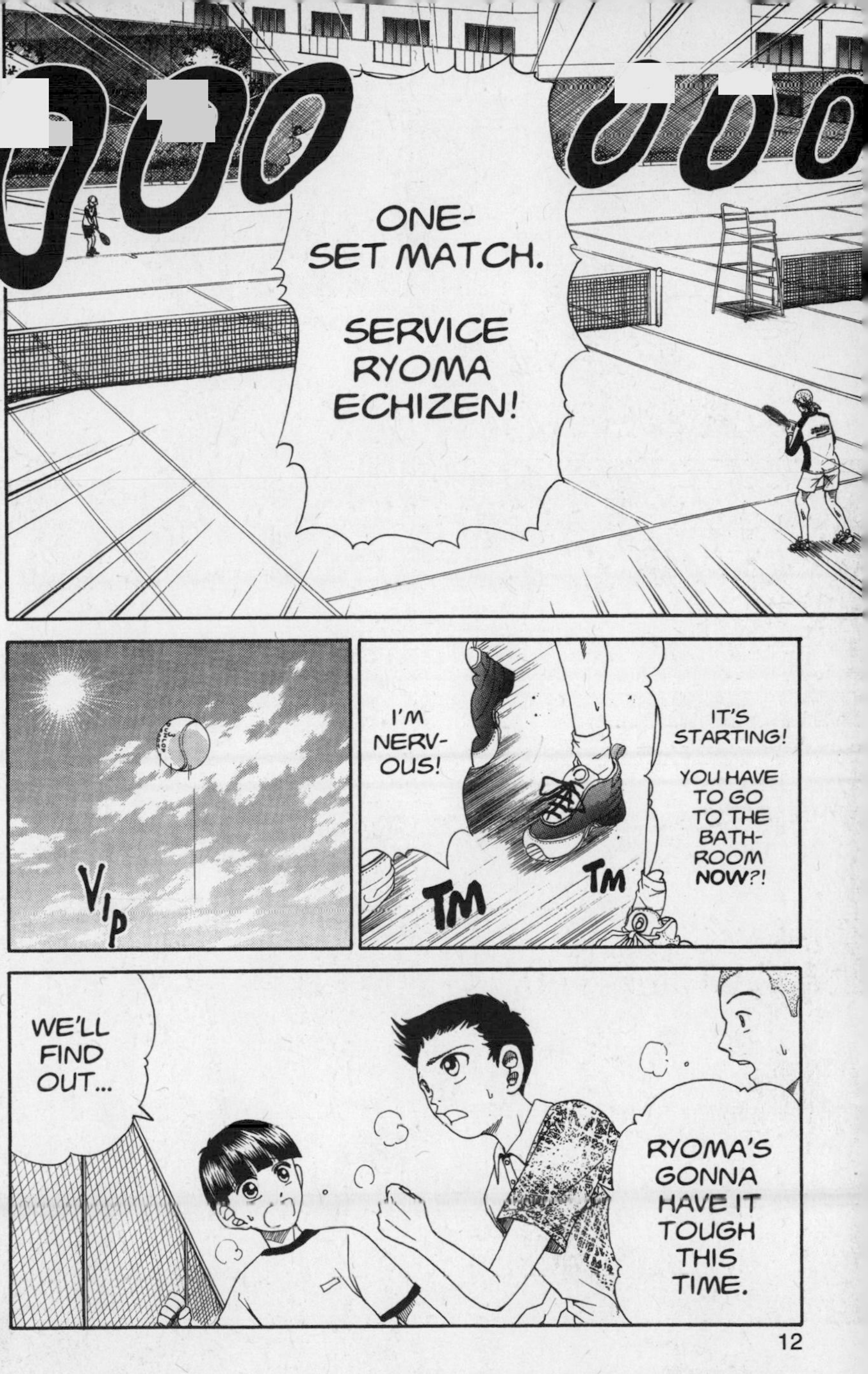
ONE-SET MATCH.
SERVICE RYOMA ECHIZEN!
IT'S STARTING!
YOU HAVE TO GO TO THE BATHROOM NOW?!
I'M NERVOUS!
TM
TM
VIP
RYOMA'S GONNA HAVE IT TOUGH THIS TIME.
WE'LL FIND OUT...

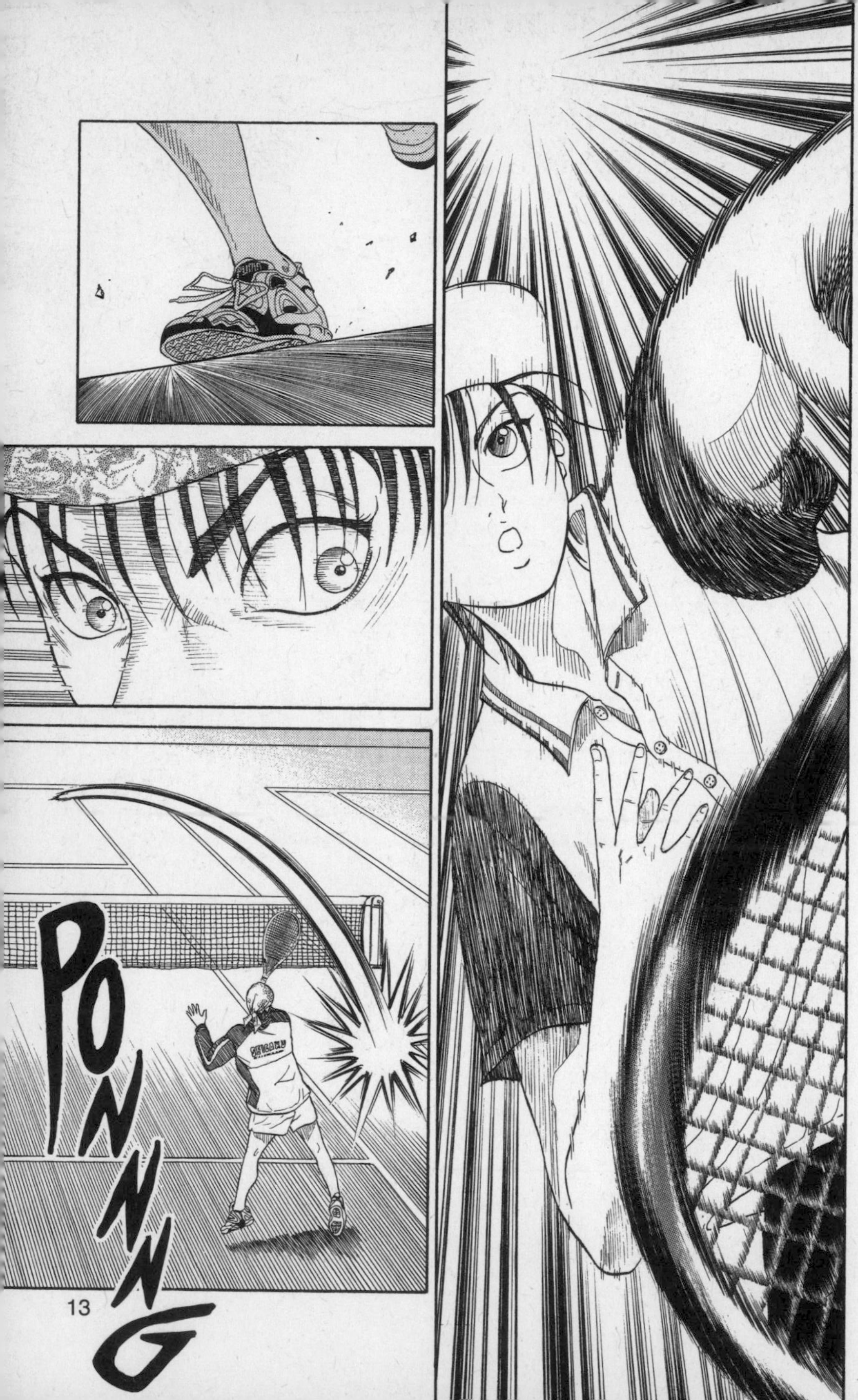
PONNNG

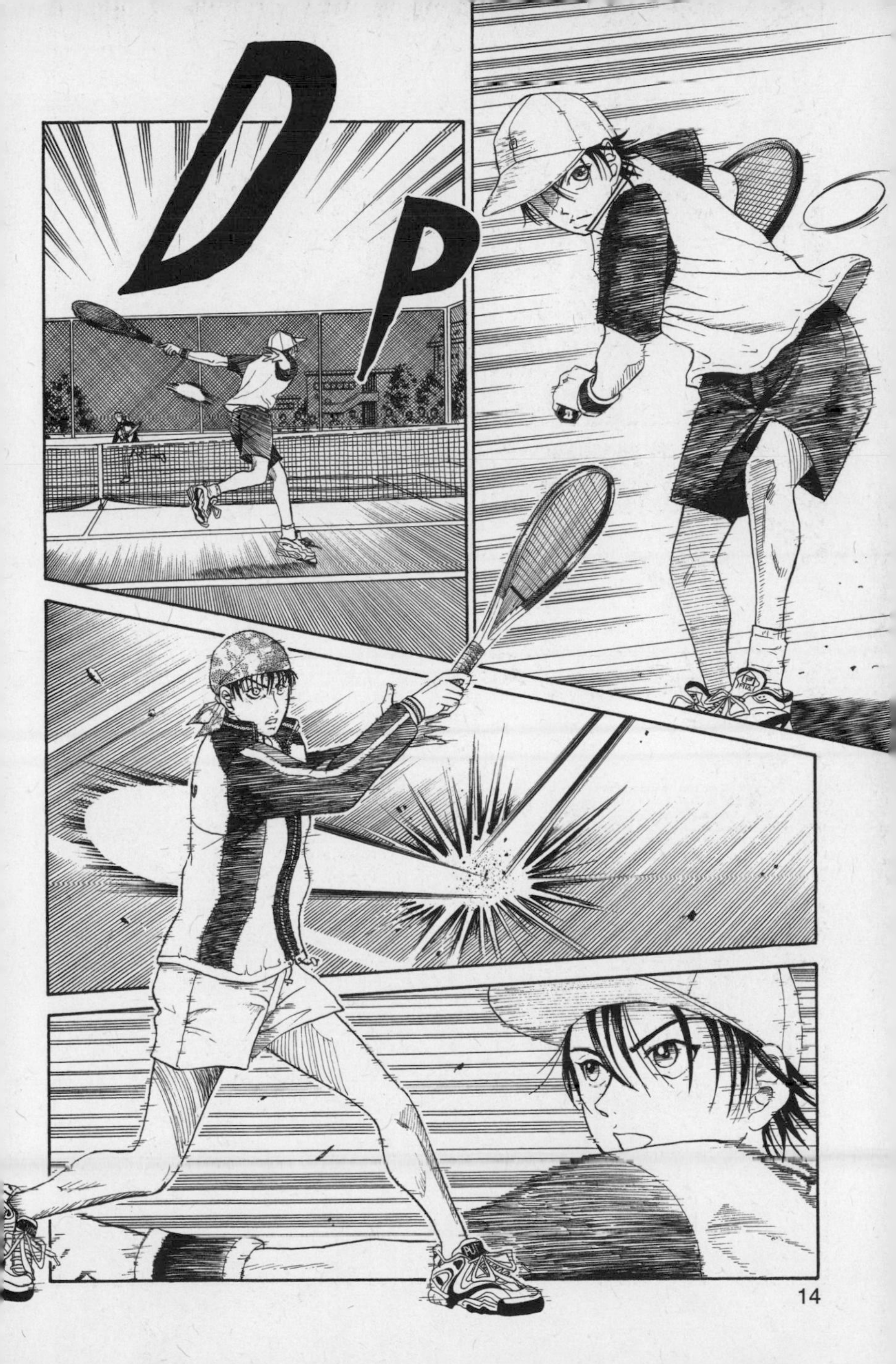
DP

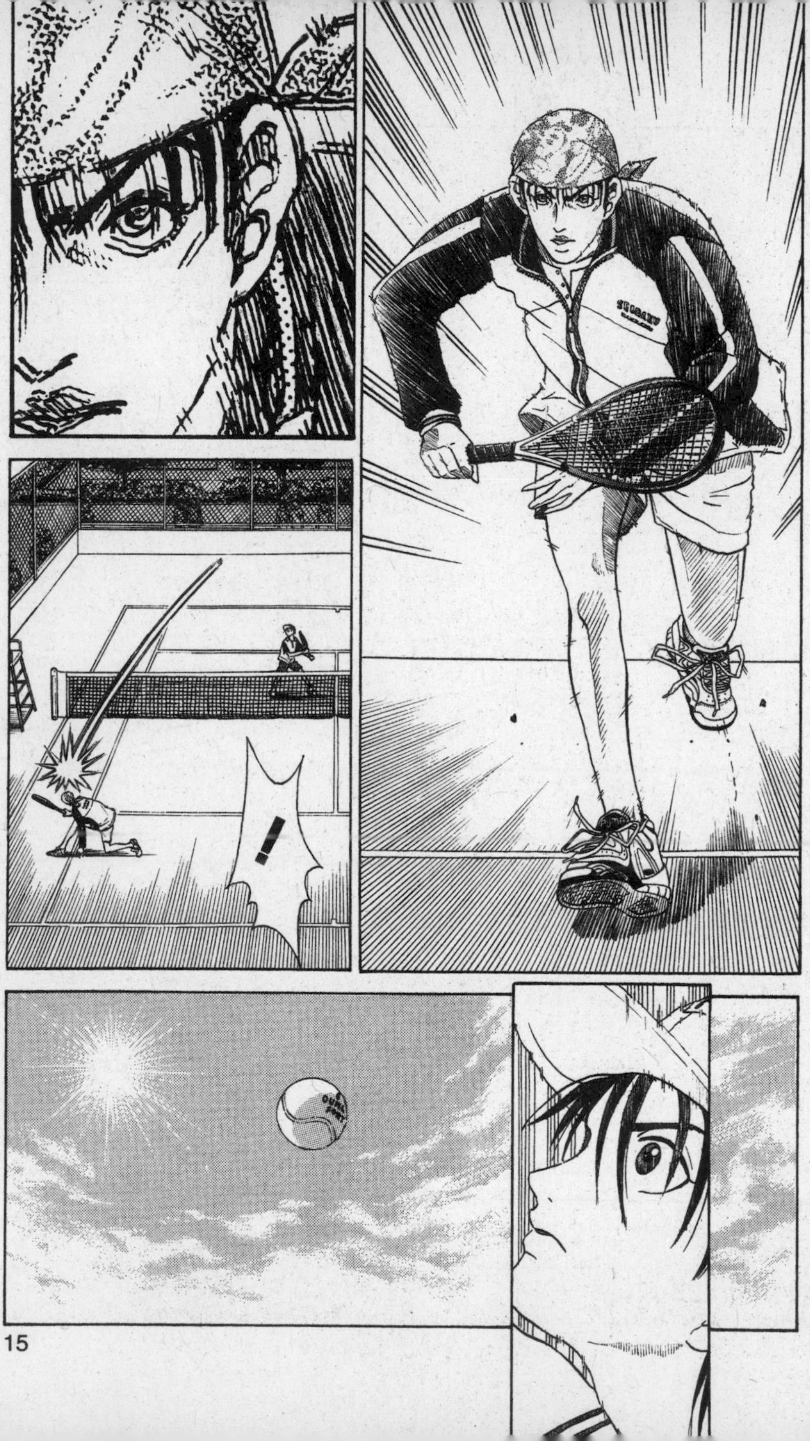
SEIGAKU
!

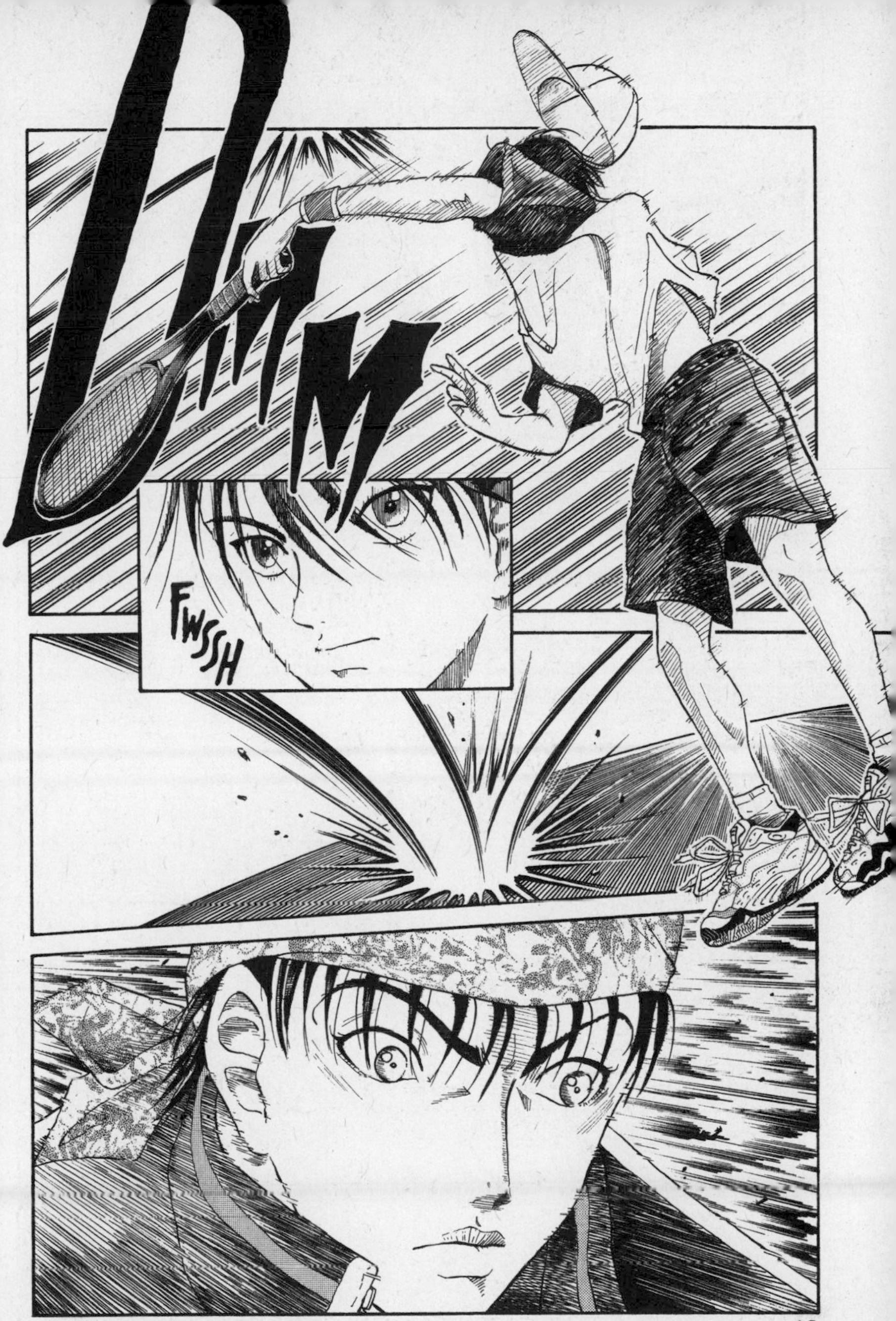
DMM
FWSSH

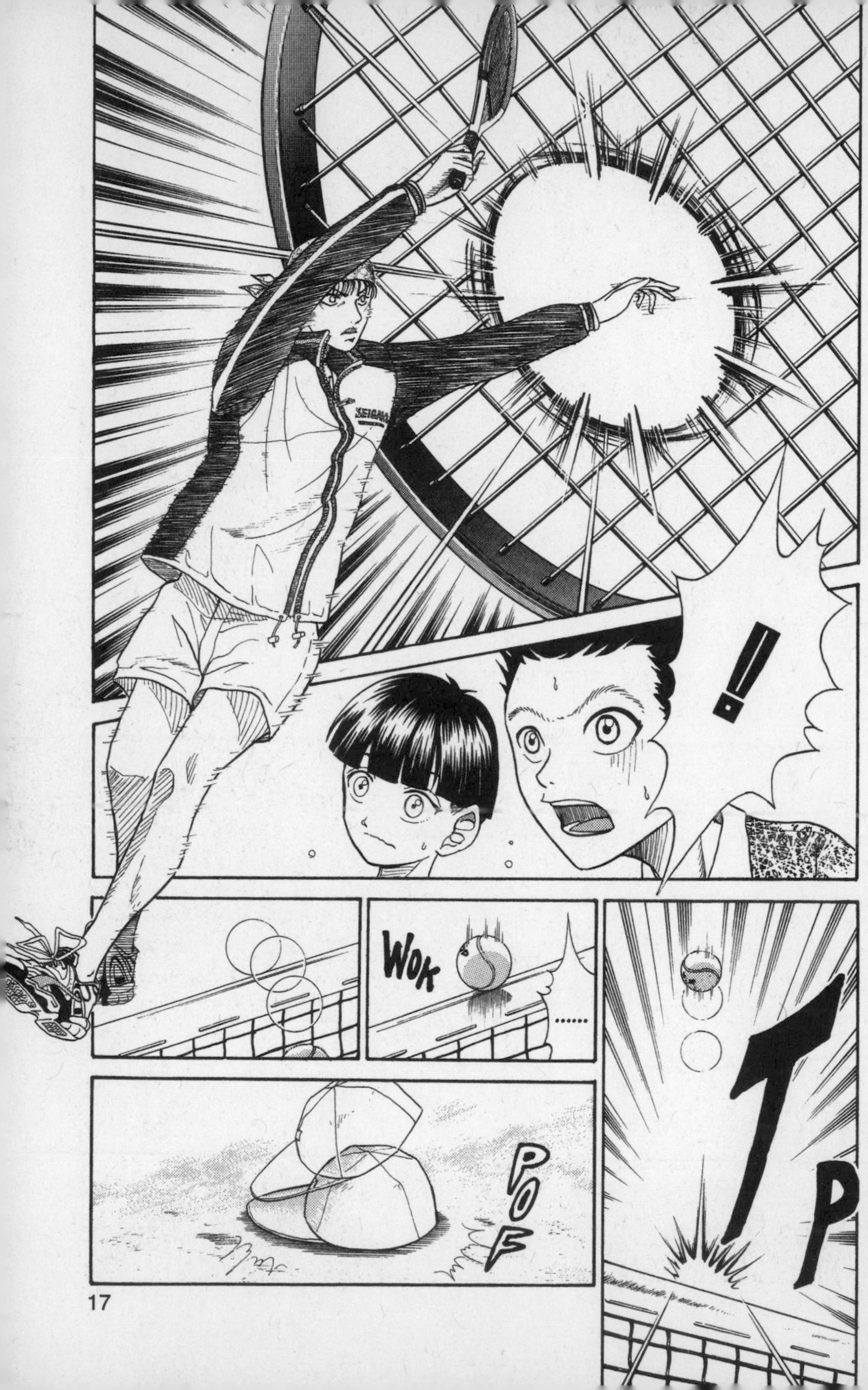
!
TP
WOK
......
POF

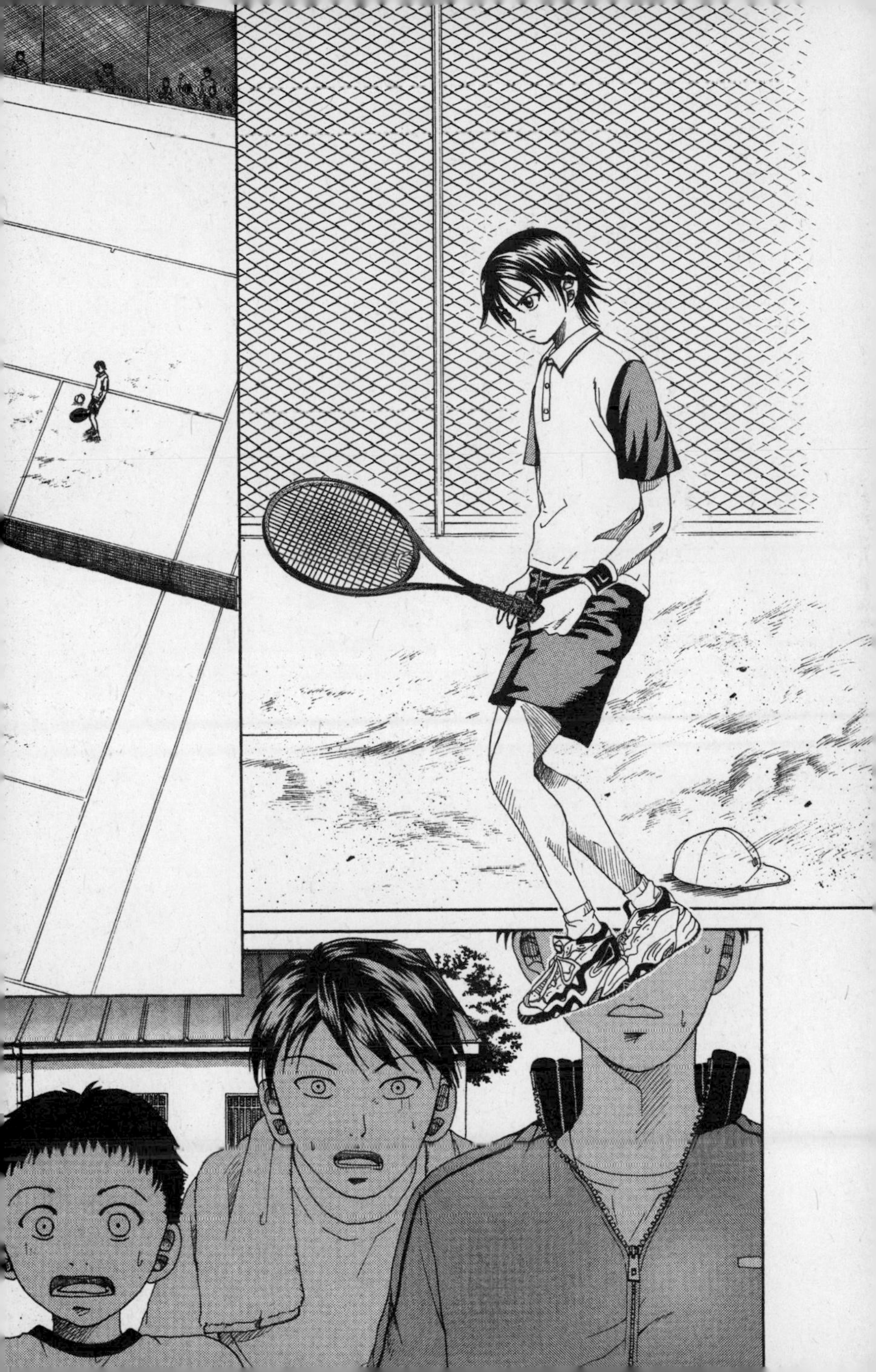

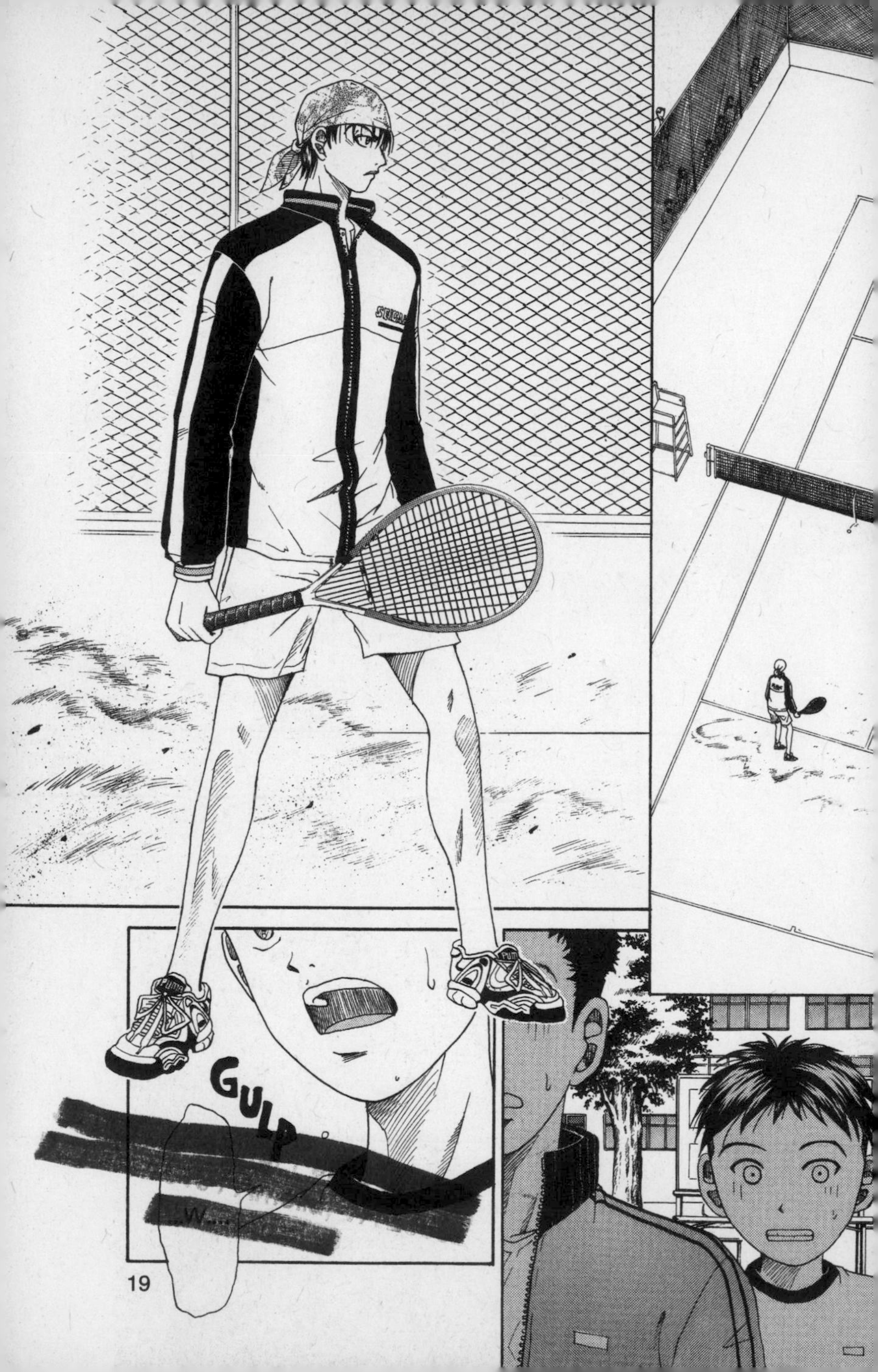
GULP
[redacted]

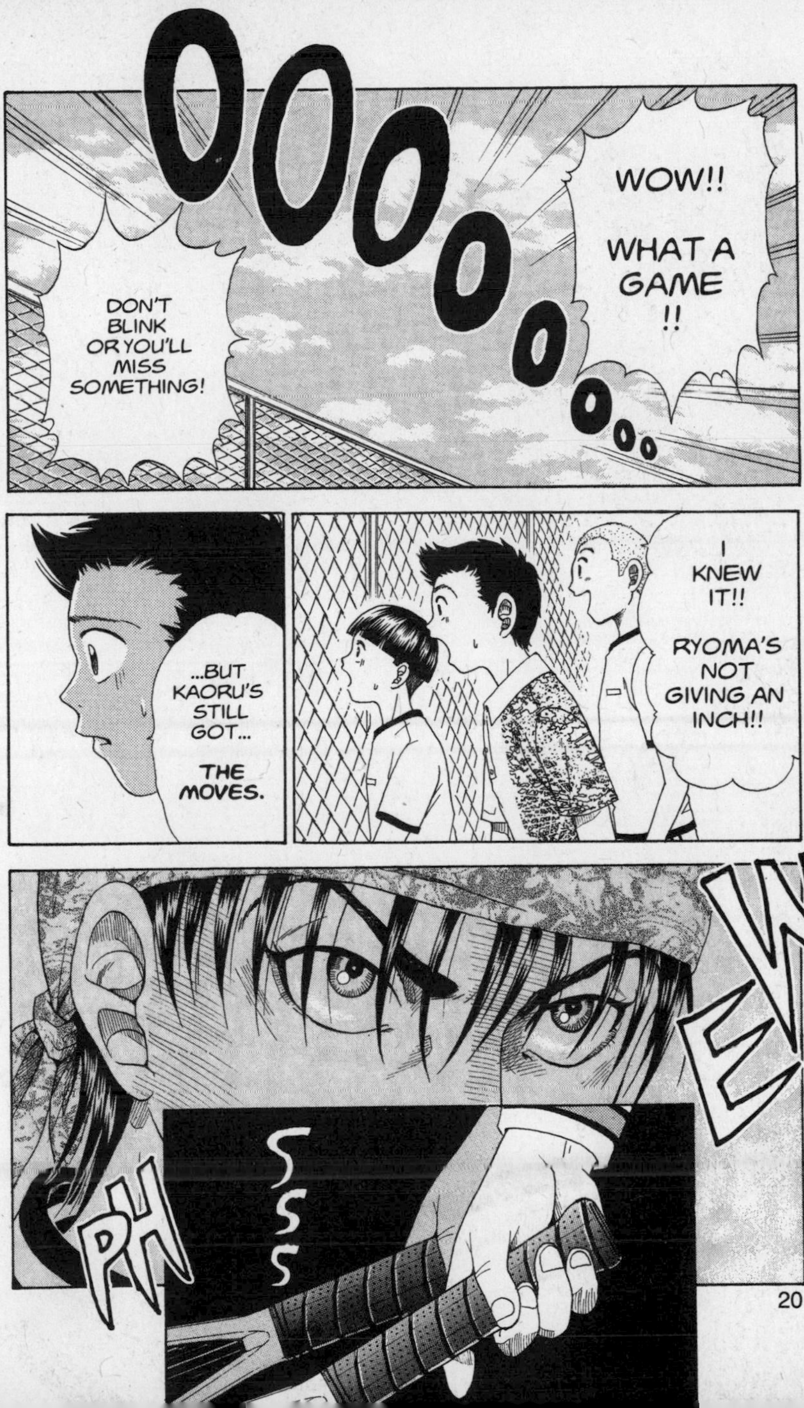
WOW!!
WHAT A GAME !!
OOOOOOOOoo
DON'T BLINK OR YOU'LL MISS SOMETHING!
I KNEW IT!!
RYOMA'S NOT GIVING AN INCH!!
...BUT KAORU'S STILL GOT...
THE MOVES.
PHSSSEWW

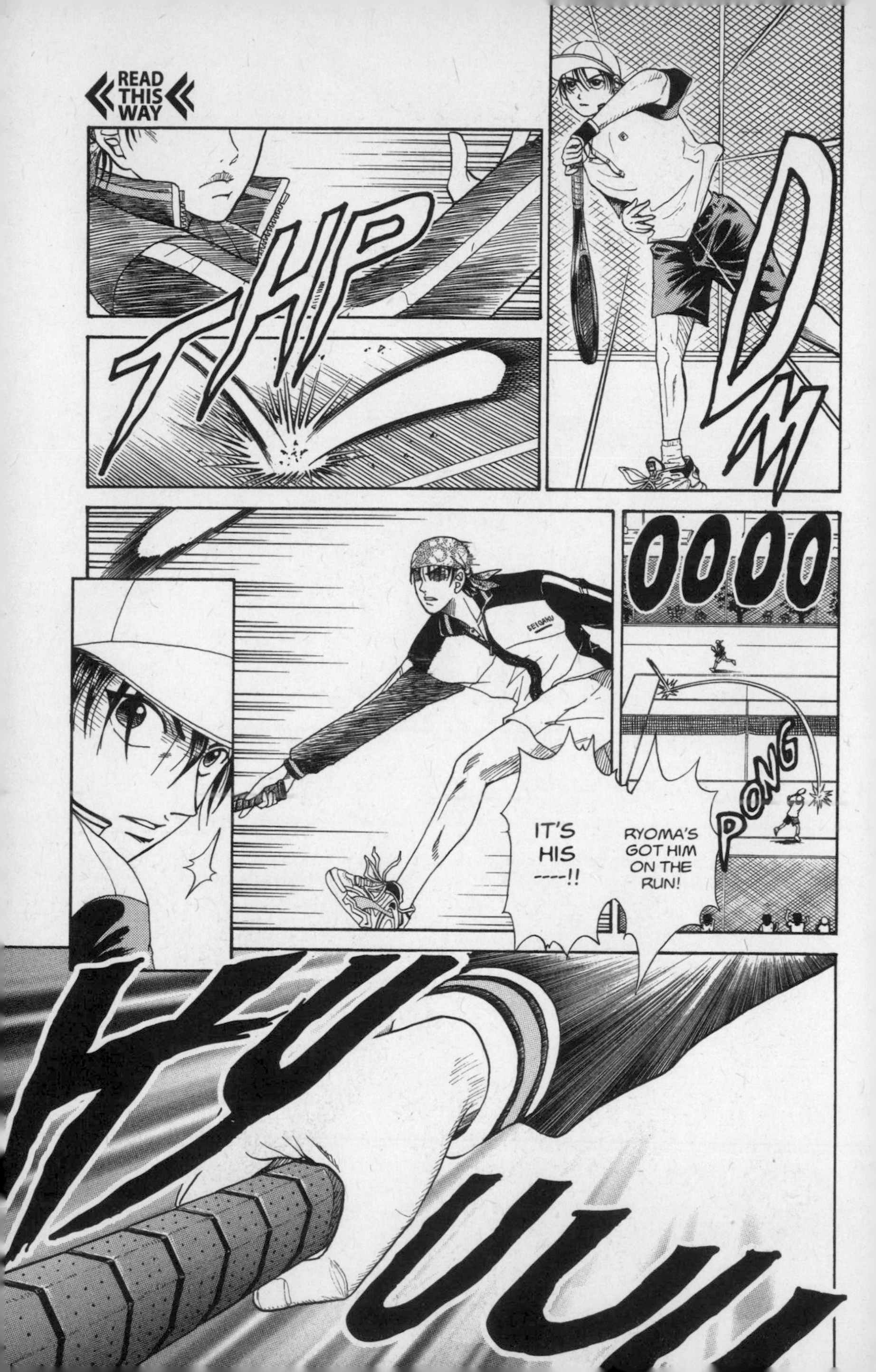
READ THIS WAY
DOM
THP
OOOO
PONG
RYOMA'S GOT HIM ON THE RUN!
IT'S HIS ----!!
KYU
UUUU

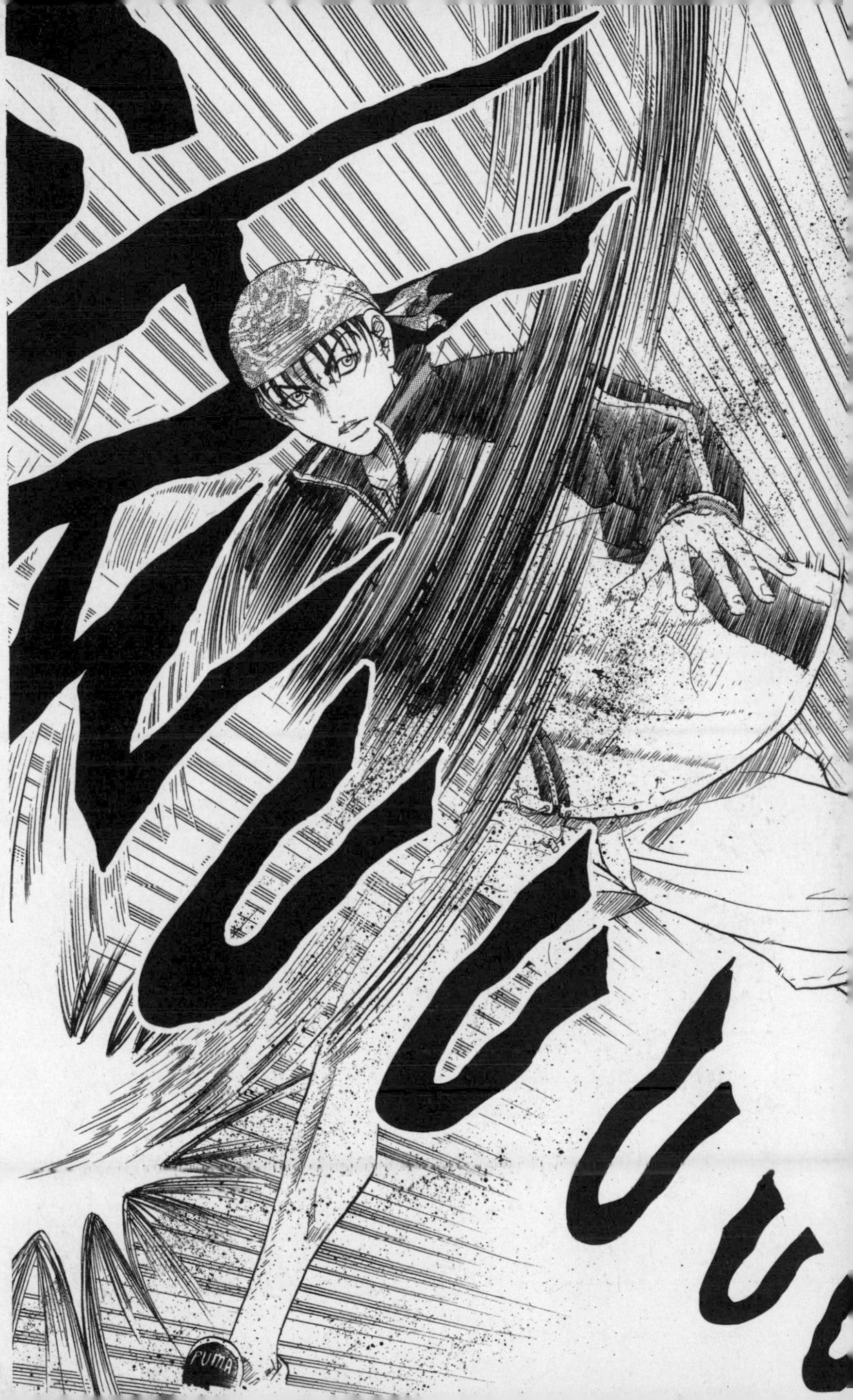
PUMA

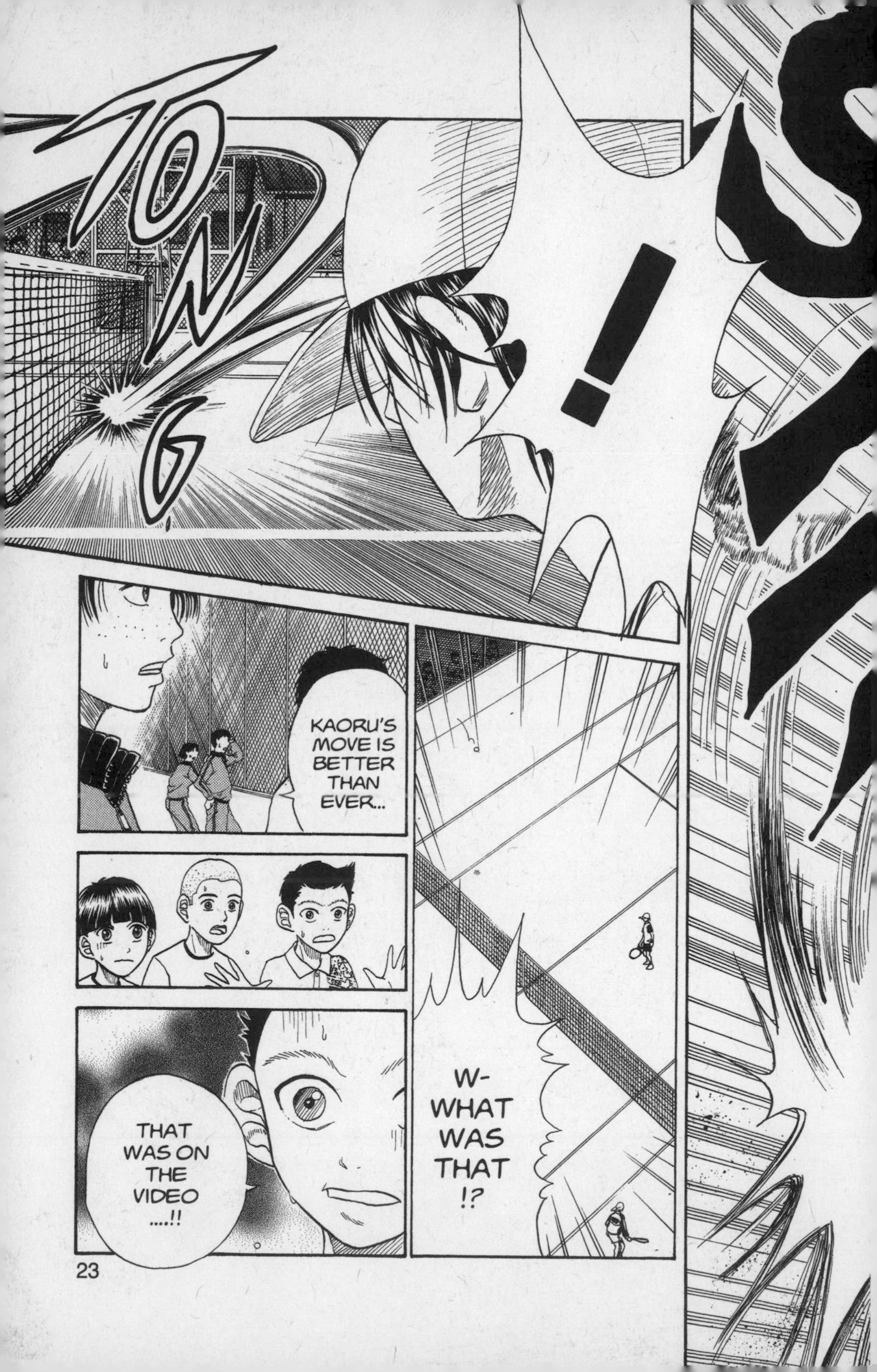
!
TONG
W- WHAT WAS THAT !?
KAORU'S MOVE IS BETTER THAN EVER...
THAT WAS ON THE VIDEO ....!!

READ THIS WAY

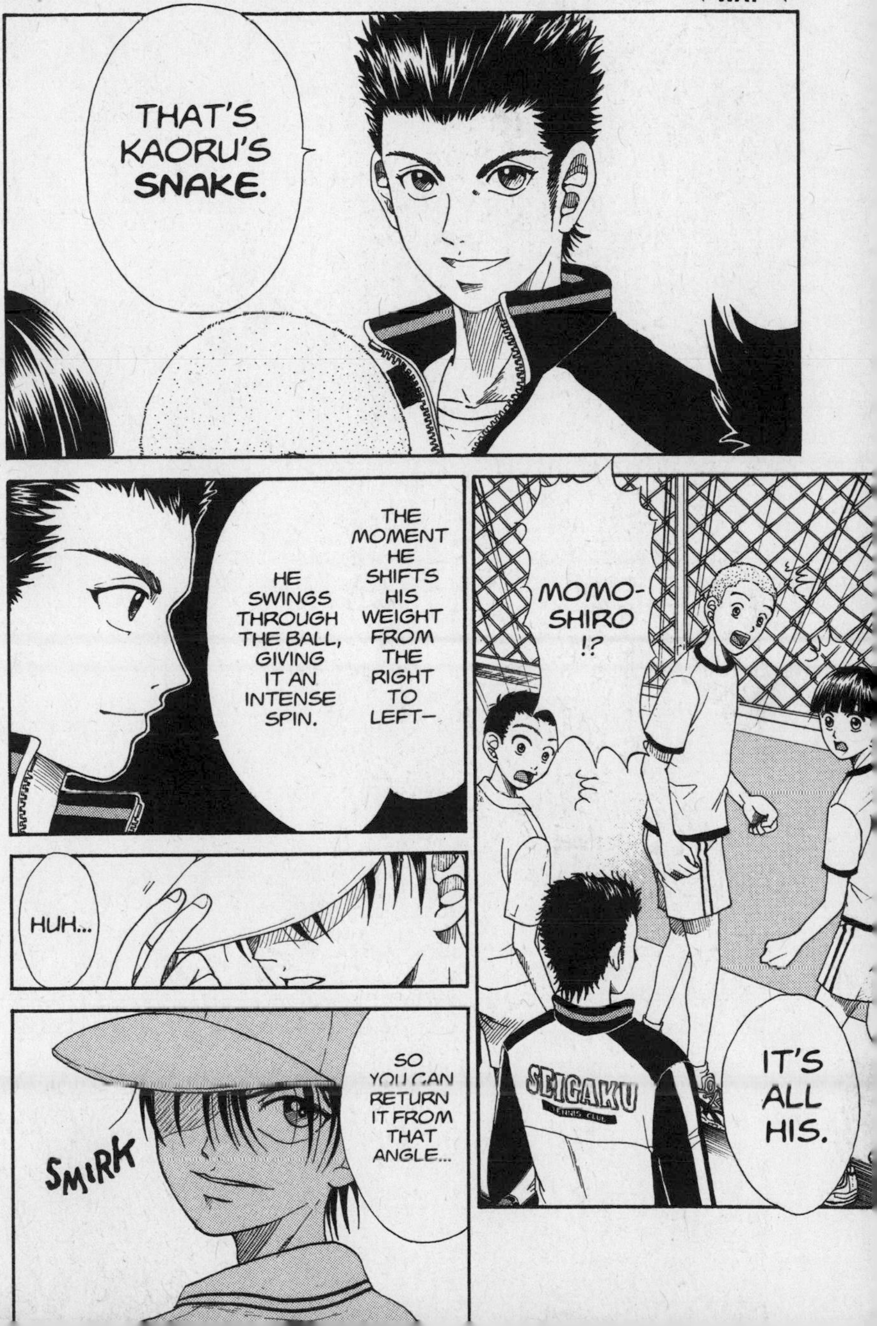
THAT'S KAORU'S SNAKE.
MOMO-SHIRO !?
SEIGAKU
TENNIS CLUB
IT'S ALL HIS.
THE MOMENT HE SHIFTS HIS WEIGHT FROM THE RIGHT TO LEFT—
HE SWINGS THROUGH THE BALL, GIVING IT AN INTENSE SPIN.
HUH...
SO YOU CAN RETURN IT FROM THAT ANGLE...
SMIRK

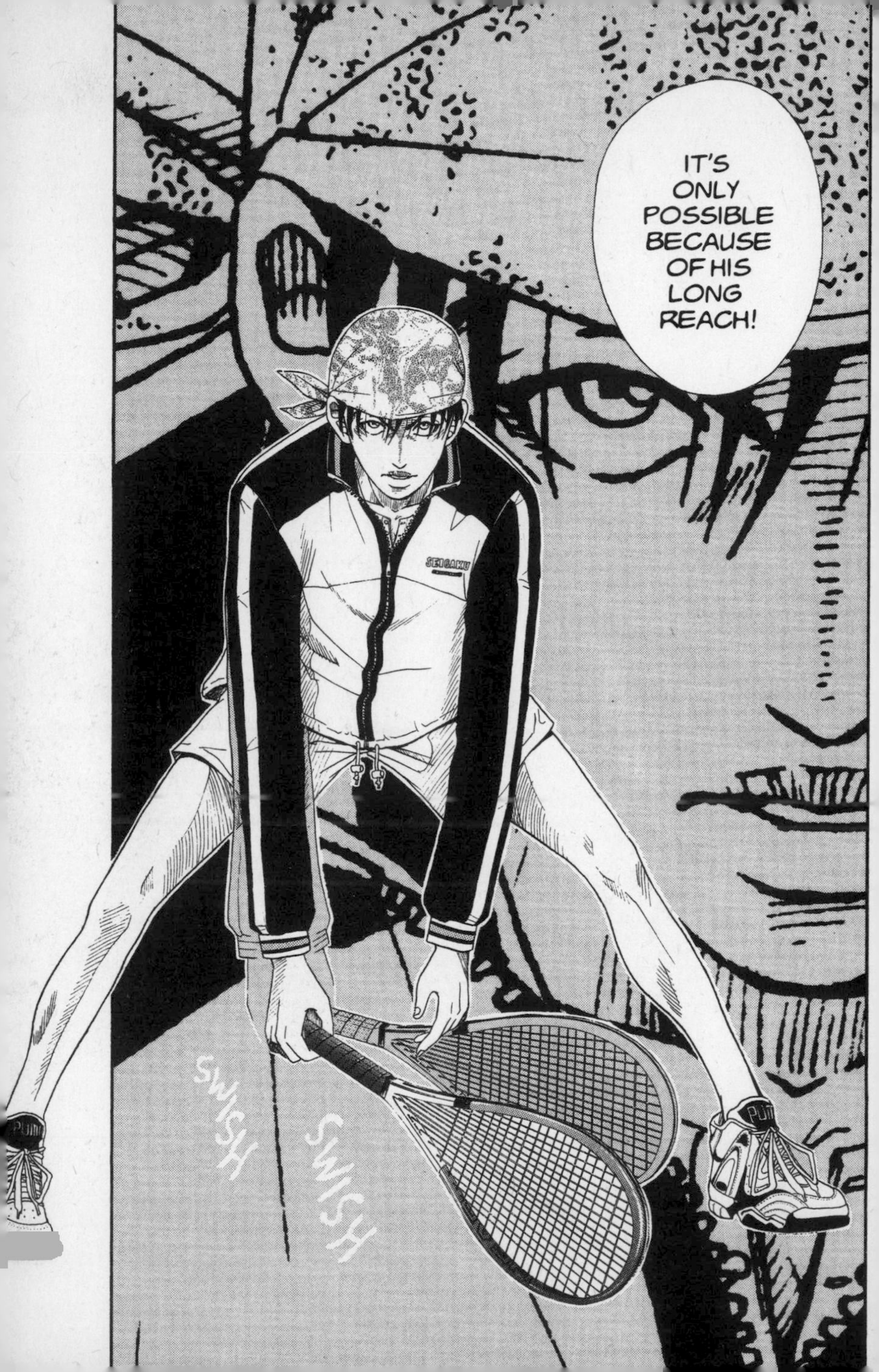
IT'S ONLY POSSIBLE BECAUSE OF HIS LONG REACH!
SEIGAKU
SWISH
SWISH

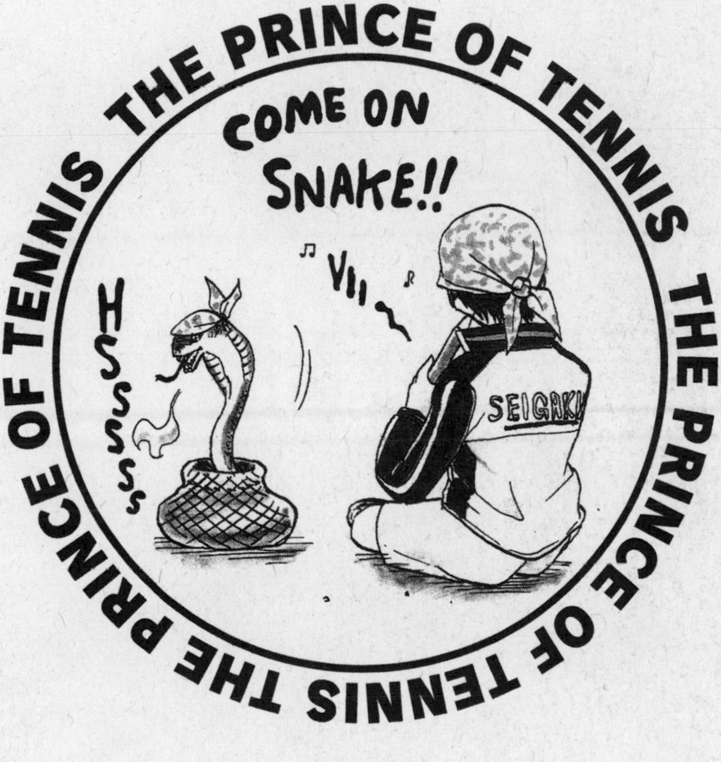
THE PRINCE OF TENNIS THE PRINCE OF TENNIS THE PRINCE OF TENNIS
COME ON SNAKE!!
Vii~
HSSSSSS
SEIGAKU

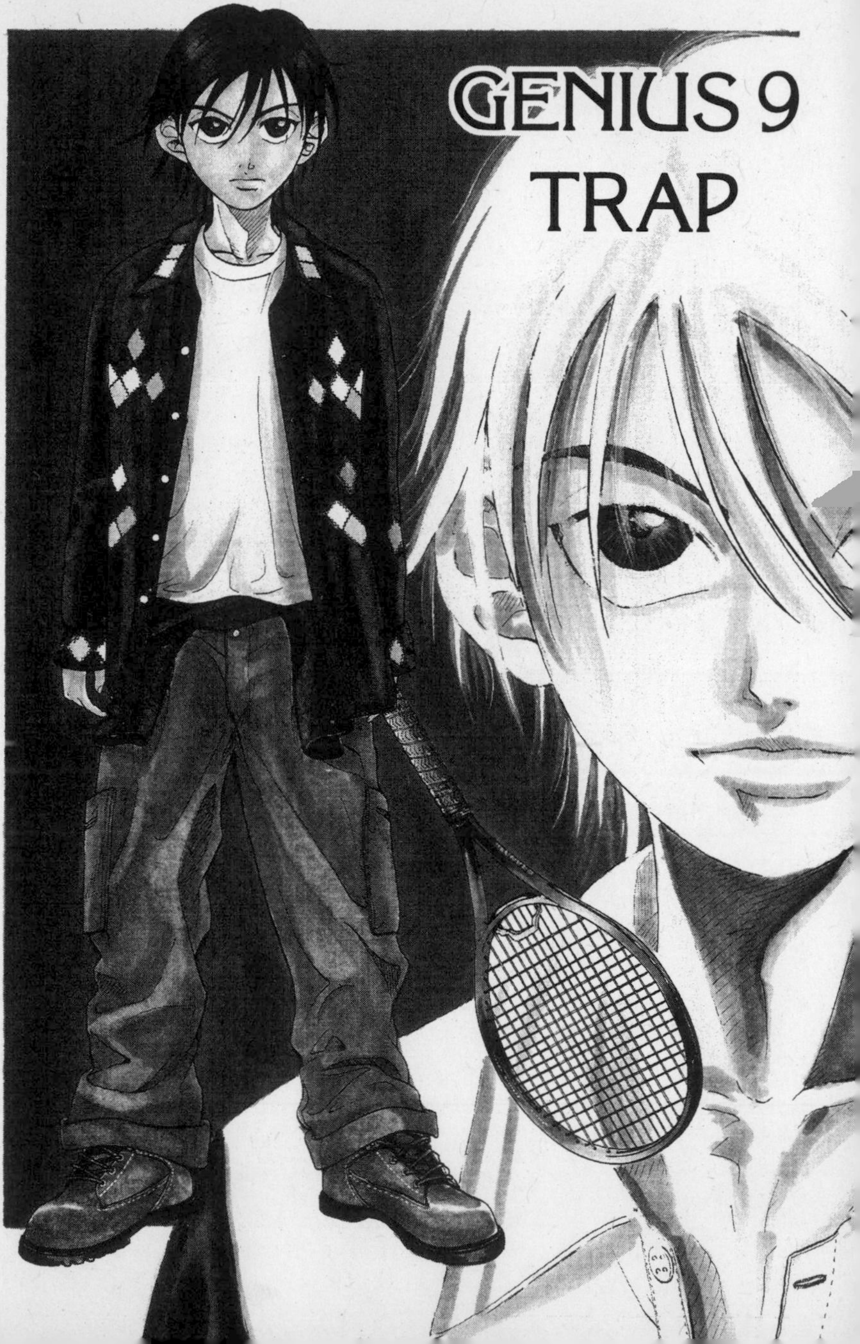
GENIUS 9
TRAP

READ THIS WAY

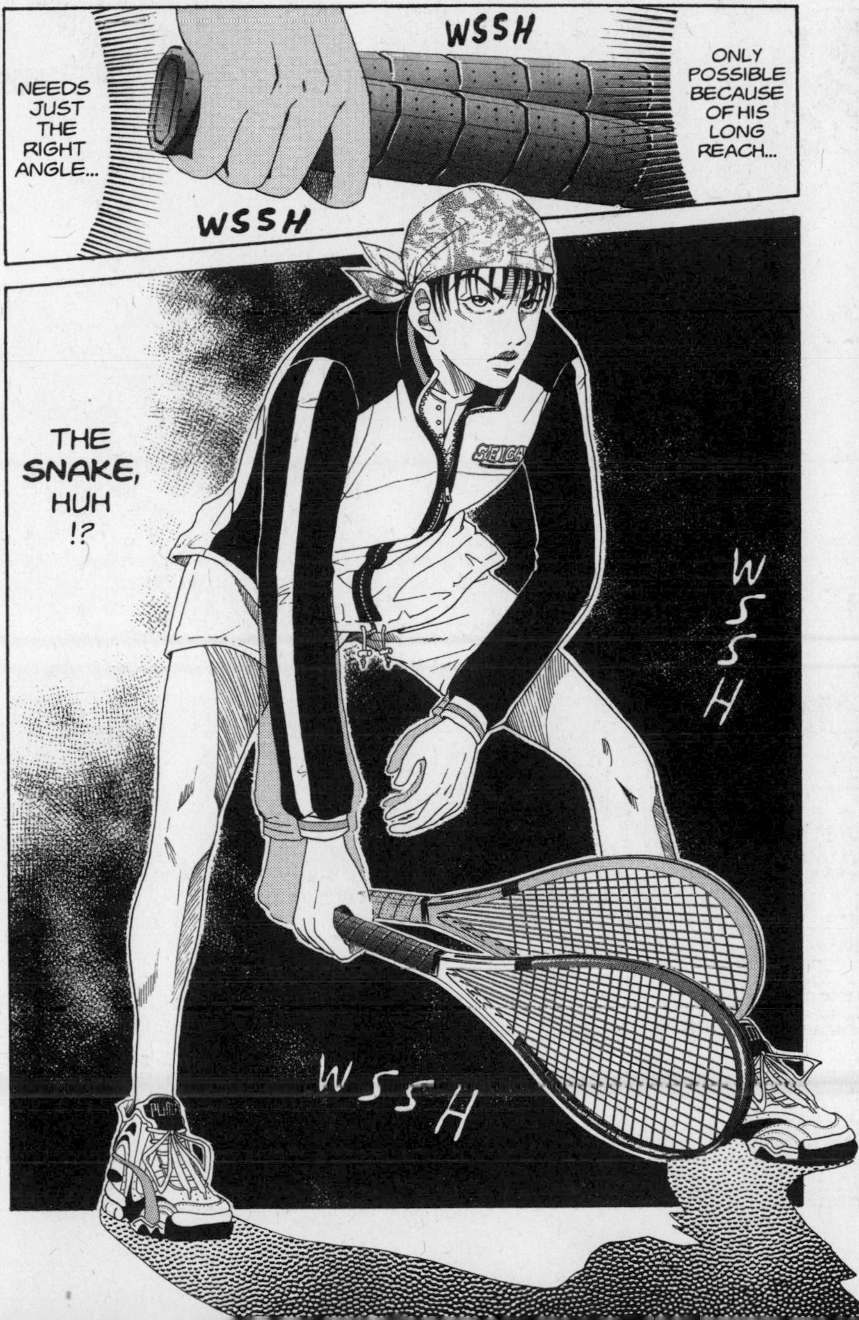

ONLY POSSIBLE BECAUSE OF HIS LONG REACH...
WSSH
NEEDS JUST THE RIGHT ANGLE...
WSSH
WSSH
THE SNAKE, HUH !?
WSSH

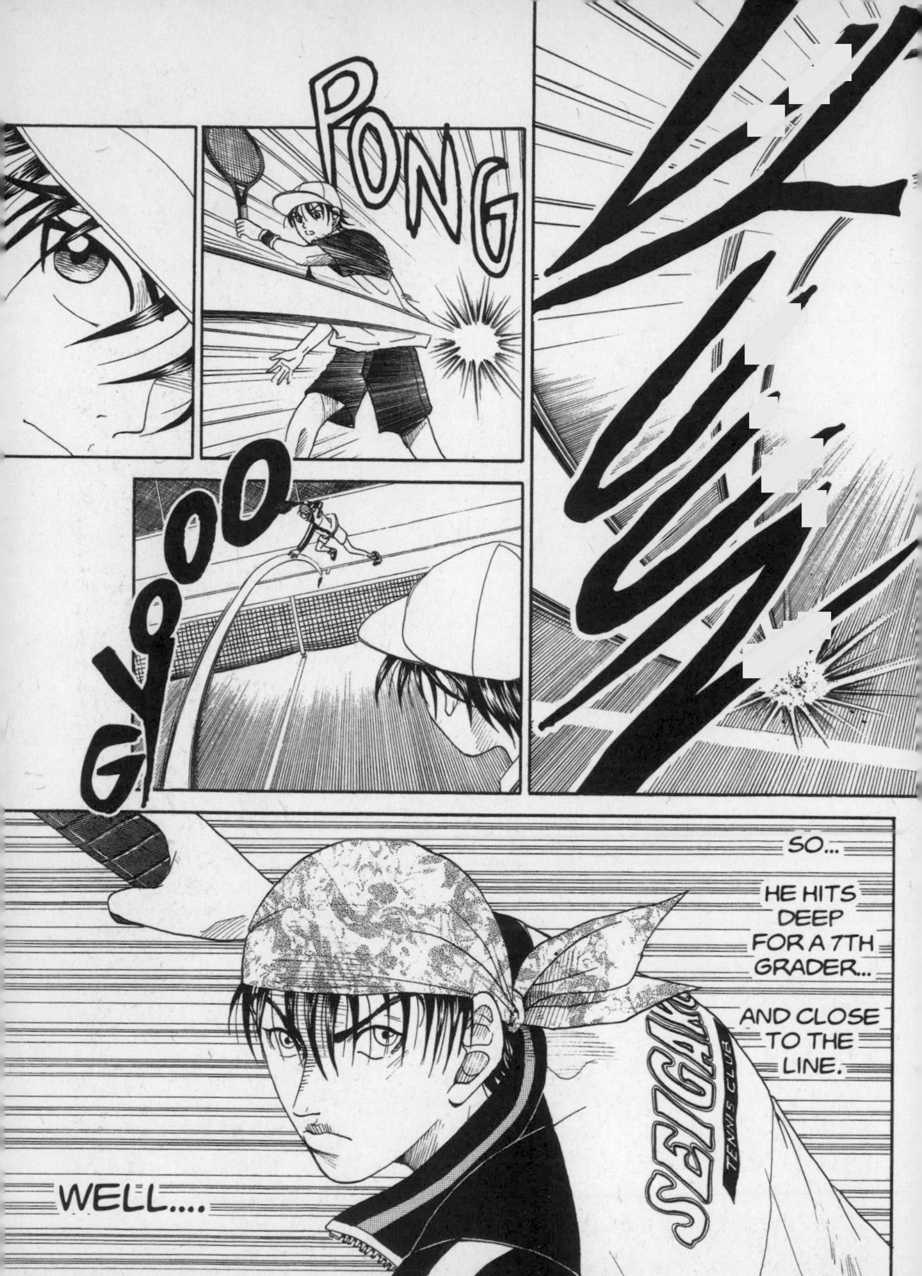
PONG
GYOOO
SO...
HE HITS DEEP FOR A 7TH GRADER...
AND CLOSE TO THE LINE.
TENNIS CLUB
WELL....

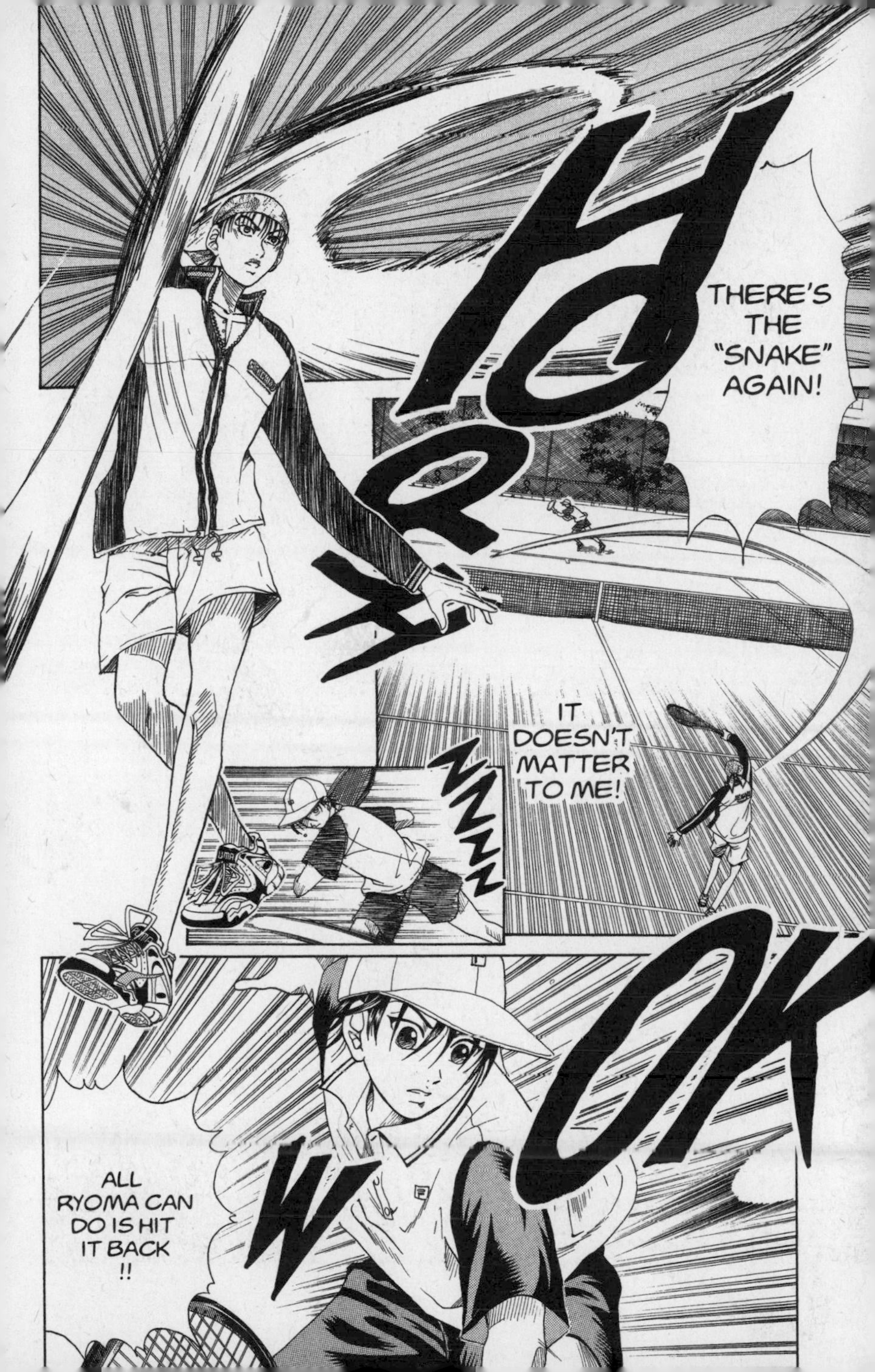
THERE'S THE "SNAKE" AGAIN!
IT DOESN'T MATTER TO ME!
ALL RYOMA CAN DO IS HIT IT BACK !!

READ THIS WAY

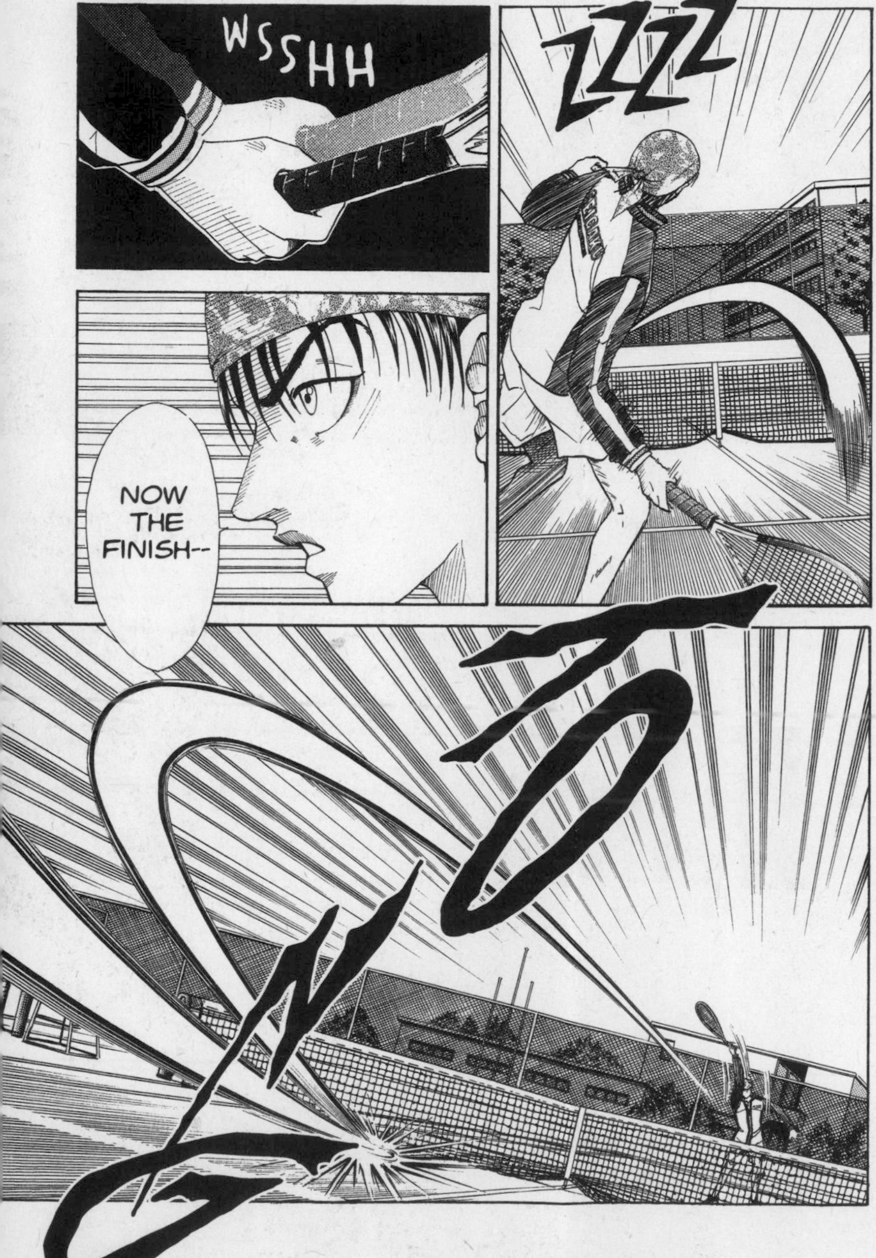
ZZZZ
WSSHH
NOW THE FINISH--

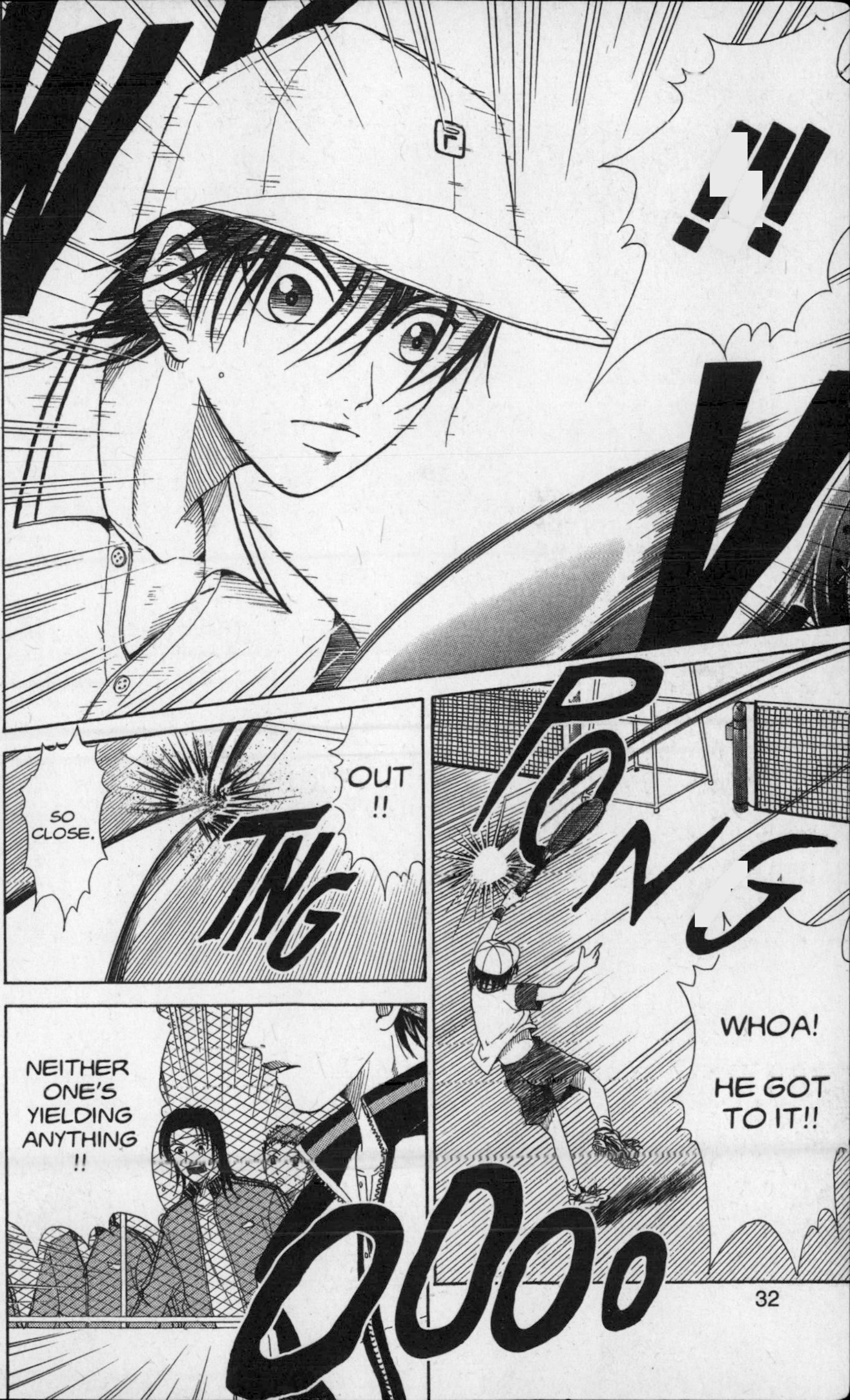
!!
PONG
WHOA!
HE GOT TO IT!!
OUT !!
SO CLOSE.
TING
NEITHER ONE'S YIELDING ANYTHING !!
OOOO

READ THIS WAY

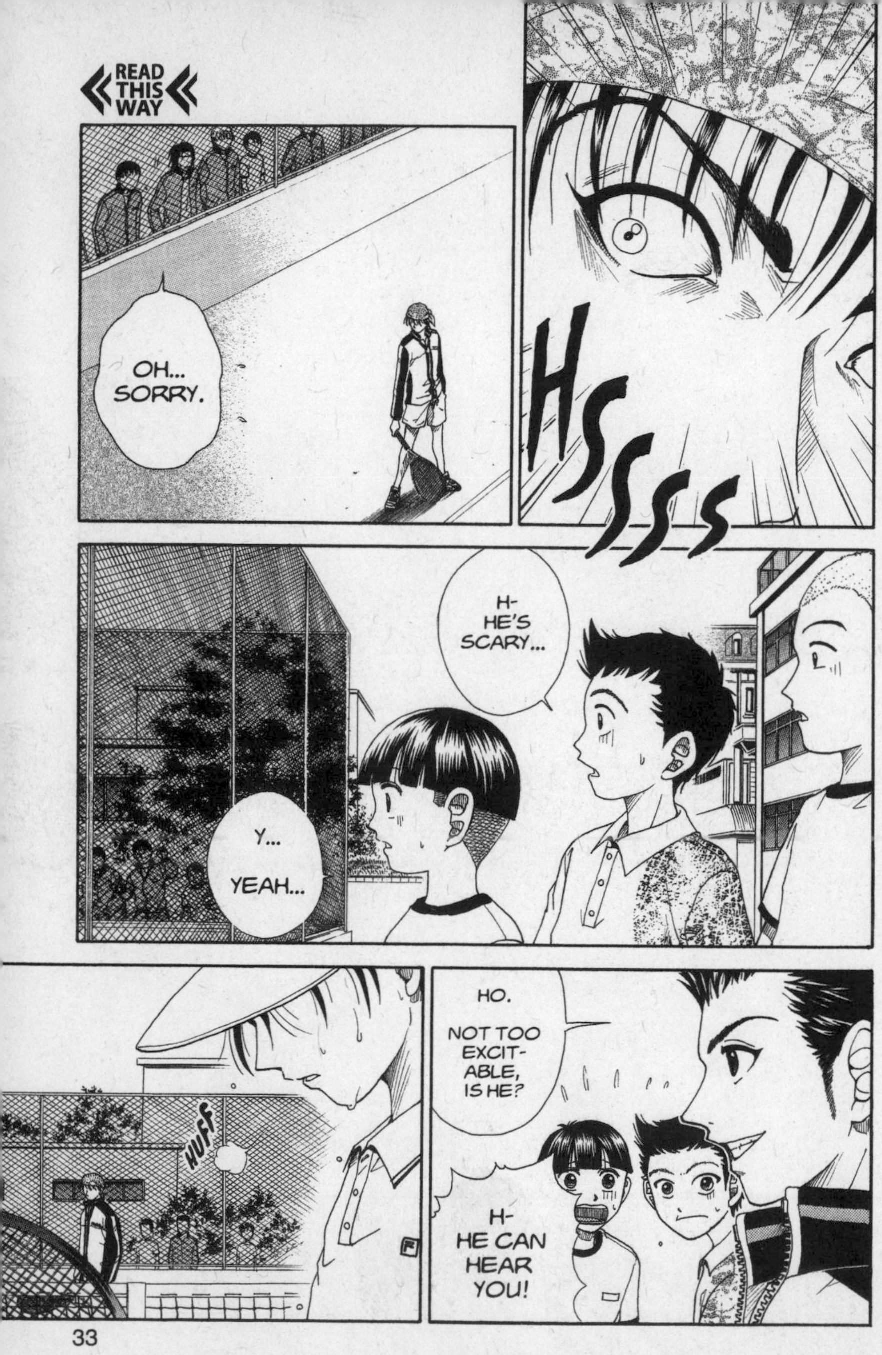
HSSSS
OH... SORRY.
H- HE'S SCARY...
Y... YEAH...
HO. NOT TOO EXCIT-ABLE, IS HE?
H- HE CAN HEAR YOU!
HUFF

READ THIS WAY

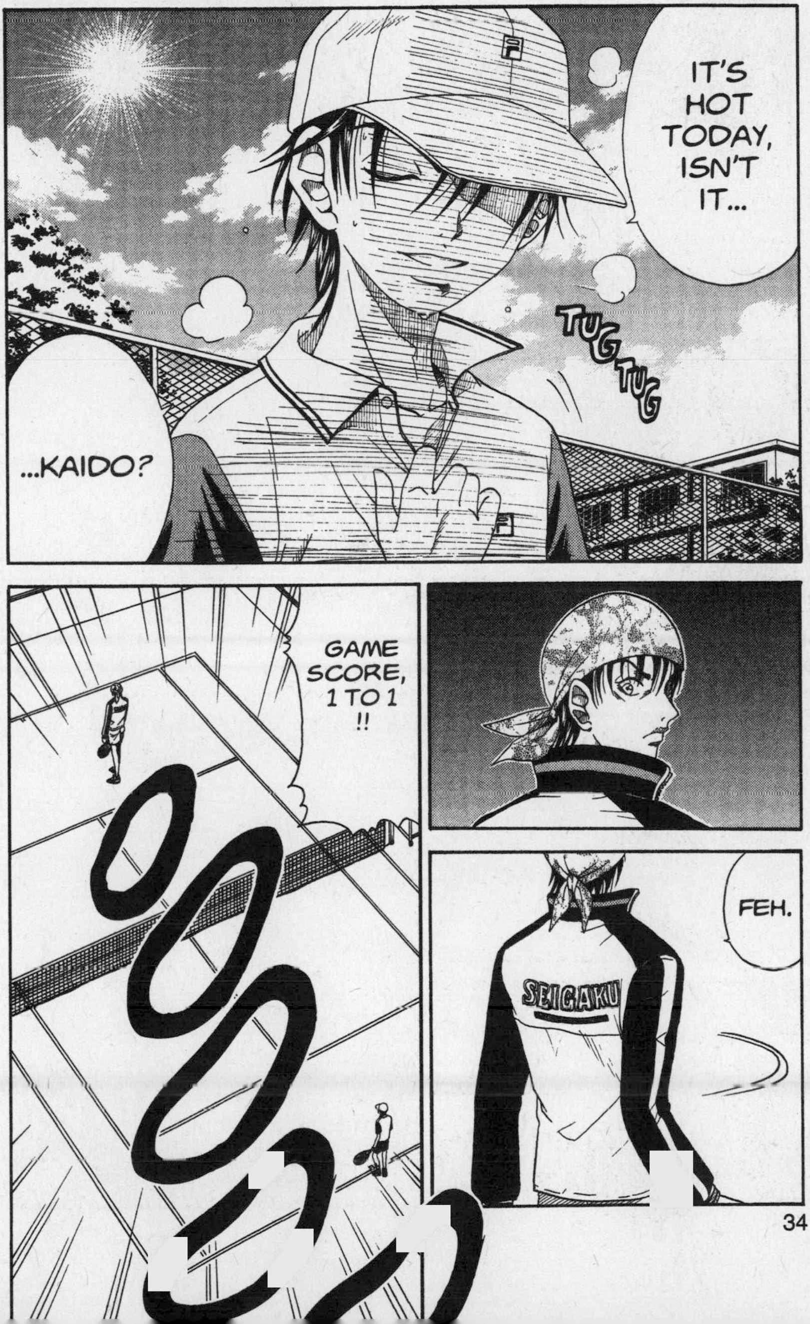
IT'S HOT TODAY, ISN'T IT...
TUG TUG
...KAIDO?
FEH.
GAME SCORE, 1 TO 1 !!

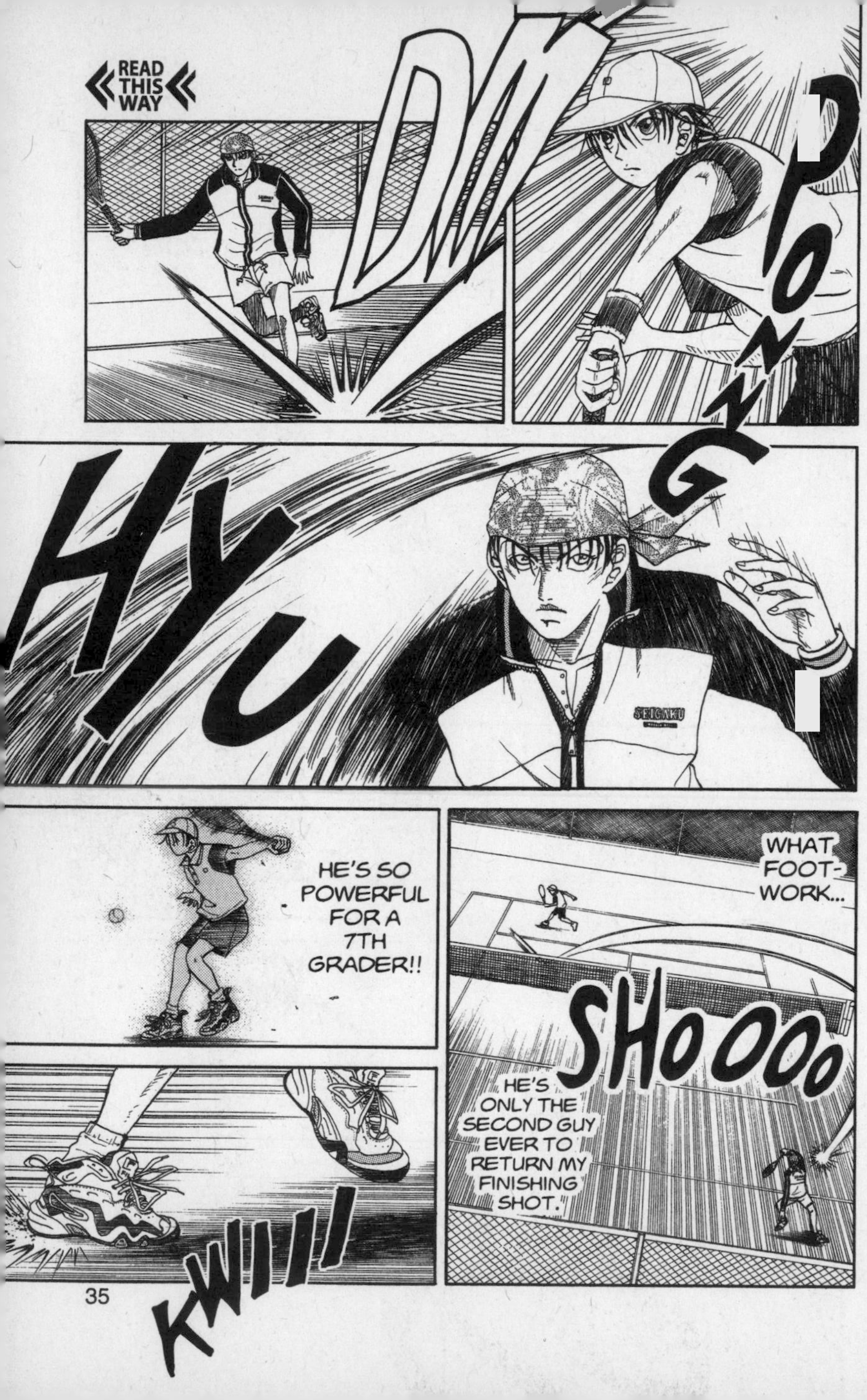
READ THIS WAY
PONNG
DM
HYU
WHAT FOOT-WORK...
SHOOOO
HE'S ONLY THE SECOND GUY EVER TO RETURN MY FINISHING SHOT.
HE'S SO POWERFUL FOR A 7TH GRADER!!
KWIIII

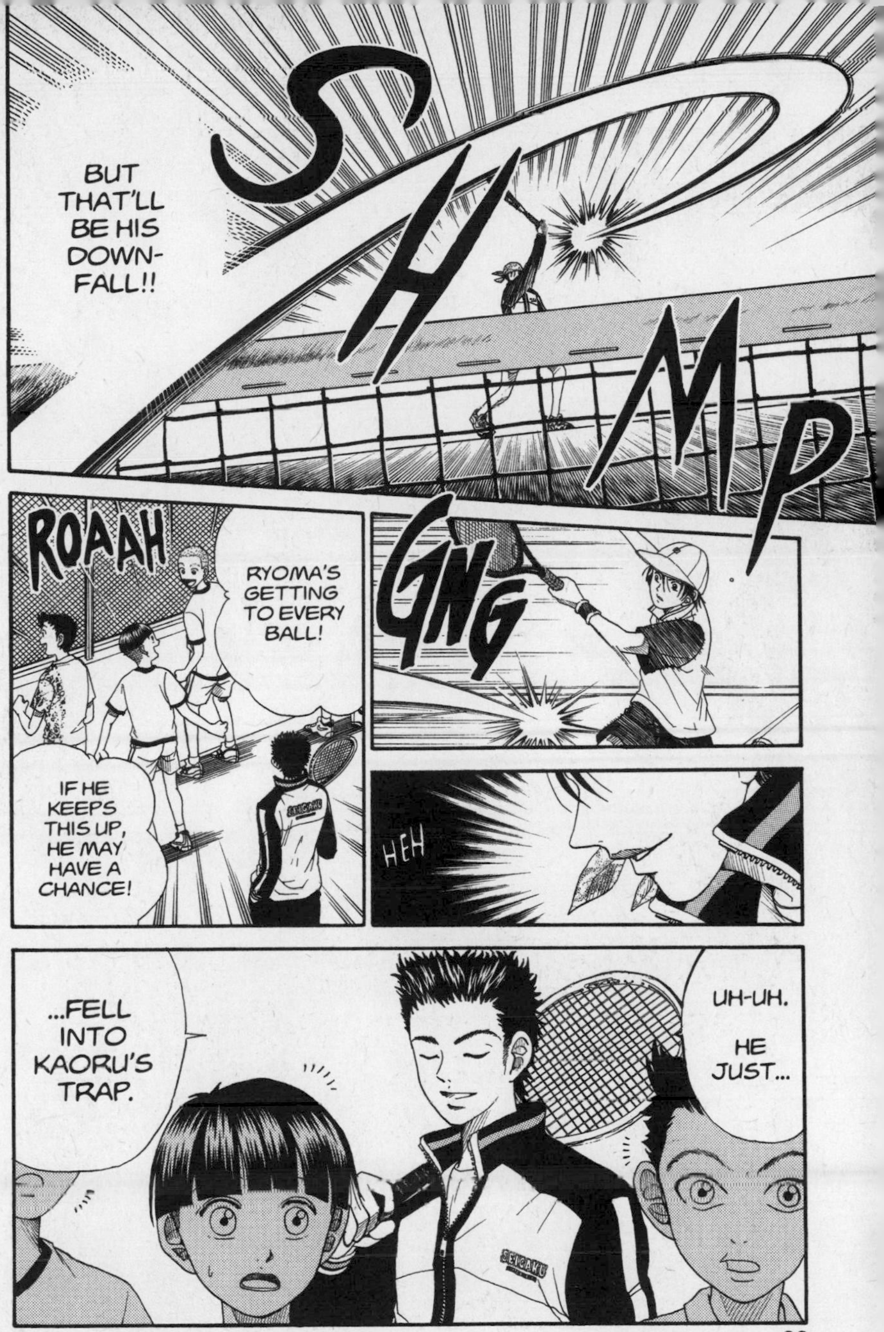
SHMP
BUT THAT'LL BE HIS DOWN-FALL!!
GNG
HEH
ROAAH
RYOMA'S GETTING TO EVERY BALL!
IF HE KEEPS THIS UP, HE MAY HAVE A CHANCE!
UH-UH.
HE JUST...
...FELL INTO KAORU'S TRAP.

READ THIS WAY

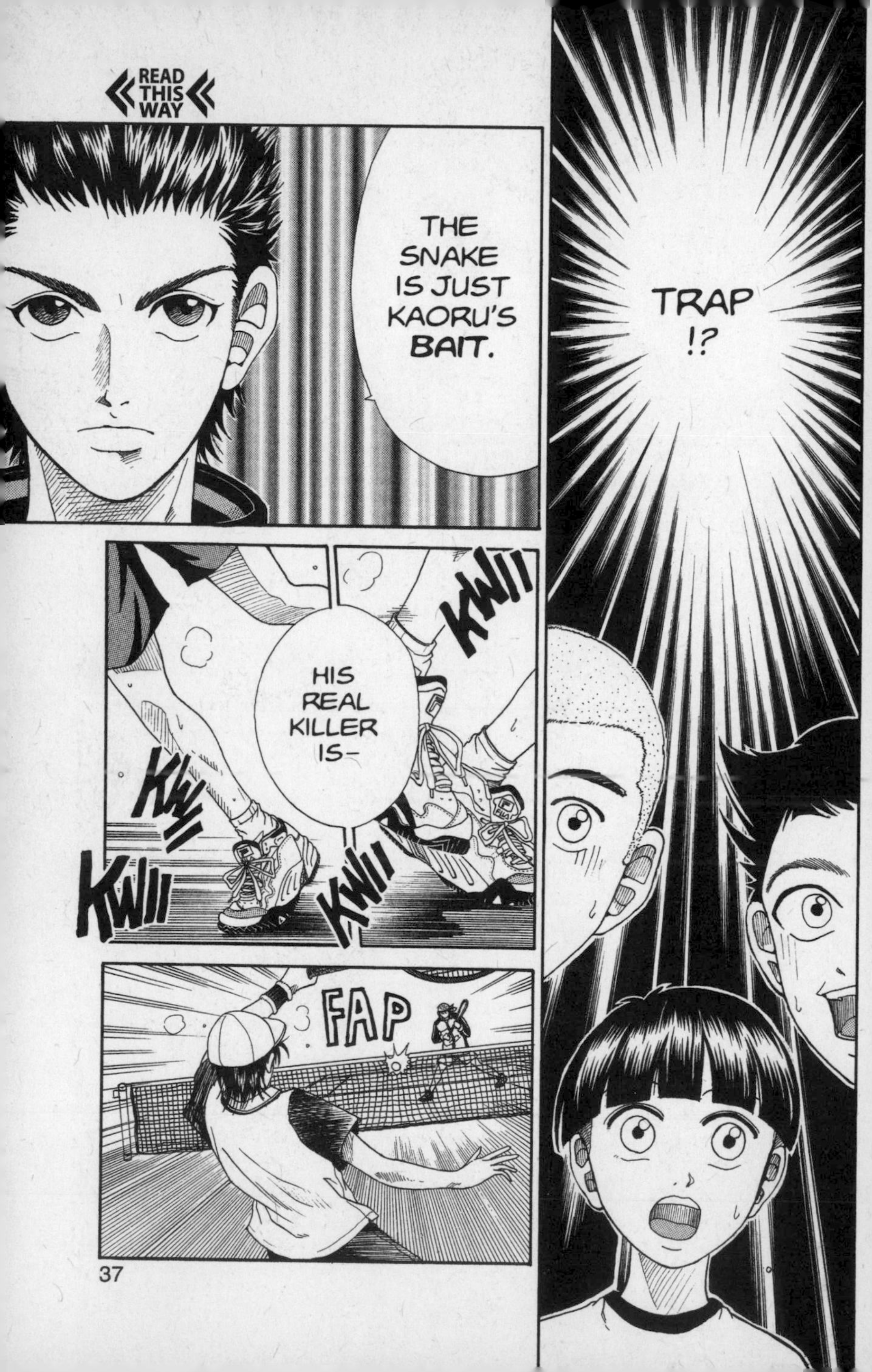
TRAP !?
THE SNAKE IS JUST KAORU'S BAIT.
KWII
HIS REAL KILLER IS—
KWII
KWII
KWII
FAP

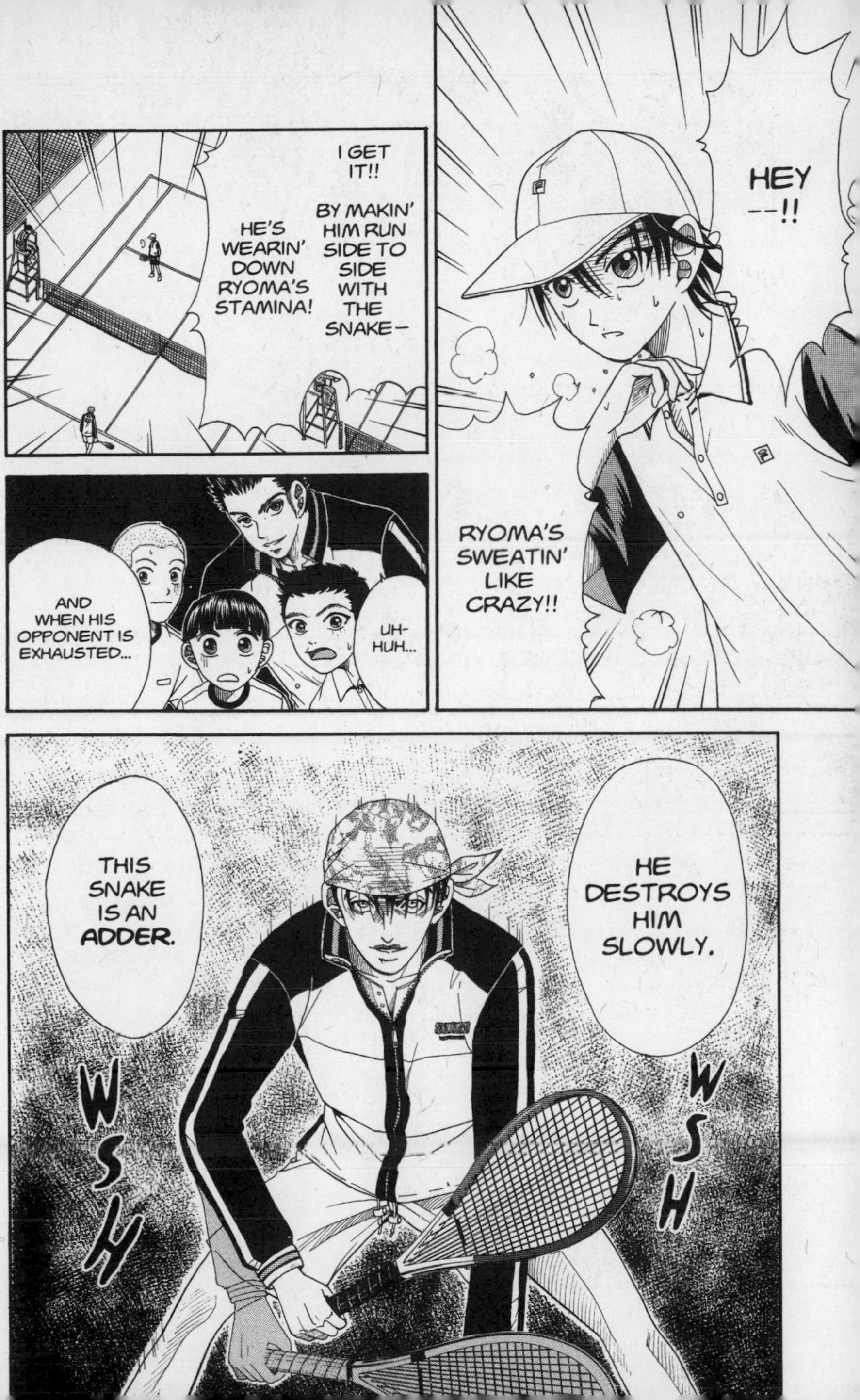
HEY --!!
RYOMA'S SWEATIN' LIKE CRAZY!!
I GET IT!!
BY MAKIN' HIM RUN SIDE TO SIDE WITH THE SNAKE—
HE'S WEARIN' DOWN RYOMA'S STAMINA!
AND WHEN HIS OPPONENT IS EXHAUSTED...
UH-HUH...
HE DESTROYS HIM SLOWLY.
THIS SNAKE IS AN ADDER.
WSH
WSH

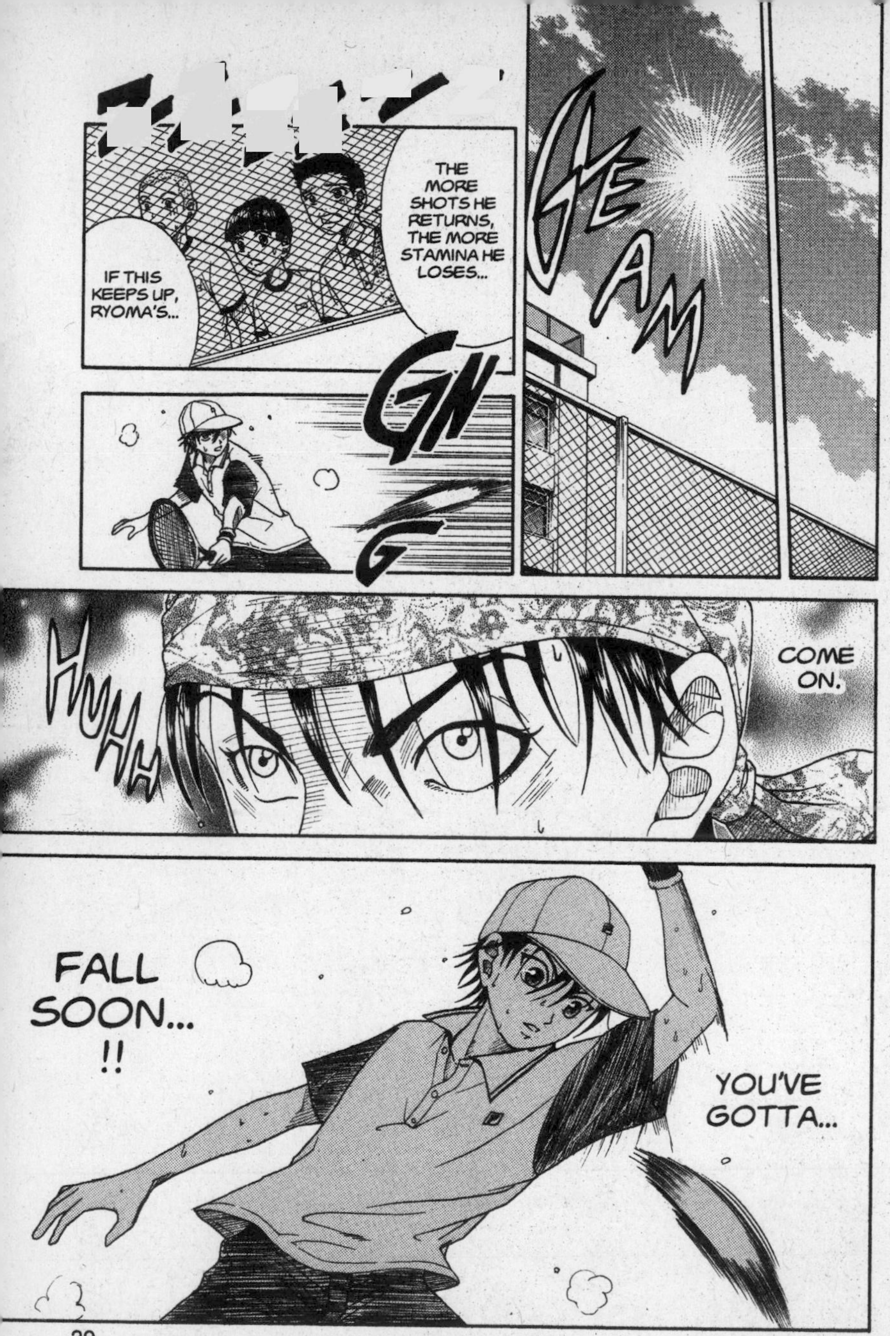
GLEAM
THE MORE SHOTS HE RETURNS, THE MORE STAMINA HE LOSES...
IF THIS KEEPS UP, RYOMA'S...
GNG
COME ON.
HUHHH
YOU'VE GOTTA...
FALL SOON... !!

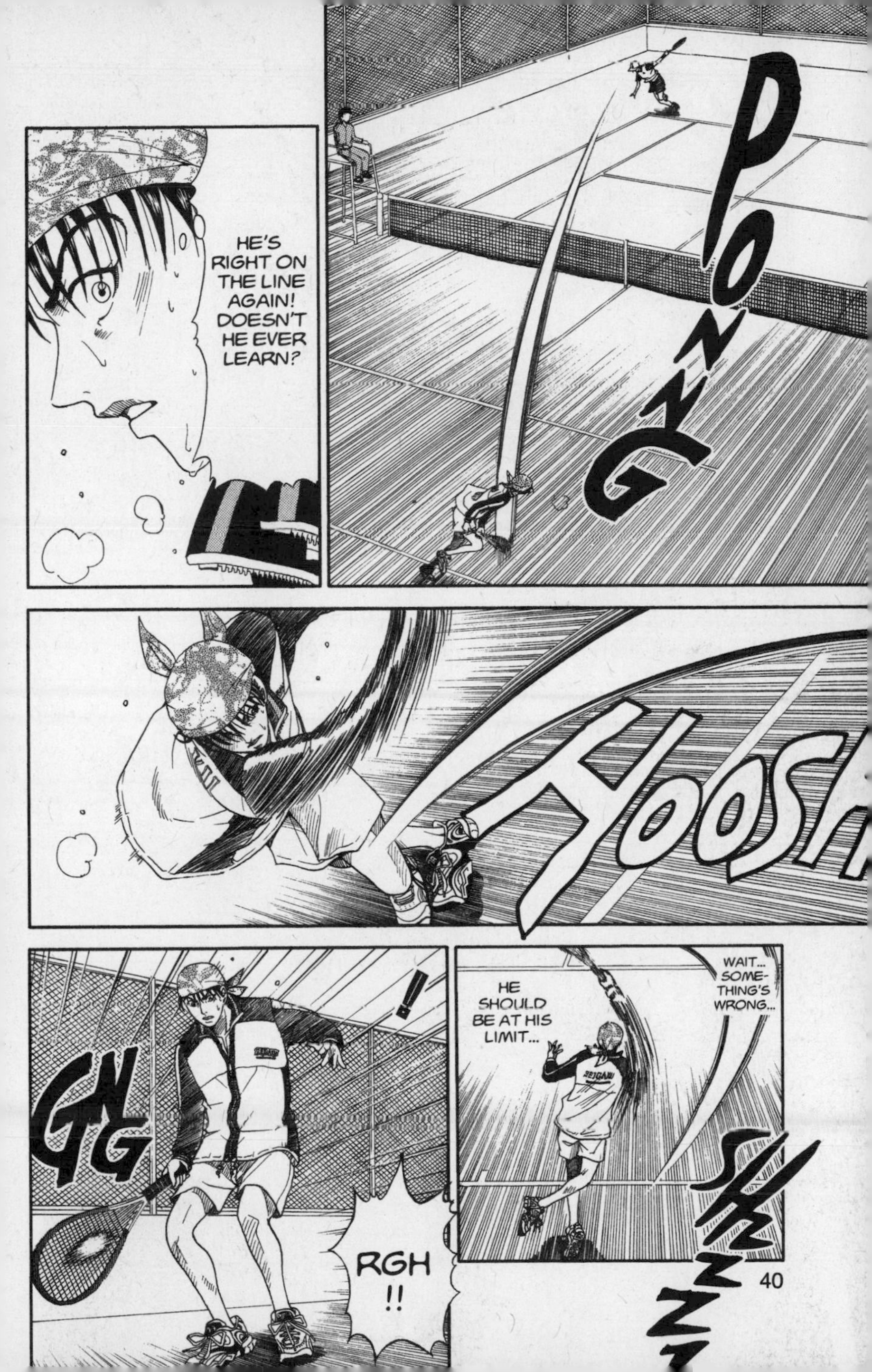
PONNNG
HE'S RIGHT ON THE LINE AGAIN! DOESN'T HE EVER LEARN?
HOOSH
WAIT... SOMETHING'S WRONG...
HE SHOULD BE AT HIS LIMIT...
SHZZZ
!
GNG
RGH !!

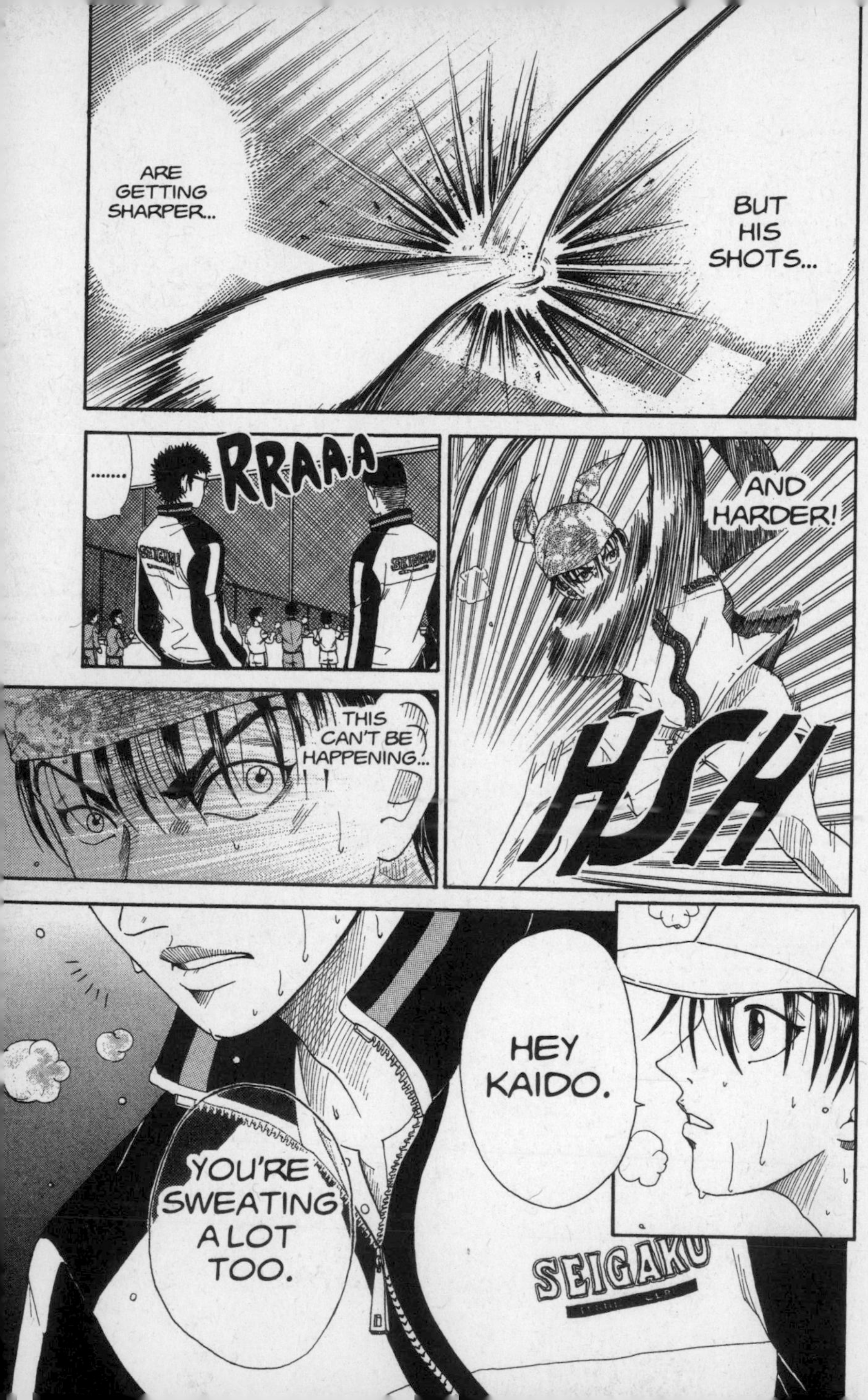
BUT HIS SHOTS...
ARE GETTING SHARPER...
AND HARDER!
HSH
....
RRAAA
THIS CAN'T BE HAPPENING...
HEY KAIDO.
SEIGAKU
YOU'RE SWEATING A LOT TOO.

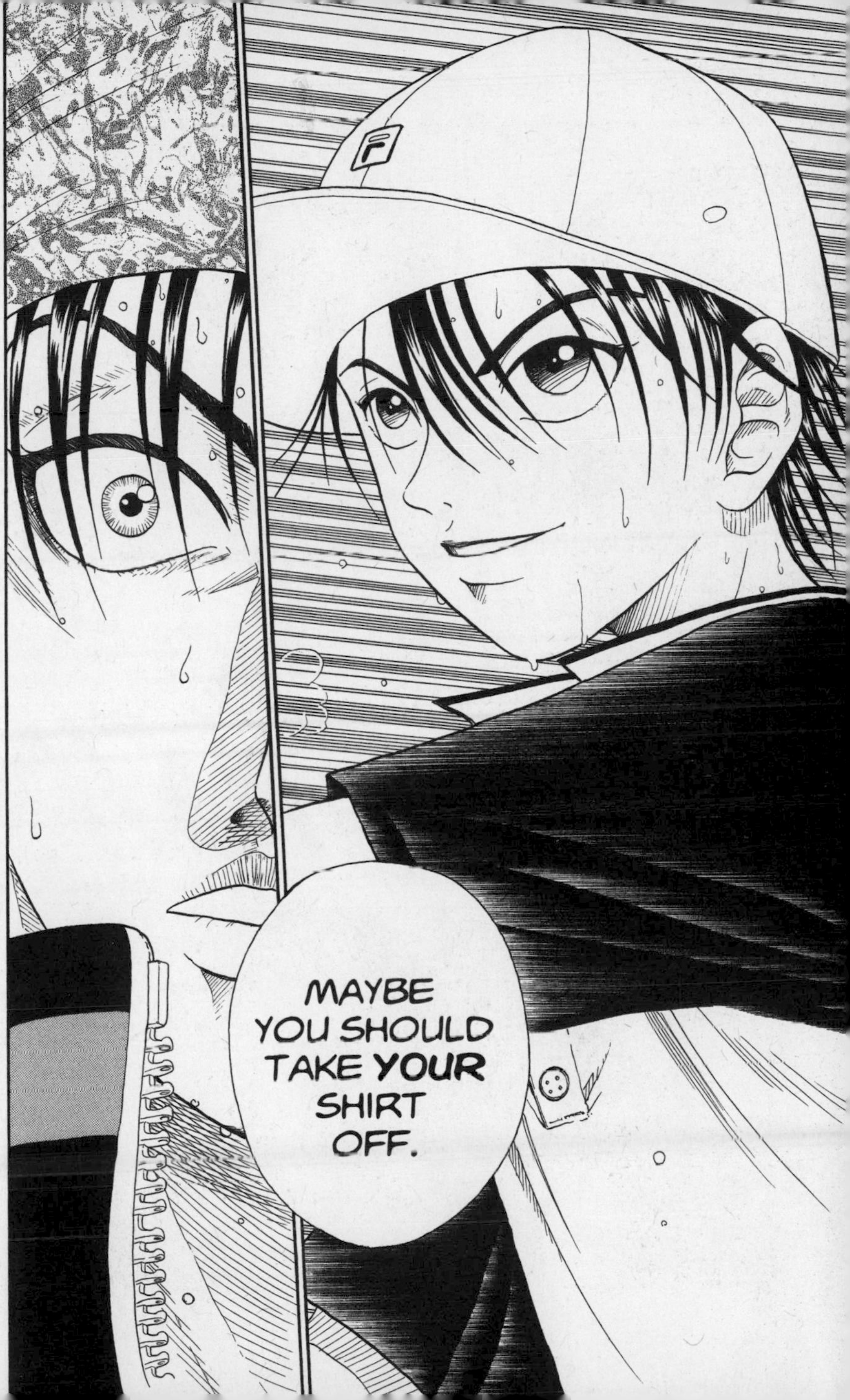
MAYBE YOU SHOULD TAKE YOUR SHIRT OFF.

READ THIS WAY

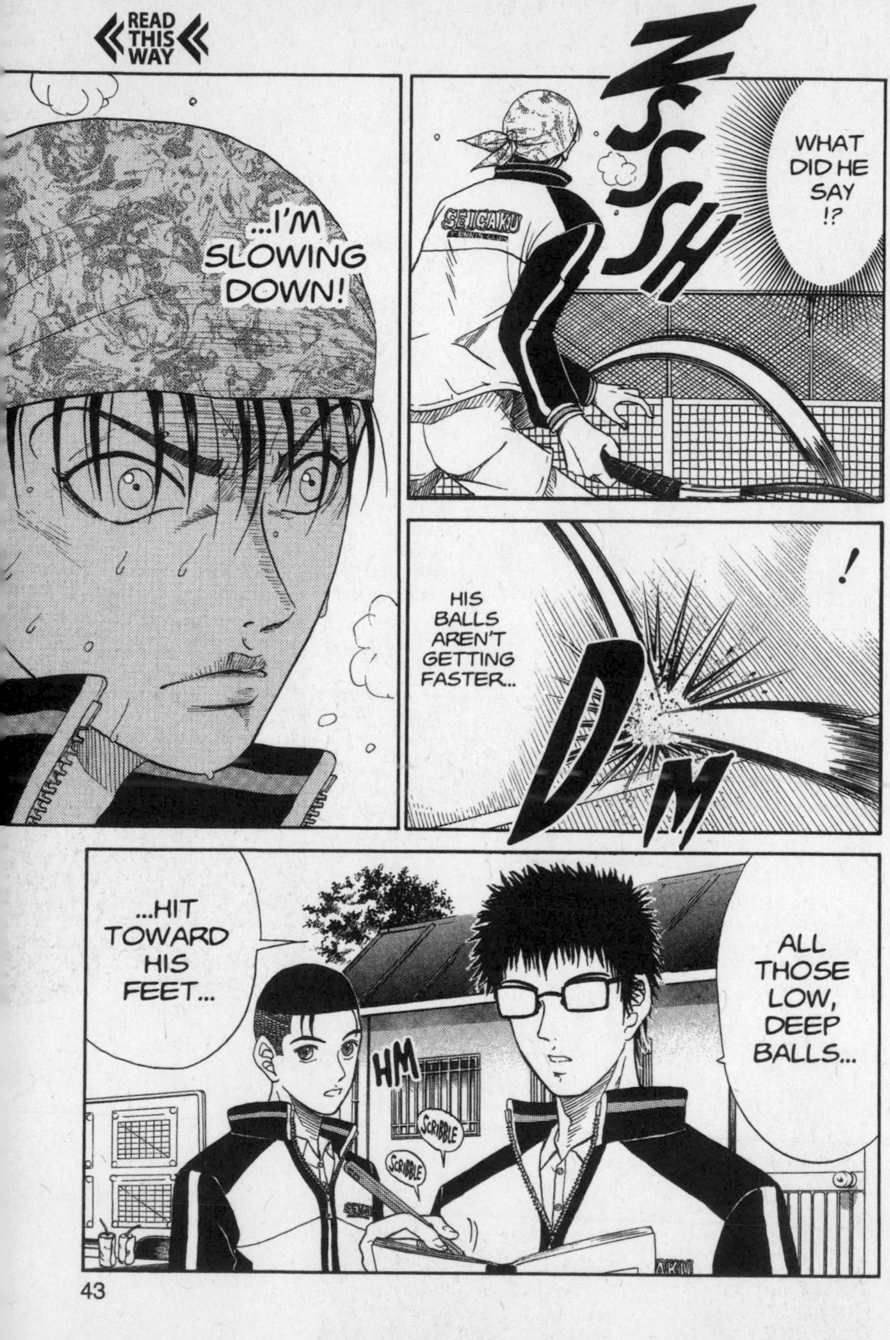
ZSSH
WHAT DID HE SAY !?
DM
!
HIS BALLS AREN'T GETTING FASTER...
...I'M SLOWING DOWN!
ALL THOSE LOW, DEEP BALLS...
HM
SCRIBBLE
SCRIBBLE
...HIT TOWARD HIS FEET...

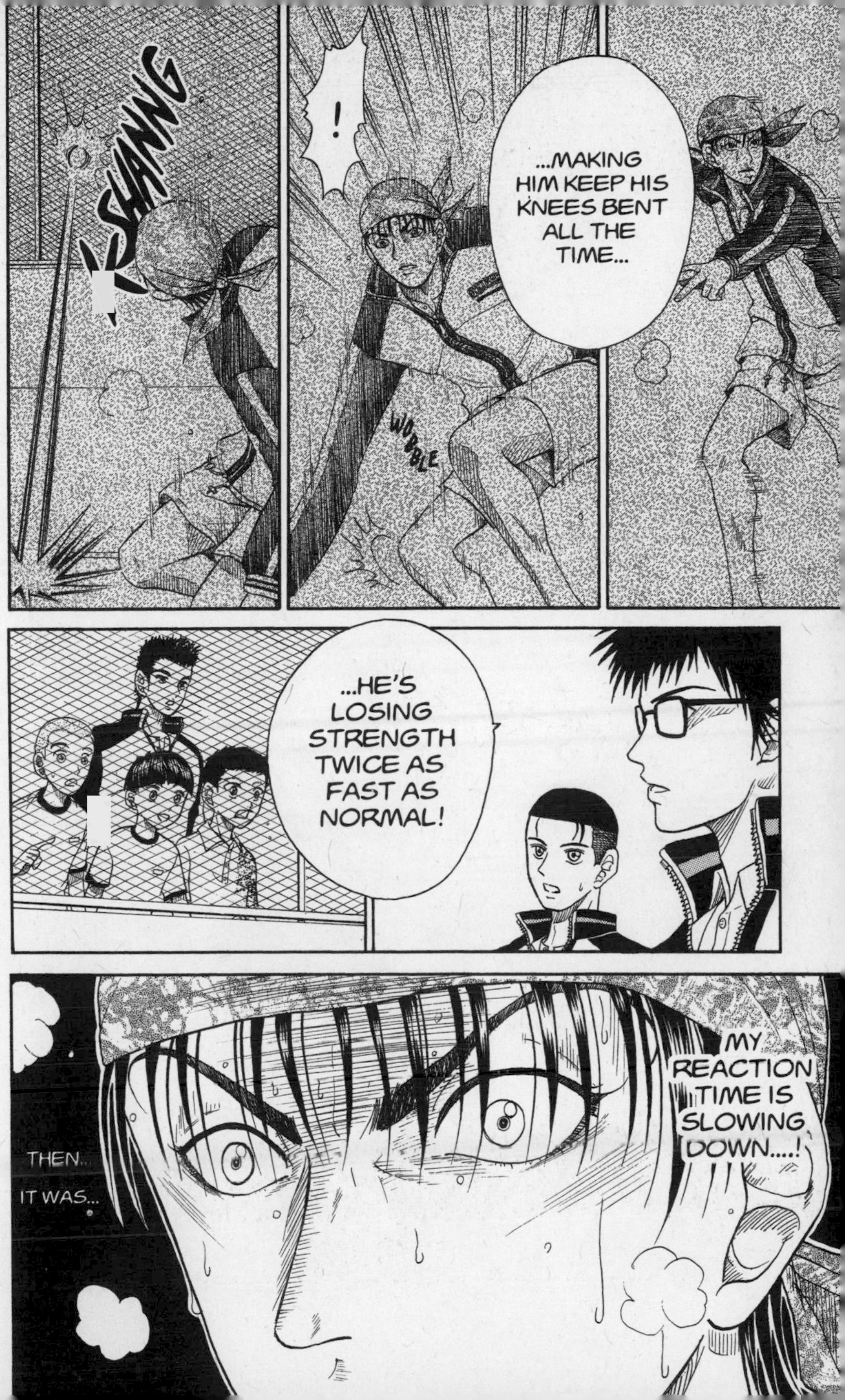
...MAKING HIM KEEP HIS KNEES BENT ALL THE TIME...
!
WOBBLE
SHANG
...HE'S LOSING STRENGTH TWICE AS FAST AS NORMAL!
MY REACTION TIME IS SLOWING DOWN....!
THEN...
IT WAS...

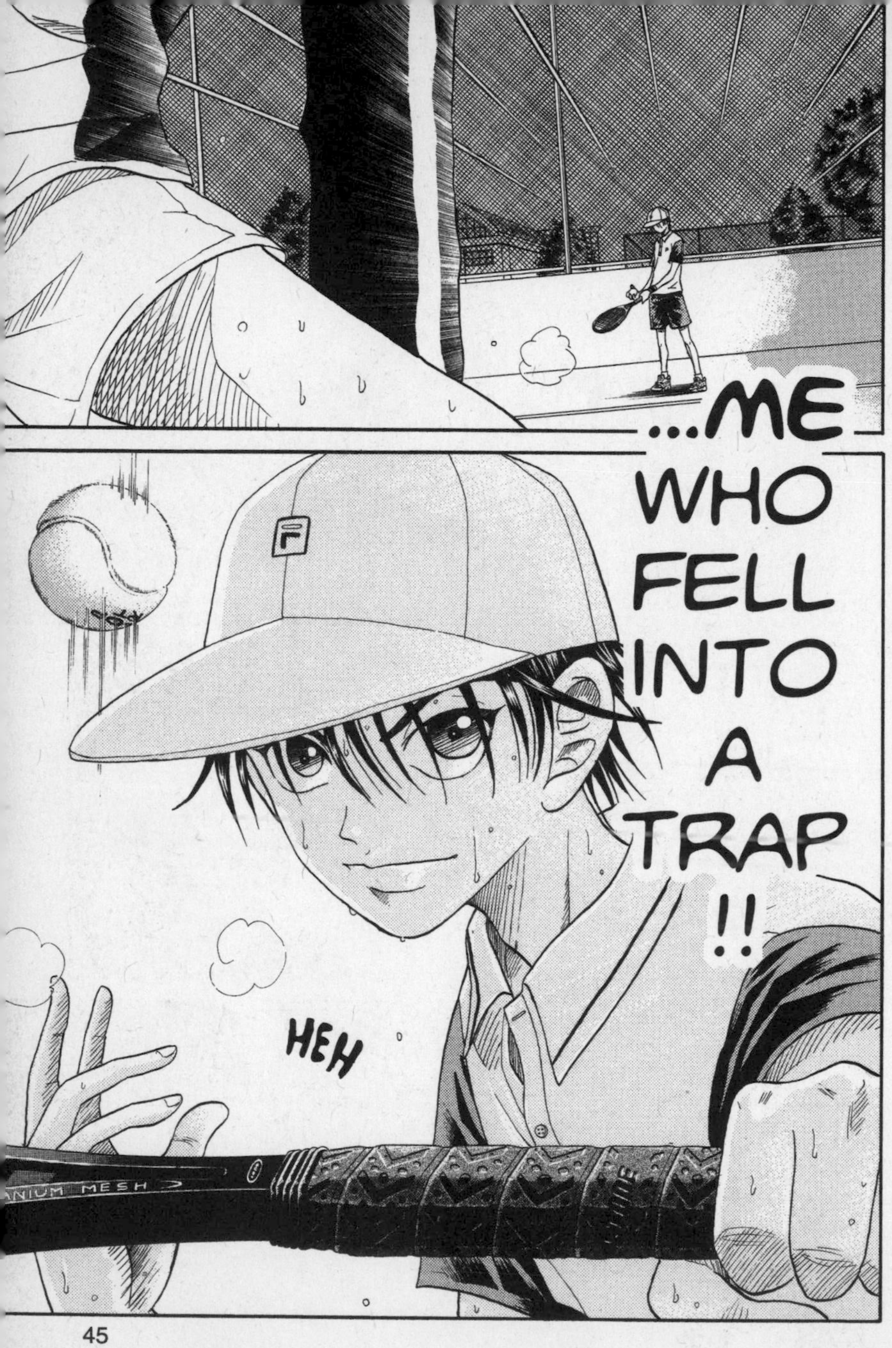
...ME WHO FELL INTO A TRAP !!
HEH
ANIUM MESH

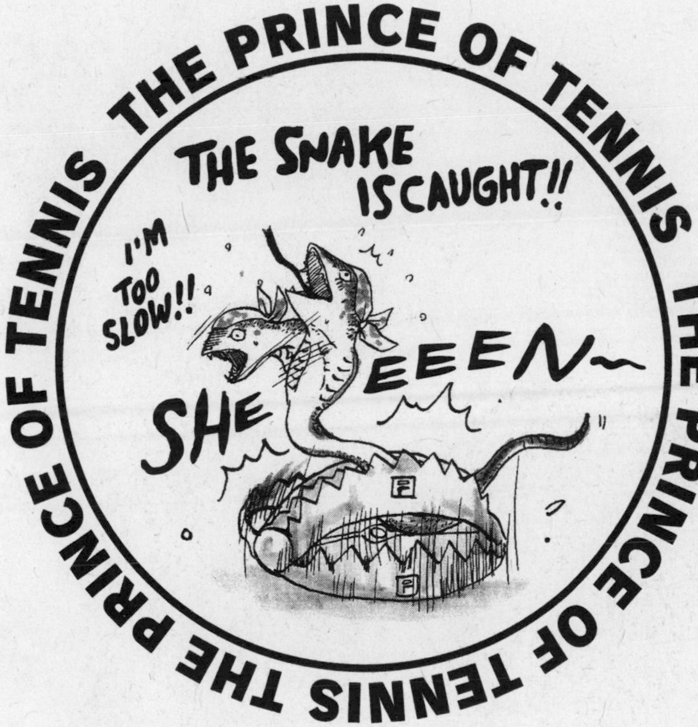
THE PRINCE OF TENNIS THE PRINCE OF TENNIS THE PRINCE OF TENNIS
THE SNAKE IS CAUGHT!!
I'M TOO SLOW!!
SHEEEEN~

GENIUS 10

MIND GAME

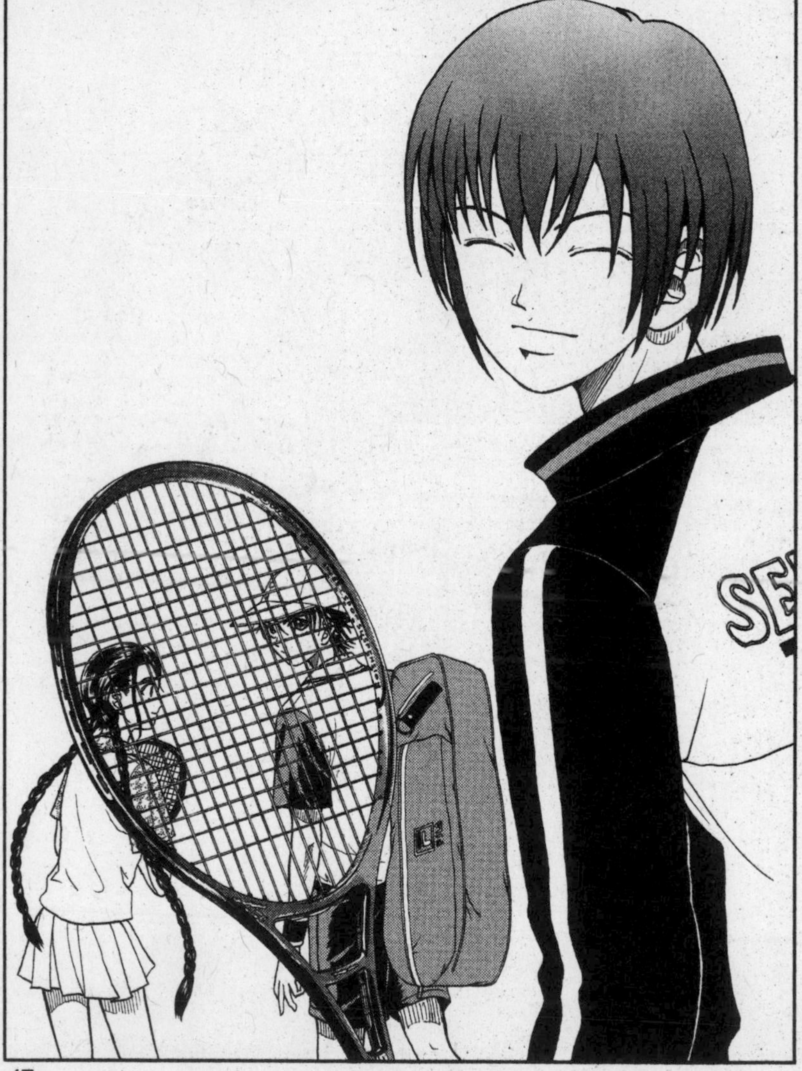

READ THIS WAY

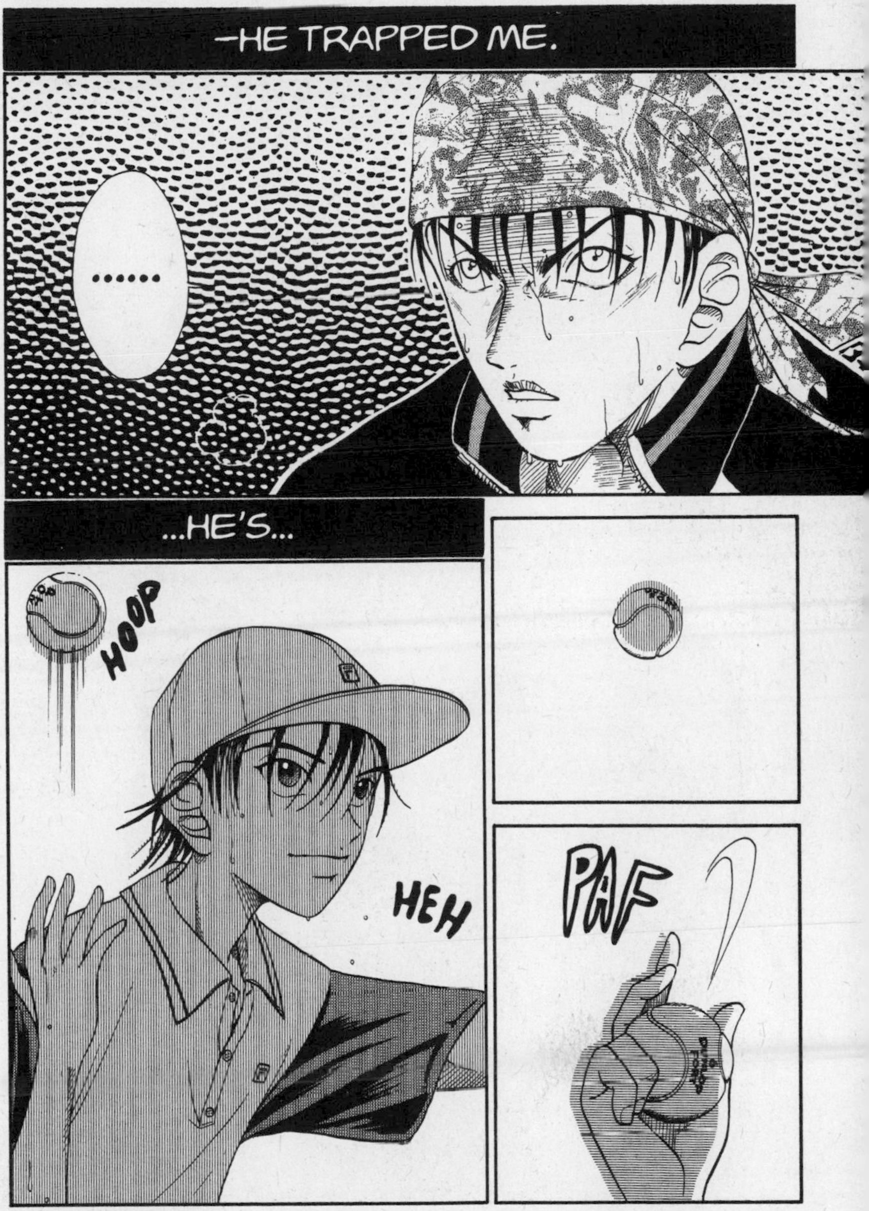
—HE TRAPPED ME.
......
PAF
...HE'S...
HOOP
HEH

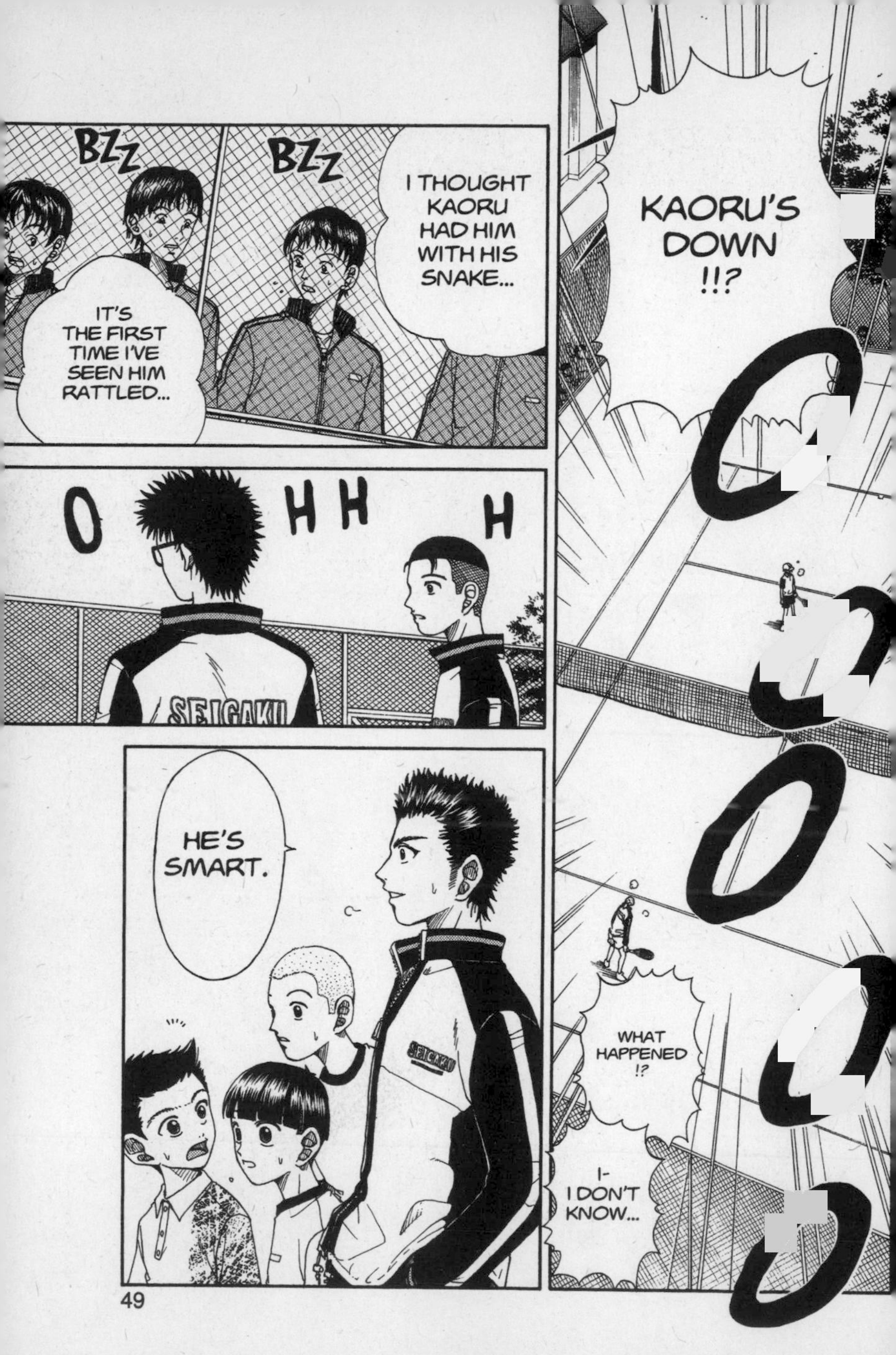
KAORU'S DOWN !!?
WHAT HAPPENED !?
I- I DON'T KNOW...
I THOUGHT KAORU HAD HIM WITH HIS SNAKE...
BZZ
BZZ
IT'S THE FIRST TIME I'VE SEEN HIM RATTLED...
O HH H
SEIGAKU
HE'S SMART.
SEIGAKU

READ THIS WAY

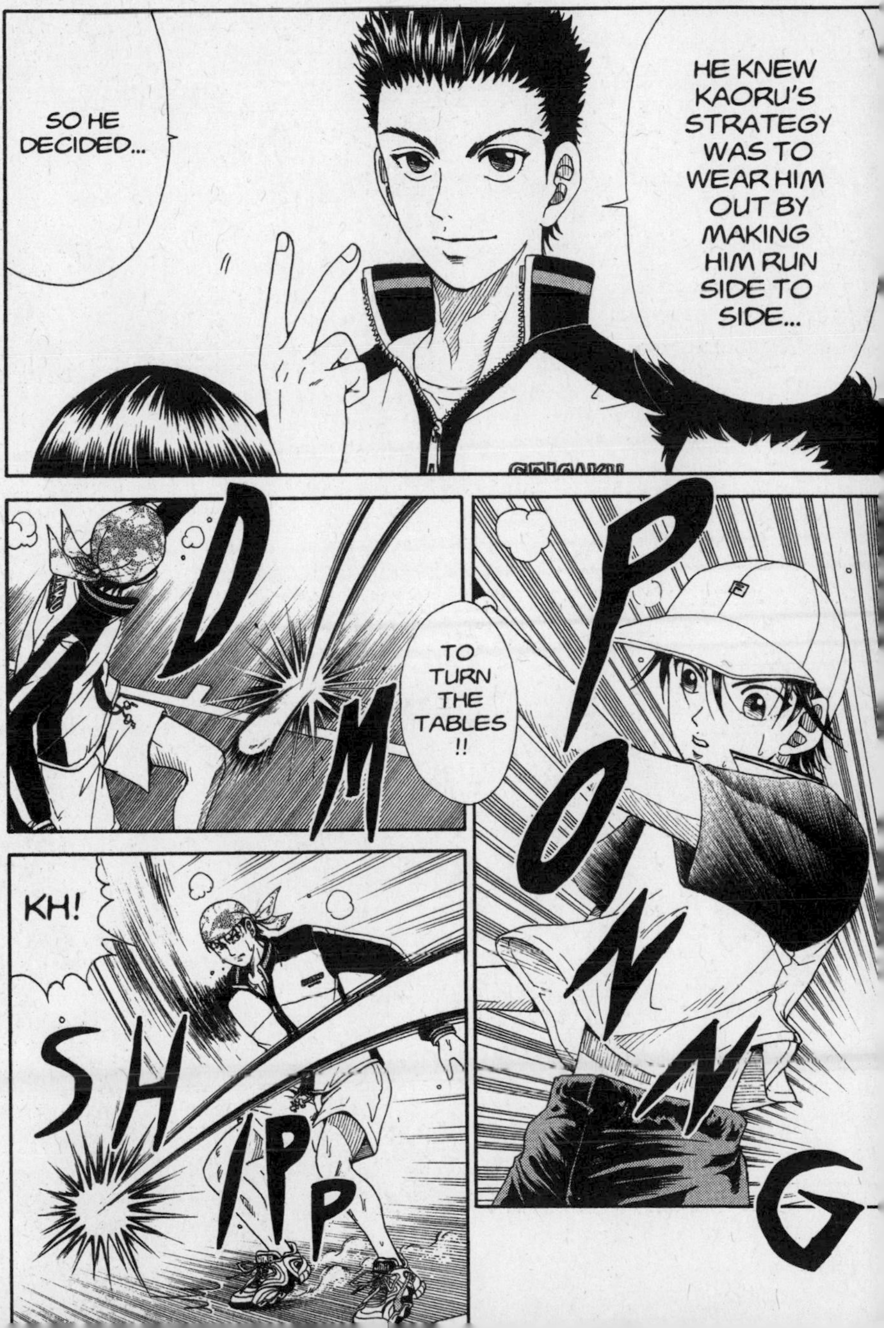
HE KNEW KAORU'S STRATEGY WAS TO WEAR HIM OUT BY MAKING HIM RUN SIDE TO SIDE...
SO HE DECIDED...
TO TURN THE TABLES !!
PONNG
DM
KH!
SHIPP

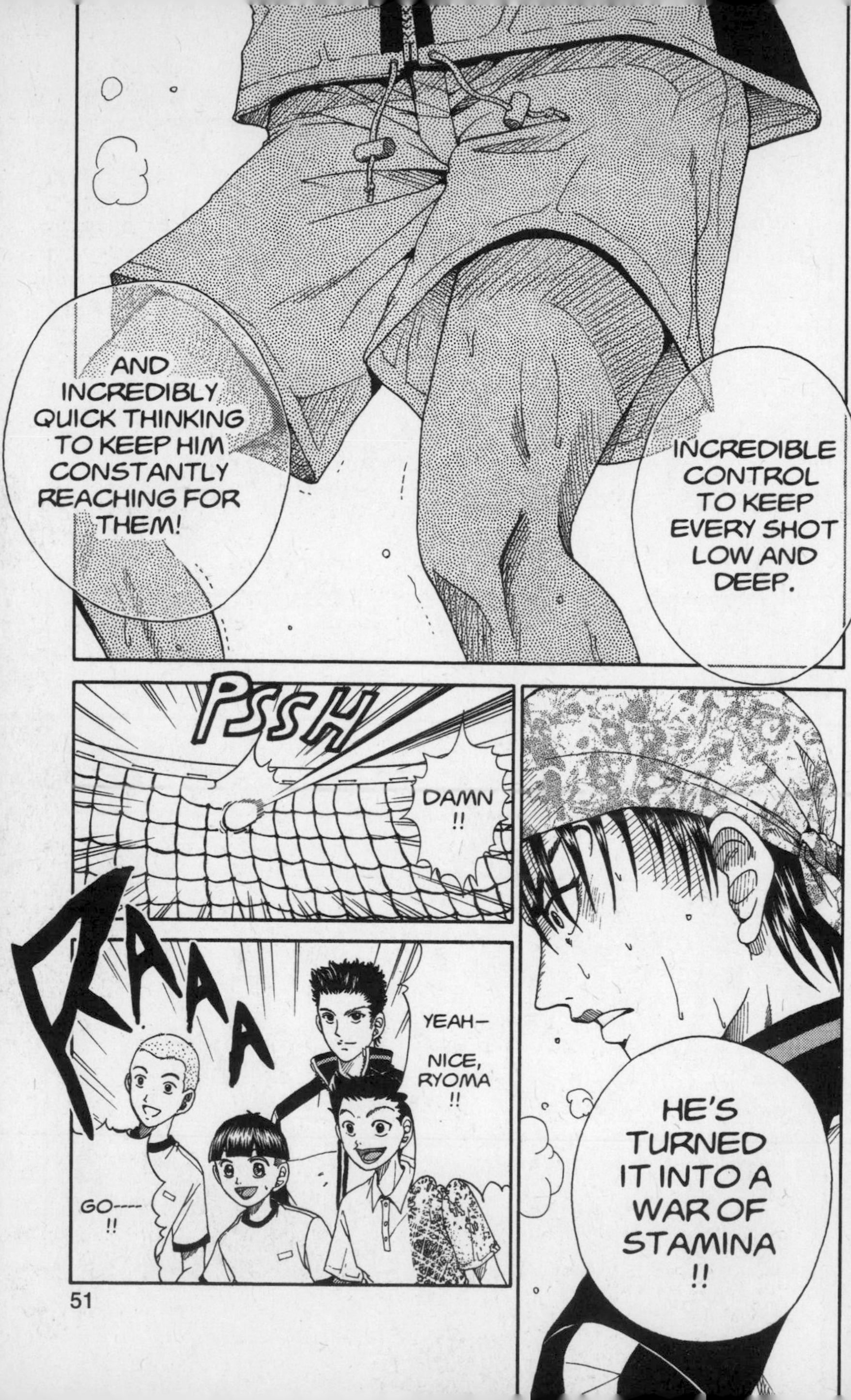
INCREDIBLE CONTROL TO KEEP EVERY SHOT LOW AND DEEP.
AND INCREDIBLY QUICK THINKING TO KEEP HIM CONSTANTLY REACHING FOR THEM!
HE'S TURNED IT INTO A WAR OF STAMINA !!
PSSH
DAMN !!
RAAA
YEAH—
NICE, RYOMA !!
GO---- !!

READ THIS WAY

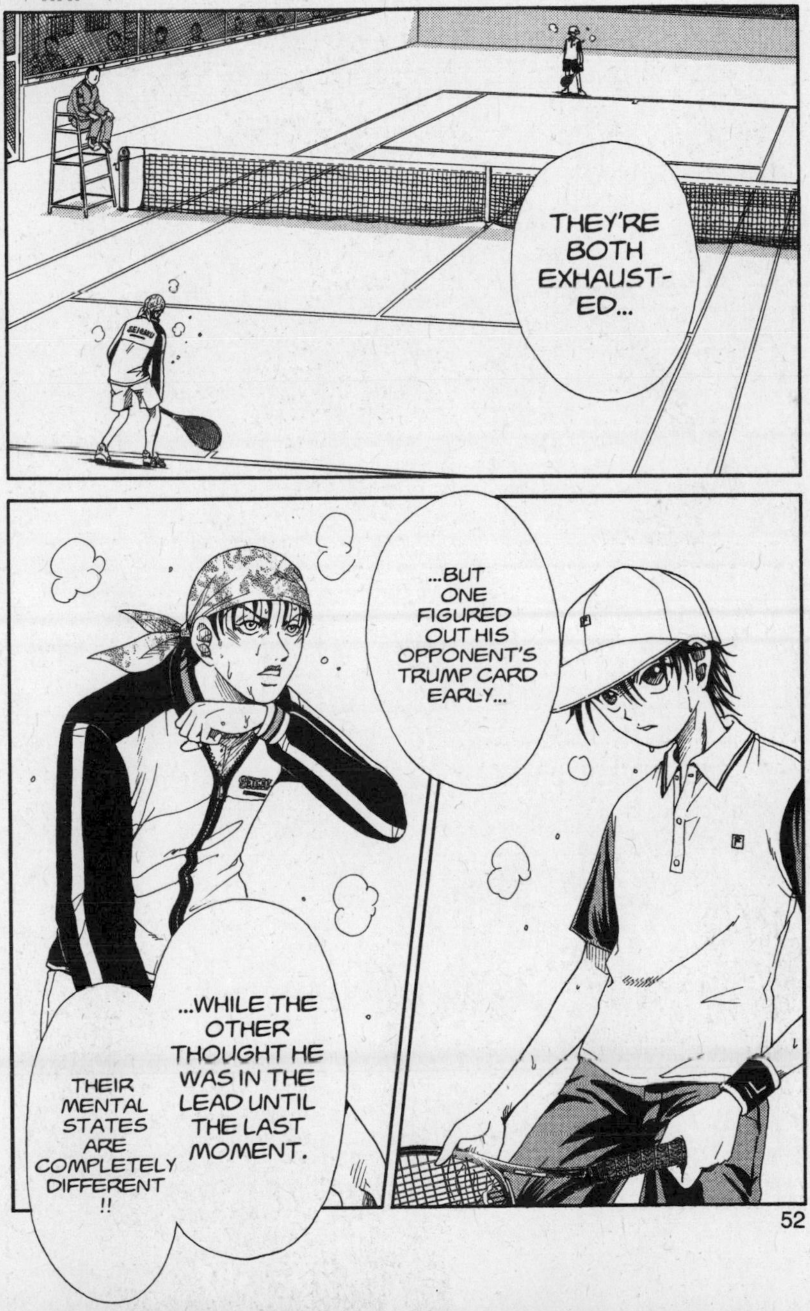
THEY'RE BOTH EXHAUST-ED...
...BUT ONE FIGURED OUT HIS OPPONENT'S TRUMP CARD EARLY...
...WHILE THE OTHER THOUGHT HE WAS IN THE LEAD UNTIL THE LAST MOMENT.
THEIR MENTAL STATES ARE COMPLETELY DIFFERENT !!

READ THIS WAY

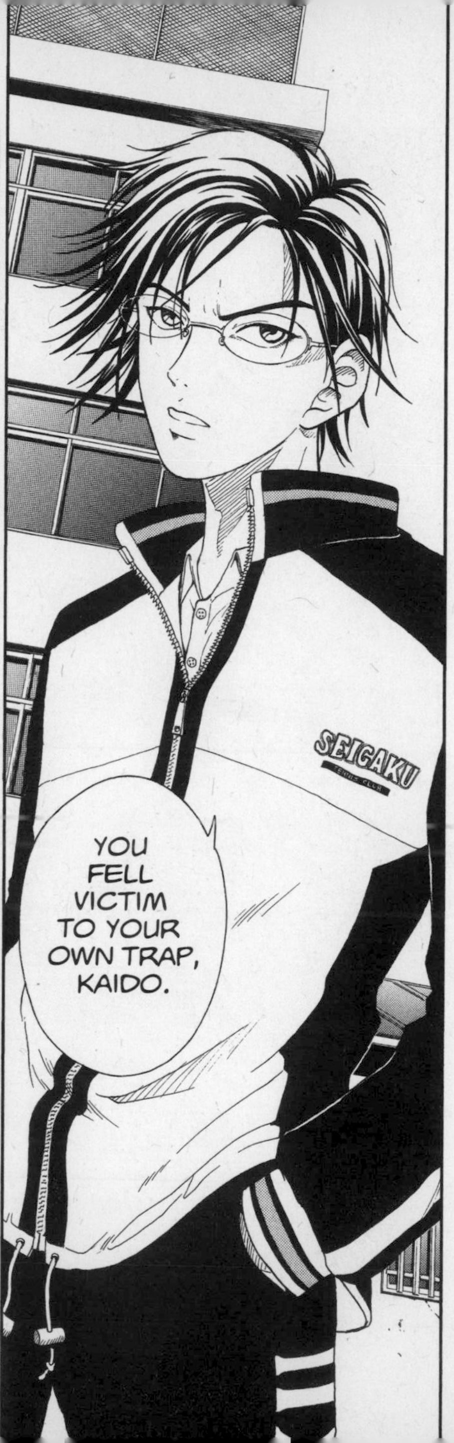
YOU FELL VICTIM TO YOUR OWN TRAP, KAIDO.
SEIGAKU

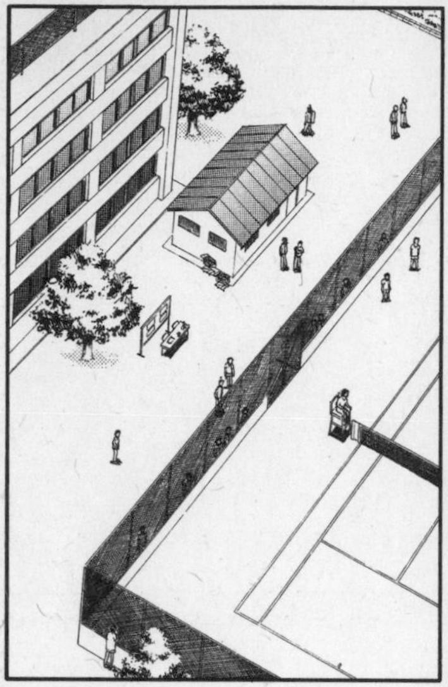

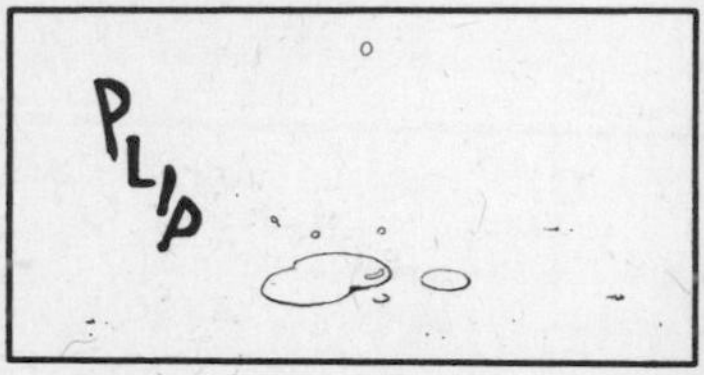
PLIP

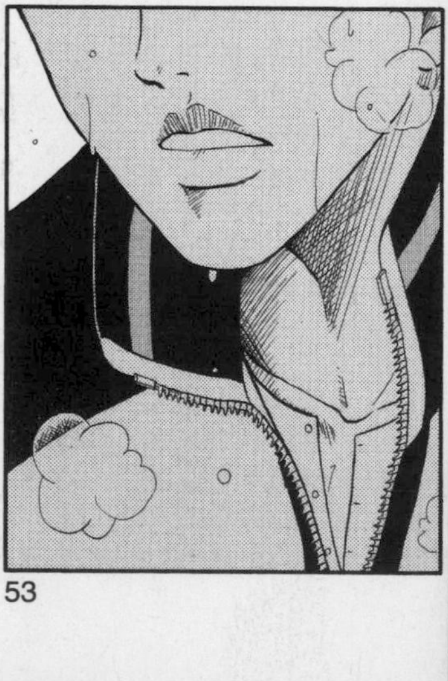

READ THIS WAY

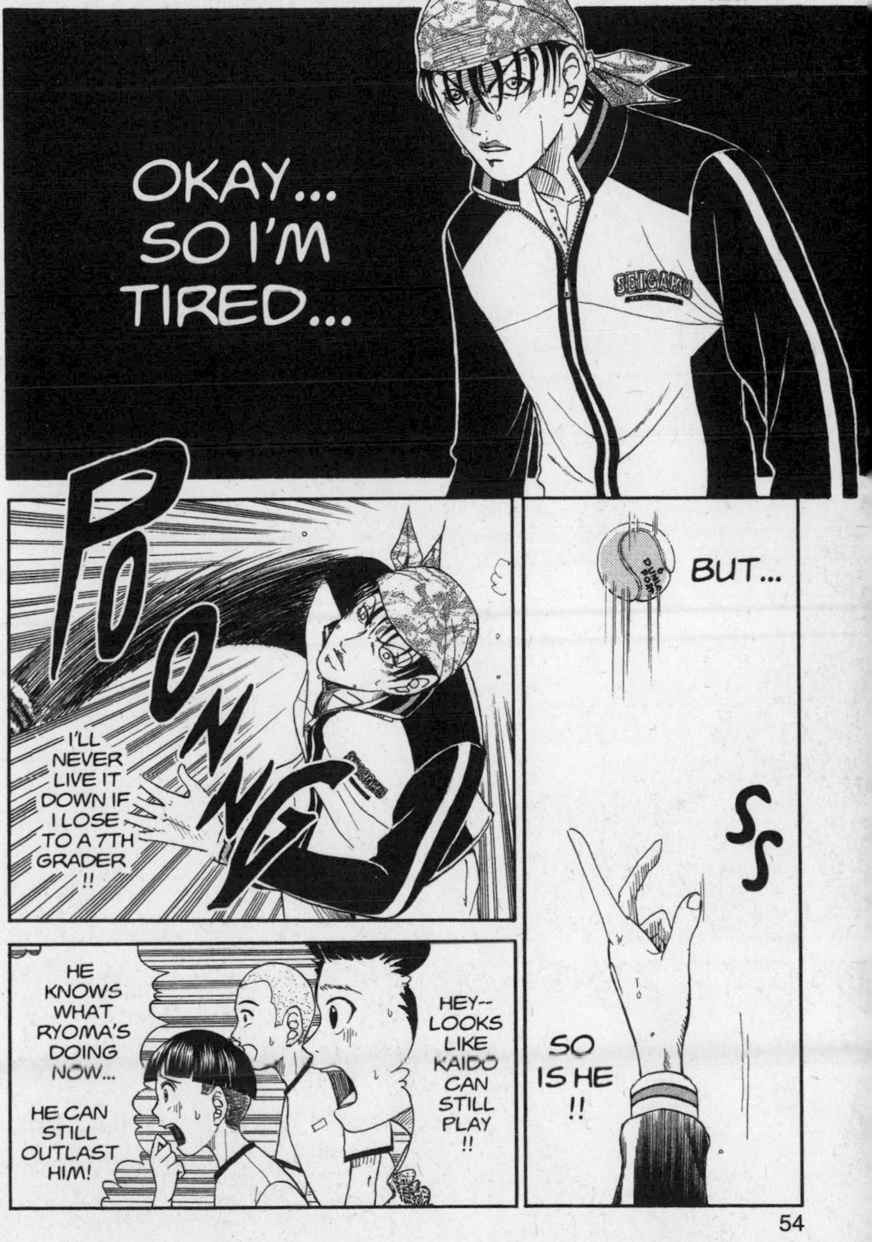
OKAY... SO I'M TIRED...
BUT...
SS
SO IS HE !!
POONNG
I'LL NEVER LIVE IT DOWN IF I LOSE TO A 7TH GRADER !!
HEY-- LOOKS LIKE KAIDO CAN STILL PLAY !!
HE KNOWS WHAT RYOMA'S DOING NOW...
HE CAN STILL OUTLAST HIM!

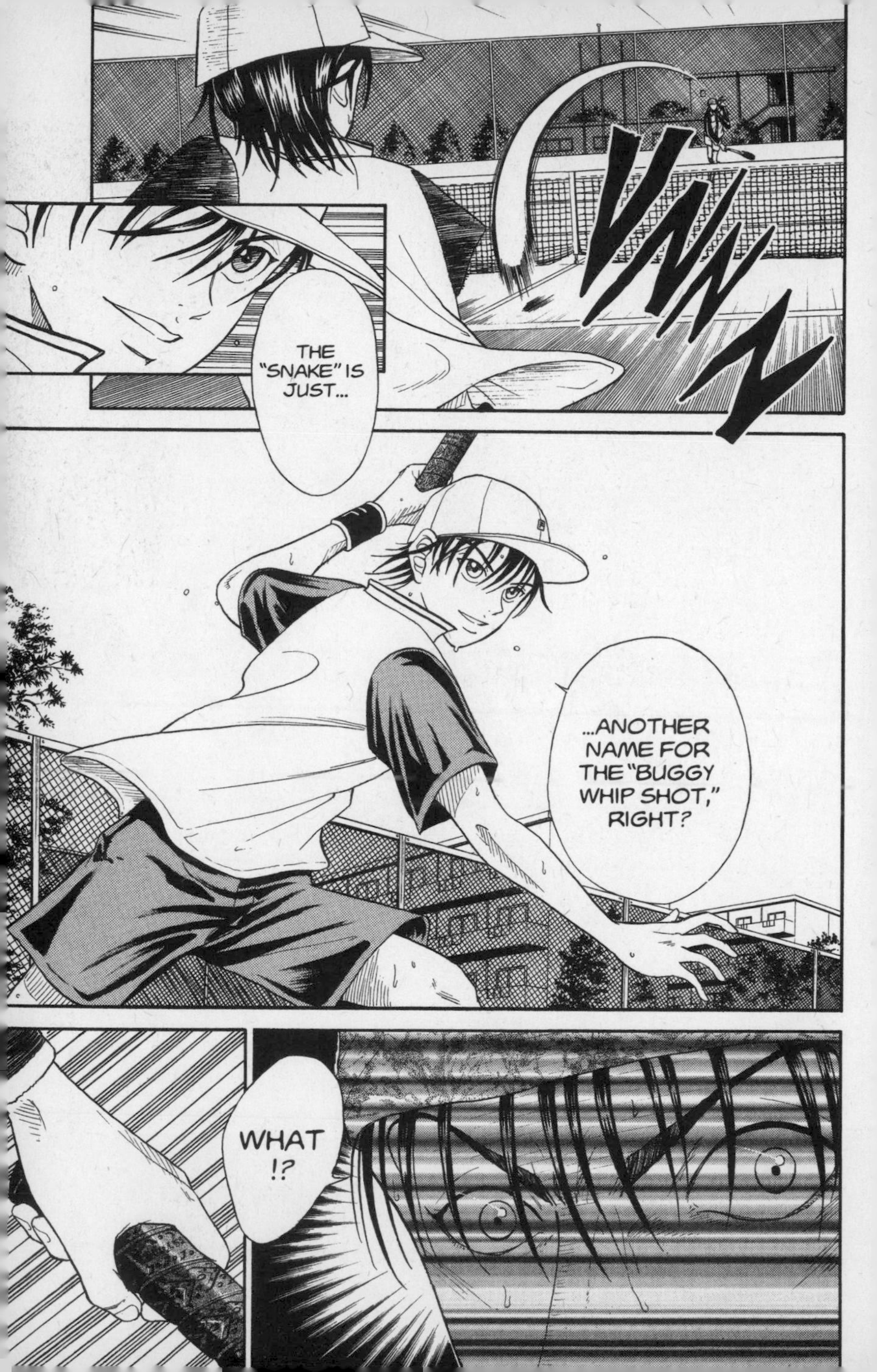
VWW
THE "SNAKE" IS JUST...
...ANOTHER NAME FOR THE "BUGGY WHIP SHOT," RIGHT?
WHAT !?

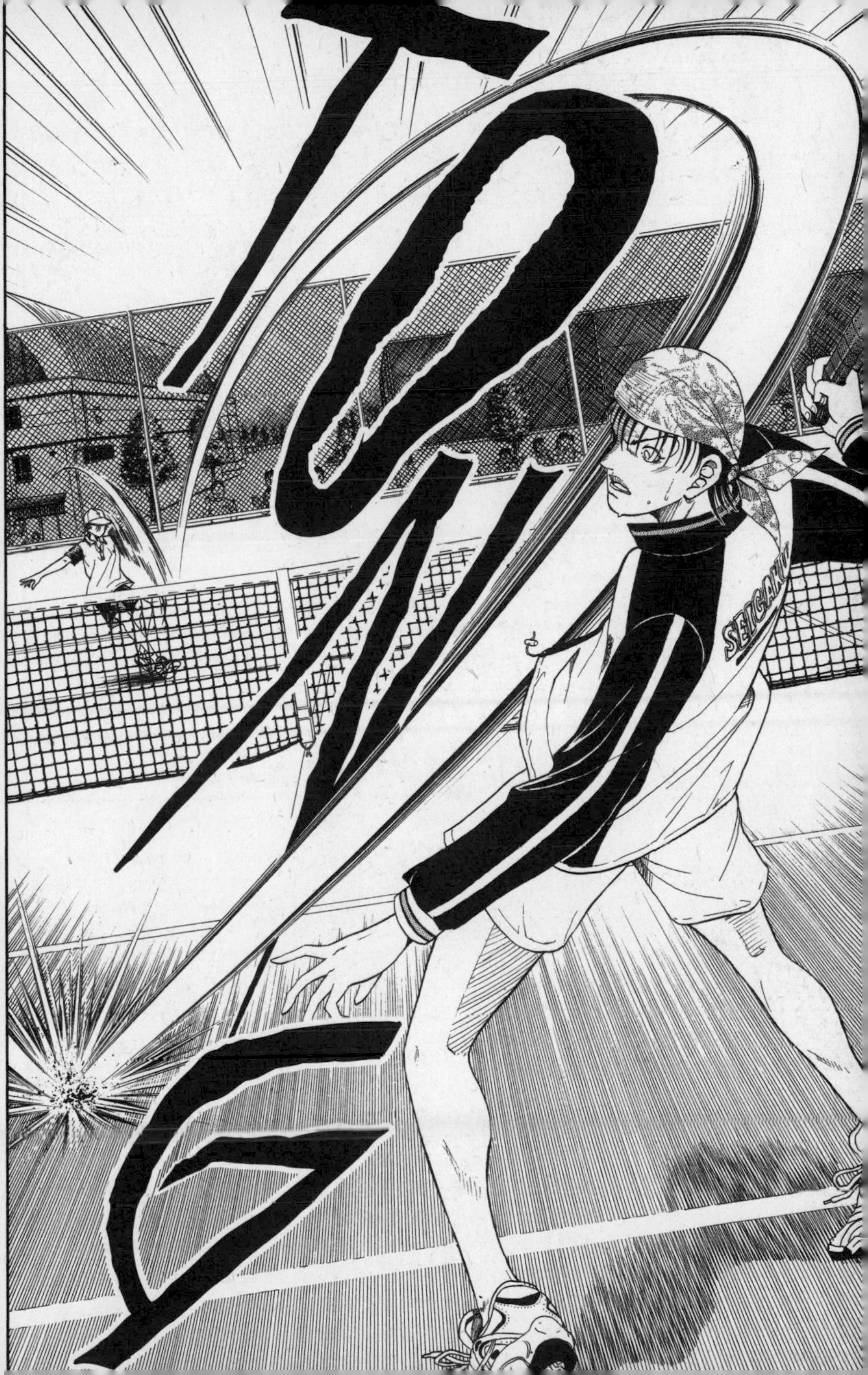
SEIGAKU

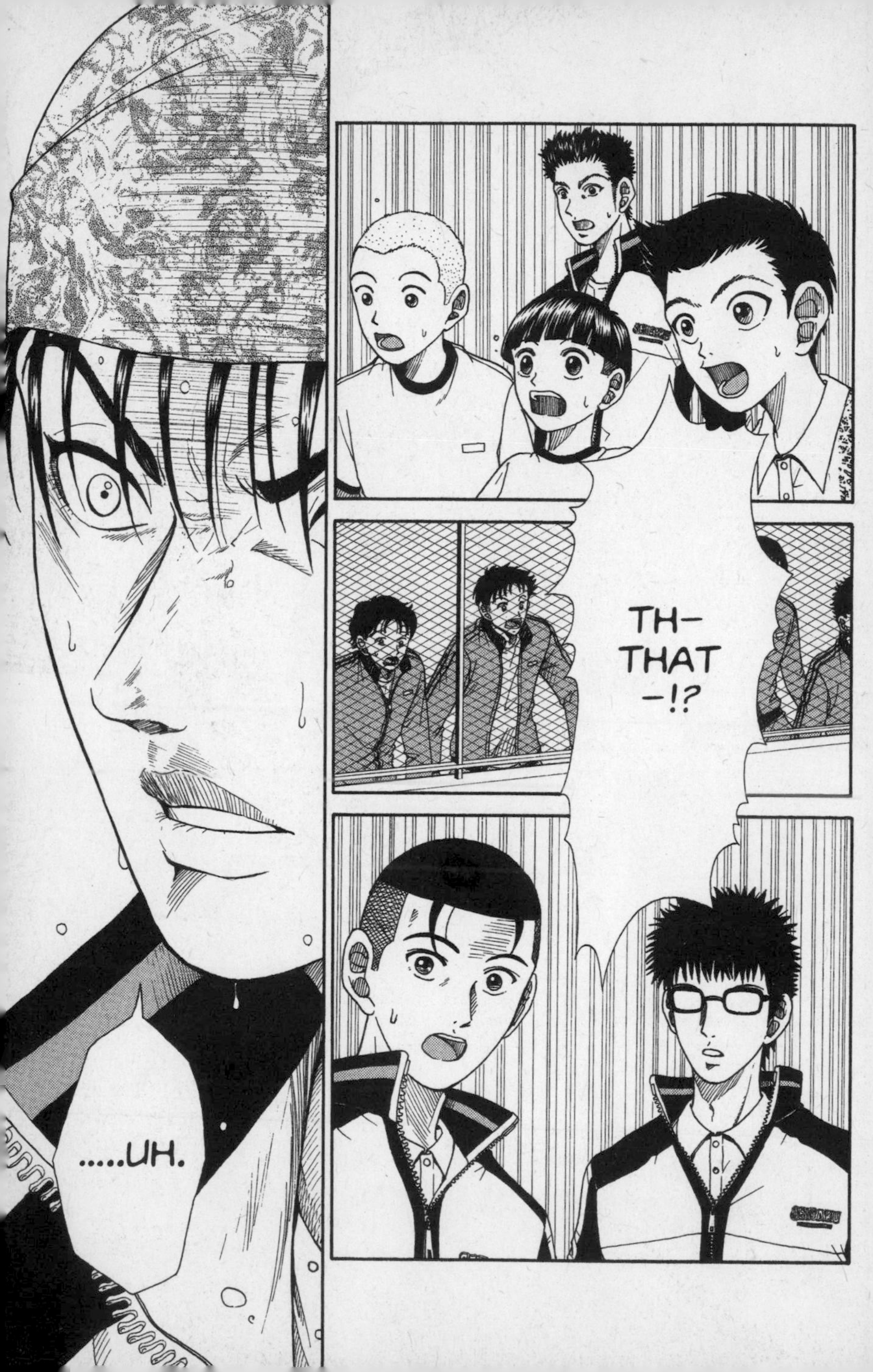
TH-THAT-!?
.....UH.

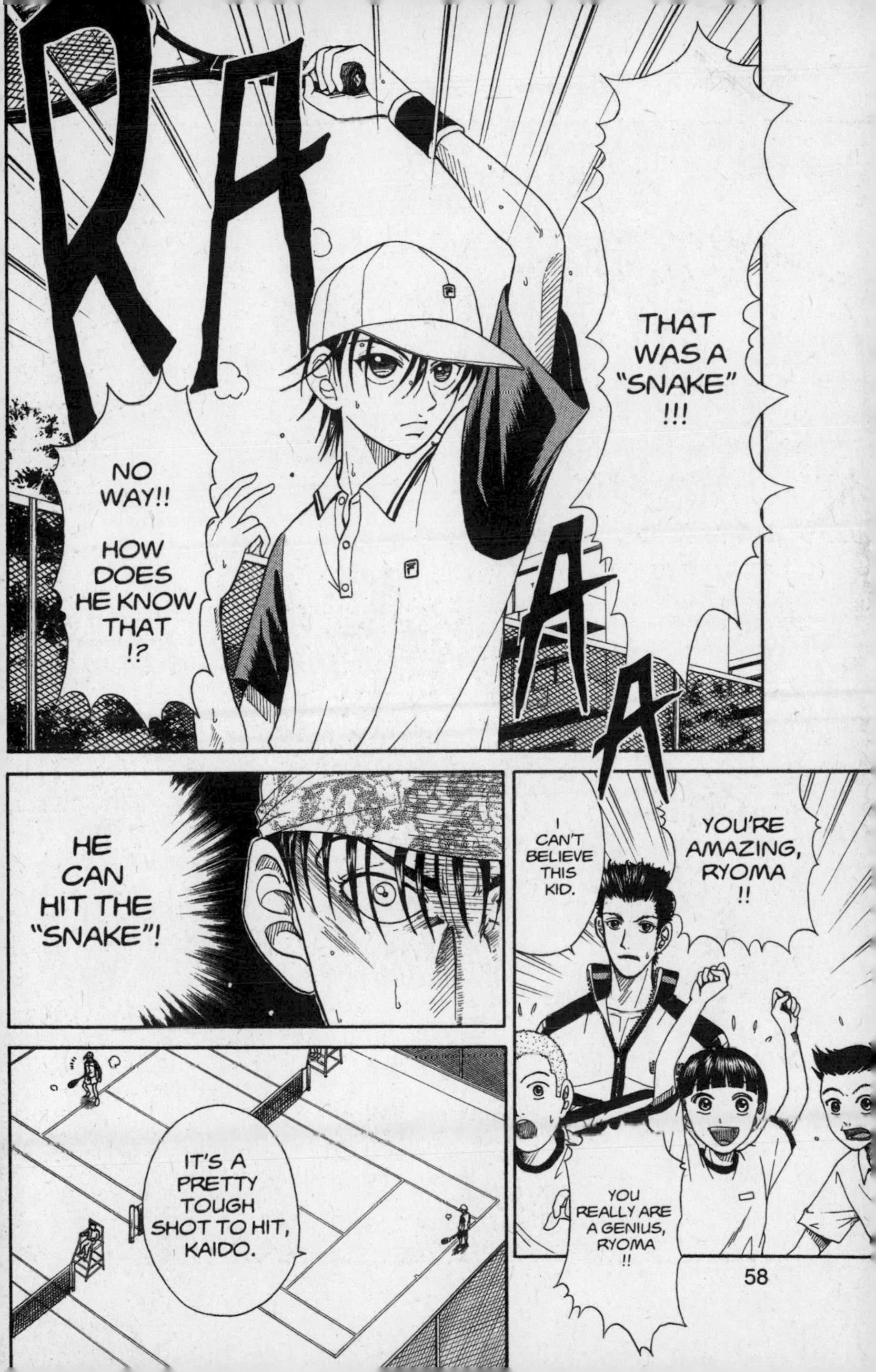
THAT WAS A "SNAKE" !!!
NO WAY!! HOW DOES HE KNOW THAT !?
RAAA
YOU'RE AMAZING, RYOMA !!
I CAN'T BELIEVE THIS KID.
YOU REALLY ARE A GENIUS, RYOMA !!
HE CAN HIT THE "SNAKE"!
IT'S A PRETTY TOUGH SHOT TO HIT, KAIDO.

READ THIS WAY

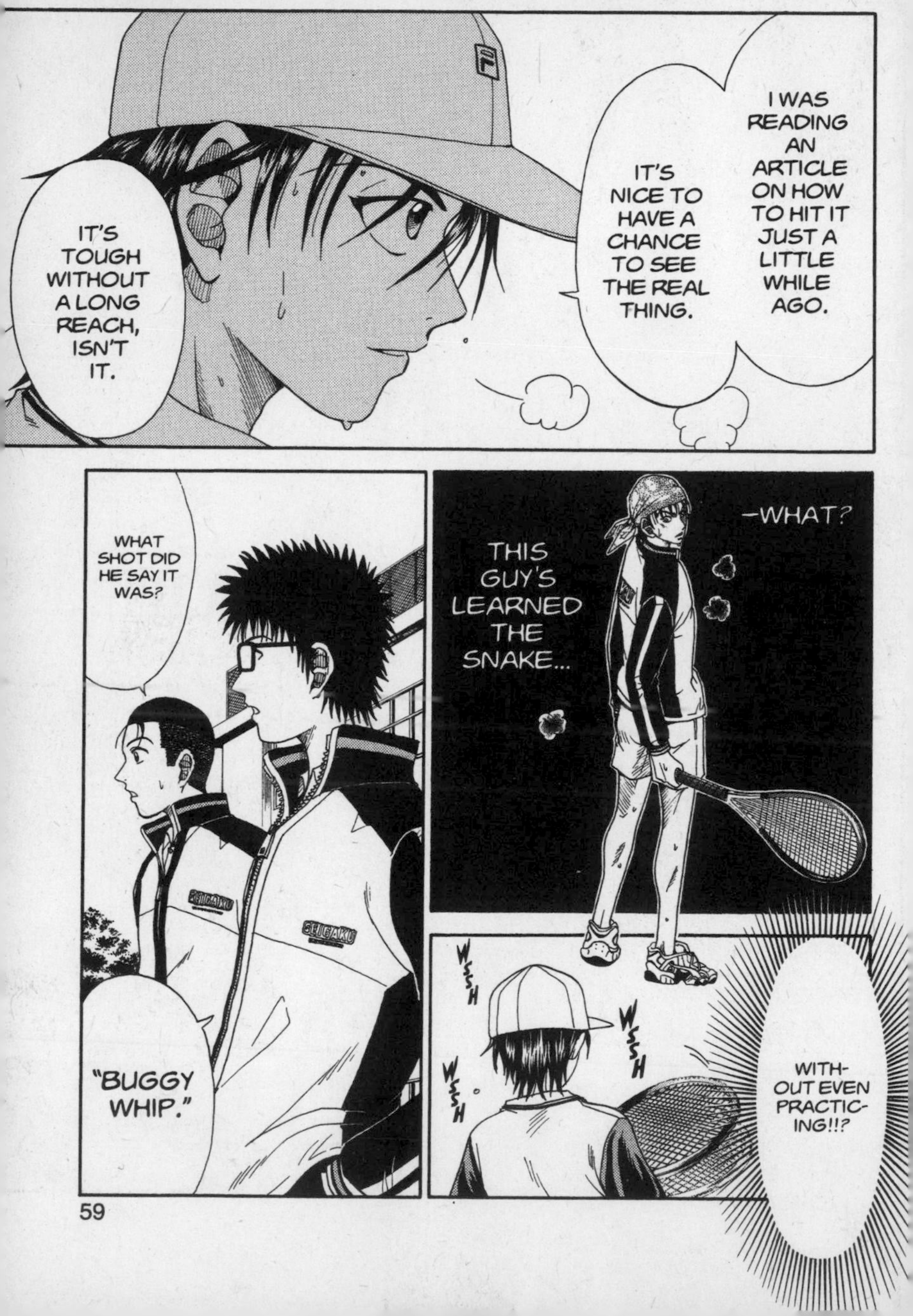

I WAS READING AN ARTICLE ON HOW TO HIT IT JUST A LITTLE WHILE AGO.
IT'S NICE TO HAVE A CHANCE TO SEE THE REAL THING.
IT'S TOUGH WITHOUT A LONG REACH, ISN'T IT.
-WHAT?
THIS GUY'S LEARNED THE SNAKE...
WITH-OUT EVEN PRACTIC-ING!!?
WSSH
WSSH
WSSH
WHAT SHOT DID HE SAY IT WAS?
"BUGGY WHIP."

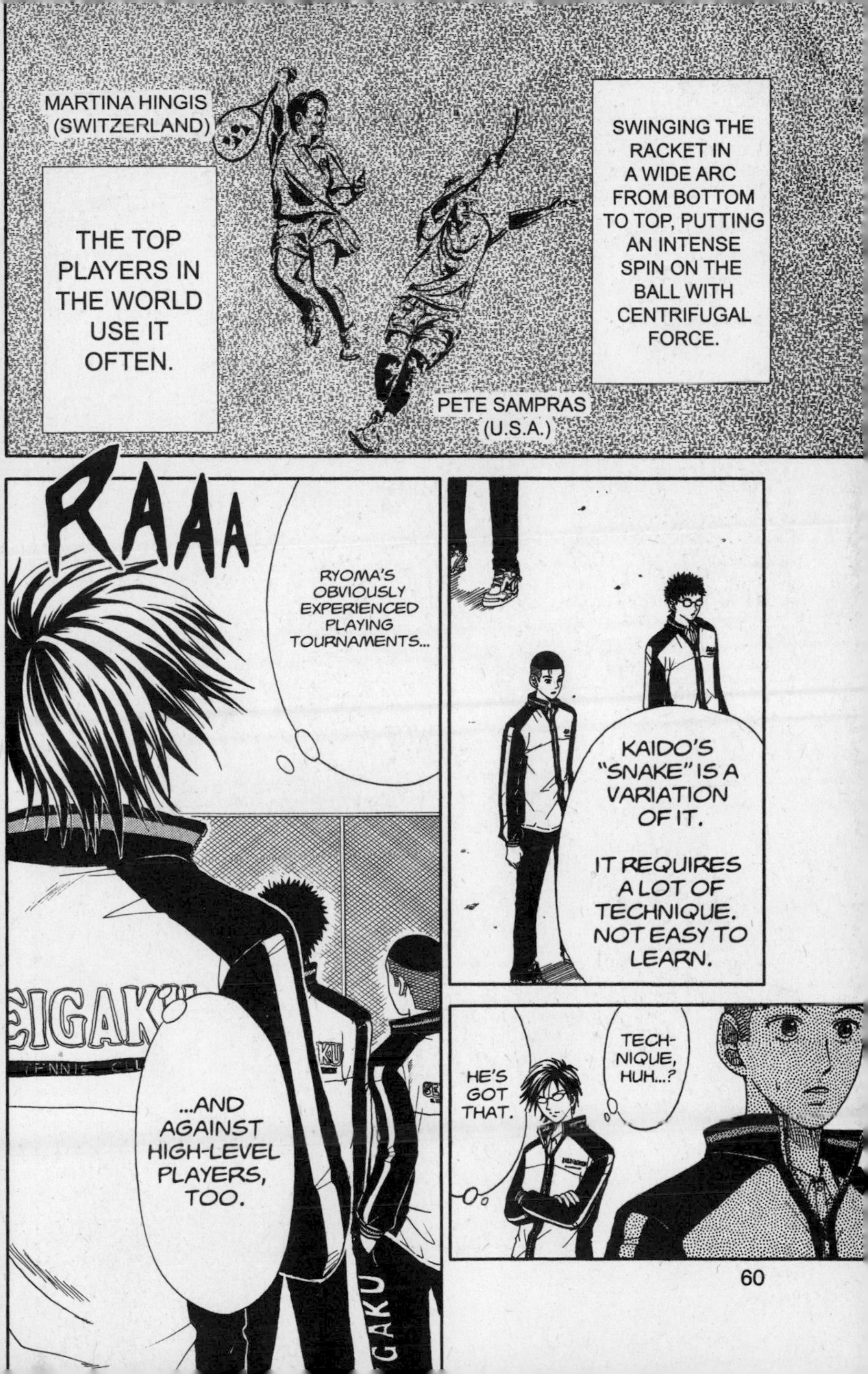
SWINGING THE RACKET IN A WIDE ARC FROM BOTTOM TO TOP, PUTTING AN INTENSE SPIN ON THE BALL WITH CENTRIFUGAL FORCE.
MARTINA HINGIS (SWITZERLAND)
THE TOP PLAYERS IN THE WORLD USE IT OFTEN.
PETE SAMPRAS (U.S.A.)
KAIDO'S "SNAKE" IS A VARIATION OF IT.
IT REQUIRES A LOT OF TECHNIQUE. NOT EASY TO LEARN.
TECH-NIQUE, HUH...?
HE'S GOT THAT.
RAAA
RYOMA'S OBVIOUSLY EXPERIENCED PLAYING TOURNAMENTS...
...AND AGAINST HIGH-LEVEL PLAYERS, TOO.
SEIGAKU
TENNIS CLUB

READ THIS WAY

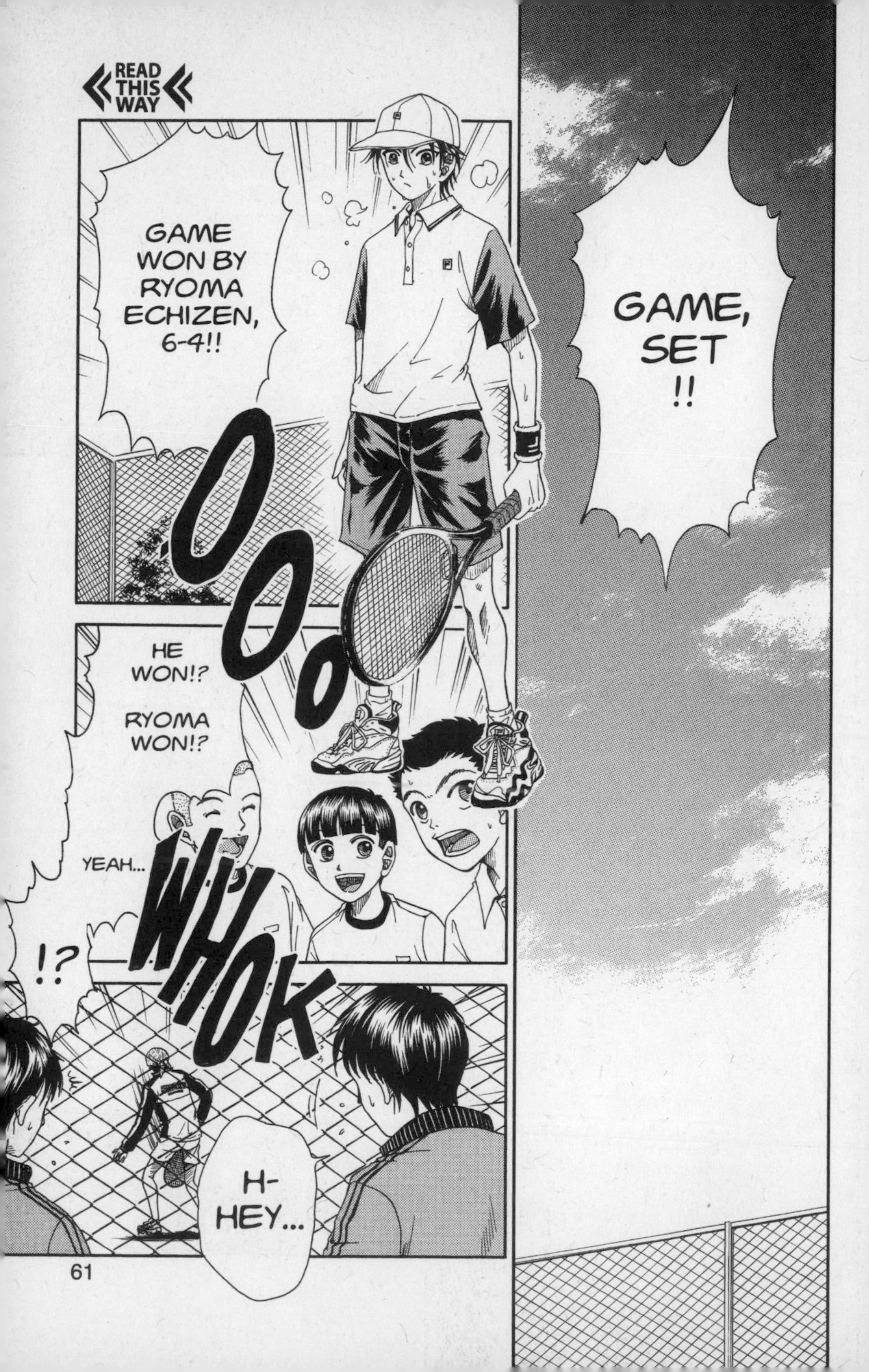
GAME, SET !!
GAME WON BY RYOMA ECHIZEN, 6-4!!
OOOO
HE WON!?
RYOMA WON!?
YEAH...
WHOK
!?
H- HEY...

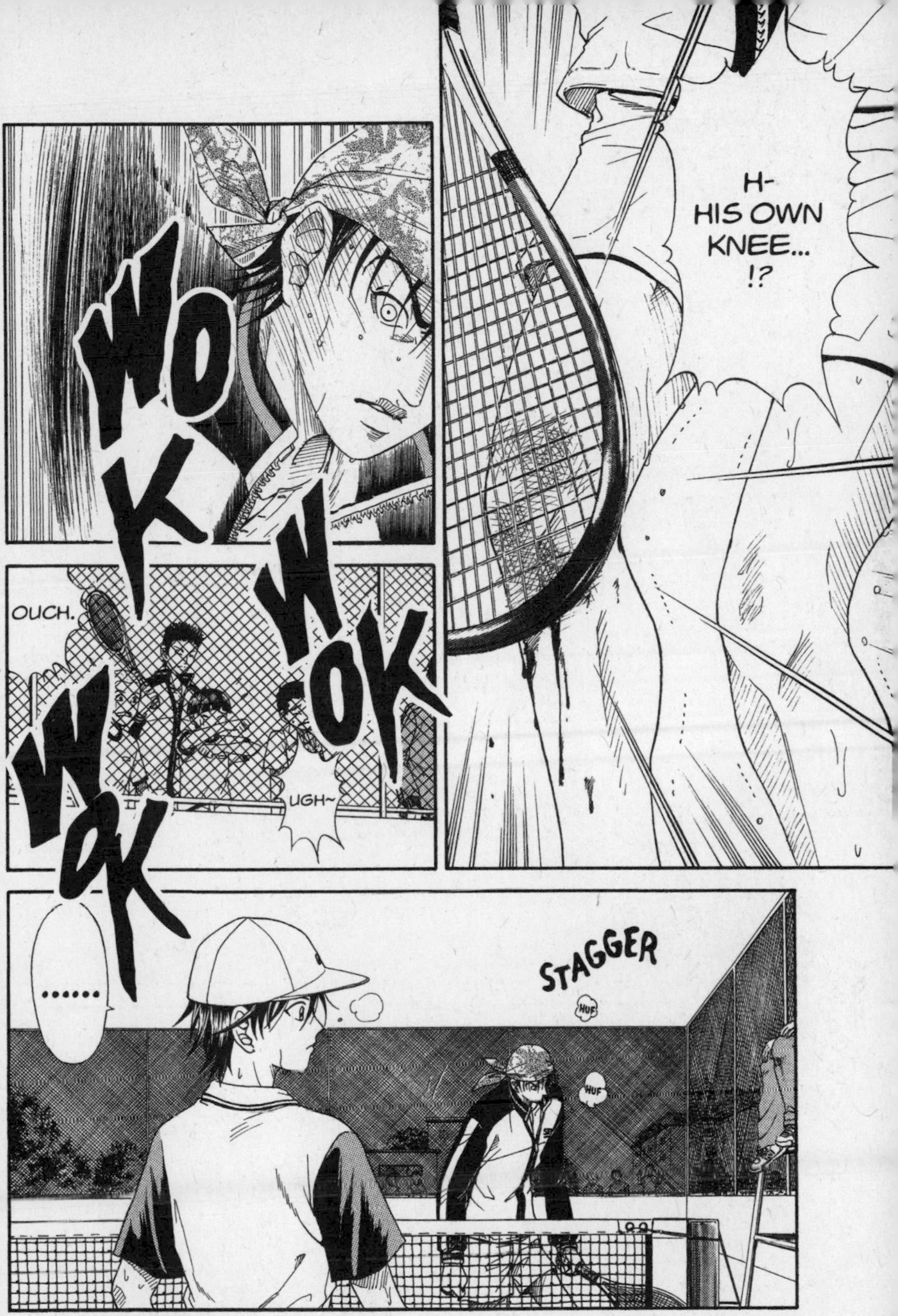
H-
HIS OWN KNEE...
!?
WOK
WOK
OUCH.
WOK
UGH~
......
STAGGER
HUF
HUF

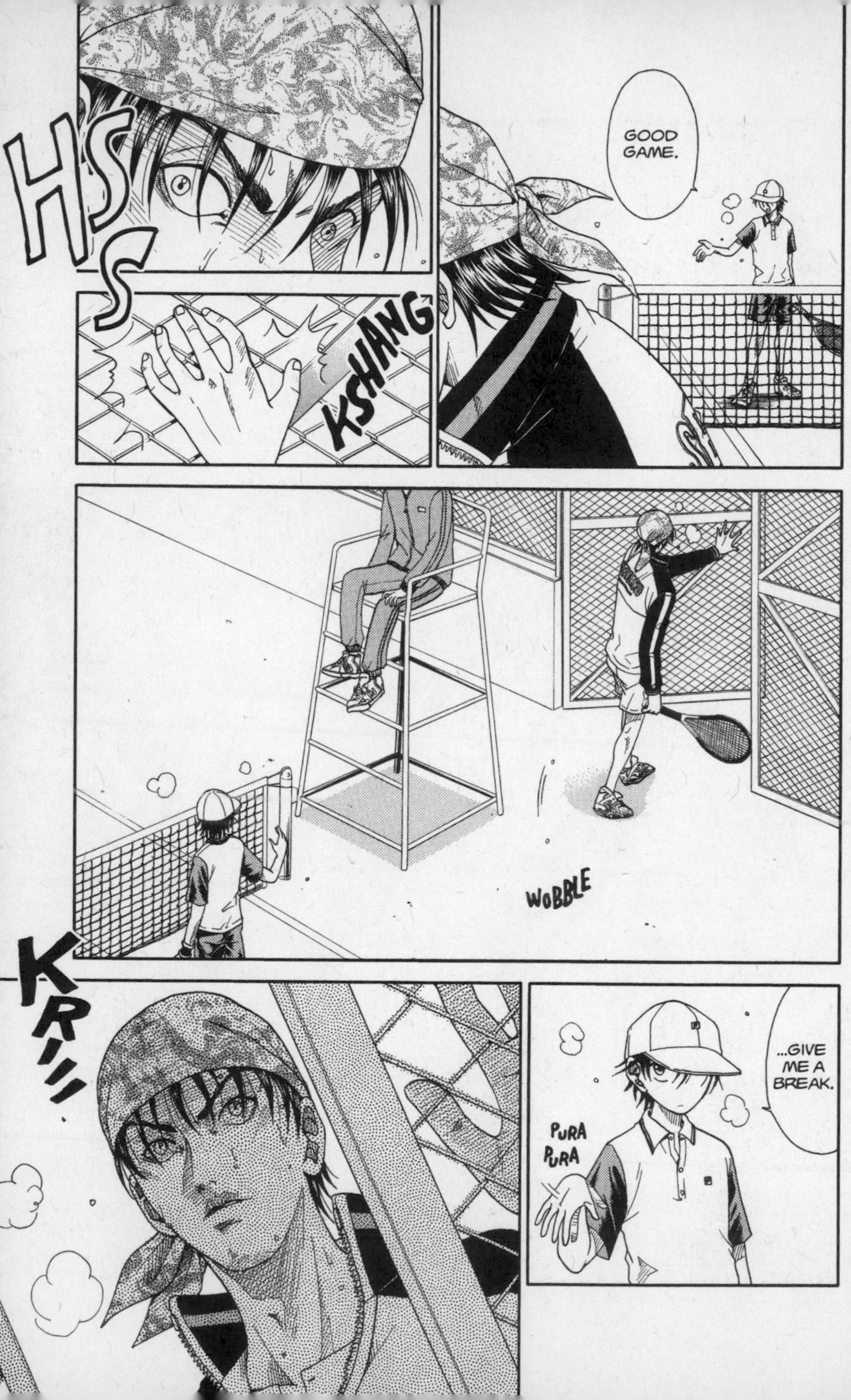
GOOD GAME.
HSS
KSHANG
WOBBLE
...GIVE ME A BREAK.
PURA PURA
KRIII

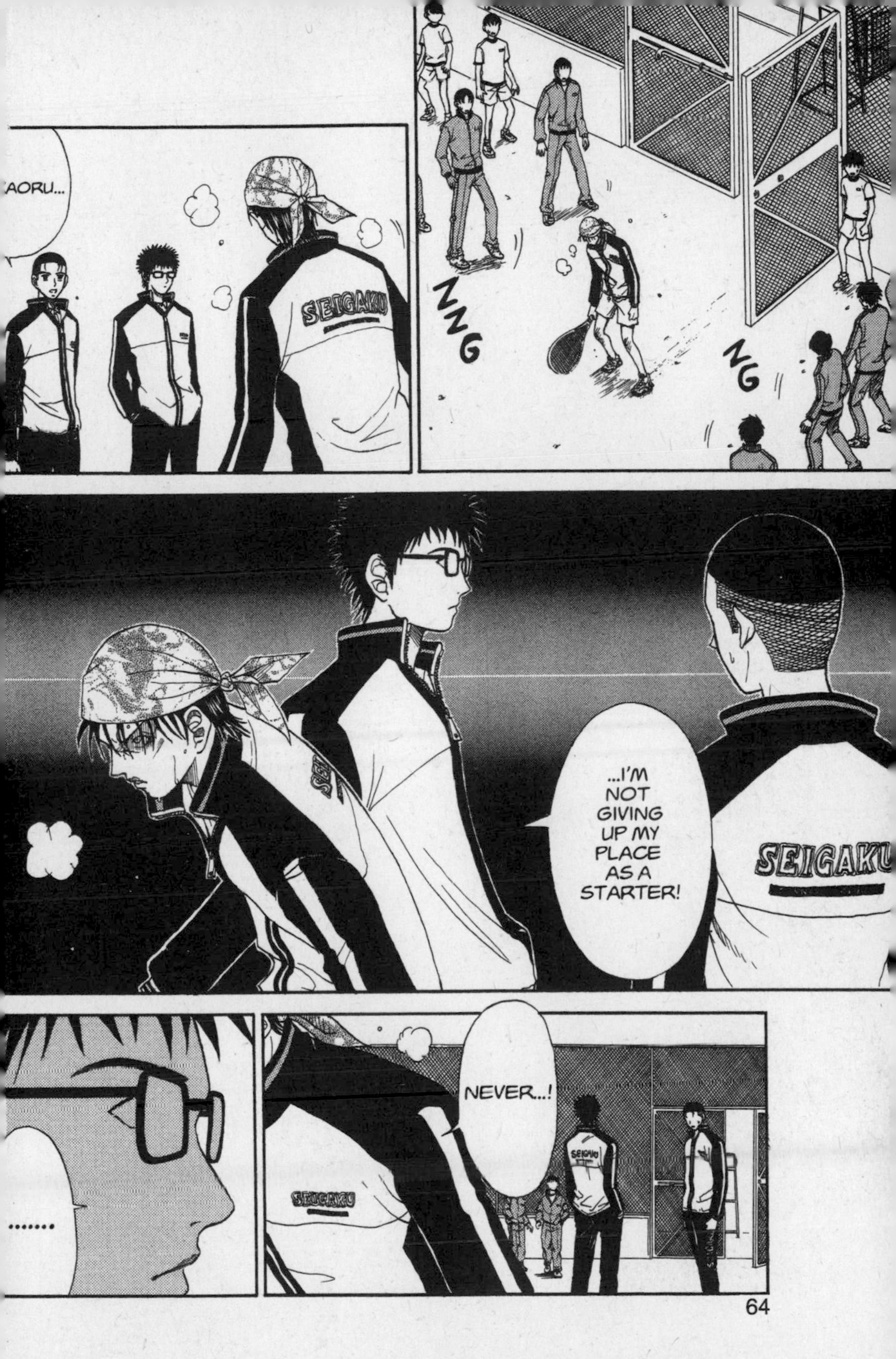
ZNG
ZNG
AORU...
...I'M NOT GIVING UP MY PLACE AS A STARTER!
SEIGAKU
NEVER...!
SEIGAKU
....

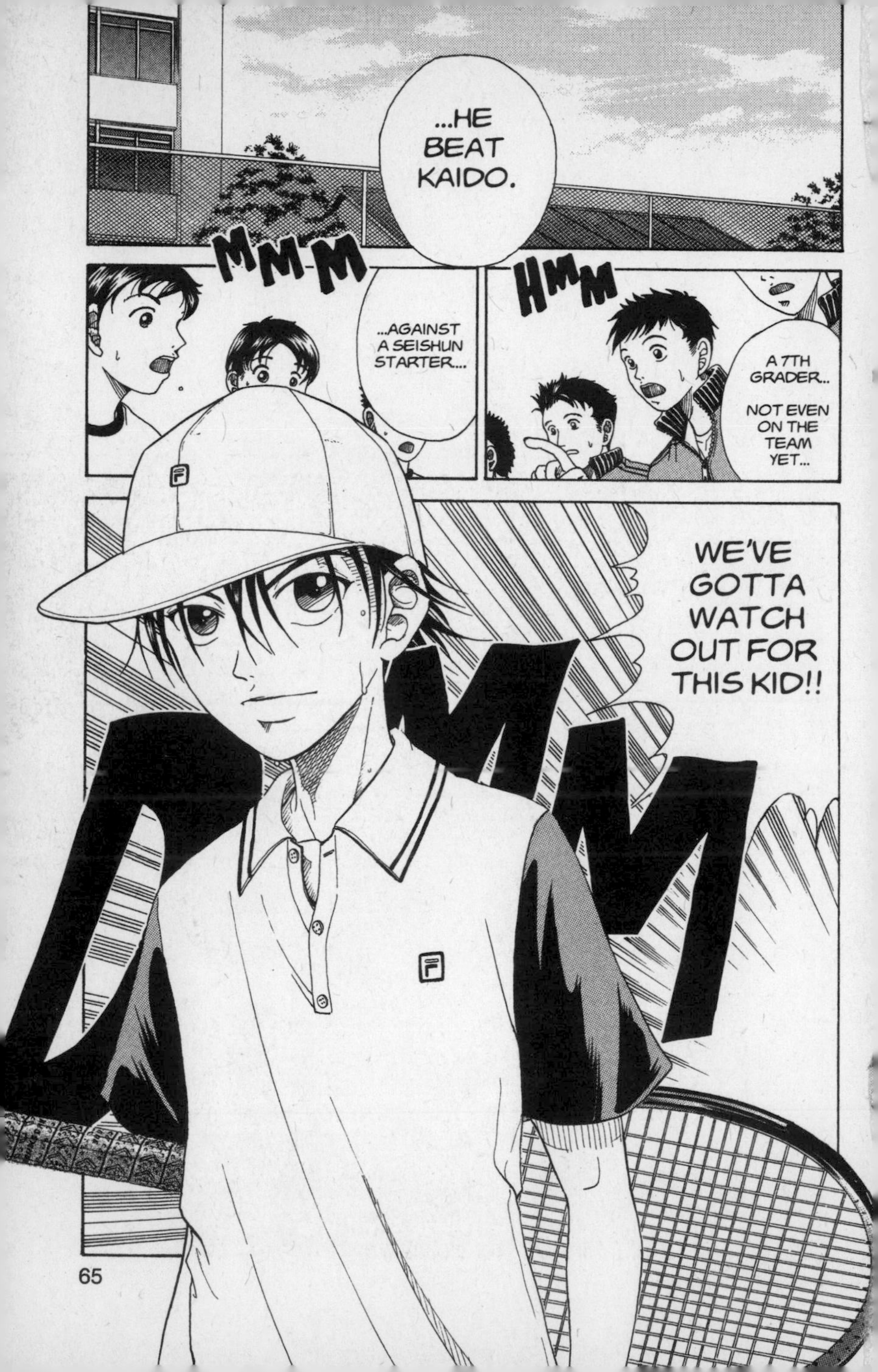
...HE BEAT KAIDO.
MMM
HMM
A 7TH GRADER...
NOT EVEN ON THE TEAM YET...
...AGAINST A SEISHUN STARTER...
WE'VE GOTTA WATCH OUT FOR THIS KID!!
MMM

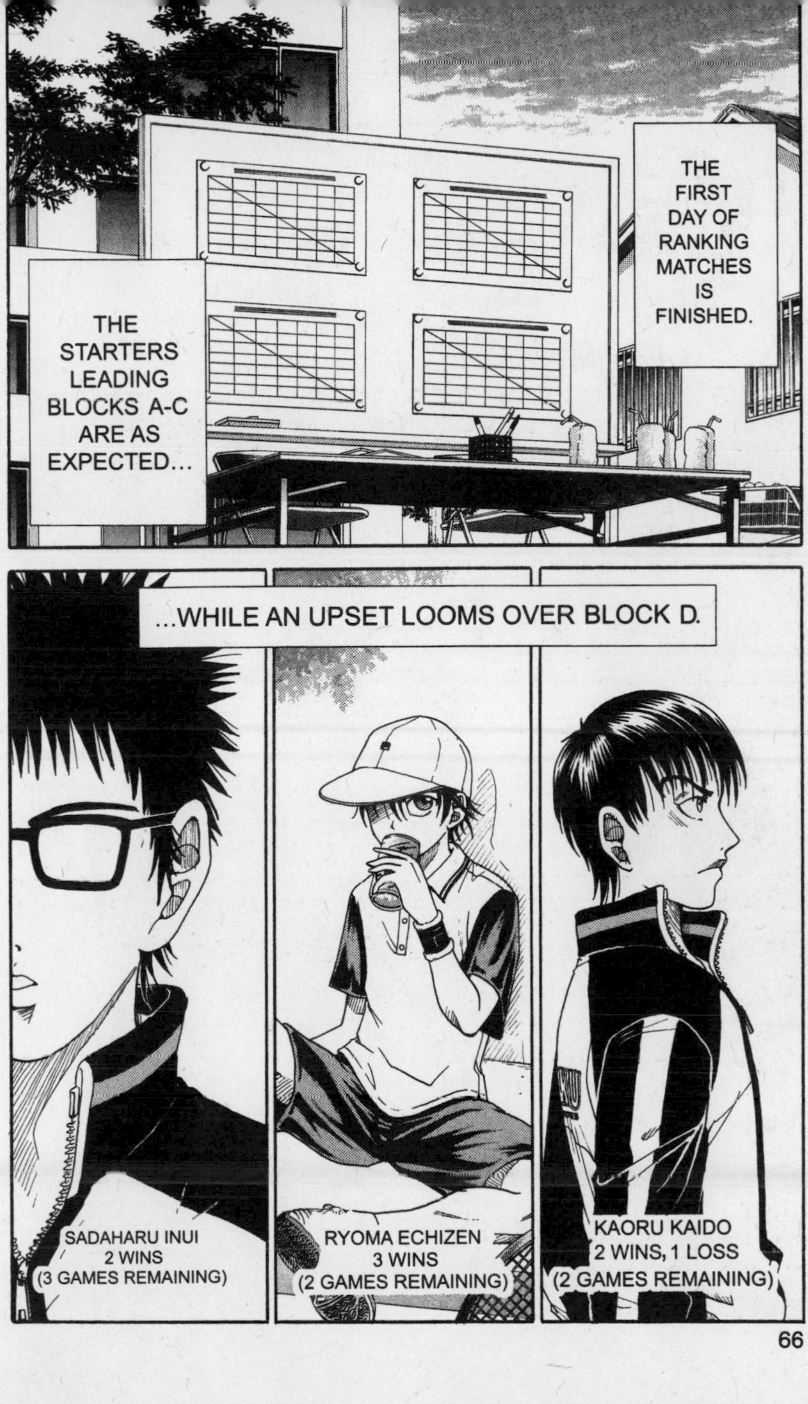
THE FIRST DAY OF RANKING MATCHES IS FINISHED.
THE STARTERS LEADING BLOCKS A-C ARE AS EXPECTED...
...WHILE AN UPSET LOOMS OVER BLOCK D.
KAORU KAIDO 2 WINS, 1 LOSS (2 GAMES REMAINING)
RYOMA ECHIZEN 3 WINS (2 GAMES REMAINING)
SADAHARU INUI 2 WINS (3 GAMES REMAINING)

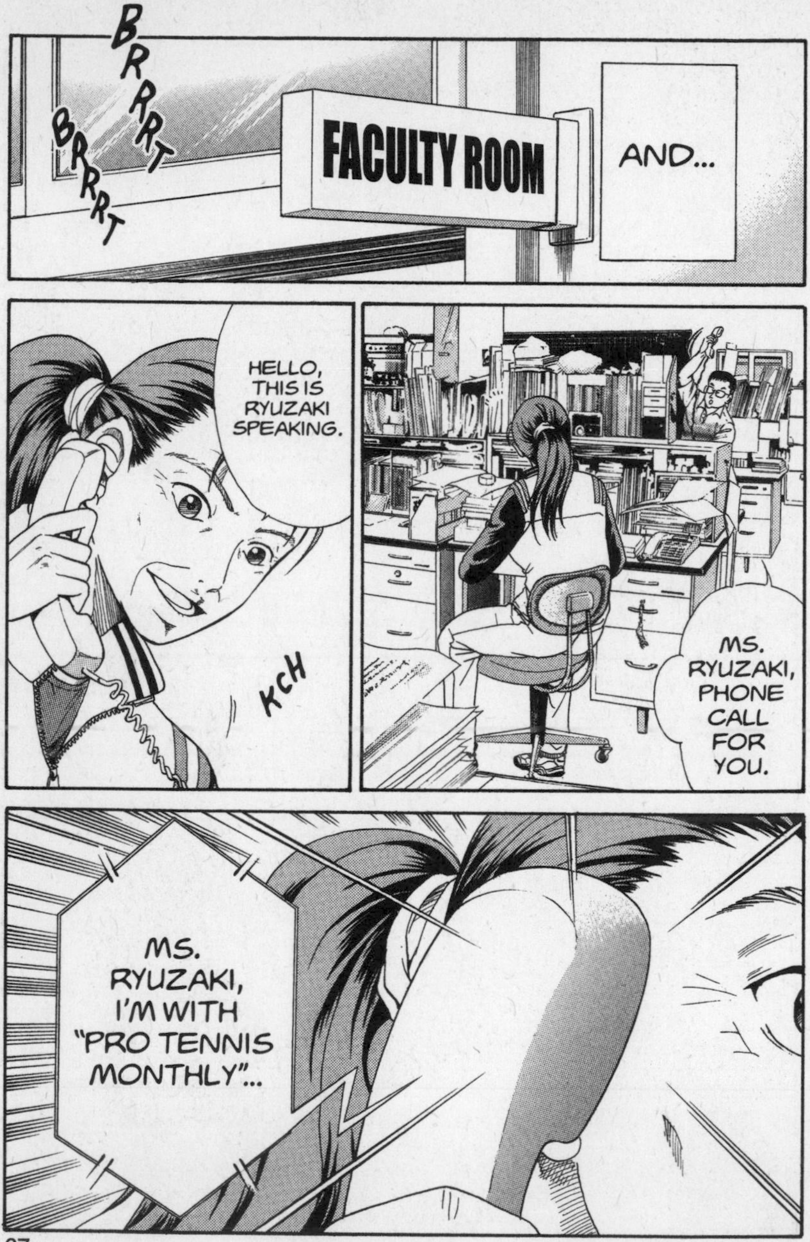
AND...
FACULTY ROOM
BRRRT
BRRRT
MS. RYUZAKI, PHONE CALL FOR YOU.
HELLO, THIS IS RYUZAKI SPEAKING.
KCH
MS. RYUZAKI, I'M WITH "PRO TENNIS MONTHLY"...

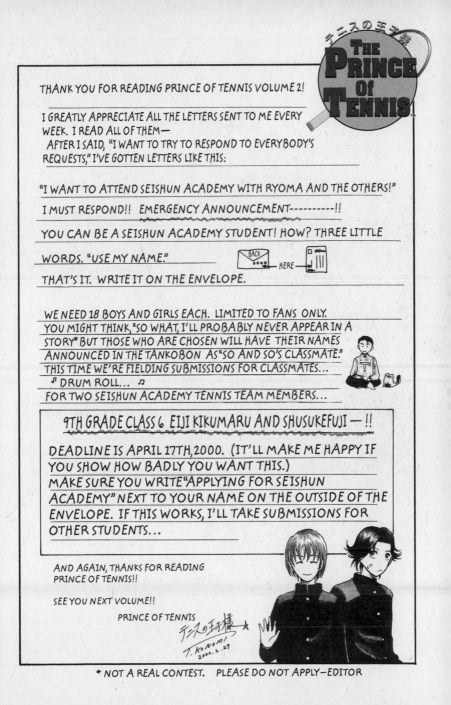

THE PRINCE OF TENNIS

THANK YOU FOR READING PRINCE OF TENNIS VOLUME 2!

I GREATLY APPRECIATE ALL THE LETTERS SENT TO ME EVERY WEEK. I READ ALL OF THEM—
    AFTER I SAID, "I WANT TO TRY TO RESPOND TO EVERYBODY'S REQUESTS," I'VE GOTTEN LETTERS LIKE THIS:

"I WANT TO ATTEND SEISHUN ACADEMY WITH RYOMA AND THE OTHERS!"

I MUST RESPOND!! EMERGENCY ANNOUNCEMENT----------!!

YOU CAN BE A SEISHUN ACADEMY STUDENT! HOW? THREE LITTLE

WORDS. "USE MY NAME."

THAT'S IT. WRITE IT ON THE ENVELOPE.

WE NEED 18 BOYS AND GIRLS EACH. LIMITED TO FANS ONLY.
YOU MIGHT THINK, "SO WHAT, I'LL PROBABLY NEVER APPEAR IN A STORY" BUT THOSE WHO ARE CHOSEN WILL HAVE THEIR NAMES ANNOUNCED IN THE TANKOBON AS "SO AND SO'S CLASSMATE." THIS TIME WE'RE FIELDING SUBMISSIONS FOR CLASSMATES...
♪ DRUM ROLL... ♫
FOR TWO SEISHUN ACADEMY TENNIS TEAM MEMBERS...

9TH GRADE CLASS 6 EIJI KIKUMARU AND SHUSUKE FUJI —!!

DEADLINE IS APRIL 17TH, 2000. (IT'LL MAKE ME HAPPY IF YOU SHOW HOW BADLY YOU WANT THIS.)
MAKE SURE YOU WRITE "APPLYING FOR SEISHUN ACADEMY" NEXT TO YOUR NAME ON THE OUTSIDE OF THE ENVELOPE. IF THIS WORKS, I'LL TAKE SUBMISSIONS FOR OTHER STUDENTS...

AND AGAIN, THANKS FOR READING PRINCE OF TENNIS!!

SEE YOU NEXT VOLUME!!

PRINCE OF TENNIS

T. KONOMI
2000.2.27

* NOT A REAL CONTEST. PLEASE DO NOT APPLY—EDITOR

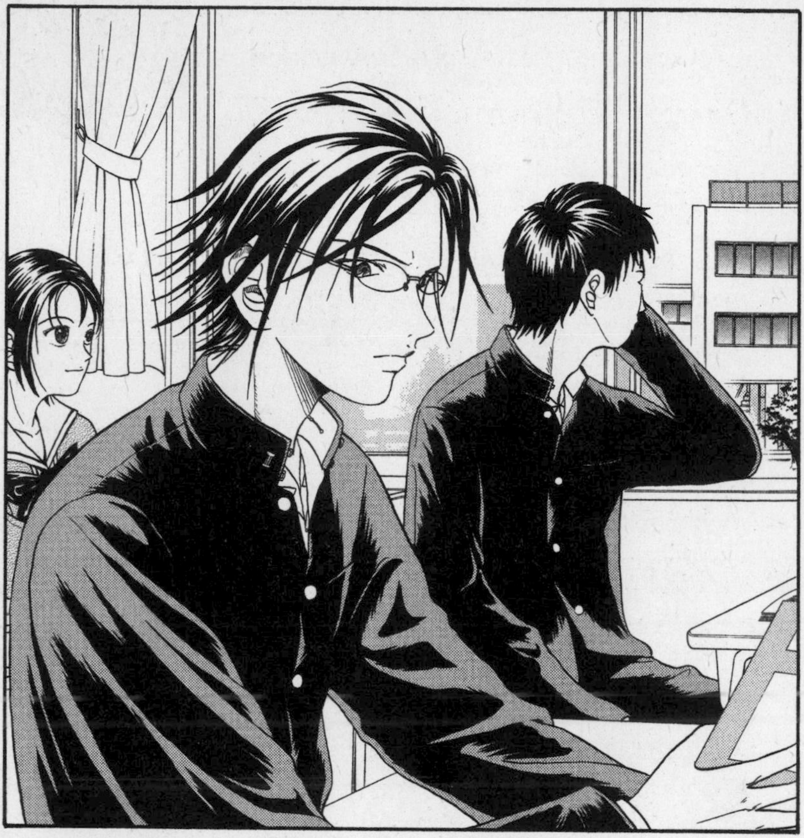

GENIUS 11
SOMEONE I WANT TO BEAT

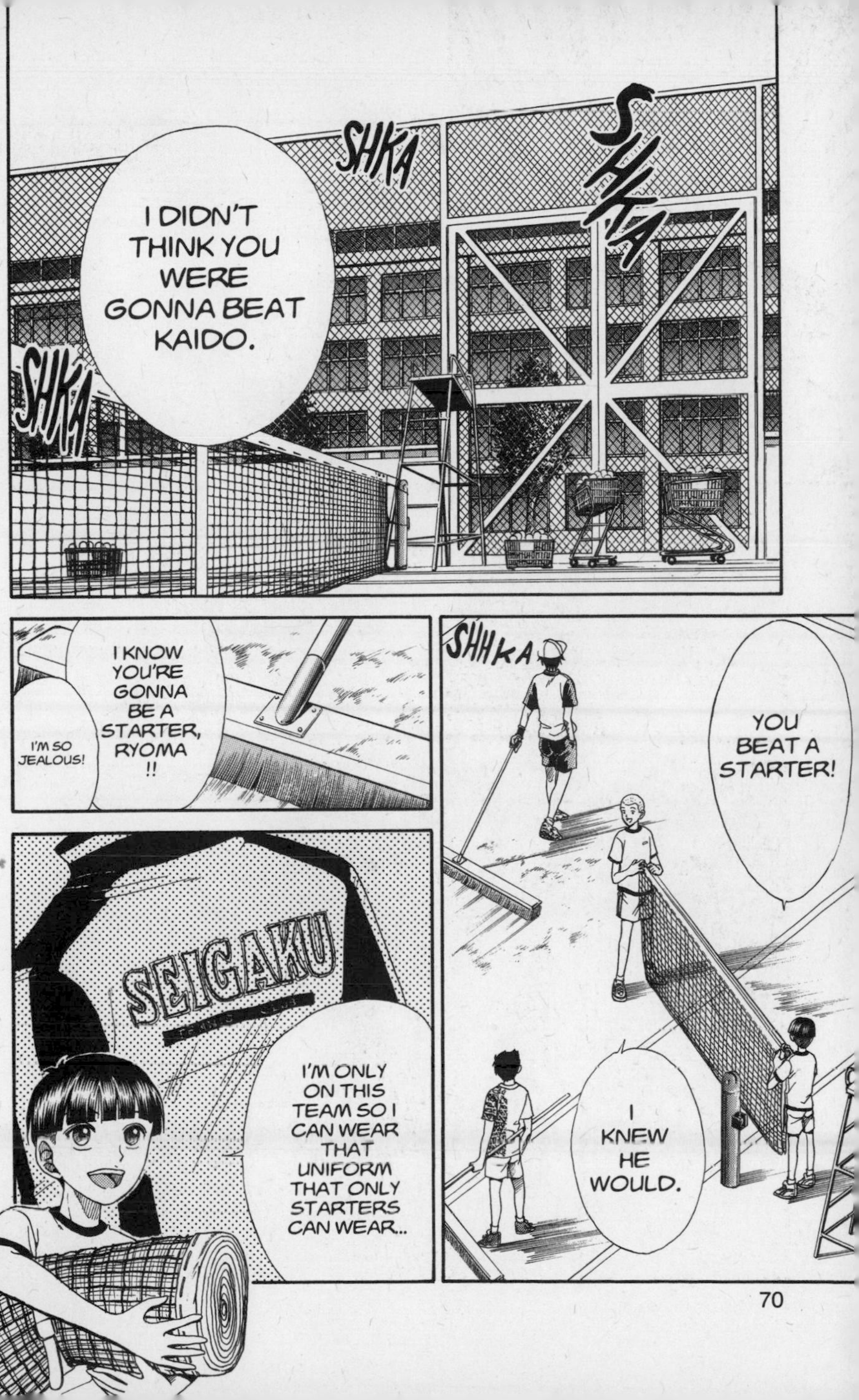
SHKA
SHKA
I DIDN'T THINK YOU WERE GONNA BEAT KAIDO.
SHKA
SHHKA
YOU BEAT A STARTER!
I KNEW HE WOULD.
I KNOW YOU'RE GONNA BE A STARTER, RYOMA !!
I'M SO JEALOUS!
SEIGAKU
I'M ONLY ON THIS TEAM SO I CAN WEAR THAT UNIFORM THAT ONLY STARTERS CAN WEAR...

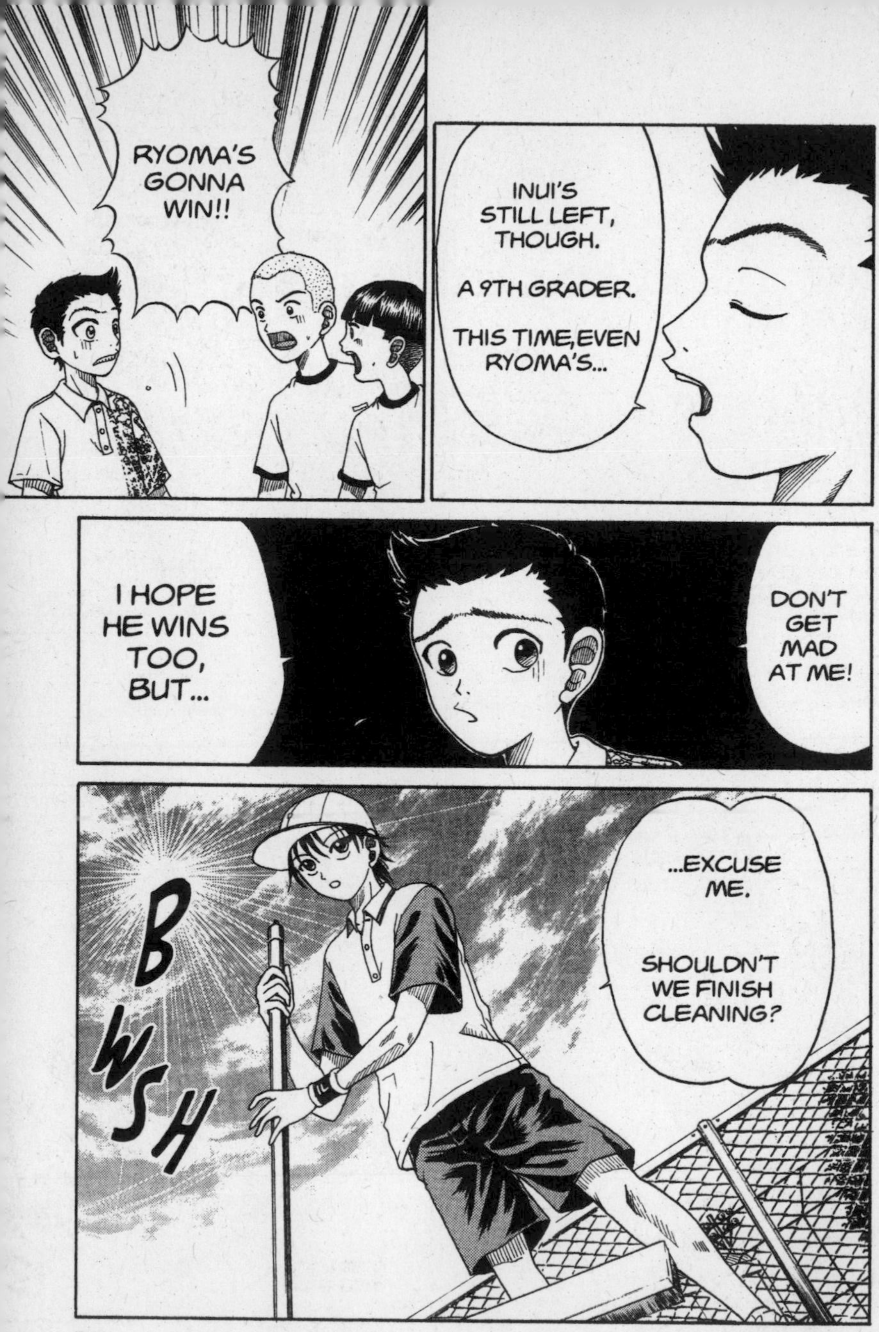
INUI'S STILL LEFT, THOUGH.
A 9TH GRADER.
THIS TIME, EVEN RYOMA'S...
RYOMA'S GONNA WIN!!
DON'T GET MAD AT ME!
I HOPE HE WINS TOO, BUT...
...EXCUSE ME.
SHOULDN'T WE FINISH CLEANING?
BWSH

READ THIS WAY

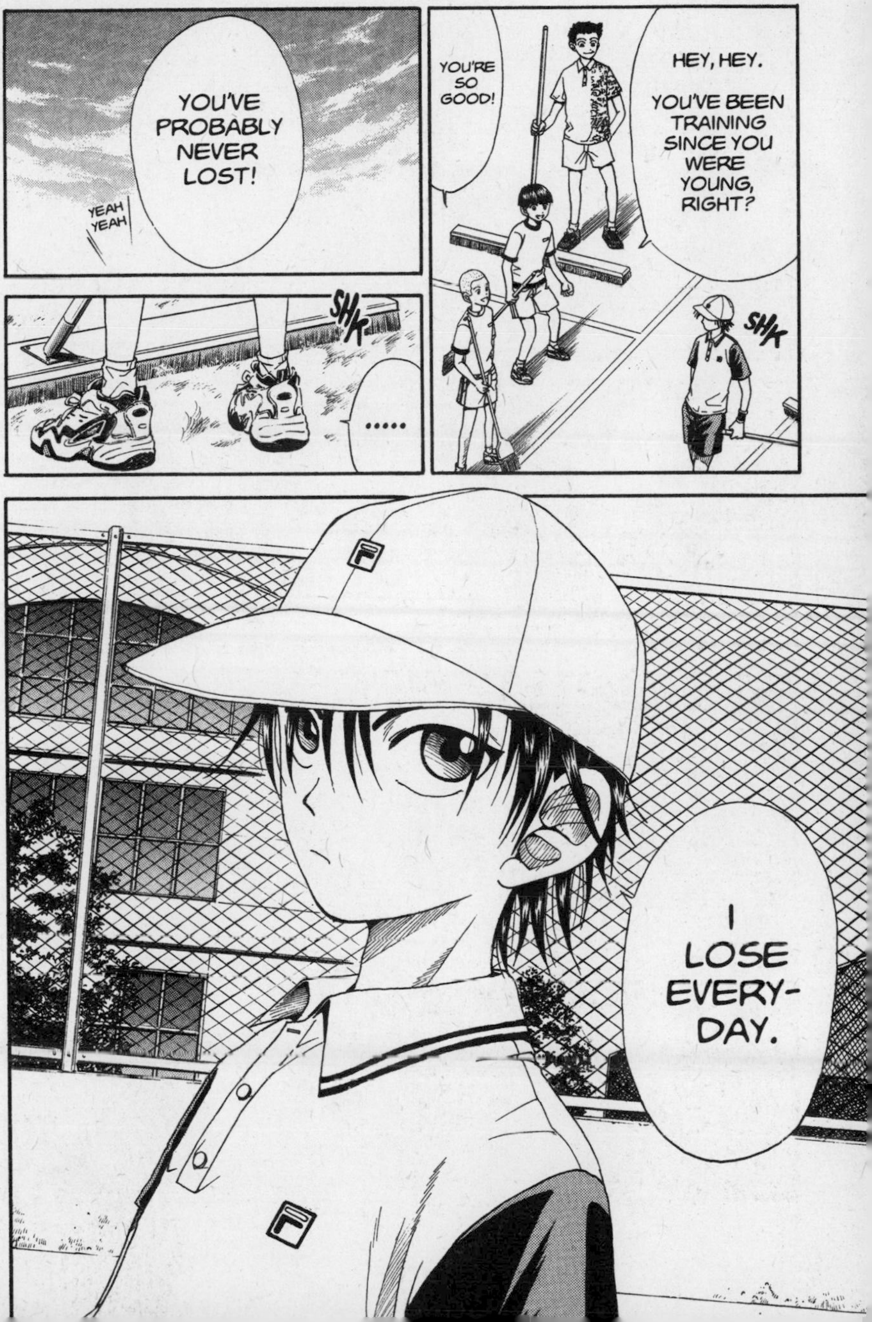
HEY, HEY.
YOU'VE BEEN TRAINING SINCE YOU WERE YOUNG, RIGHT?
YOU'RE SO GOOD!
SHK
YOU'VE PROBABLY NEVER LOST!
YEAH YEAH
SHK
.....
I LOSE EVERY-DAY.

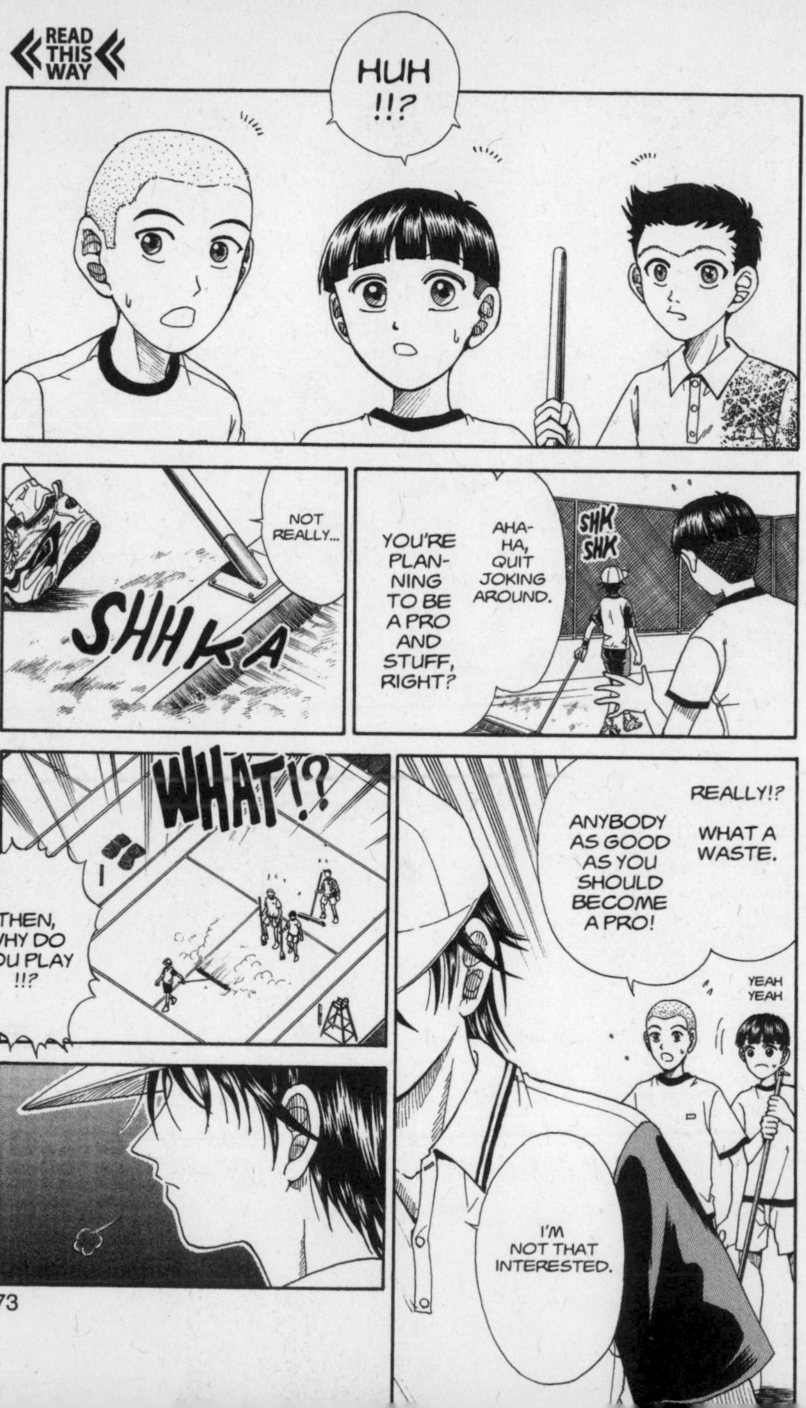
READ THIS WAY
HUH !!?
AHA-HA, QUIT JOKING AROUND.
YOU'RE PLANNING TO BE A PRO AND STUFF, RIGHT?
SHK SHK
NOT REALLY...
SHHKA
REALLY!?
WHAT A WASTE.
ANYBODY AS GOOD AS YOU SHOULD BECOME A PRO!
YEAH YEAH
I'M NOT THAT INTERESTED.
WHAT!?
THEN, WHY DO YOU PLAY !!?

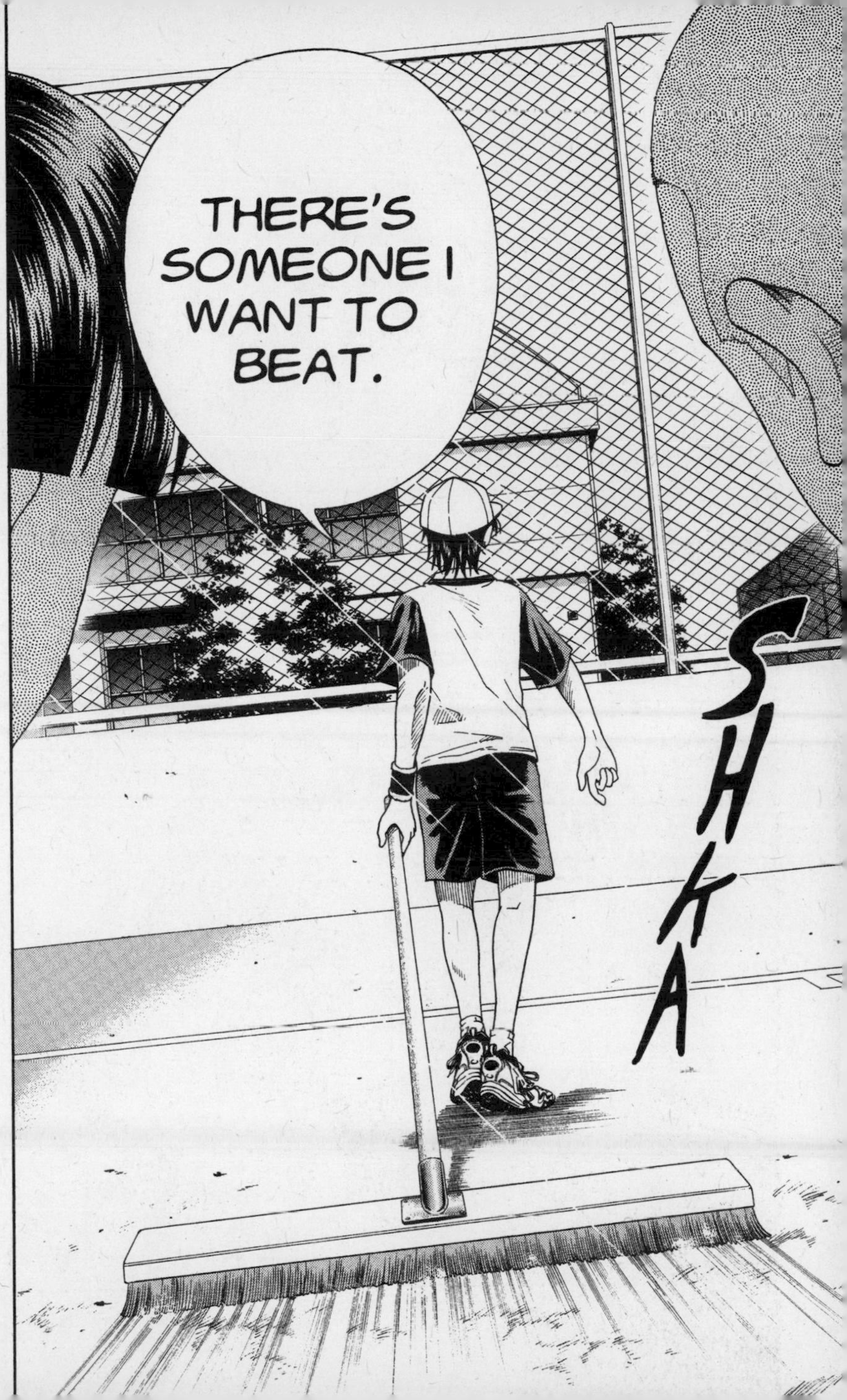
THERE'S SOMEONE I WANT TO BEAT.
SHKA

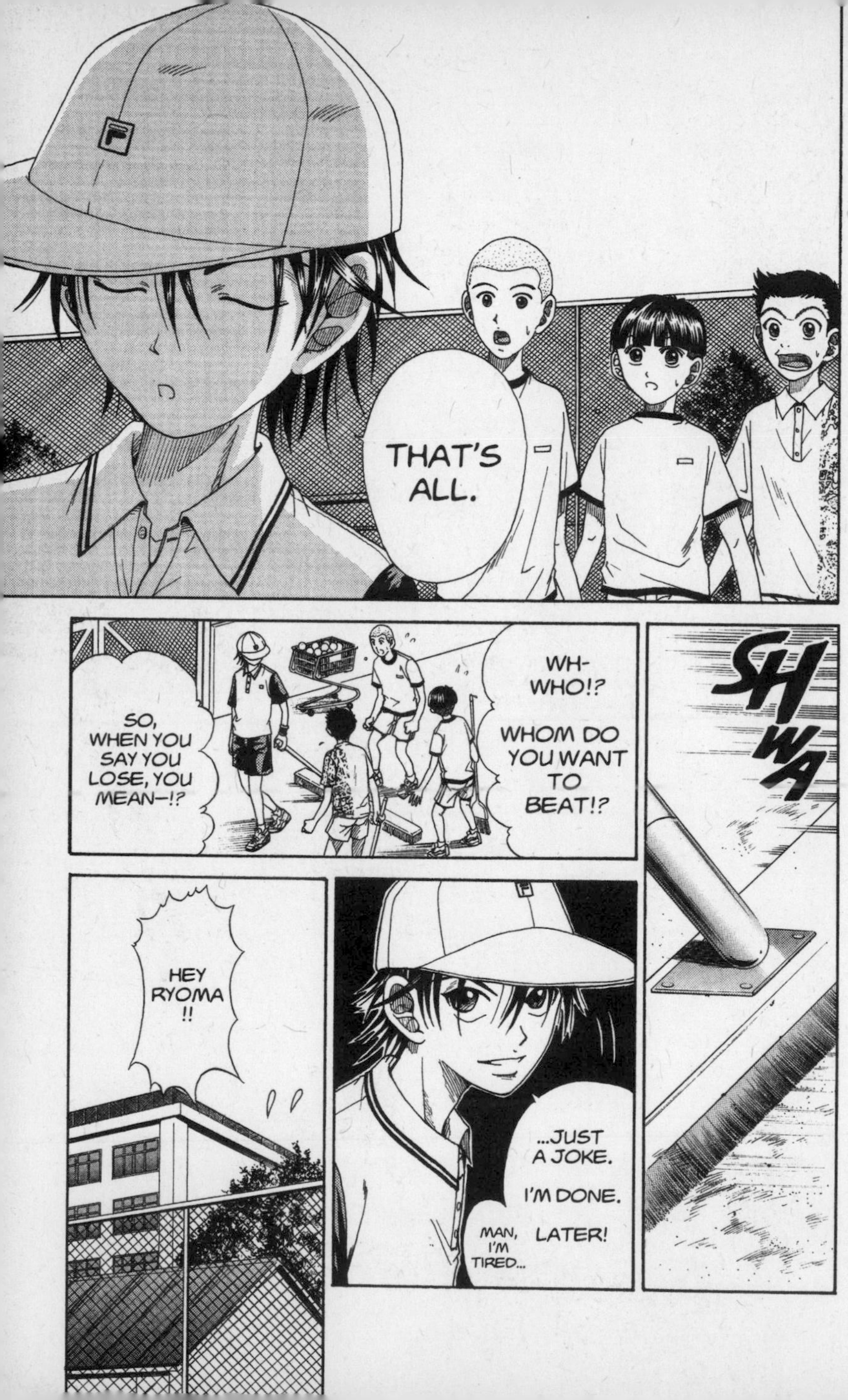
THAT'S ALL.
SHWA
WH- WHO!? WHOM DO YOU WANT TO BEAT!?
SO, WHEN YOU SAY YOU LOSE, YOU MEAN—!?
...JUST A JOKE. I'M DONE. LATER!
MAN, I'M TIRED...
HEY RYOMA !!

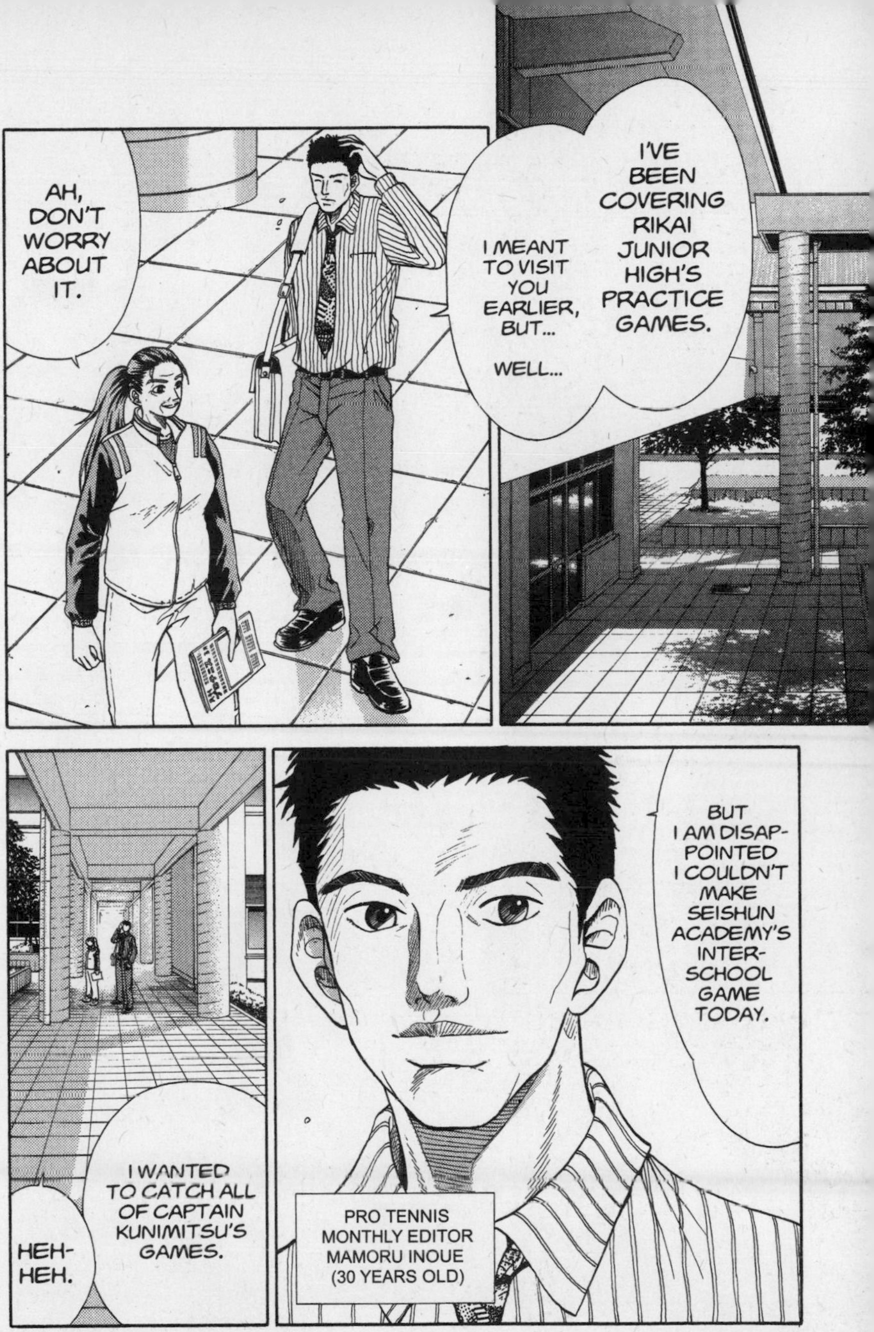
I'VE BEEN COVERING RIKAI JUNIOR HIGH'S PRACTICE GAMES.
I MEANT TO VISIT YOU EARLIER, BUT...
WELL...
AH, DON'T WORRY ABOUT IT.
BUT I AM DISAP-POINTED I COULDN'T MAKE SEISHUN ACADEMY'S INTER-SCHOOL GAME TODAY.
PRO TENNIS MONTHLY EDITOR MAMORU INOUE (30 YEARS OLD)
I WANTED TO CATCH ALL OF CAPTAIN KUNIMITSU'S GAMES.
HEH-HEH.

READ THIS WAY

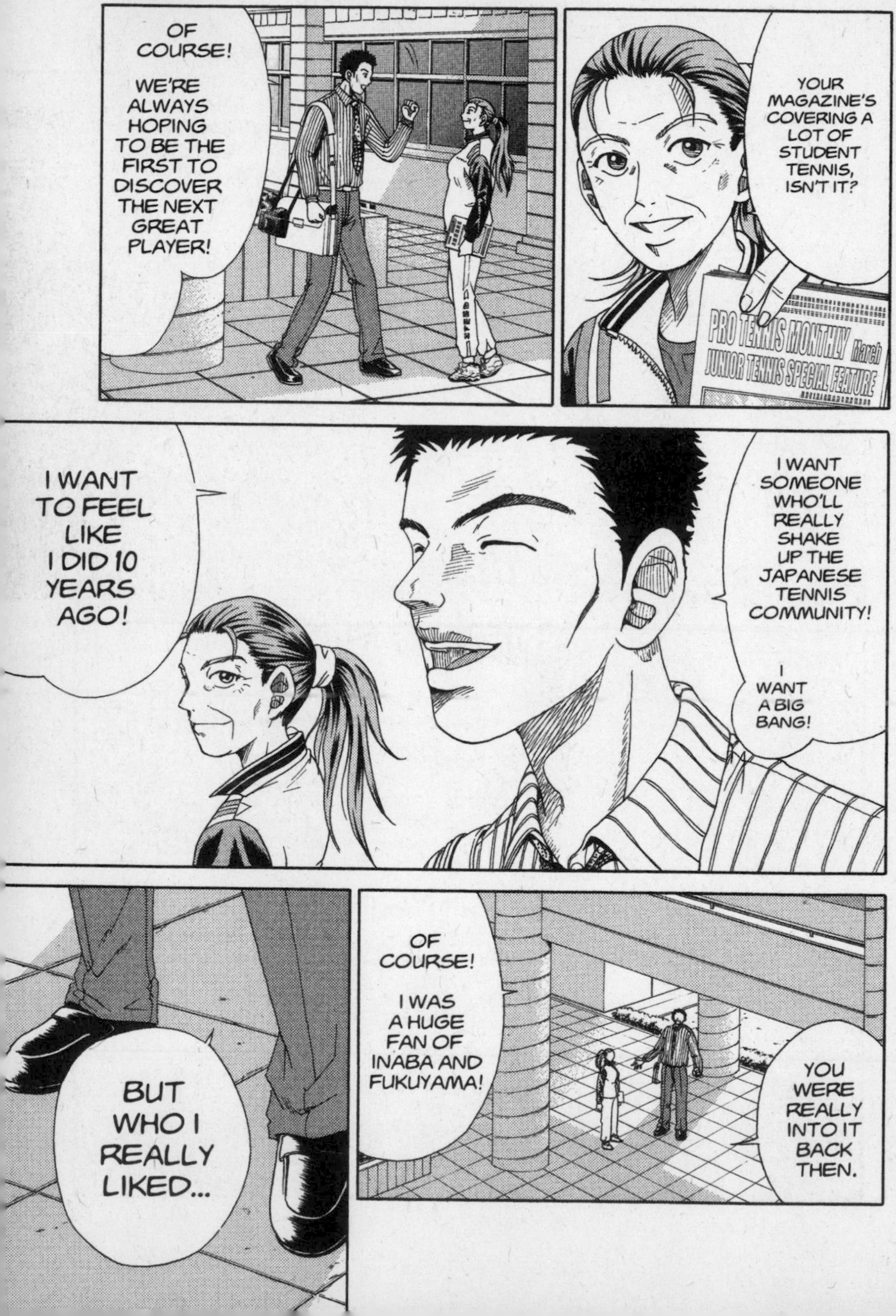
YOUR MAGAZINE'S COVERING A LOT OF STUDENT TENNIS, ISN'T IT?
PRO TENNIS MONTHLY March
JUNIOR TENNIS SPECIAL FEATURE
OF COURSE! WE'RE ALWAYS HOPING TO BE THE FIRST TO DISCOVER THE NEXT GREAT PLAYER!
I WANT SOMEONE WHO'LL REALLY SHAKE UP THE JAPANESE TENNIS COMMUNITY!
I WANT A BIG BANG!
I WANT TO FEEL LIKE I DID 10 YEARS AGO!
YOU WERE REALLY INTO IT BACK THEN.
OF COURSE! I WAS A HUGE FAN OF INABA AND FUKUYAMA!
BUT WHO I REALLY LIKED...

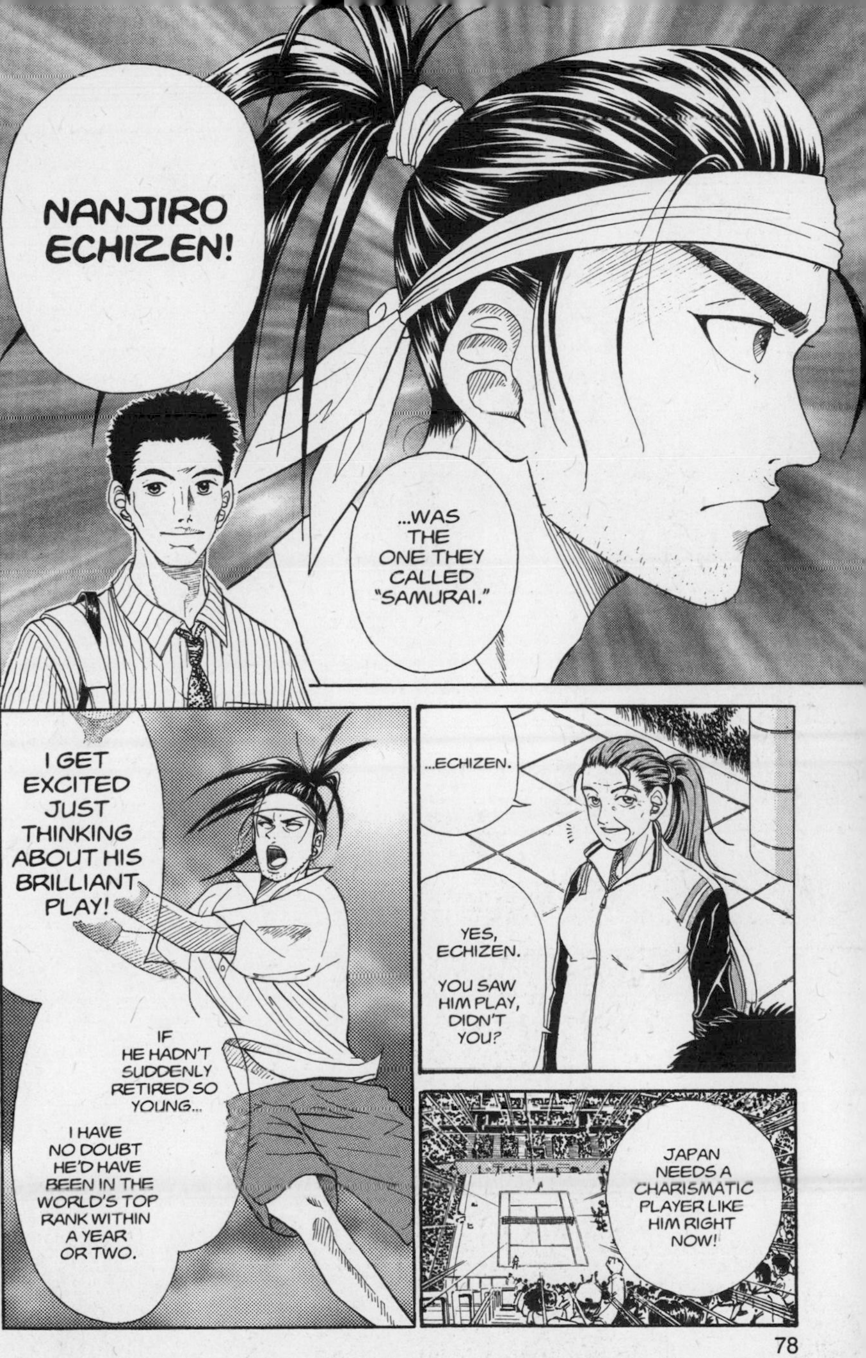
NANJIRO ECHIZEN!
...WAS THE ONE THEY CALLED "SAMURAI."
...ECHIZEN.
YES, ECHIZEN.
YOU SAW HIM PLAY, DIDN'T YOU?
JAPAN NEEDS A CHARISMATIC PLAYER LIKE HIM RIGHT NOW!
I GET EXCITED JUST THINKING ABOUT HIS BRILLIANT PLAY!
IF HE HADN'T SUDDENLY RETIRED SO YOUNG...
I HAVE NO DOUBT HE'D HAVE BEEN IN THE WORLD'S TOP RANK WITHIN A YEAR OR TWO.

READ THIS WAY

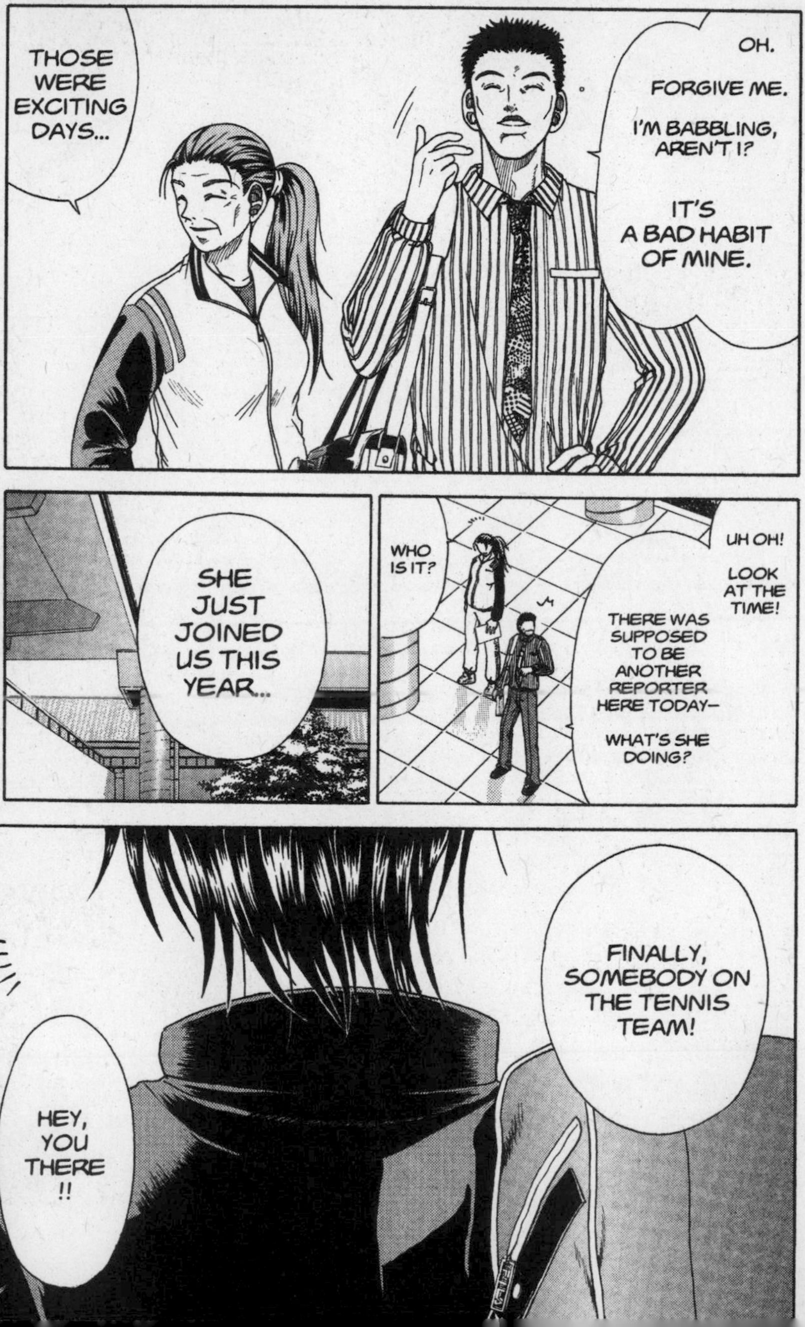
OH.
FORGIVE ME.
I'M BABBLING, AREN'T I?
IT'S A BAD HABIT OF MINE.
THOSE WERE EXCITING DAYS...
UH OH!
LOOK AT THE TIME!
THERE WAS SUPPOSED TO BE ANOTHER REPORTER HERE TODAY—
WHAT'S SHE DOING?
WHO IS IT?
SHE JUST JOINED US THIS YEAR...
FINALLY, SOMEBODY ON THE TENNIS TEAM!
HEY, YOU THERE!!

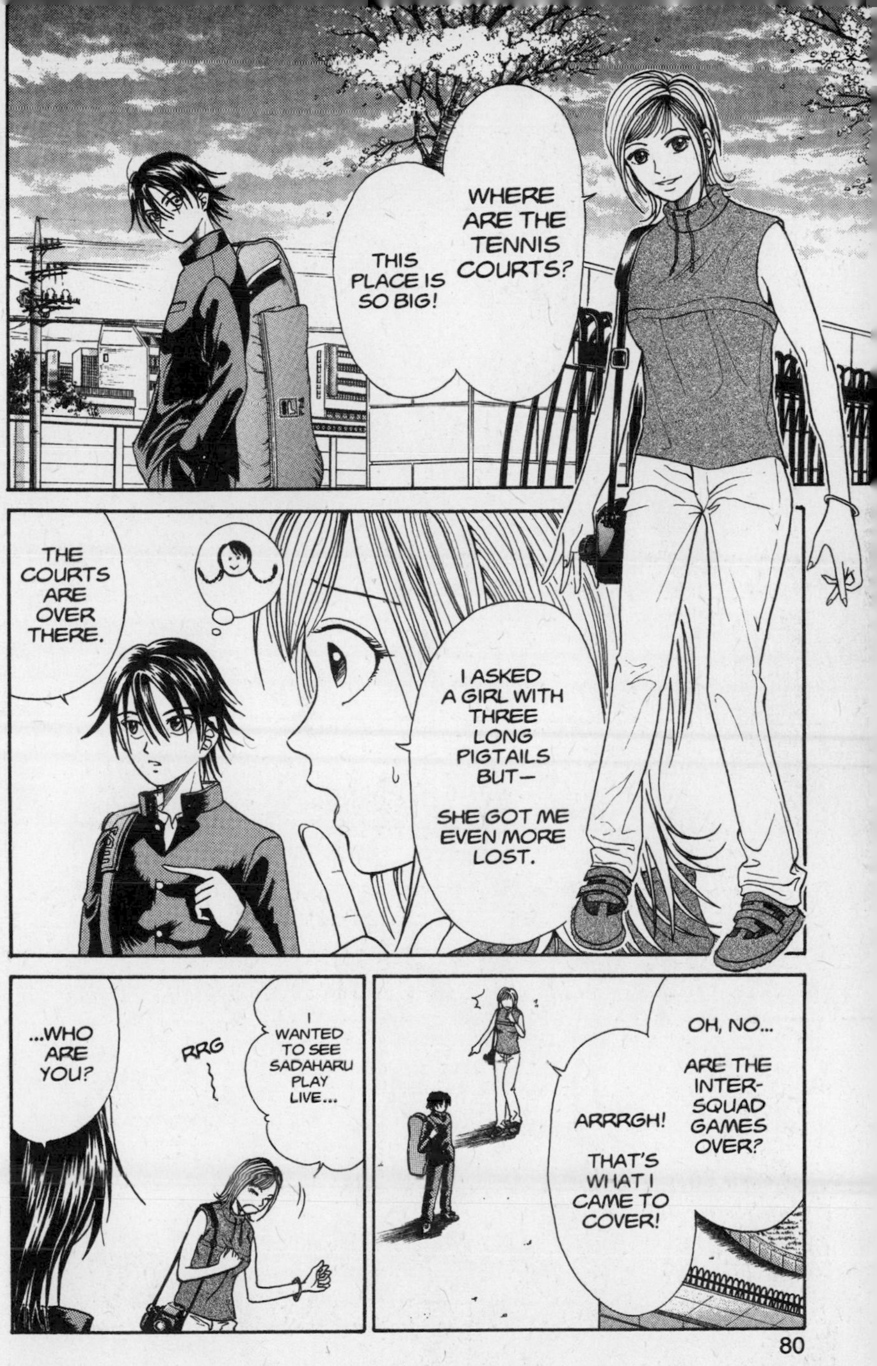
WHERE ARE THE TENNIS COURTS?
THIS PLACE IS SO BIG!
I ASKED A GIRL WITH THREE LONG PIGTAILS BUT—
SHE GOT ME EVEN MORE LOST.
THE COURTS ARE OVER THERE.
OH, NO...
ARE THE INTER-SQUAD GAMES OVER?
ARRRGH!
THAT'S WHAT I CAME TO COVER!
I WANTED TO SEE SADAHARU PLAY LIVE...
RRG
...WHO ARE YOU?

READ THIS WAY

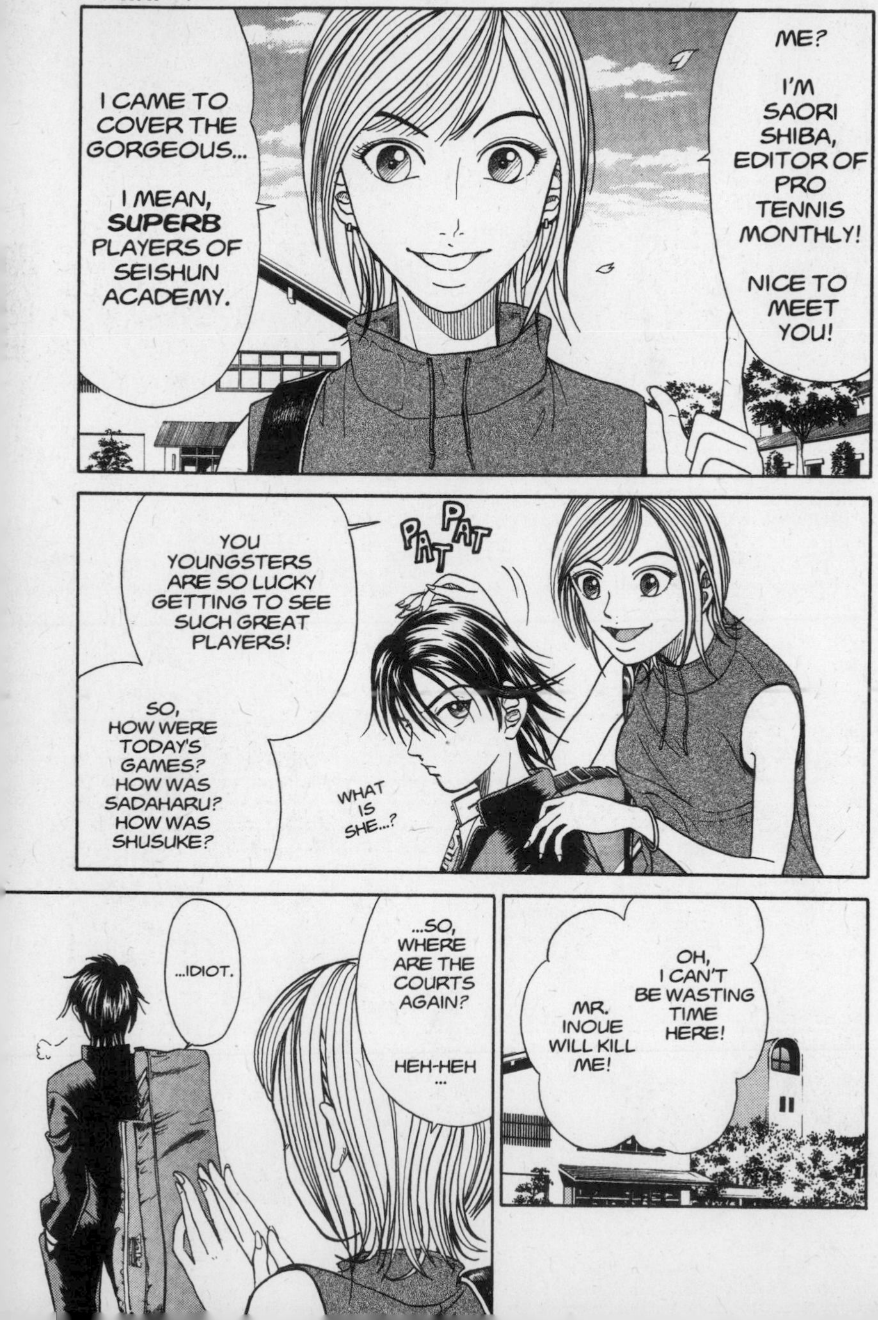

ME? I'M SAORI SHIBA, EDITOR OF PRO TENNIS MONTHLY! NICE TO MEET YOU!
I CAME TO COVER THE GORGEOUS... I MEAN, **SUPERB** PLAYERS OF SEISHUN ACADEMY.
PAT PAT
YOU YOUNGSTERS ARE SO LUCKY GETTING TO SEE SUCH GREAT PLAYERS!
SO, HOW WERE TODAY'S GAMES? HOW WAS SADAHARU? HOW WAS SHUSUKE?
WHAT IS SHE...?
OH, I CAN'T BE WASTING TIME HERE!
MR. INOUE WILL KILL ME!
...SO, WHERE ARE THE COURTS AGAIN?
HEH-HEH ...
...IDIOT.

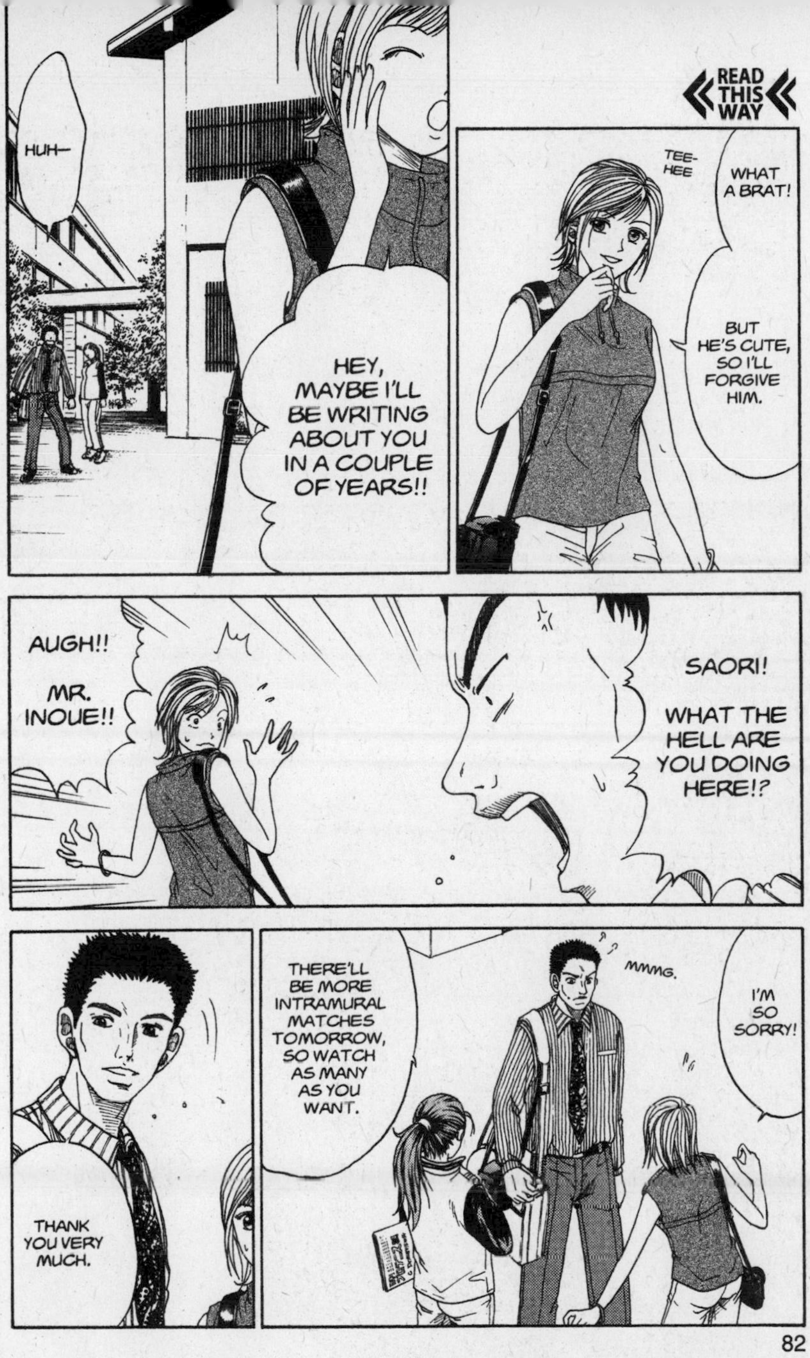
READ THIS WAY
TEE-HEE
WHAT A BRAT!
BUT HE'S CUTE, SO I'LL FORGIVE HIM.
HEY, MAYBE I'LL BE WRITING ABOUT YOU IN A COUPLE OF YEARS!!
HUH—
SAORI!
WHAT THE HELL ARE YOU DOING HERE!?
AUGH!!
MR. INOUE!!
I'M SO SORRY!
MMMG.
THERE'LL BE MORE INTRAMURAL MATCHES TOMORROW, SO WATCH AS MANY AS YOU WANT.
THANK YOU VERY MUCH.

READ THIS WAY

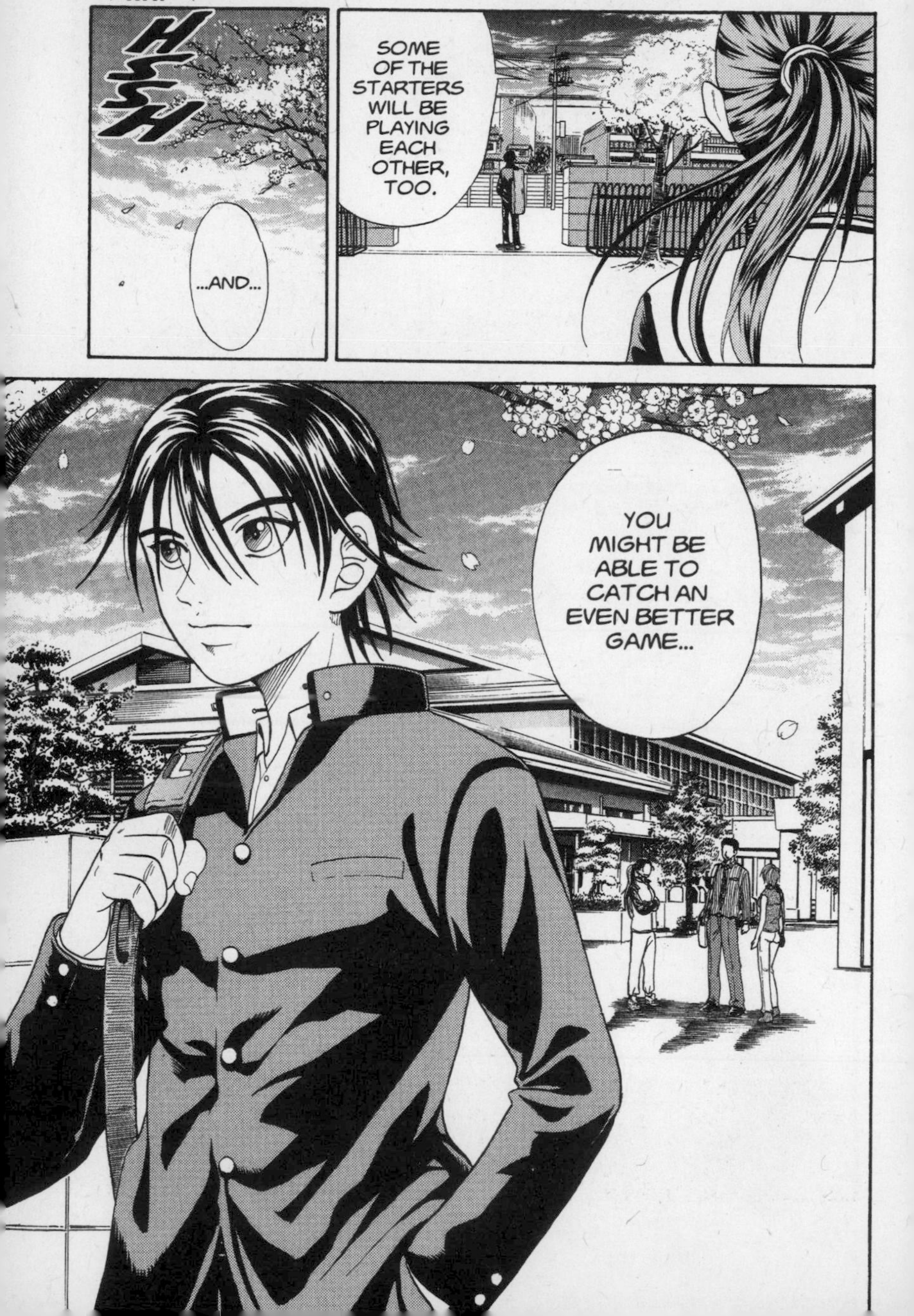
SOME OF THE STARTERS WILL BE PLAYING EACH OTHER, TOO.
HSH
...AND...
YOU MIGHT BE ABLE TO CATCH AN EVEN BETTER GAME...

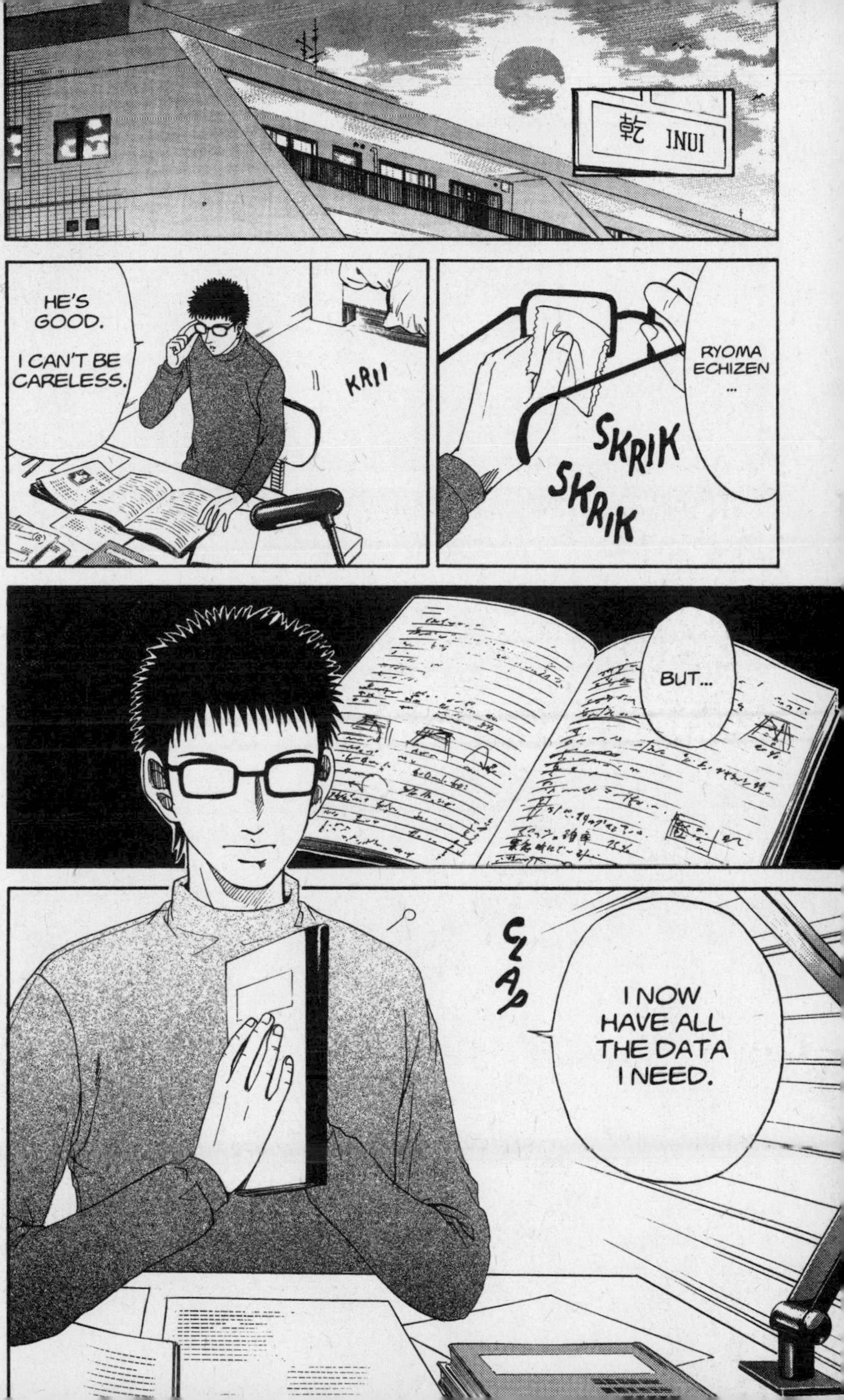
乾 INUI
RYOMA ECHIZEN ...
SKRIK
SKRIK
HE'S GOOD.
I CAN'T BE CARELESS.
KRII
BUT...
CLAP
I NOW HAVE ALL THE DATA I NEED.

READ THIS WAY

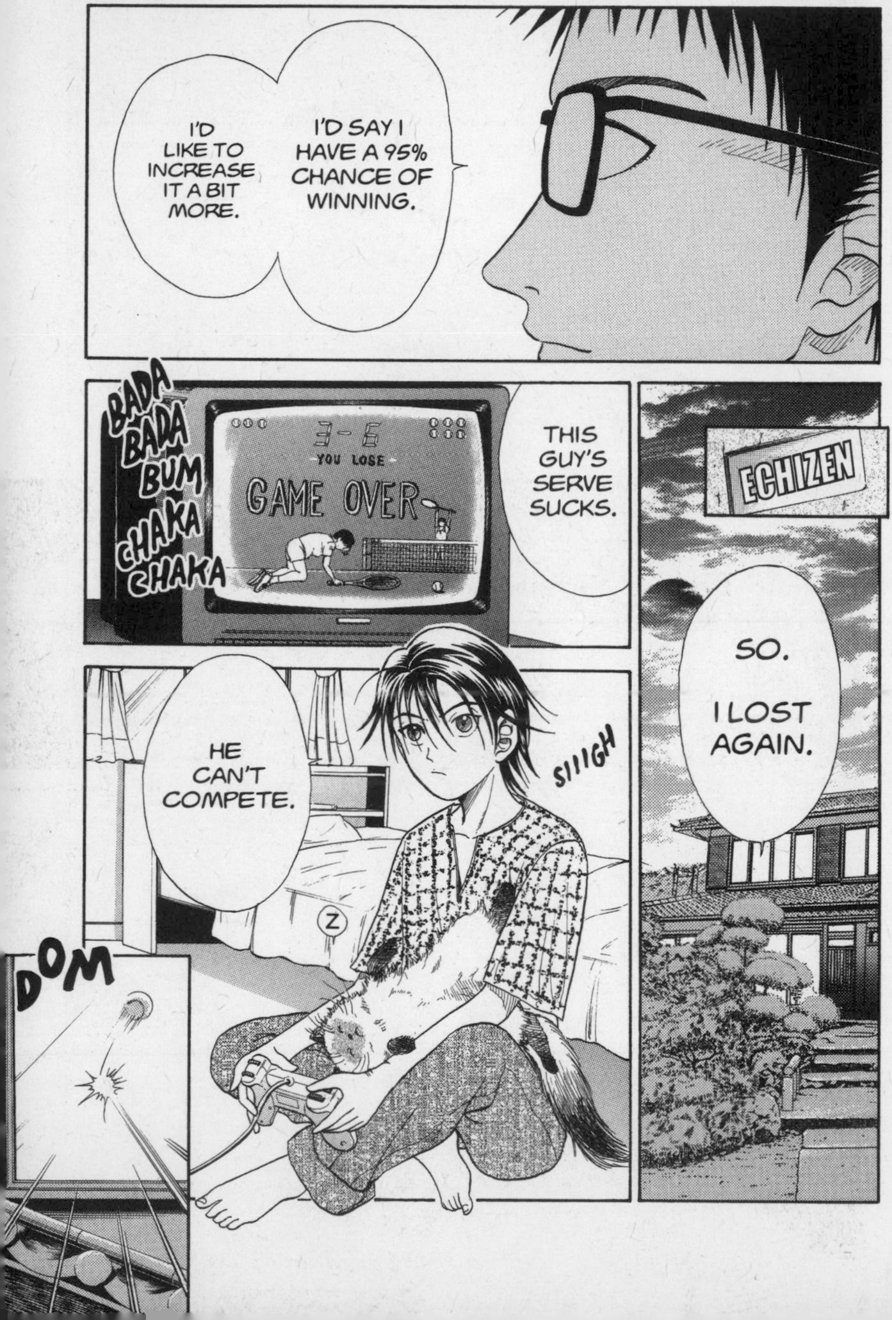
I'D SAY I HAVE A 95% CHANCE OF WINNING.
I'D LIKE TO INCREASE IT A BIT MORE.
ECHIZEN
SO.
I LOST AGAIN.
THIS GUY'S SERVE SUCKS.
YOU LOSE
GAME OVER
BADA BADA BUM CHAKA CHAKA
SIIIGH
HE CAN'T COMPETE.
Z
DOM

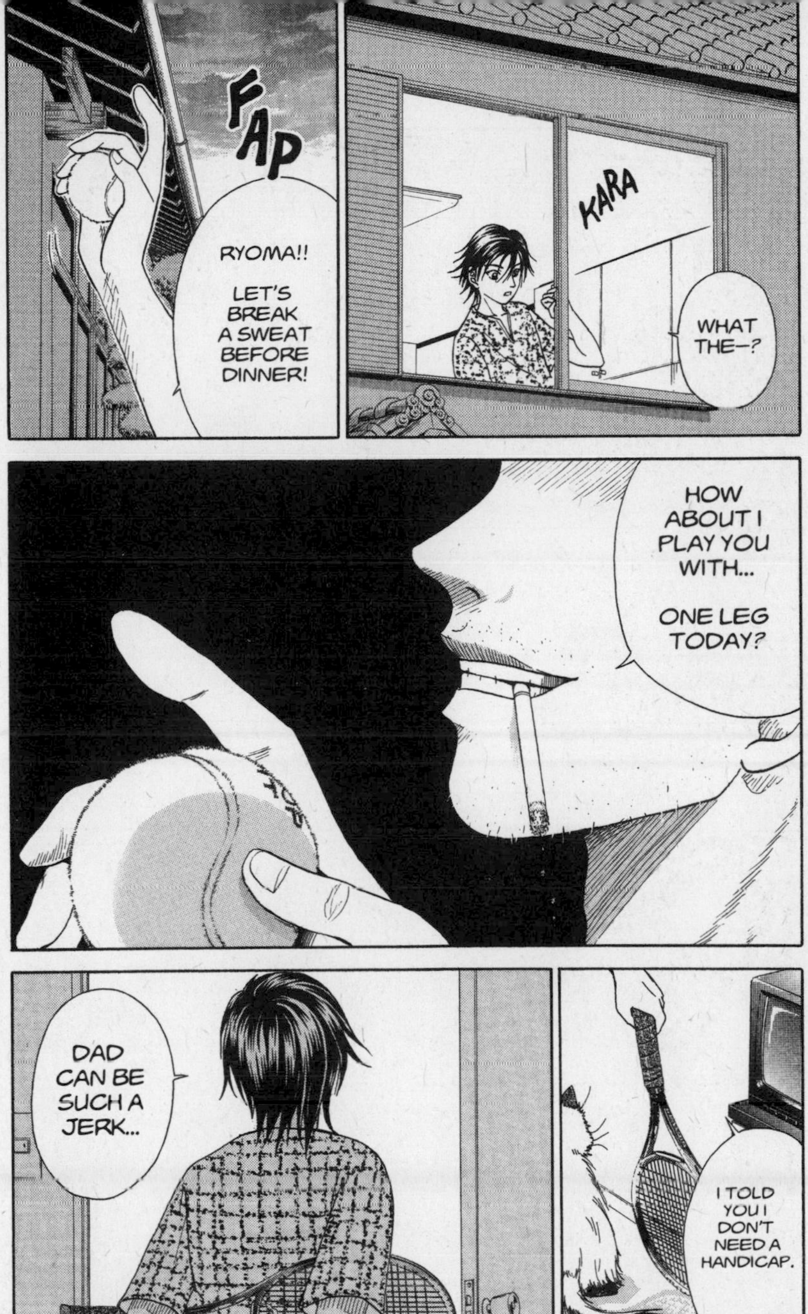
KARA
WHAT THE—?
FAP
RYOMA!! LET'S BREAK A SWEAT BEFORE DINNER!
HOW ABOUT I PLAY YOU WITH... ONE LEG TODAY?
I TOLD YOU I DON'T NEED A HANDICAP.
DAD CAN BE SUCH A JERK...

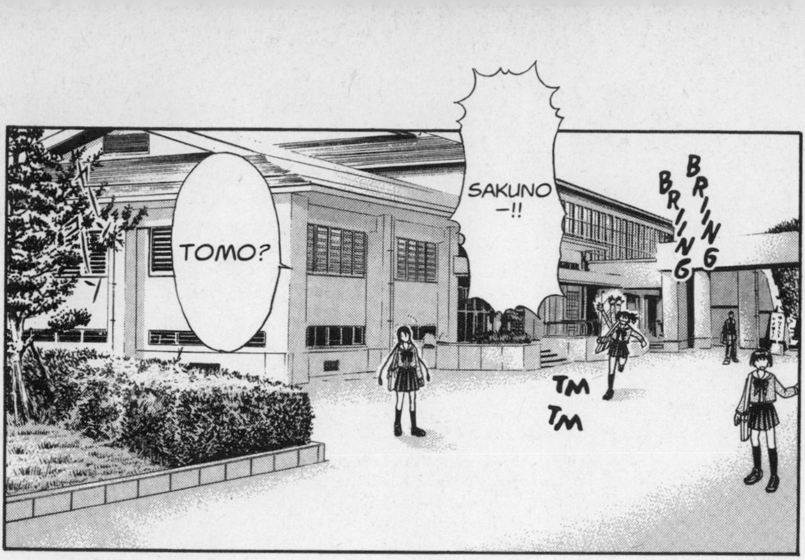
BRING BRING
SAKUNO —!!
TOMO?
TM TM

GENIUS 12 UNREACHABLE

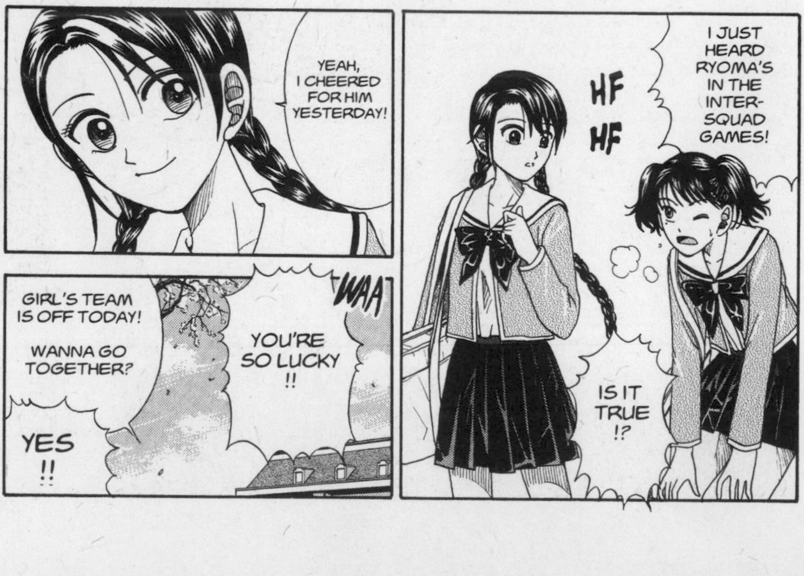
I JUST HEARD RYOMA'S IN THE INTER-SQUAD GAMES!
HF HF
IS IT TRUE !?
YEAH, I CHEERED FOR HIM YESTERDAY!
WAA
YOU'RE SO LUCKY !!
GIRL'S TEAM IS OFF TODAY!
WANNA GO TOGETHER?
YES !!

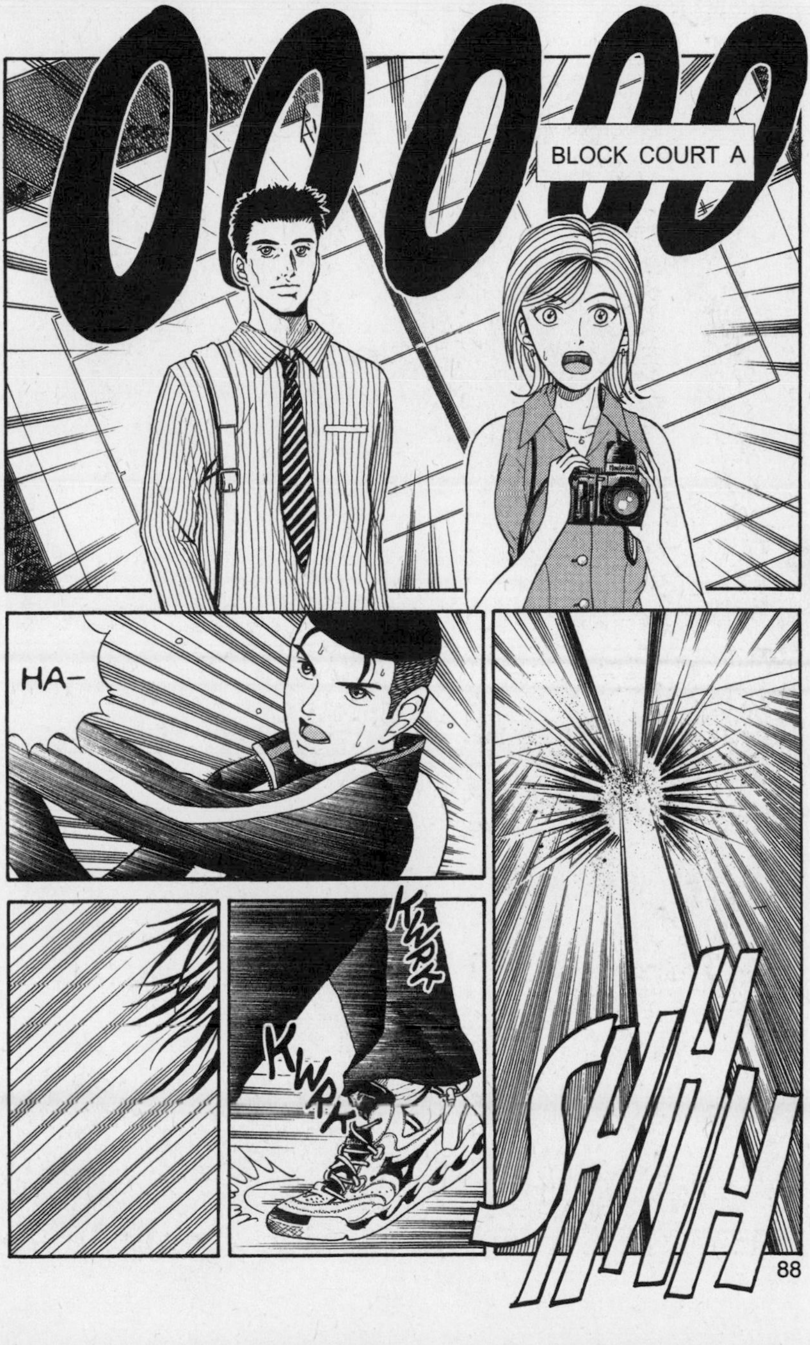
OOOOO
BLOCK COURT A
SHHA
HA-
KWRK
KWRK

READ THIS WAY

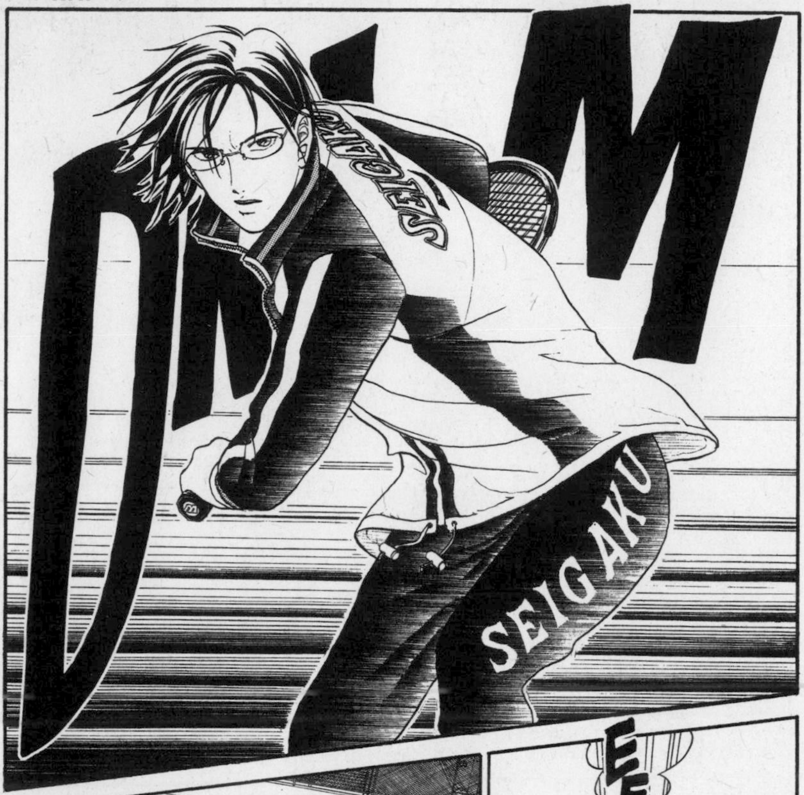
SEIGAKU
SEIGAKU

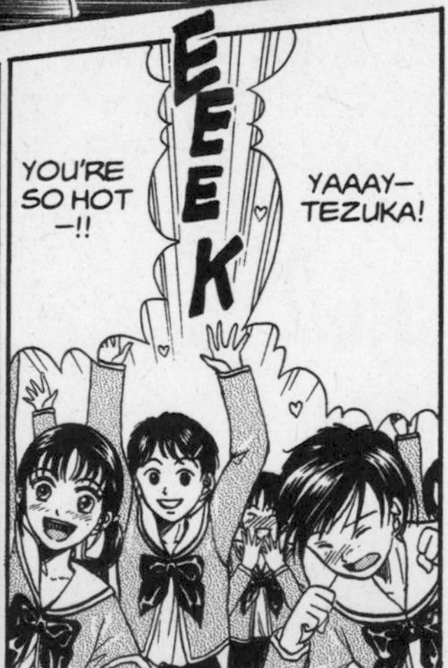
YAAAY—
TEZUKA!
EEEEK
YOU'RE SO HOT —!!

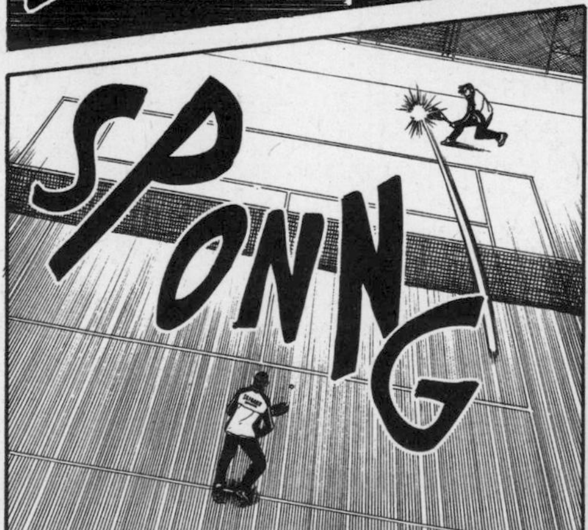
SPONNG

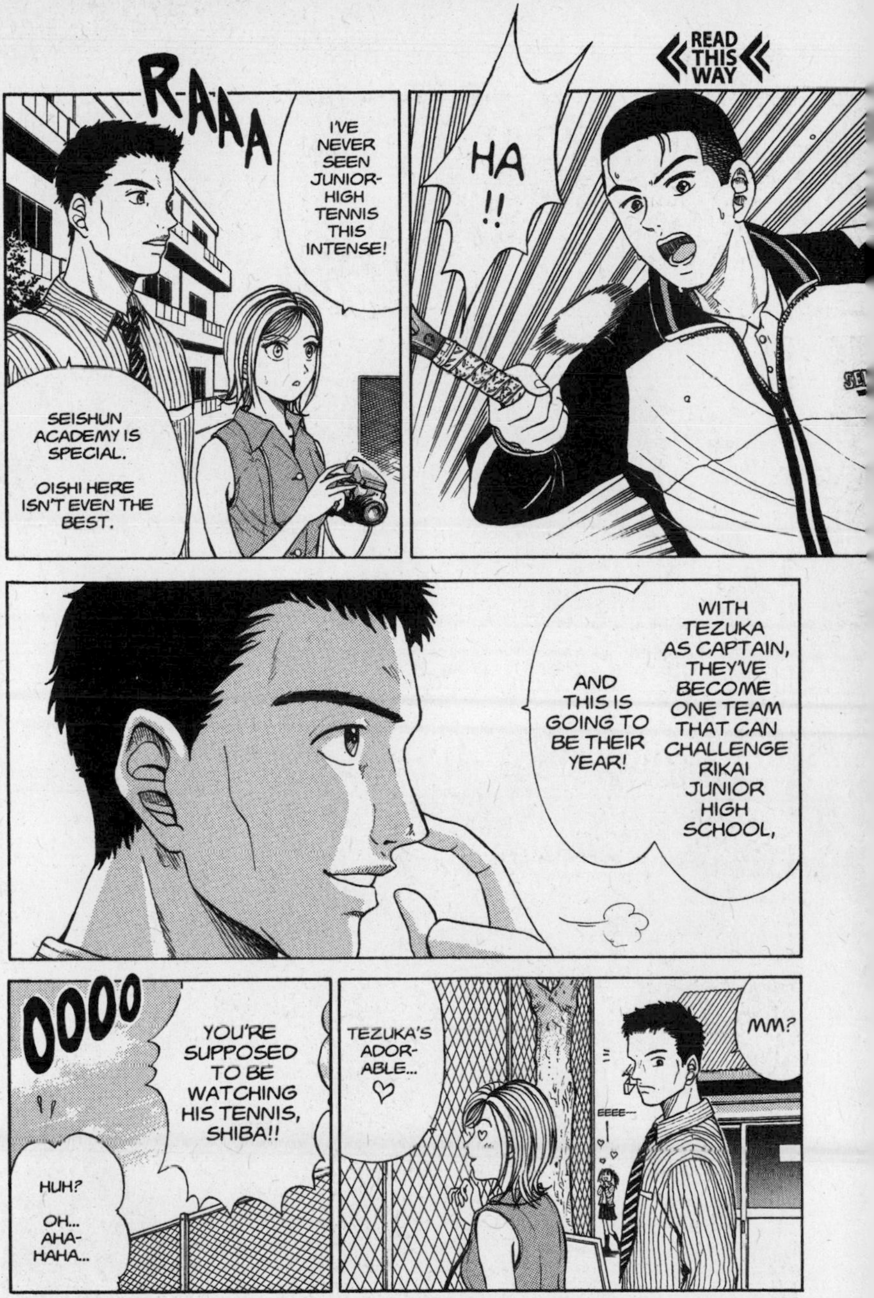
READ THIS WAY
HA!!
R-A-A-A
I'VE NEVER SEEN JUNIOR-HIGH TENNIS THIS INTENSE!
SEISHUN ACADEMY IS SPECIAL.
OISHI HERE ISN'T EVEN THE BEST.
WITH TEZUKA AS CAPTAIN, THEY'VE BECOME ONE TEAM THAT CAN CHALLENGE RIKAI JUNIOR HIGH SCHOOL,
AND THIS IS GOING TO BE THEIR YEAR!
MM?
TEZUKA'S ADOR-ABLE... ♡
EEEE---
OOOO
YOU'RE SUPPOSED TO BE WATCHING HIS TENNIS, SHIBA!!
HUH?
OH... AHA-HAHA...

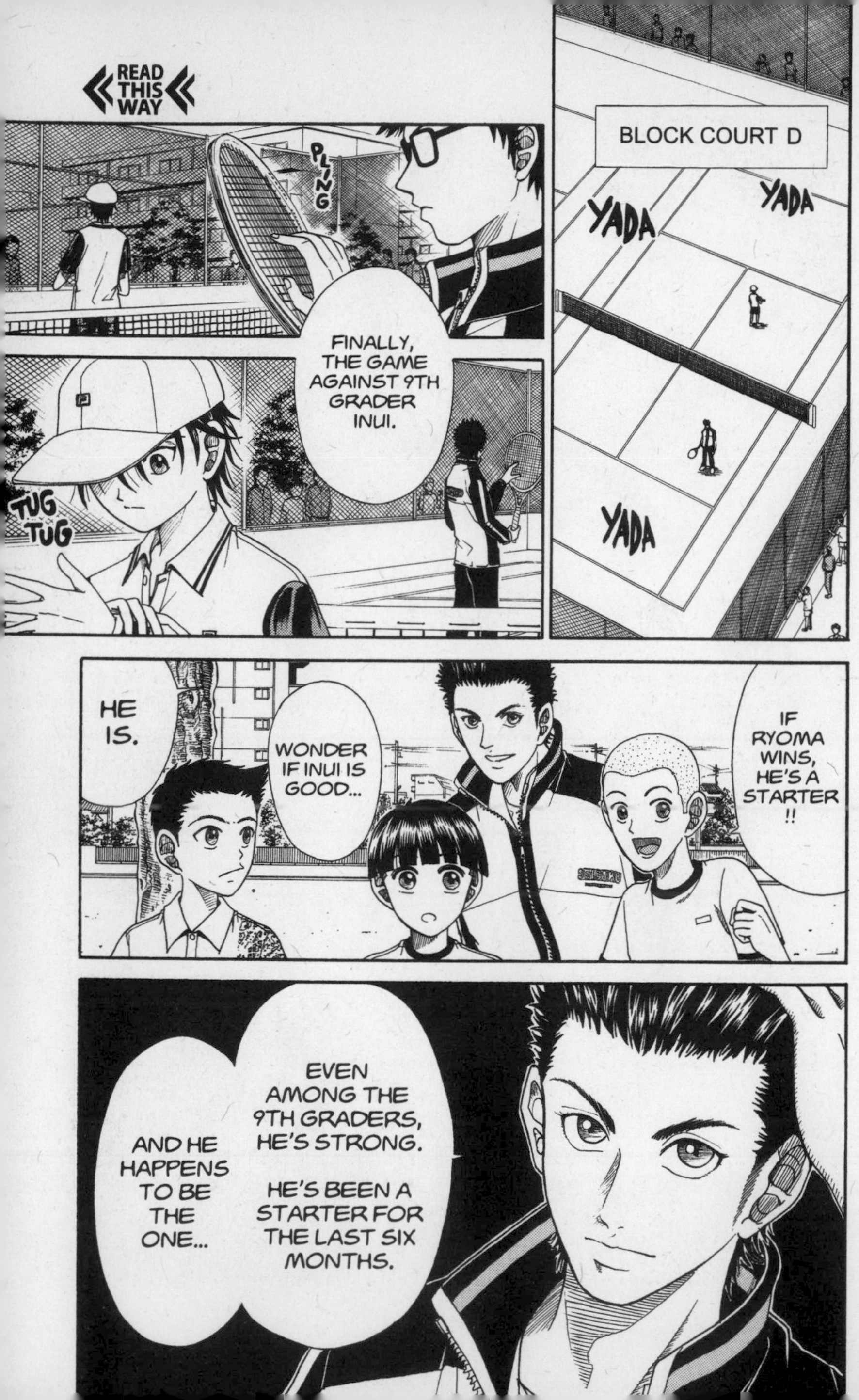
READ THIS WAY
BLOCK COURT D
YADA
YADA
YADA
PLING
FINALLY, THE GAME AGAINST 9TH GRADER INUI.
TUG TUG
IF RYOMA WINS, HE'S A STARTER !!
WONDER IF INUI IS GOOD...
HE IS.
EVEN AMONG THE 9TH GRADERS, HE'S STRONG.
HE'S BEEN A STARTER FOR THE LAST SIX MONTHS.
AND HE HAPPENS TO BE THE ONE...

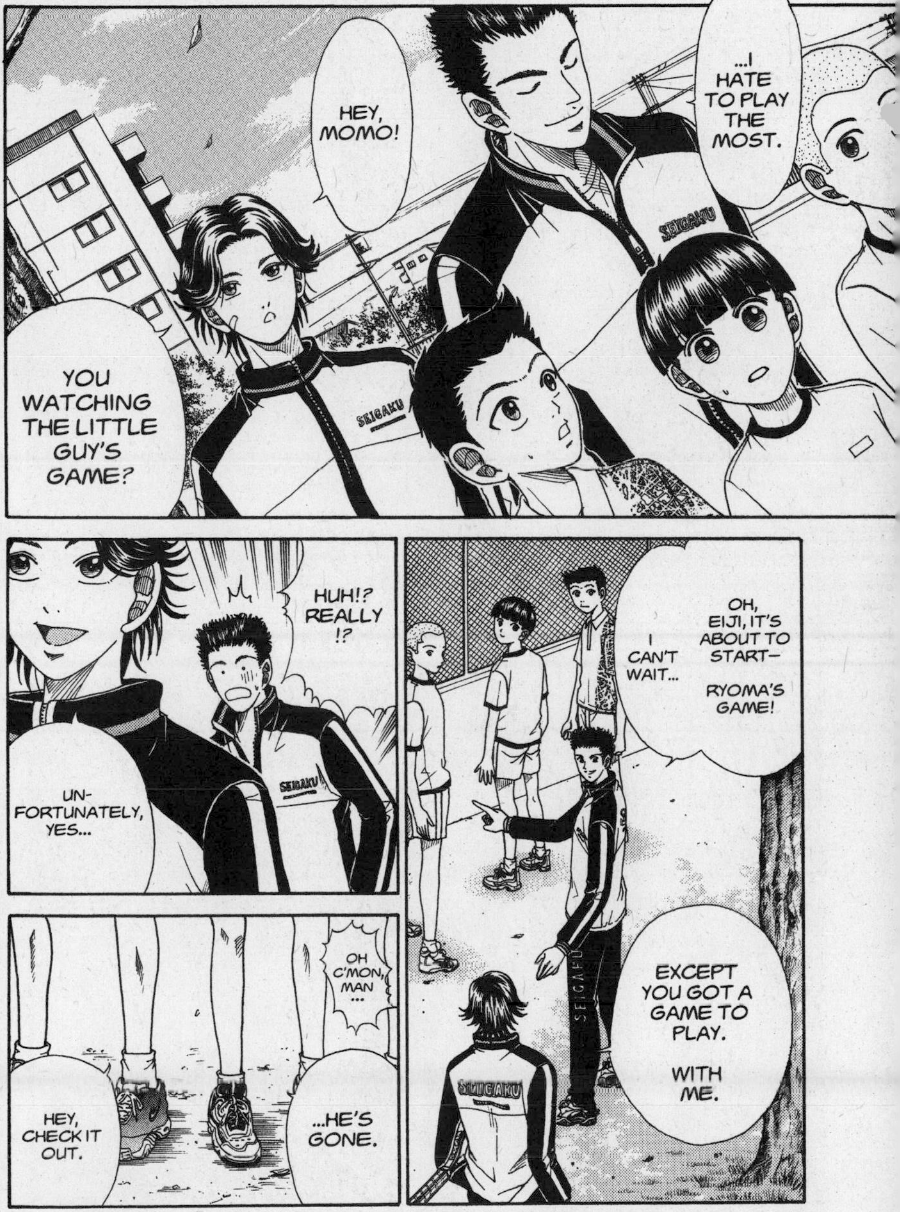
...I HATE TO PLAY THE MOST.
HEY, MOMO!
YOU WATCHING THE LITTLE GUY'S GAME?
OH, EIJI, IT'S ABOUT TO START— RYOMA'S GAME!
I CAN'T WAIT...
EXCEPT YOU GOT A GAME TO PLAY. WITH ME.
HUH!? REALLY !?
UN-FORTUNATELY, YES...
OH C'MON, MAN ...
...HE'S GONE.
HEY, CHECK IT OUT.

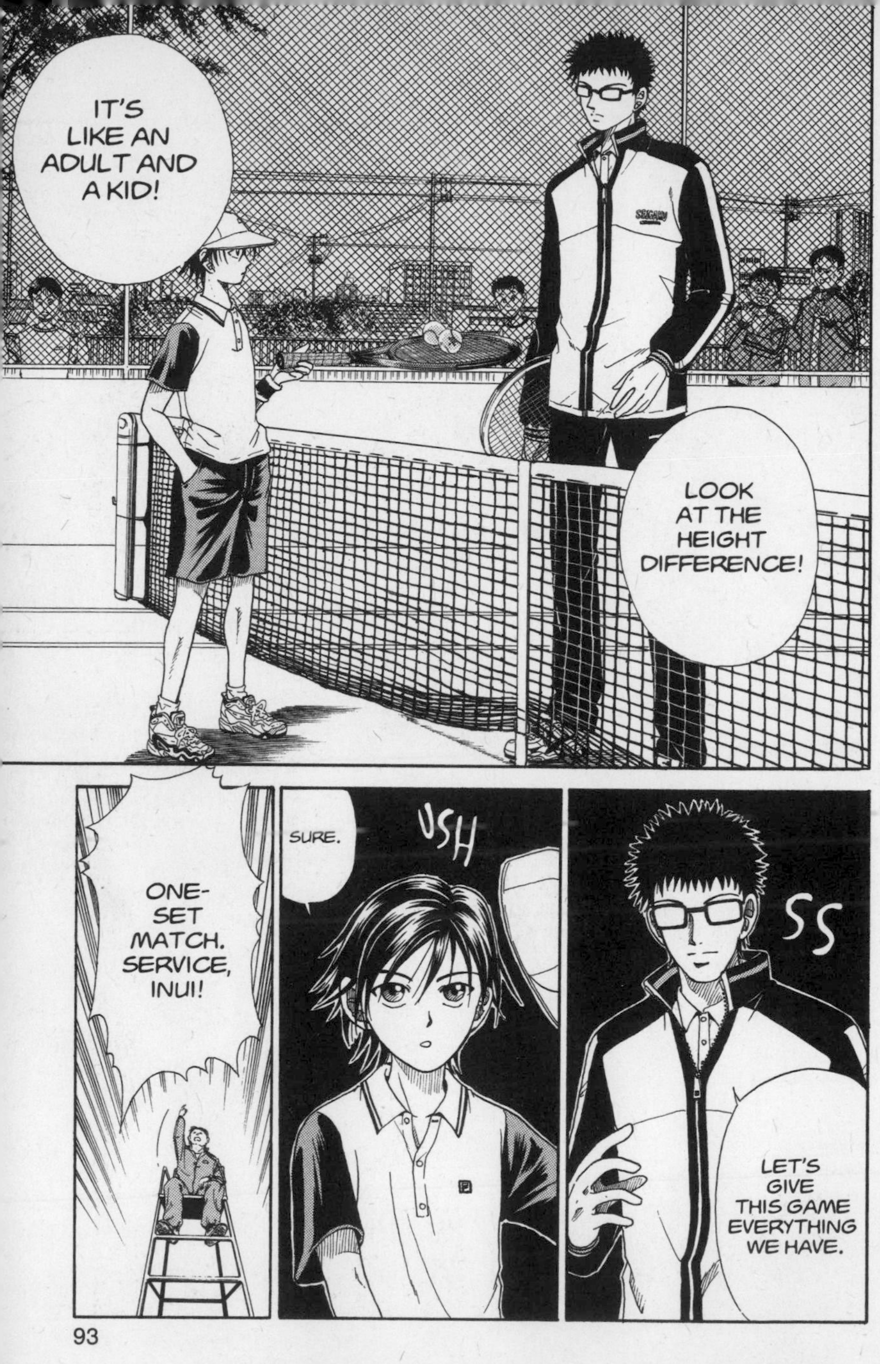
LOOK AT THE HEIGHT DIFFERENCE!
IT'S LIKE AN ADULT AND A KID!
SS
LET'S GIVE THIS GAME EVERYTHING WE HAVE.
USH
SURE.
ONE-SET MATCH. SERVICE, INUI!

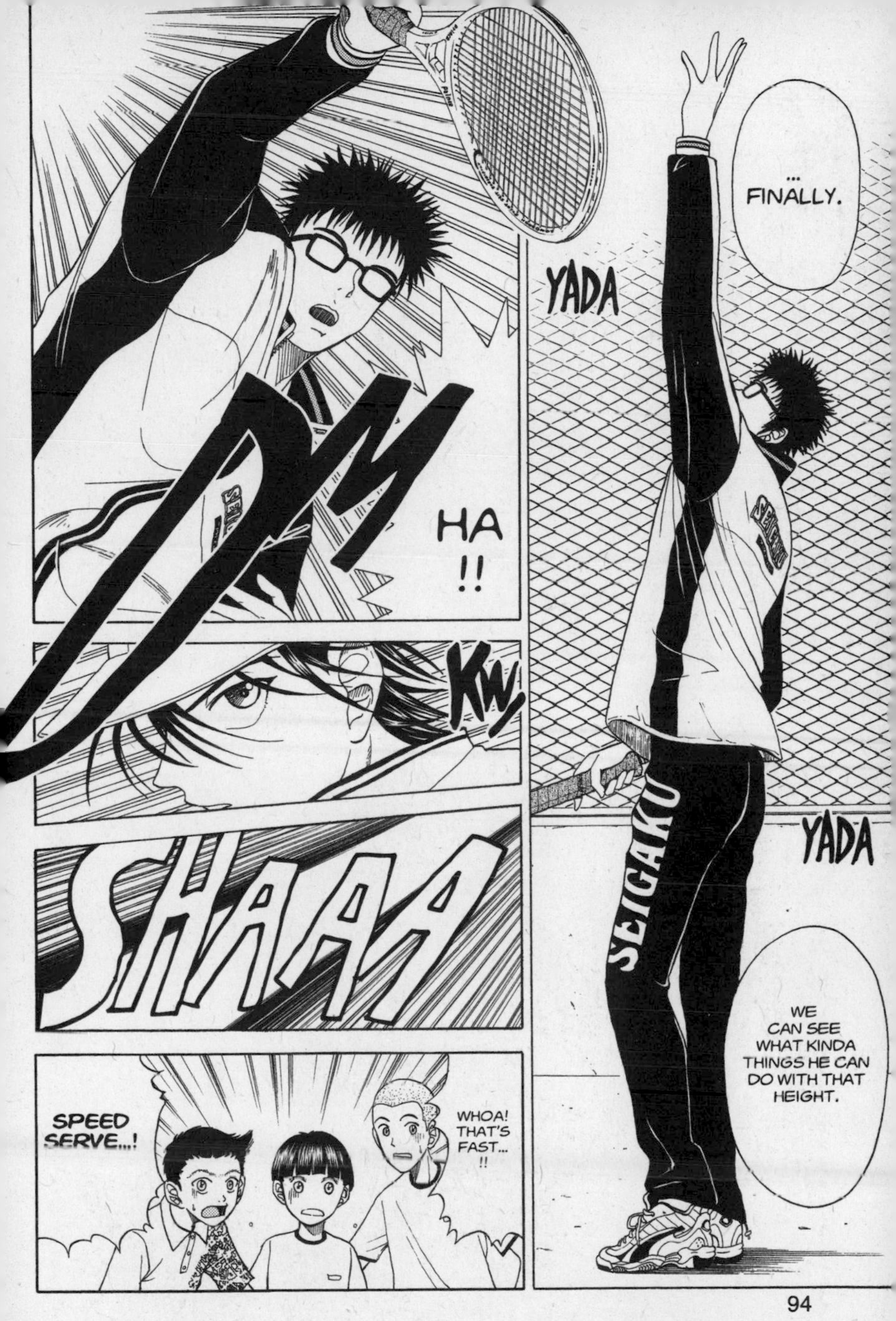

... FINALLY.
YADA
YADA
SEIGAKU
WE CAN SEE WHAT KINDA THINGS HE CAN DO WITH THAT HEIGHT.
HA !!
KW
SHAAA
WHOA! THAT'S FAST... !!
SPEED SERVE...!

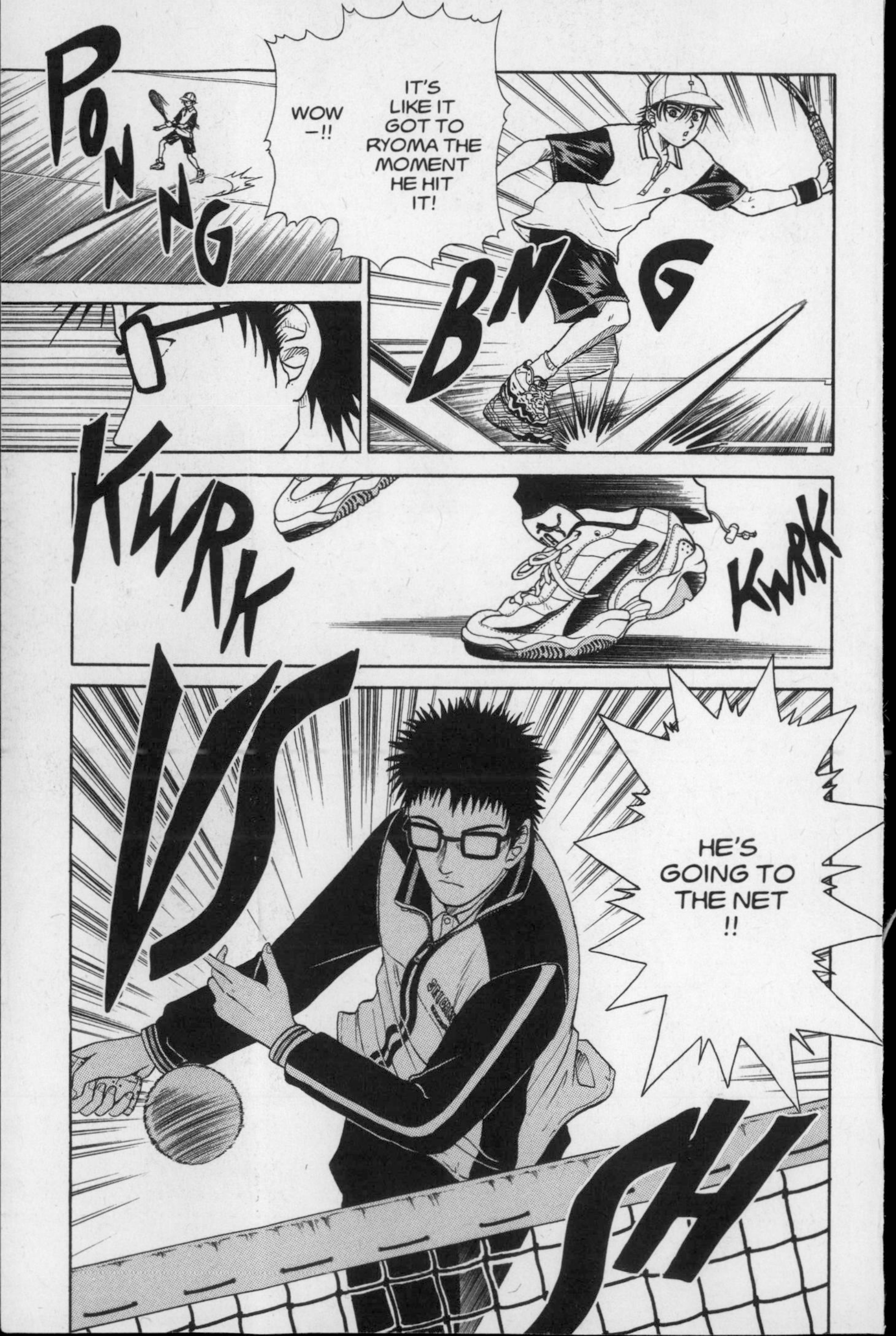
BNG
IT'S LIKE IT GOT TO RYOMA THE MOMENT HE HIT IT!
WOW—!!
PONNG
KWRK
KWRK
HE'S GOING TO THE NET !!
VS
SH

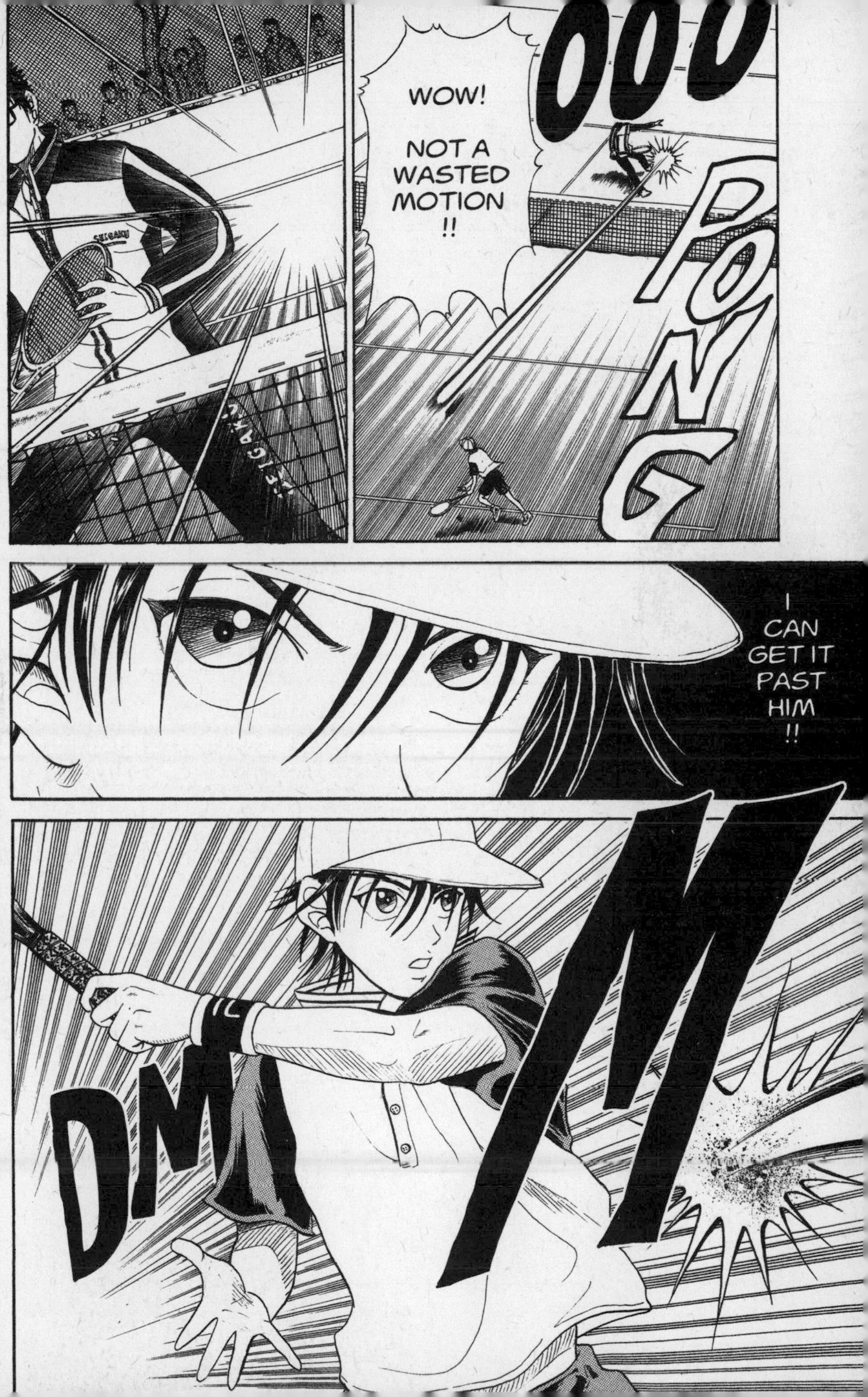
OOO
WOW!
NOT A WASTED MOTION !!
PONG
SEIGAKU
SEIGAKU
I CAN GET IT PAST HIM !!
DMM

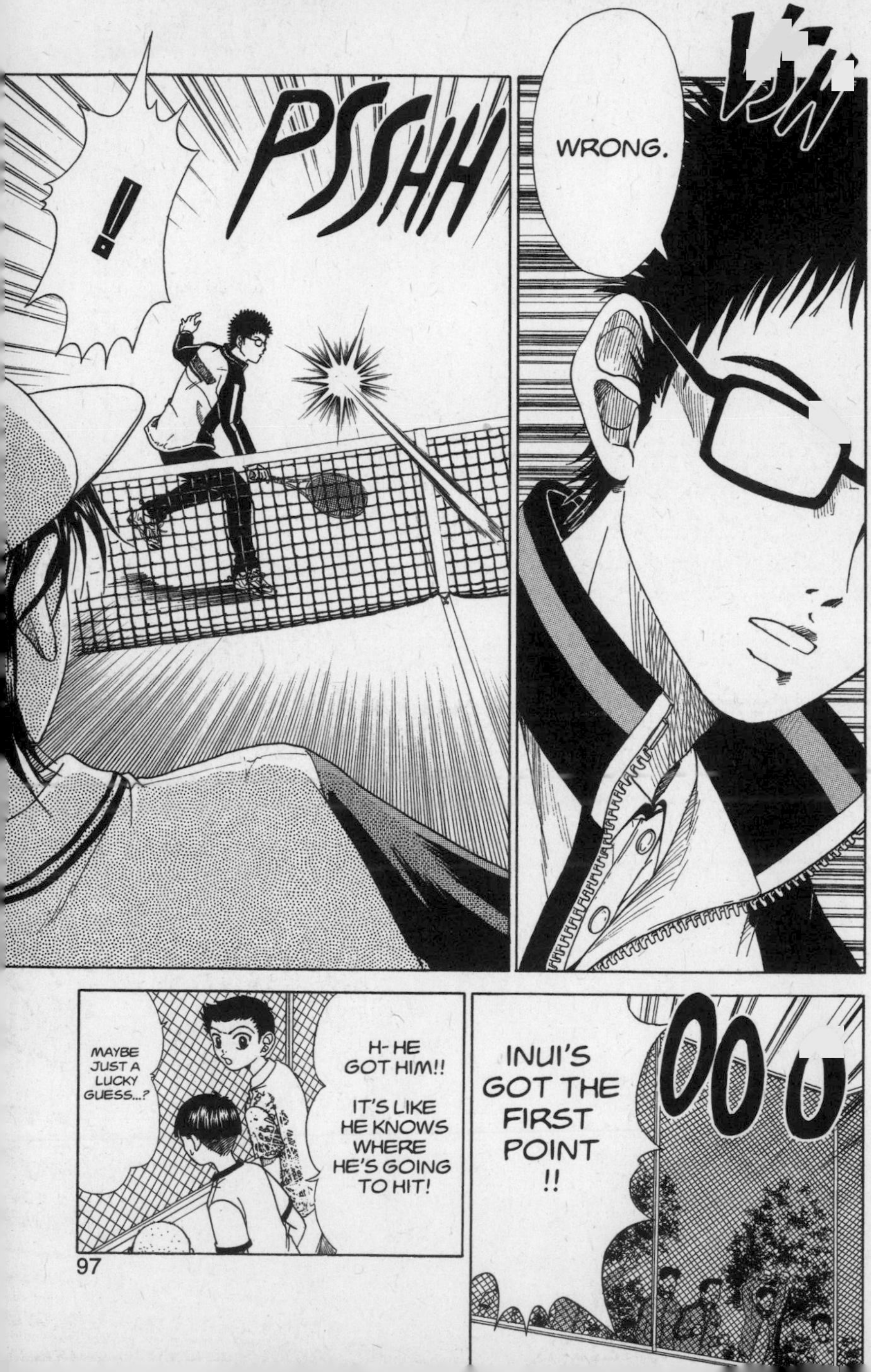
WRONG.
PSSHH
!
INUI'S GOT THE FIRST POINT !!
H- HE GOT HIM!!
IT'S LIKE HE KNOWS WHERE HE'S GOING TO HIT!
MAYBE JUST A LUCKY GUESS...?

READ THIS WAY

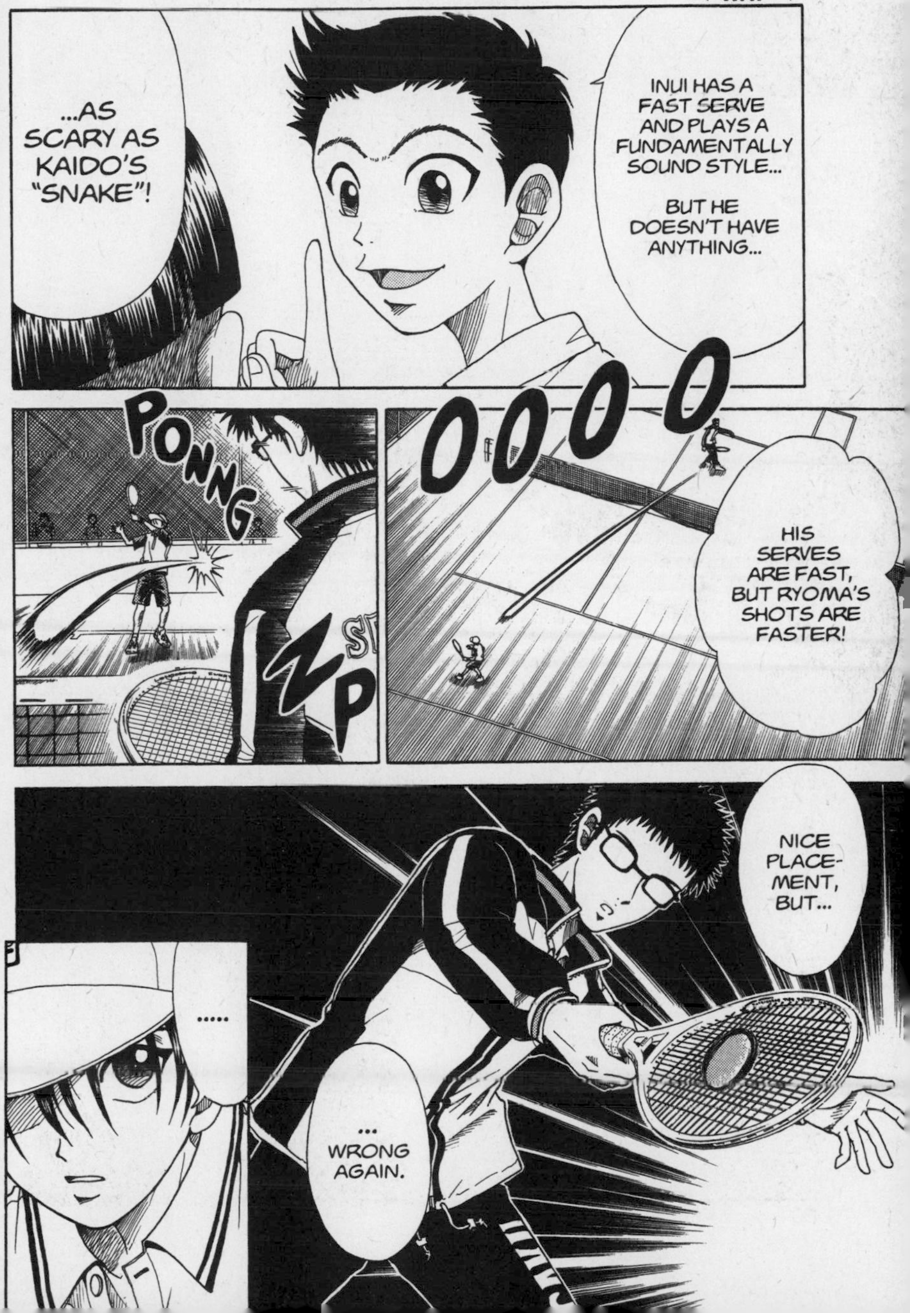

INUI HAS A FAST SERVE AND PLAYS A FUNDAMENTALLY SOUND STYLE... BUT HE DOESN'T HAVE ANYTHING...
...AS SCARY AS KAIDO'S "SNAKE"!
OOOO
HIS SERVES ARE FAST, BUT RYOMA'S SHOTS ARE FASTER!
PONNG
ZP
NICE PLACE-MENT, BUT...
... WRONG AGAIN.
......

READ THIS WAY

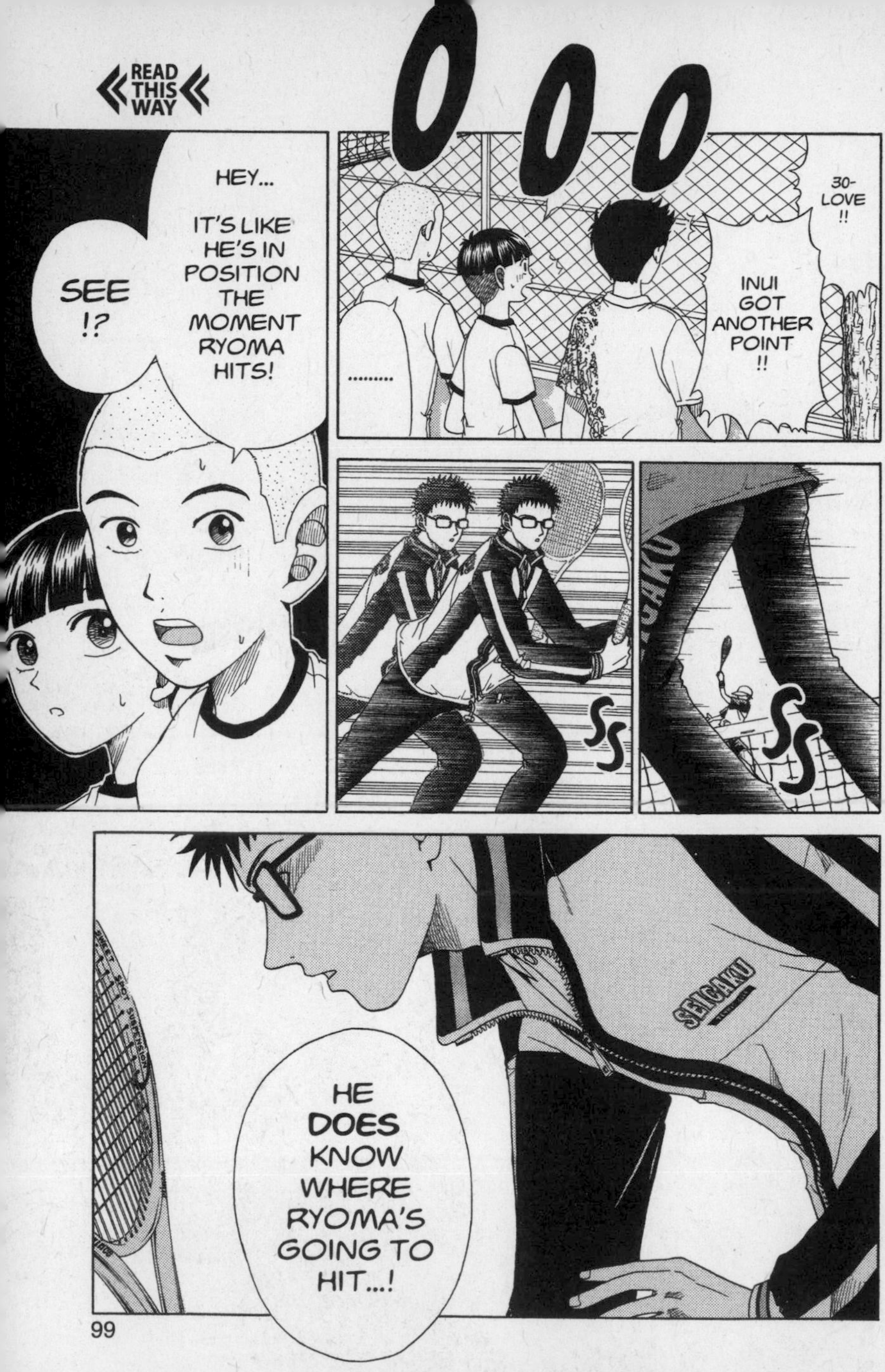
30-LOVE !!
INUI GOT ANOTHER POINT !!
....
SS
SS
HEY...
IT'S LIKE HE'S IN POSITION THE MOMENT RYOMA HITS!
SEE !?
HE DOES KNOW WHERE RYOMA'S GOING TO HIT...!

READ THIS WAY

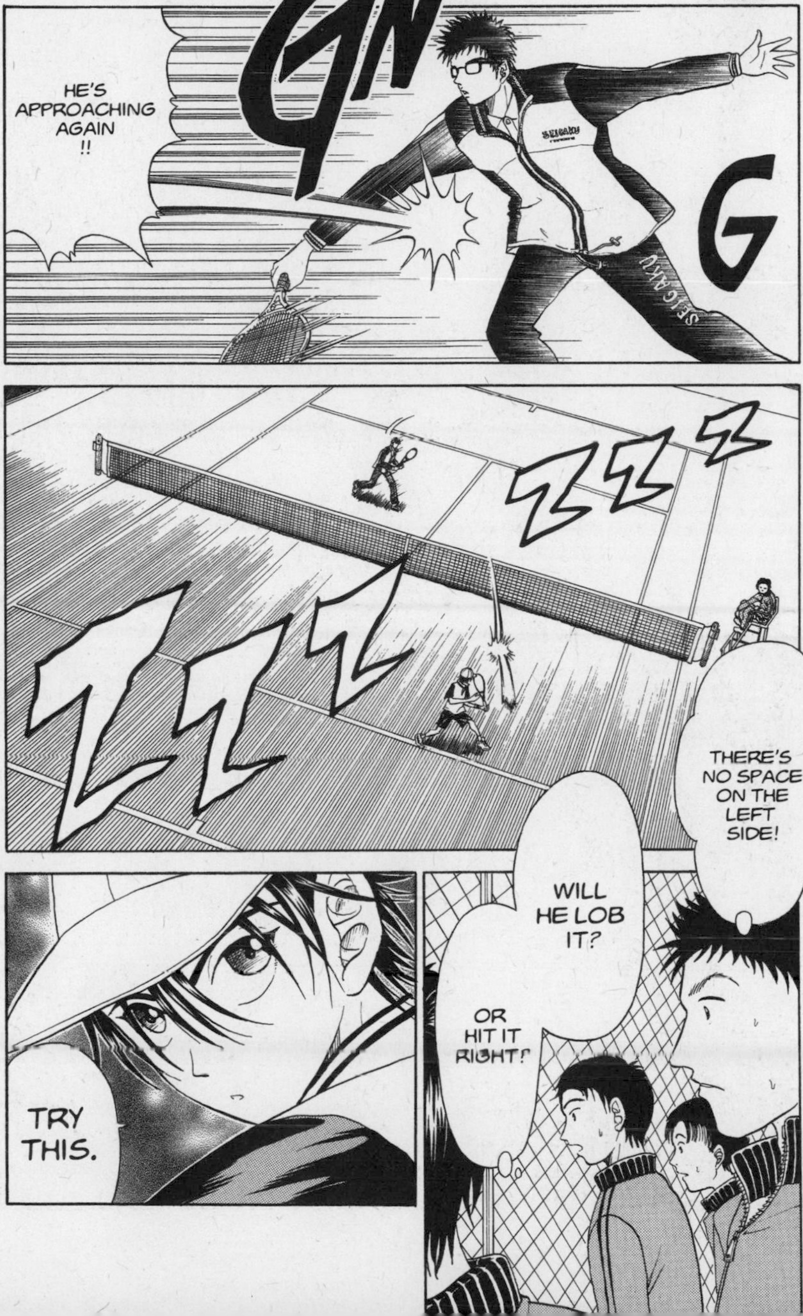
GN
G
HE'S APPROACHING AGAIN !!
THERE'S NO SPACE ON THE LEFT SIDE!
WILL HE LOB IT?
OR HIT IT RIGHT!?
TRY THIS.

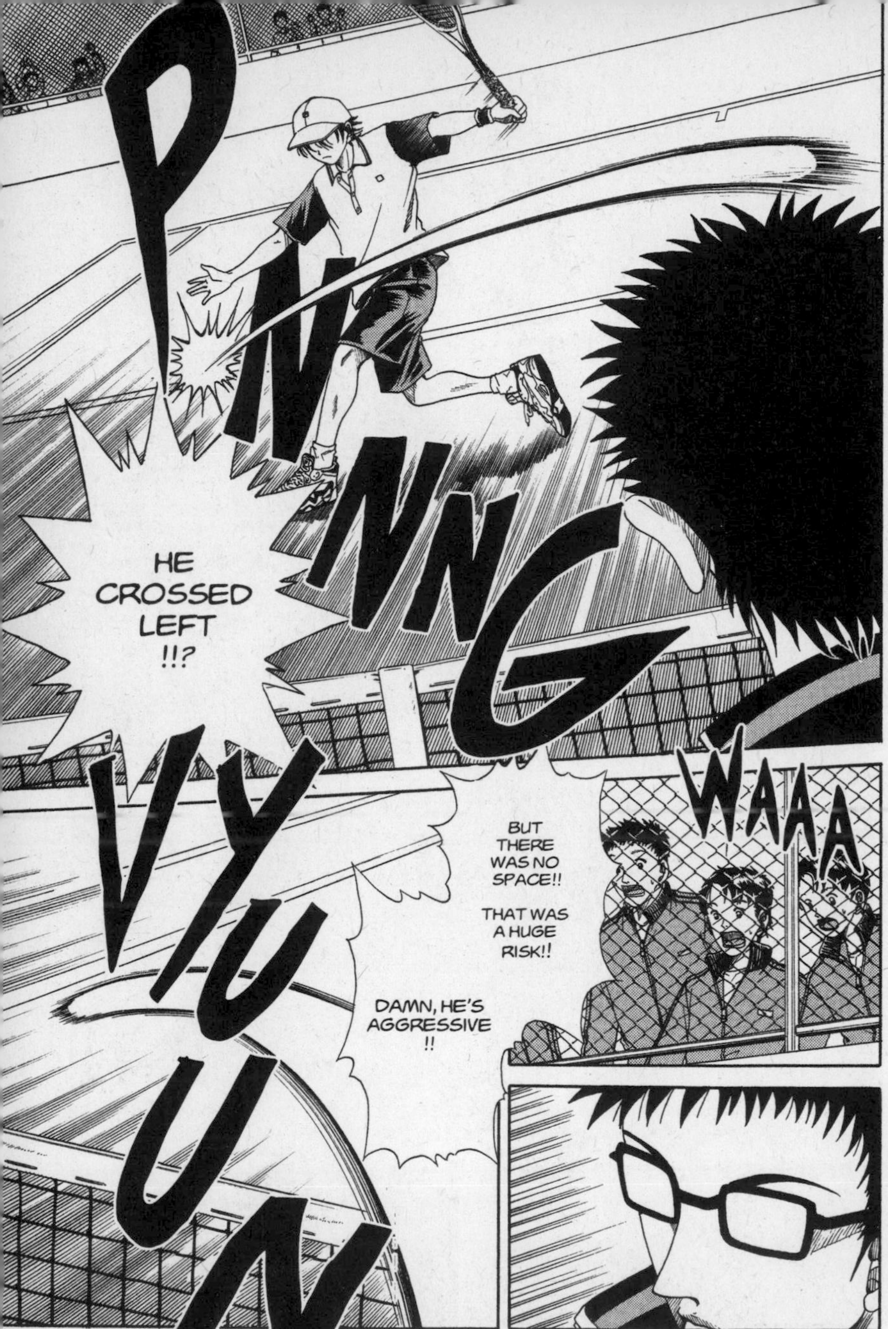
PINNNG
HE CROSSED LEFT !!?
VYUUUN
WAAA
BUT THERE WAS NO SPACE!!
THAT WAS A HUGE RISK!!
DAMN, HE'S AGGRESSIVE !!

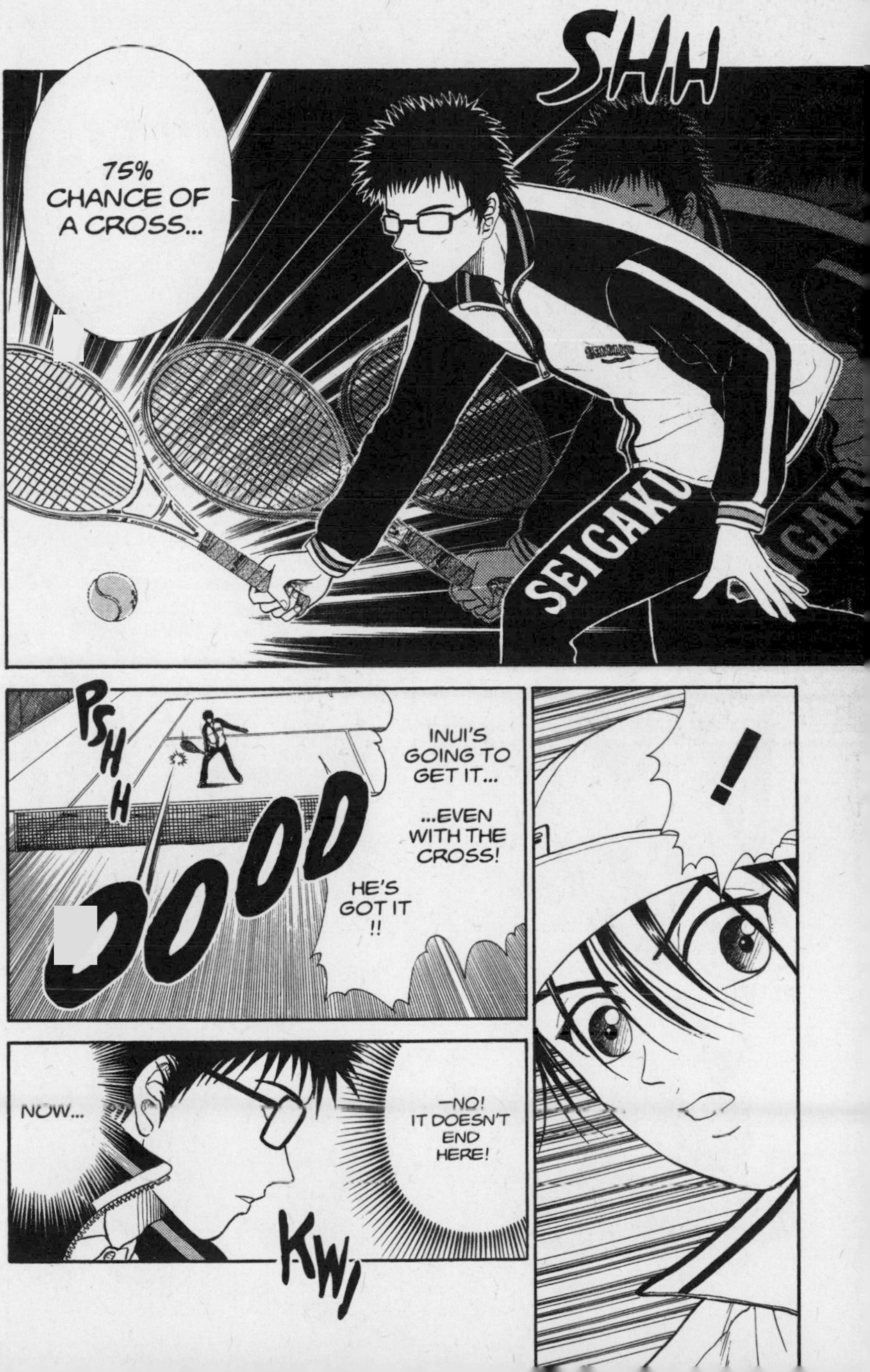
SHH
75% CHANCE OF A CROSS...
!
INUI'S GOING TO GET IT...
...EVEN WITH THE CROSS!
HE'S GOT IT !!
PSHH
—NO! IT DOESN'T END HERE!
NOW...
KWI

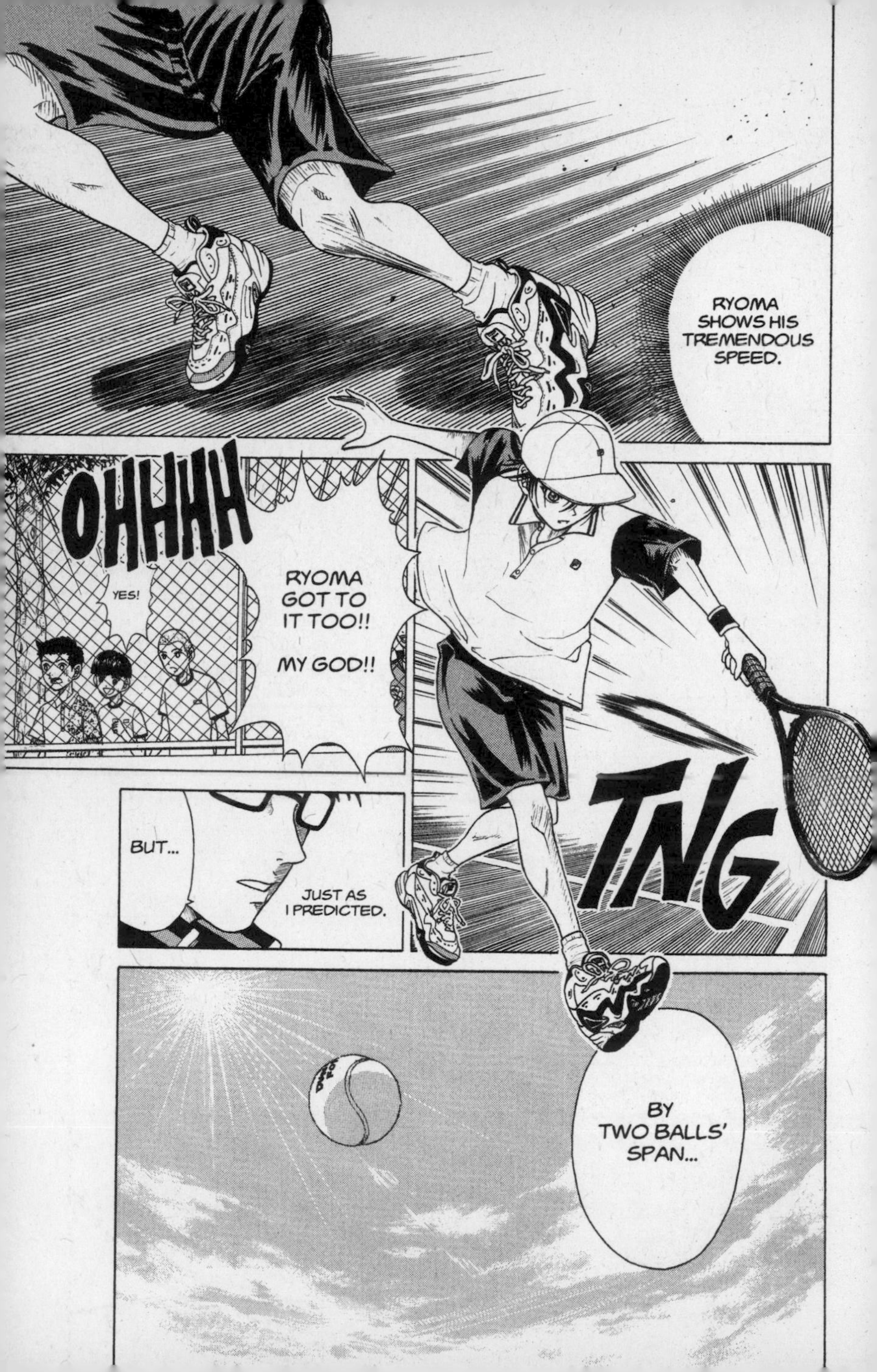
RYOMA SHOWS HIS TREMENDOUS SPEED.
TNG
OHHHH
RYOMA GOT TO IT TOO!!
MY GOD!!
YES!
BUT...
JUST AS I PREDICTED.
BY TWO BALLS' SPAN...

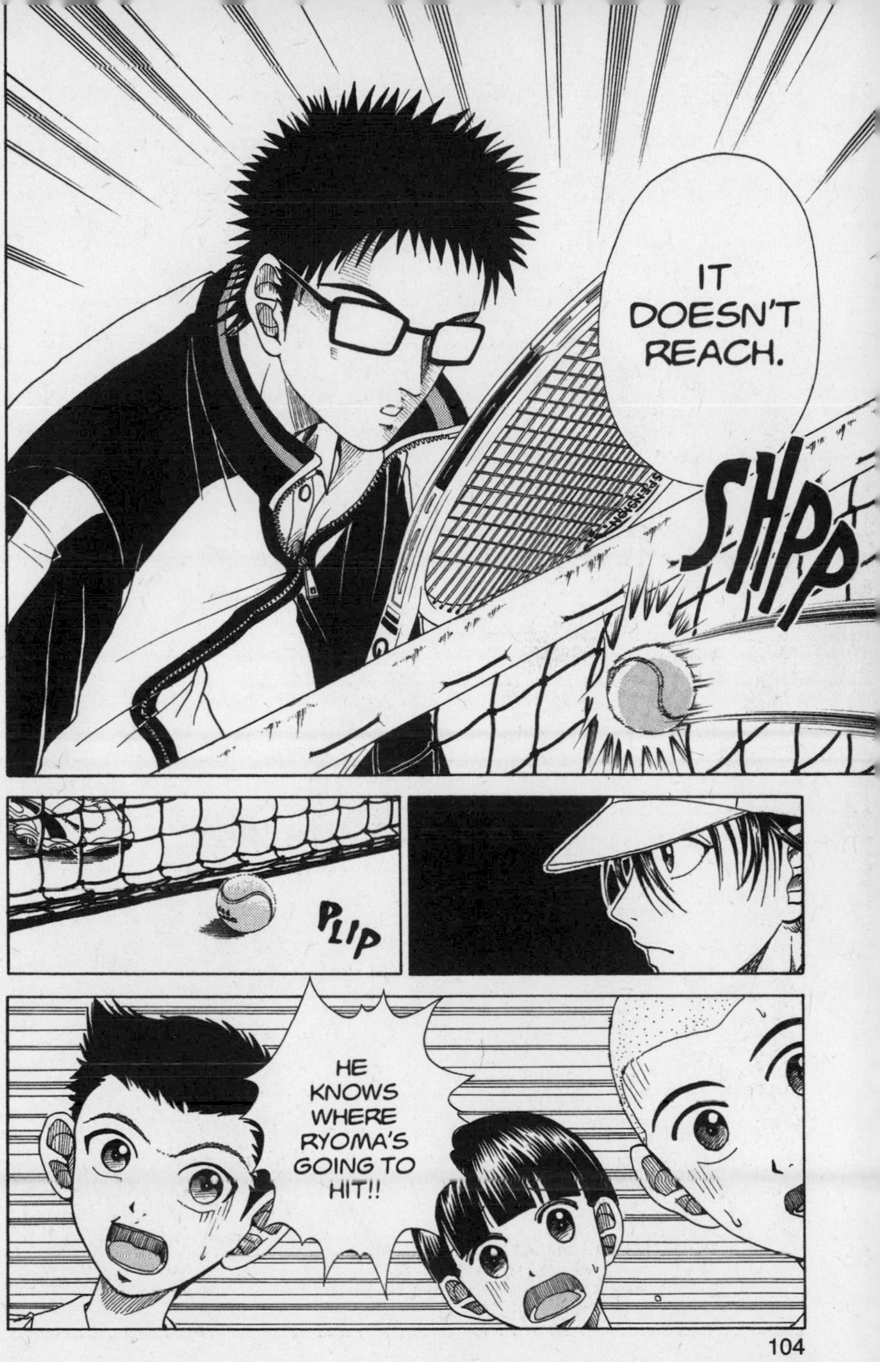
IT DOESN'T REACH.
SHPP
PLIP
HE KNOWS WHERE RYOMA'S GOING TO HIT!!

READ THIS WAY

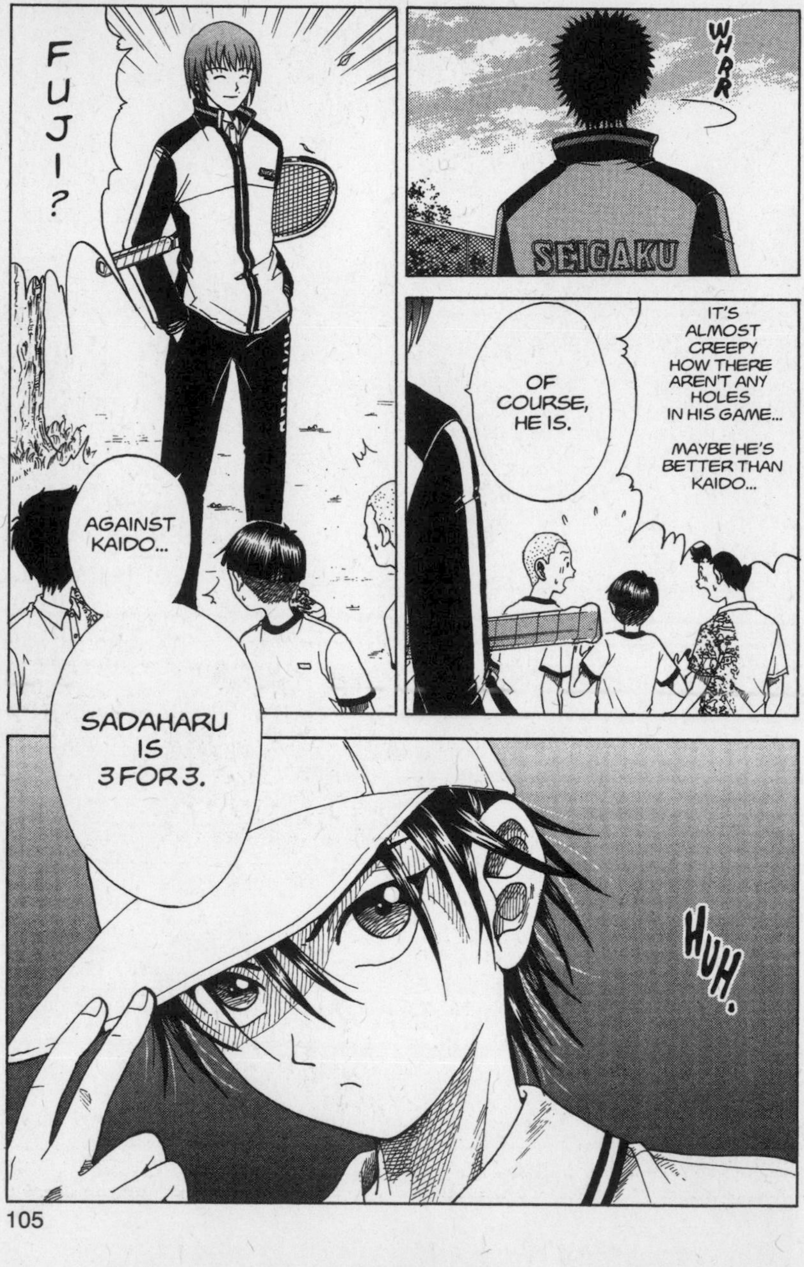
WHRR
SEIGAKU
IT'S ALMOST CREEPY HOW THERE AREN'T ANY HOLES IN HIS GAME...
MAYBE HE'S BETTER THAN KAIDO...
OF COURSE, HE IS.
FUJI?
AGAINST KAIDO...
SADAHARU IS 3 FOR 3.
HUH.

READ THIS WAY

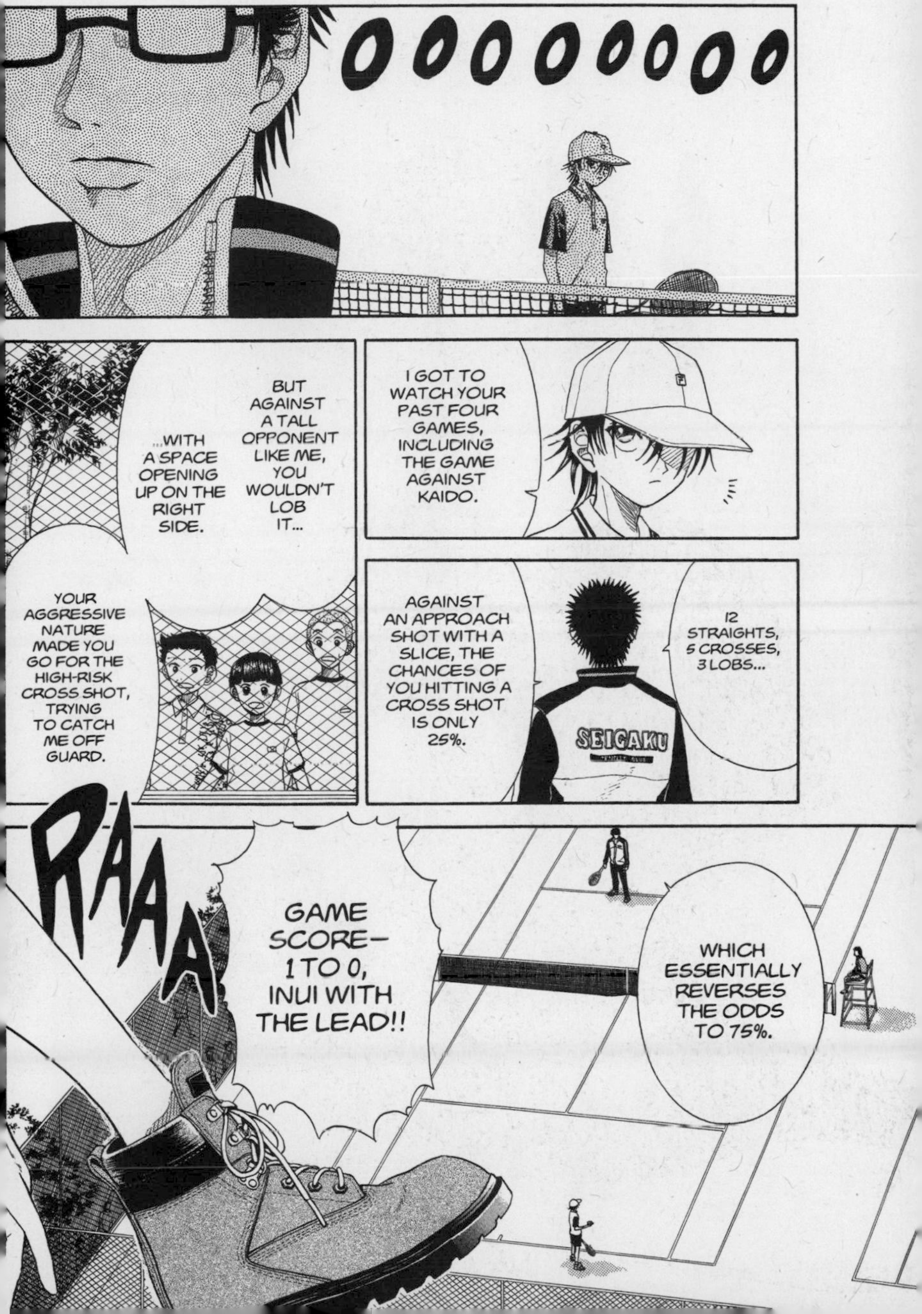
OOOOOOOO
I GOT TO WATCH YOUR PAST FOUR GAMES, INCLUDING THE GAME AGAINST KAIDO.
12 STRAIGHTS, 5 CROSSES, 3 LOBS...
AGAINST AN APPROACH SHOT WITH A SLICE, THE CHANCES OF YOU HITTING A CROSS SHOT IS ONLY 25%.
BUT AGAINST A TALL OPPONENT LIKE ME, YOU WOULDN'T LOB IT...
...WITH A SPACE OPENING UP ON THE RIGHT SIDE.
YOUR AGGRESSIVE NATURE MADE YOU GO FOR THE HIGH-RISK CROSS SHOT, TRYING TO CATCH ME OFF GUARD.
WHICH ESSENTIALLY REVERSES THE ODDS TO 75%.
GAME SCORE—1 TO 0, INUI WITH THE LEAD!!
RAAA

Genius 13
9th Grader Poise

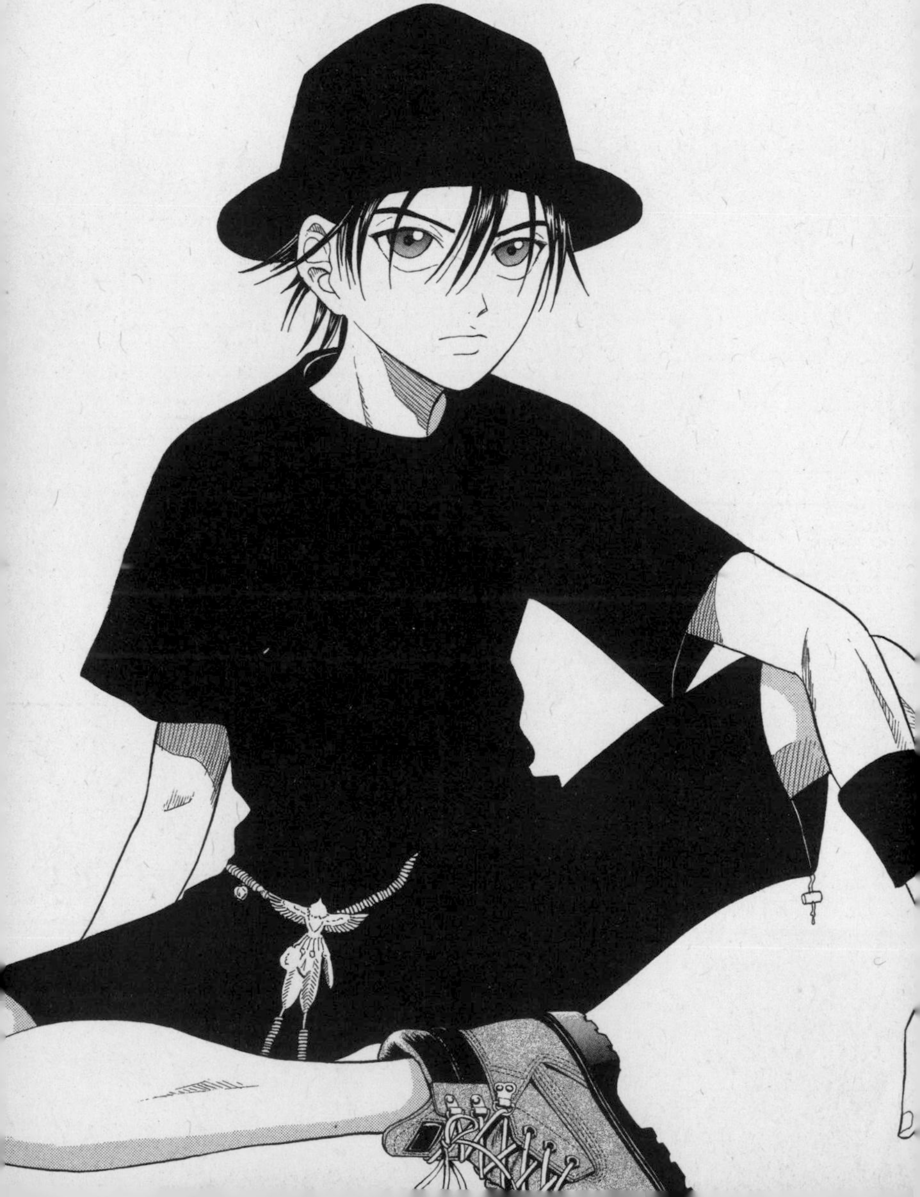

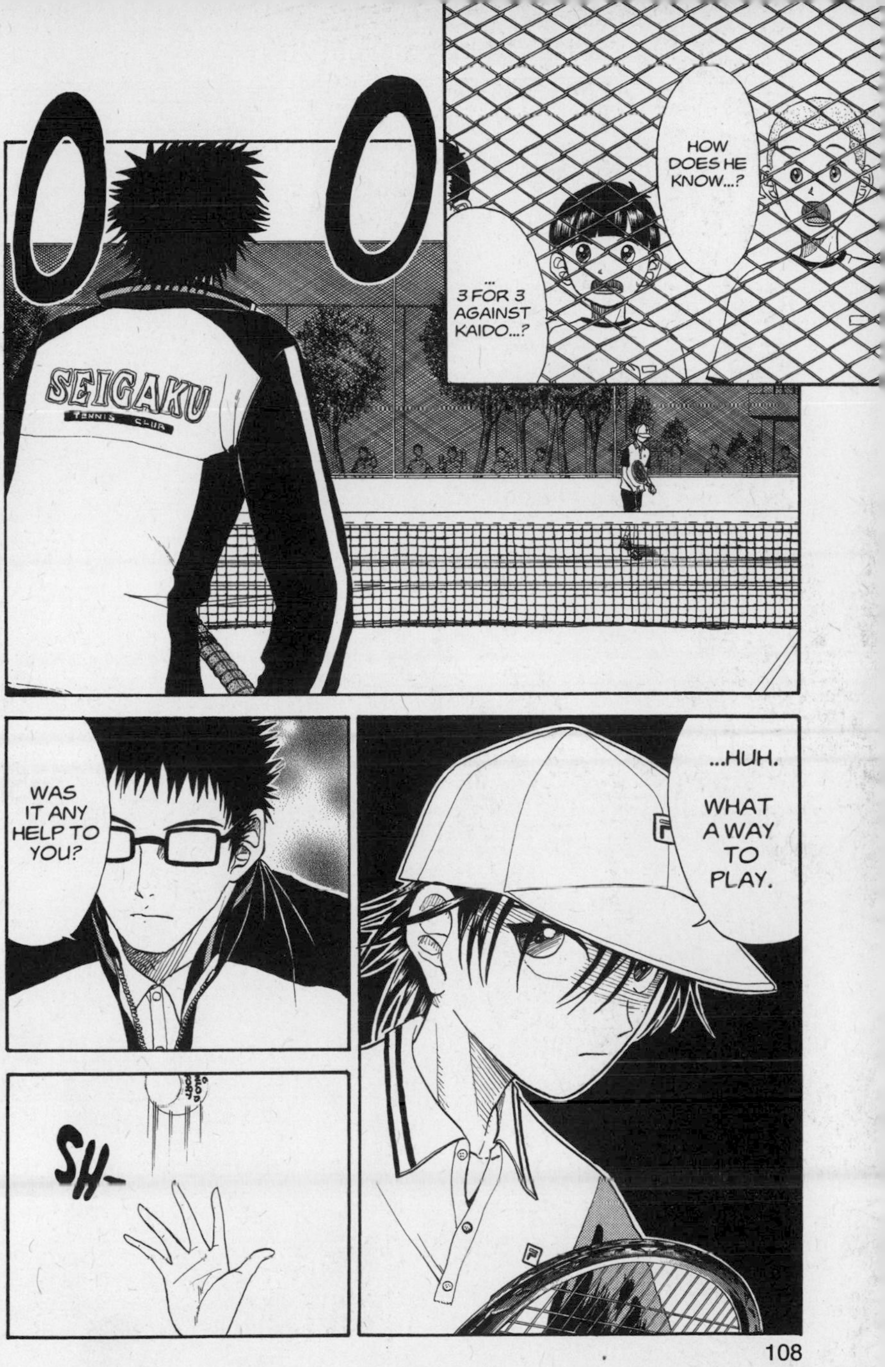
HOW DOES HE KNOW...?
... 3 FOR 3 AGAINST KAIDO...?
0
0
SEIGAKU
TENNIS CLUB
...HUH.
WHAT A WAY TO PLAY.
WAS IT ANY HELP TO YOU?
SH-

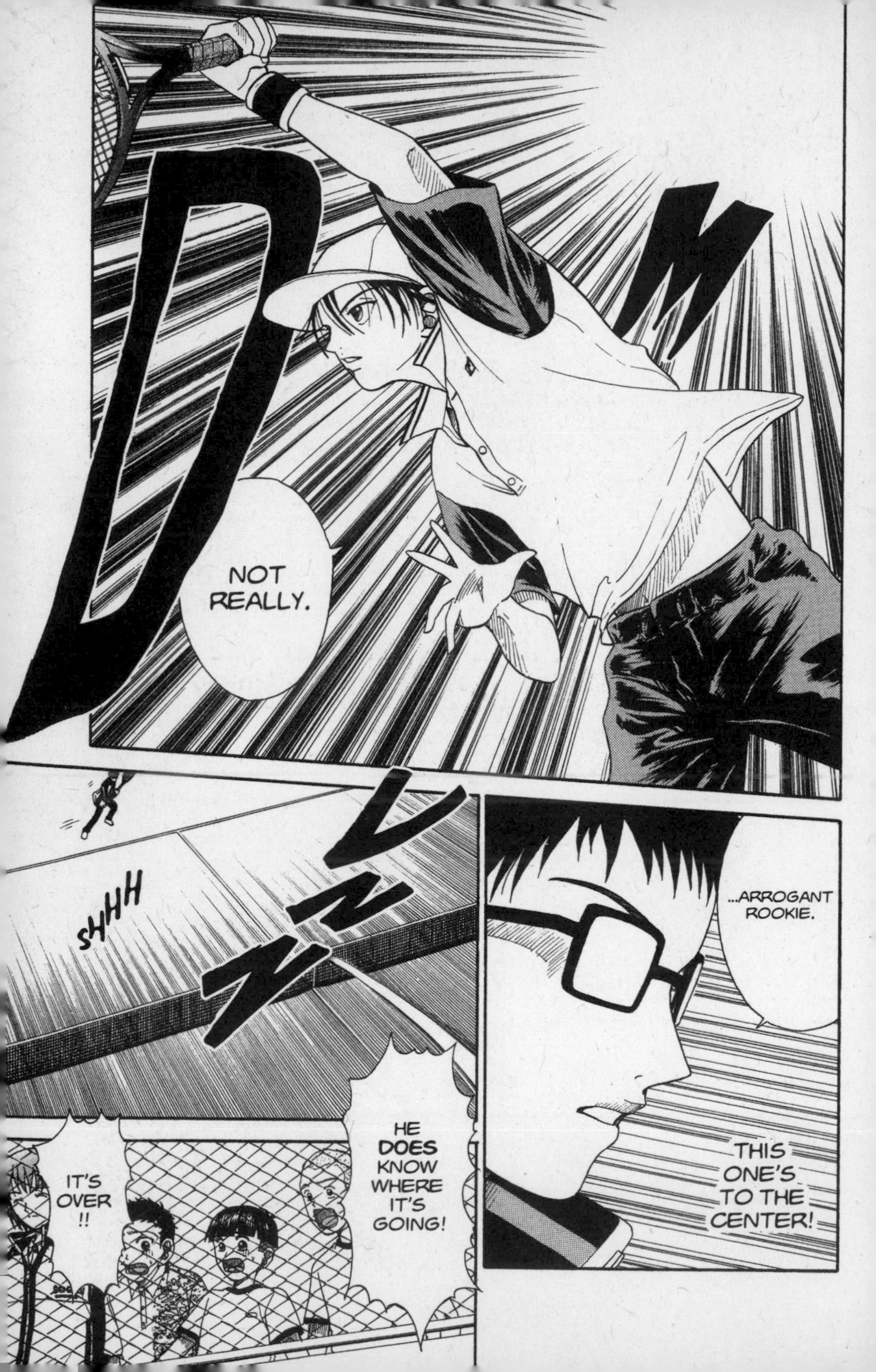
NOT REALLY.
...ARROGANT ROOKIE.
THIS ONE'S TO THE CENTER!
SHHH
HE DOES KNOW WHERE IT'S GOING!
IT'S OVER !!

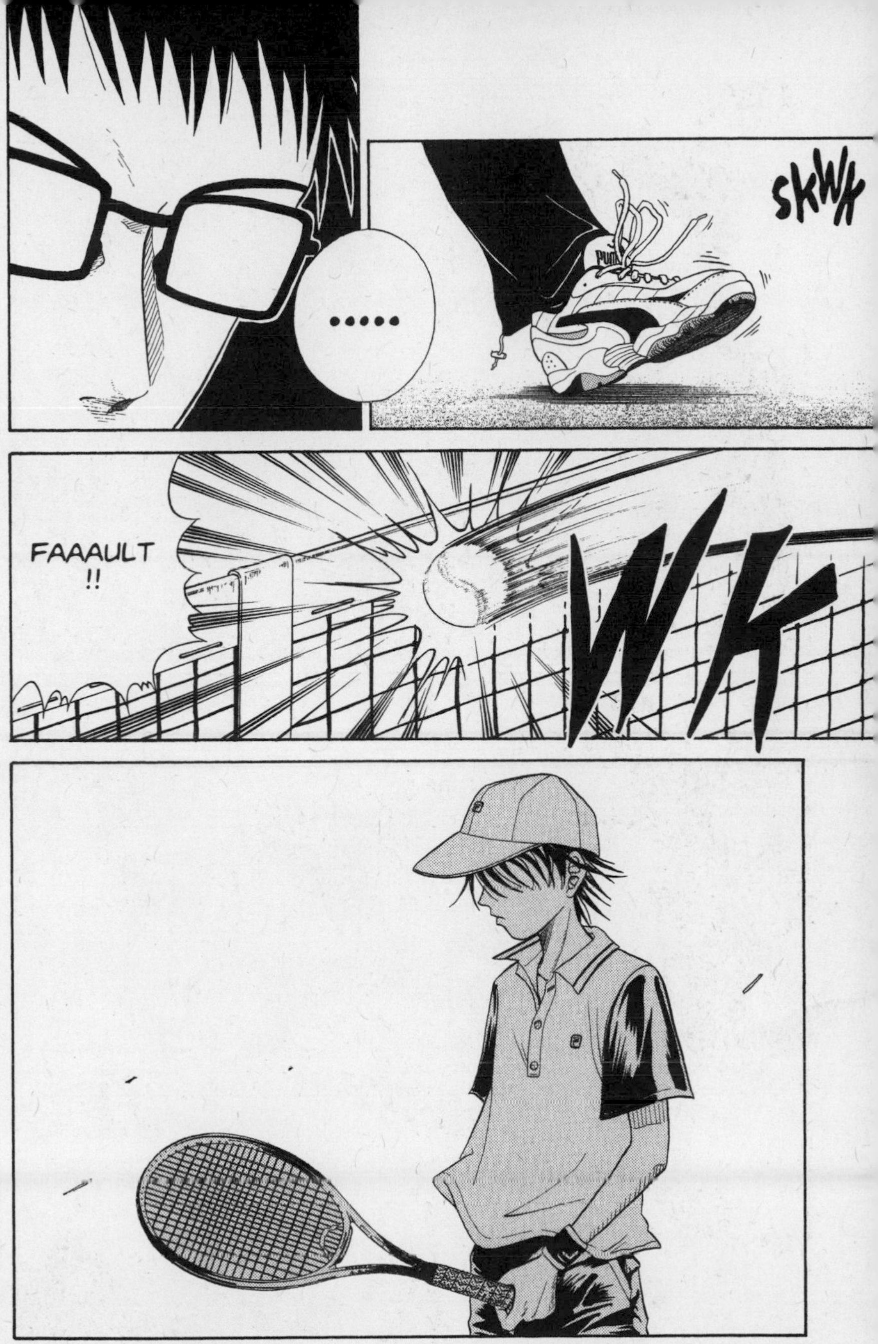
SKWK
.....
WK
FAAAULT !!

READ THIS WAY

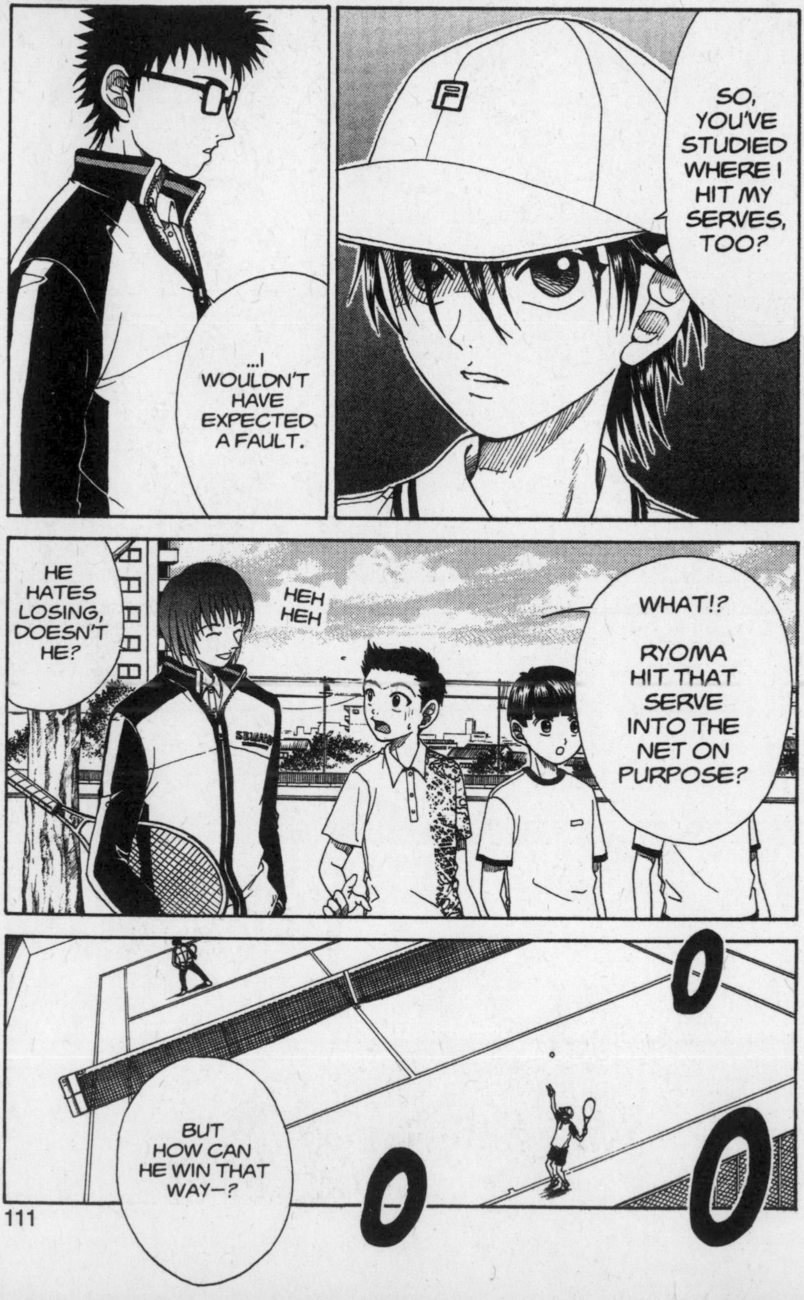
SO, YOU'VE STUDIED WHERE I HIT MY SERVES, TOO?
...I WOULDN'T HAVE EXPECTED A FAULT.
WHAT!? RYOMA HIT THAT SERVE INTO THE NET ON PURPOSE?
HEH HEH
HE HATES LOSING, DOESN'T HE?
BUT HOW CAN HE WIN THAT WAY–?

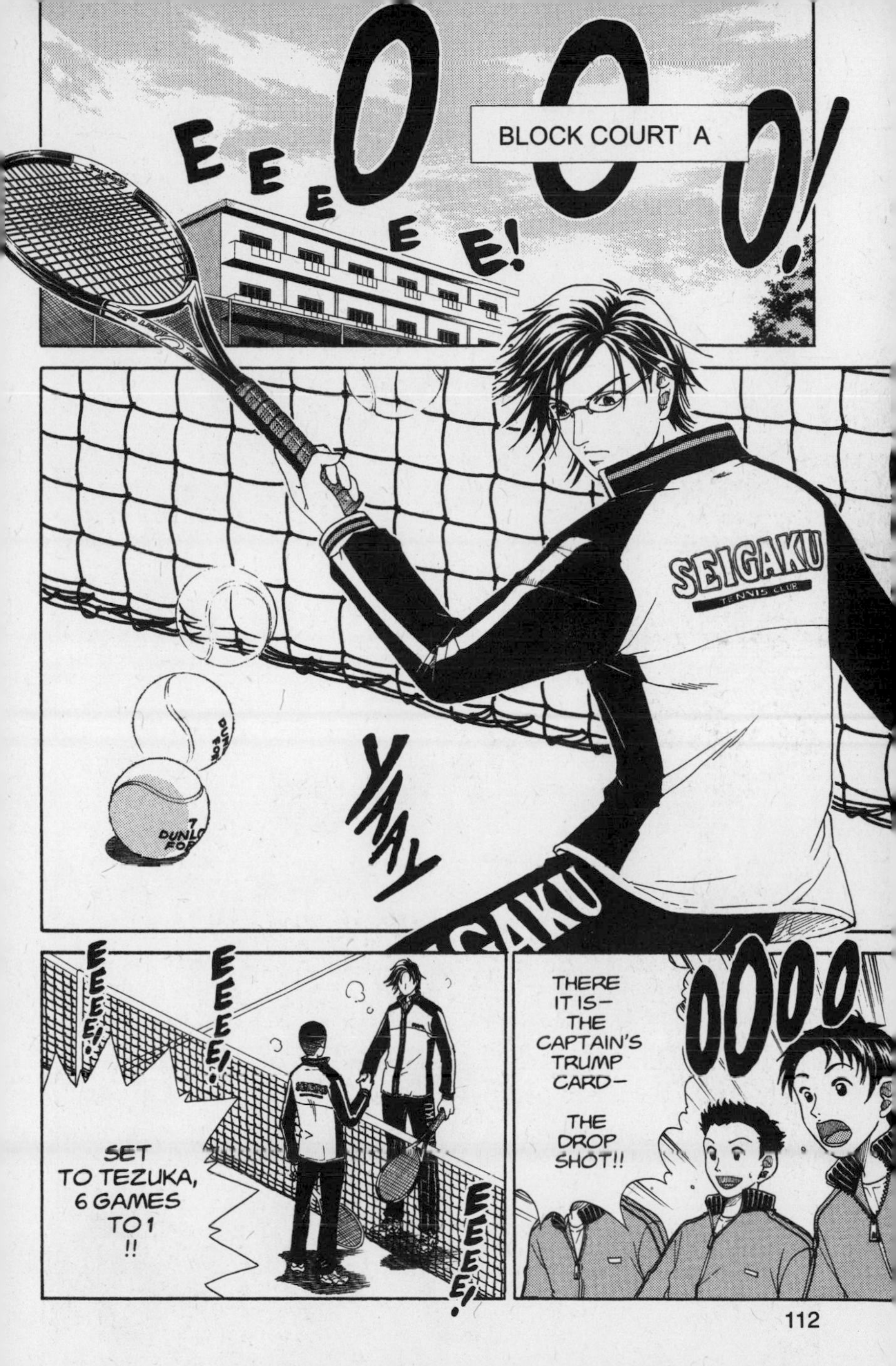
EEEEEE!
OOO!
BLOCK COURT A
SEIGAKU
TENNIS CLUB
YAAY
THERE IT IS— THE CAPTAIN'S TRUMP CARD—
THE DROP SHOT!!
OOOO
EEEEE!
EEEEE!
EEEEE!
SET TO TEZUKA, 6 GAMES TO 1 !!

READ THIS WAY

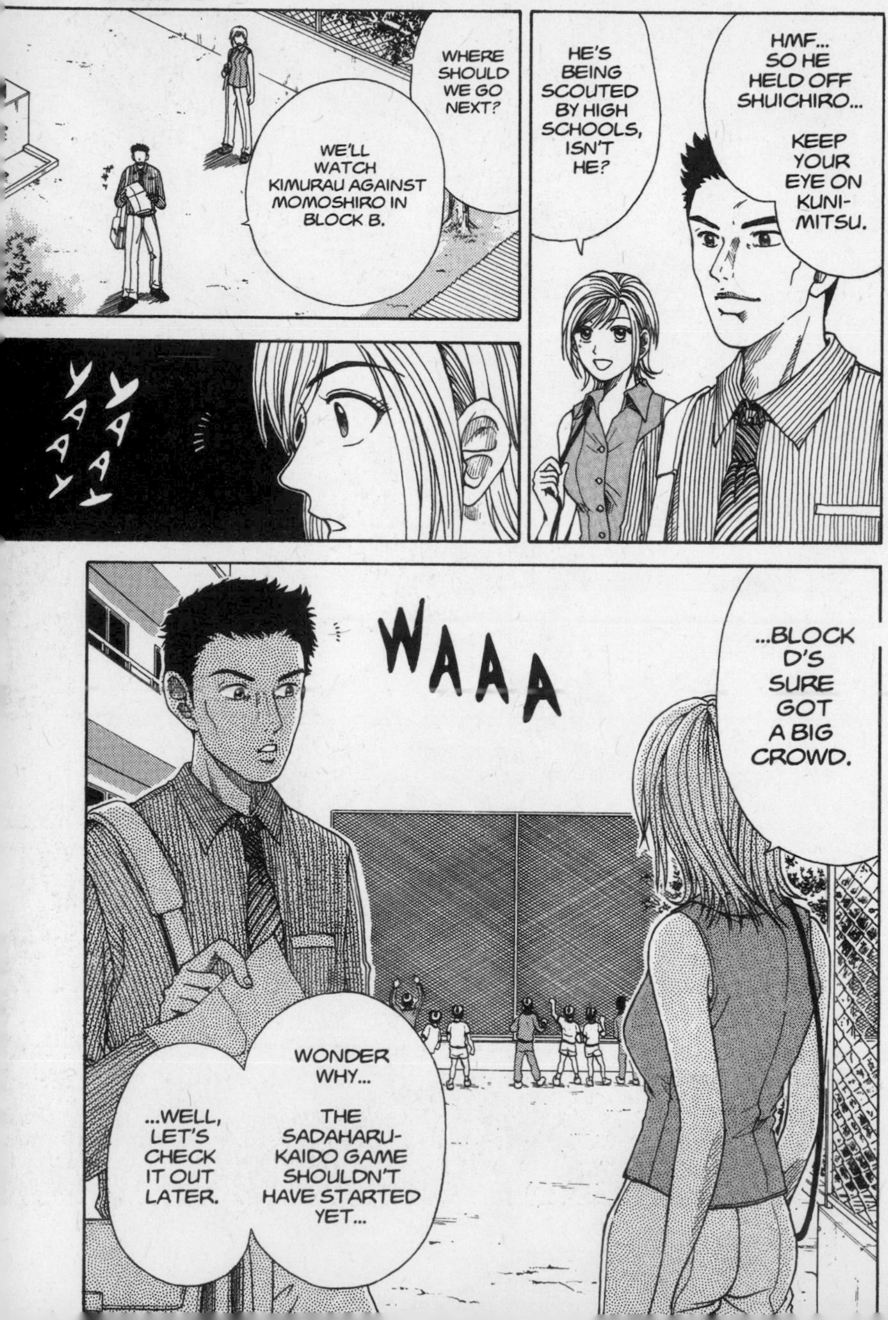

HMF... SO HE HELD OFF SHUICHIRO...
KEEP YOUR EYE ON KUNI-MITSU.
HE'S BEING SCOUTED BY HIGH SCHOOLS, ISN'T HE?
WHERE SHOULD WE GO NEXT?
WE'LL WATCH KIMURAU AGAINST MOMOSHIRO IN BLOCK B.
YAAAY
YAAAY
...BLOCK D'S SURE GOT A BIG CROWD.
WAAA
WONDER WHY...
THE SADAHARU-KAIDO GAME SHOULDN'T HAVE STARTED YET...
...WELL, LET'S CHECK IT OUT LATER.

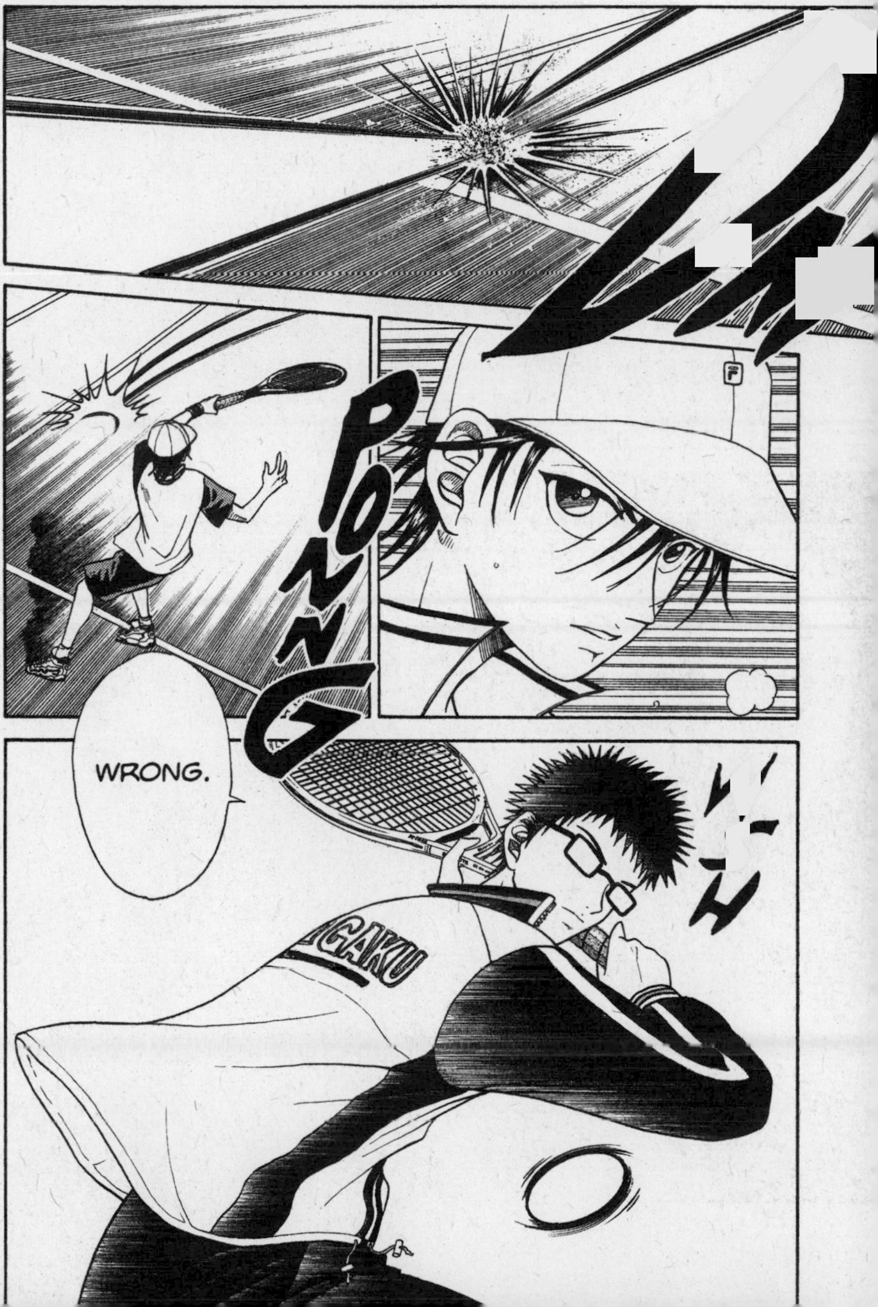
PONG
WRONG.

READ THIS WAY

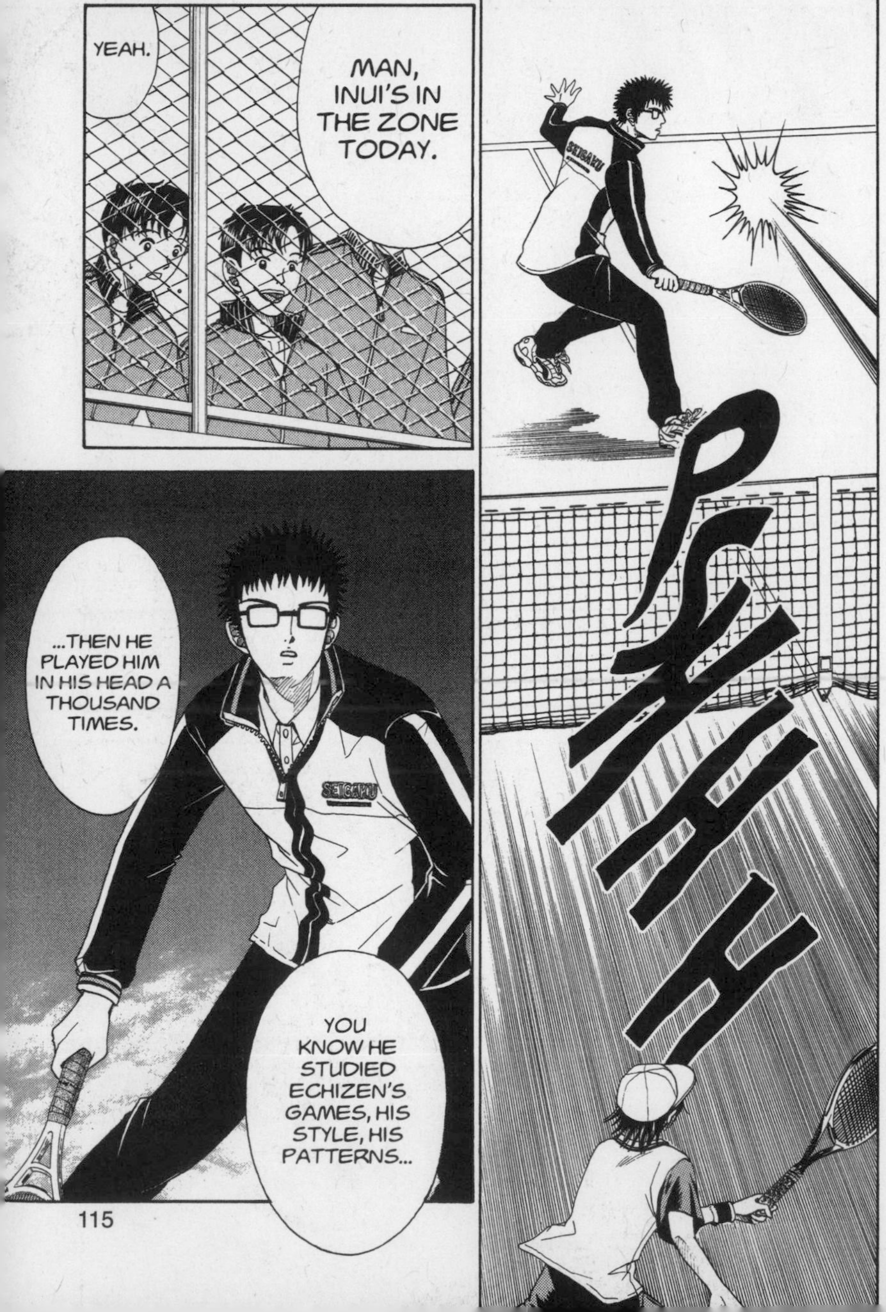
MAN, INUI'S IN THE ZONE TODAY.
YEAH.
PSHHH
YOU KNOW HE STUDIED ECHIZEN'S GAMES, HIS STYLE, HIS PATTERNS...
...THEN HE PLAYED HIM IN HIS HEAD A THOUSAND TIMES.

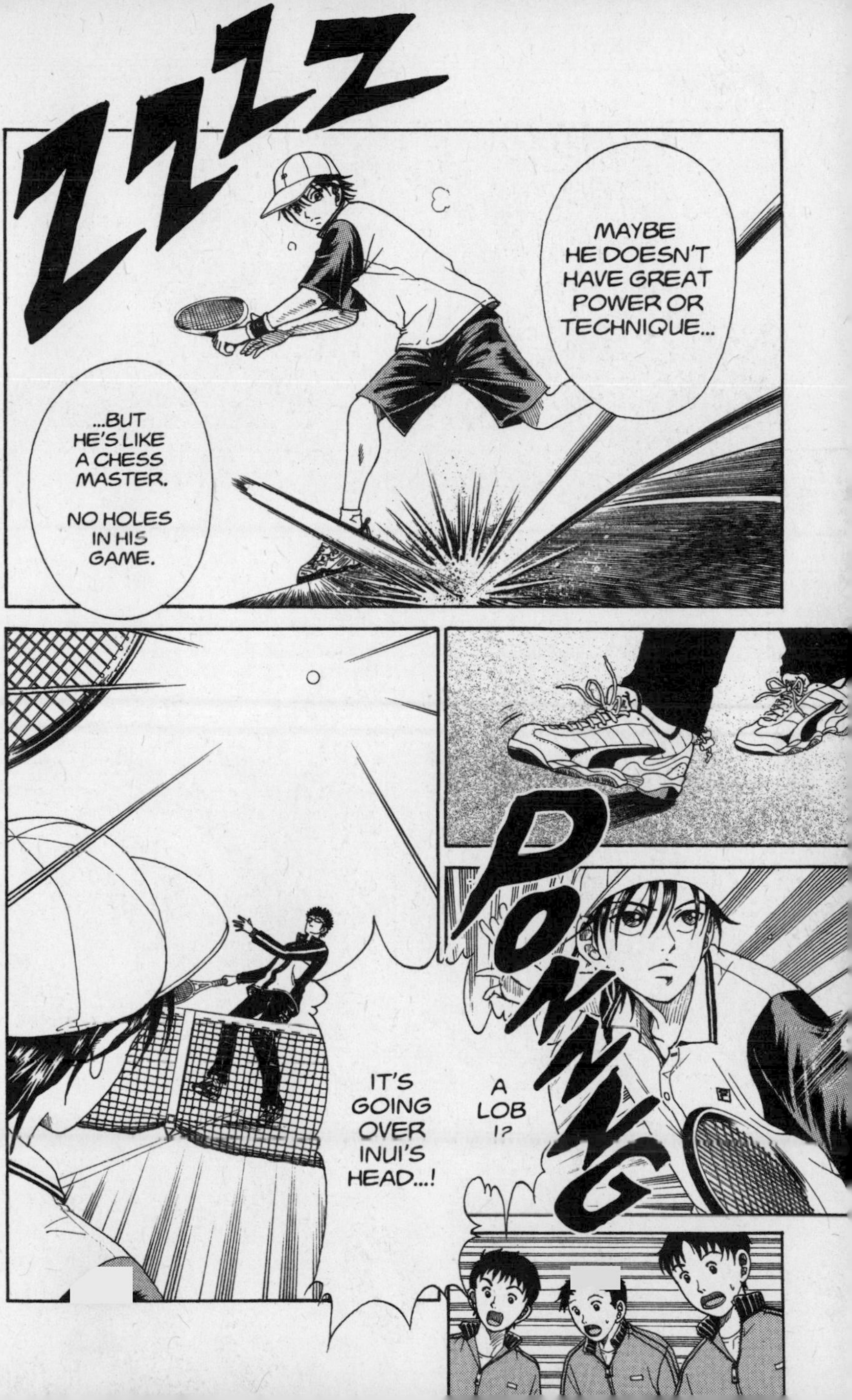
MAYBE HE DOESN'T HAVE GREAT POWER OR TECHNIQUE...
ZZZZ
...BUT HE'S LIKE A CHESS MASTER.
NO HOLES IN HIS GAME.
A LOB !?
IT'S GOING OVER INUI'S HEAD...!

READ THIS WAY

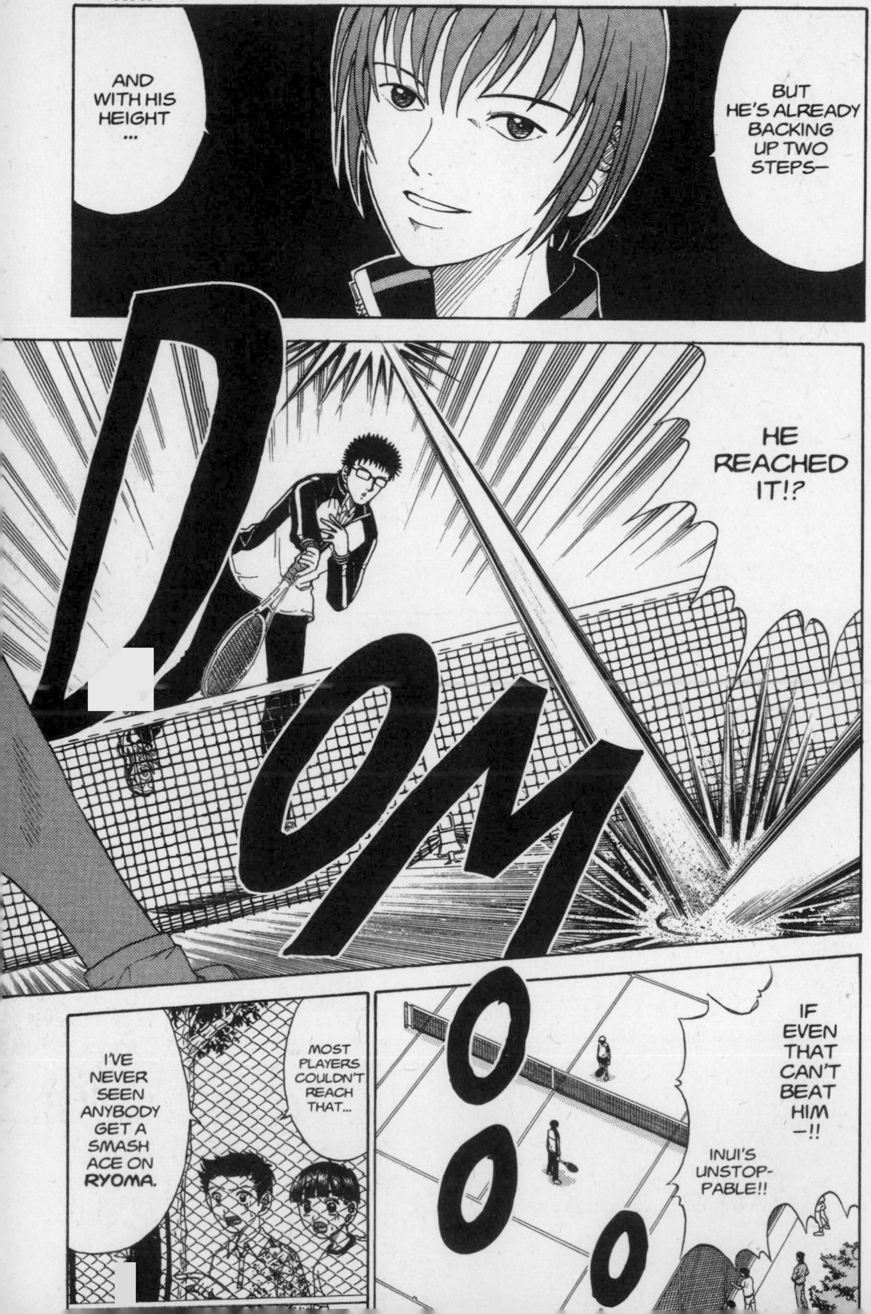
BUT HE'S ALREADY BACKING UP TWO STEPS—
AND WITH HIS HEIGHT ...
DOMOOO
HE REACHED IT!?
IF EVEN THAT CAN'T BEAT HIM —!!
INUI'S UNSTOP-PABLE!!
MOST PLAYERS COULDN'T REACH THAT...
I'VE NEVER SEEN ANYBODY GET A SMASH ACE ON RYOMA.

READ THIS WAY

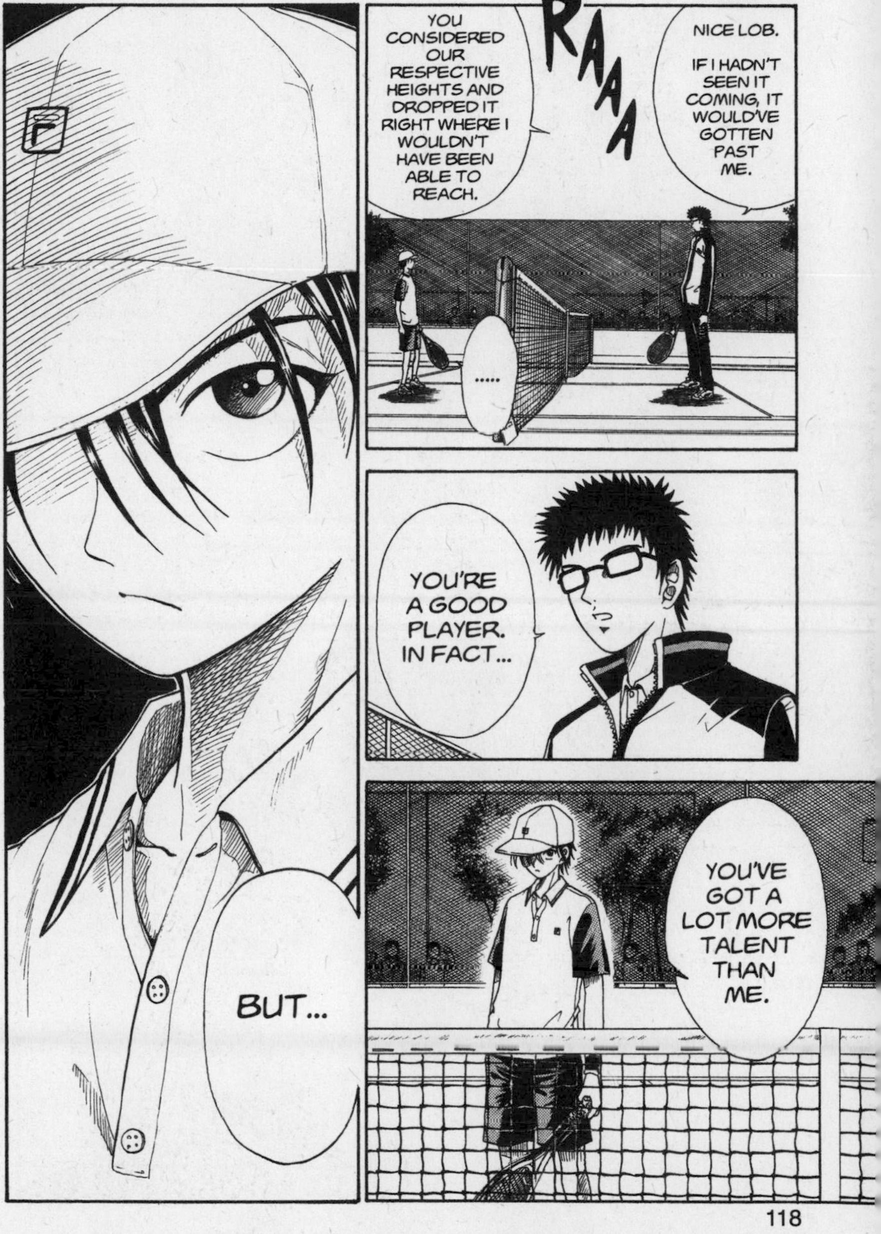
NICE LOB.
IF I HADN'T SEEN IT COMING, IT WOULD'VE GOTTEN PAST ME.
RAAAA
YOU CONSIDERED OUR RESPECTIVE HEIGHTS AND DROPPED IT RIGHT WHERE I WOULDN'T HAVE BEEN ABLE TO REACH.
......
YOU'RE A GOOD PLAYER. IN FACT...
YOU'VE GOT A LOT MORE TALENT THAN ME.
BUT...

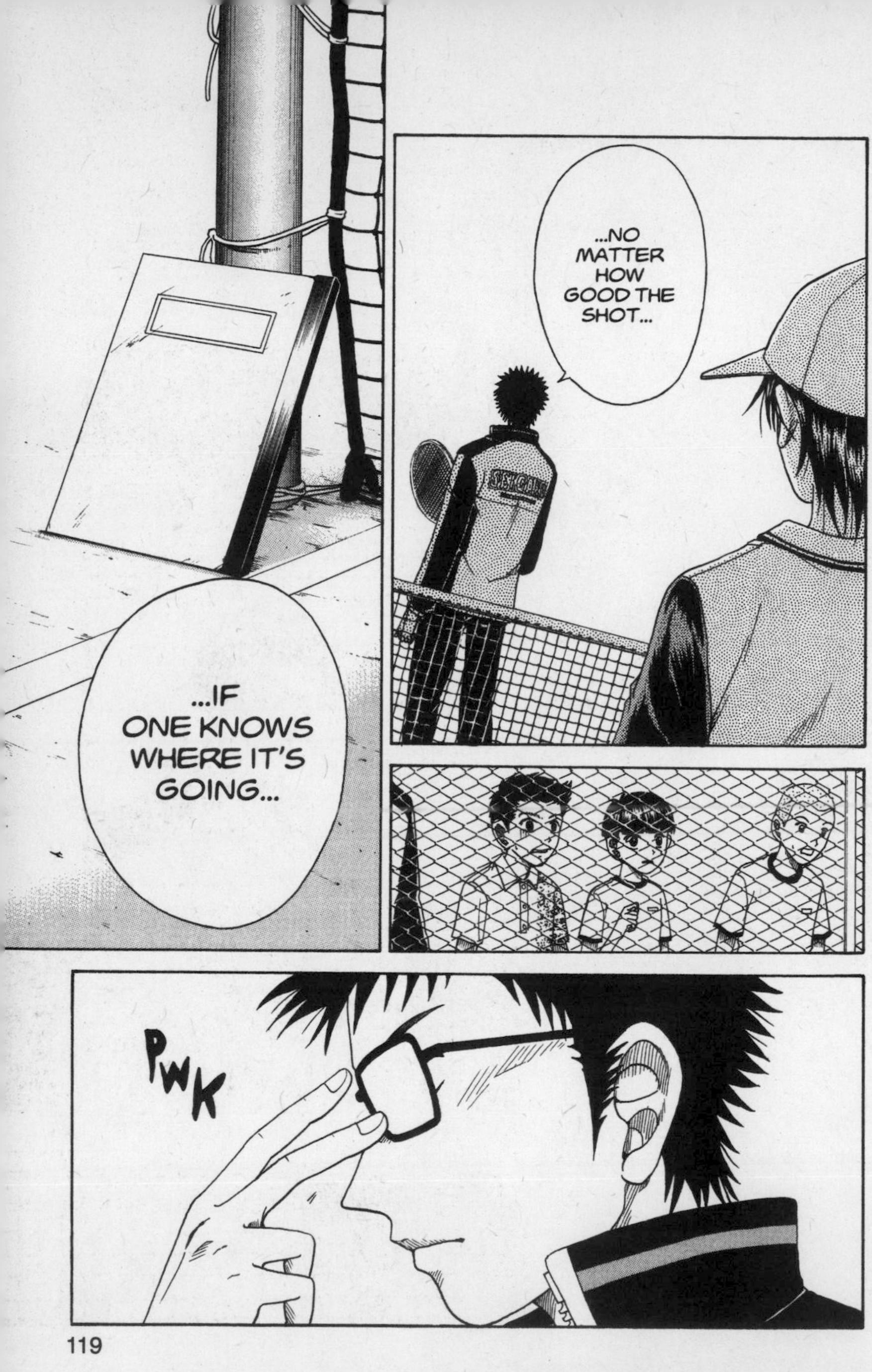
...NO MATTER HOW GOOD THE SHOT...
...IF ONE KNOWS WHERE IT'S GOING...
PWK

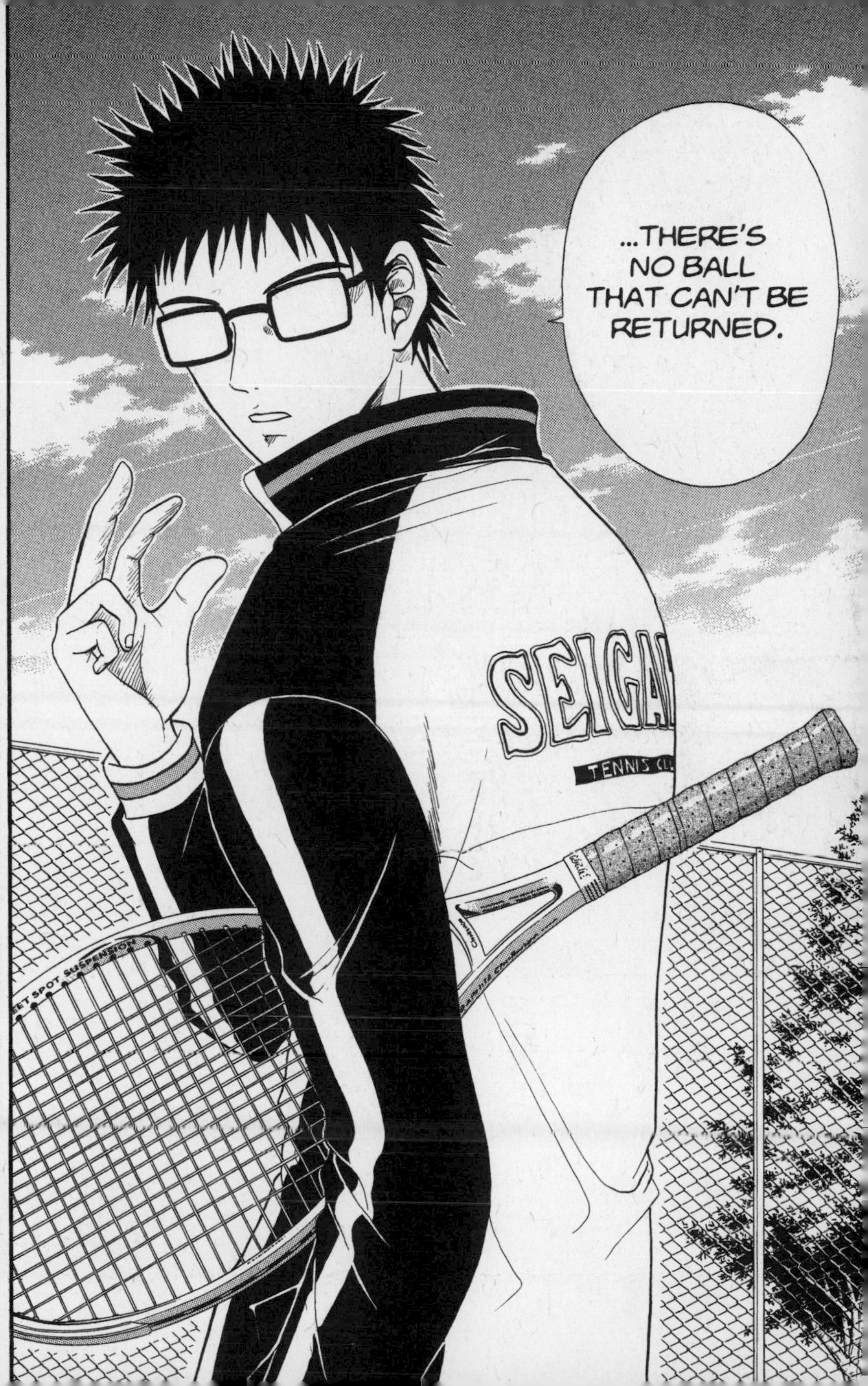
...THERE'S NO BALL THAT CAN'T BE RETURNED.

READ THIS WAY

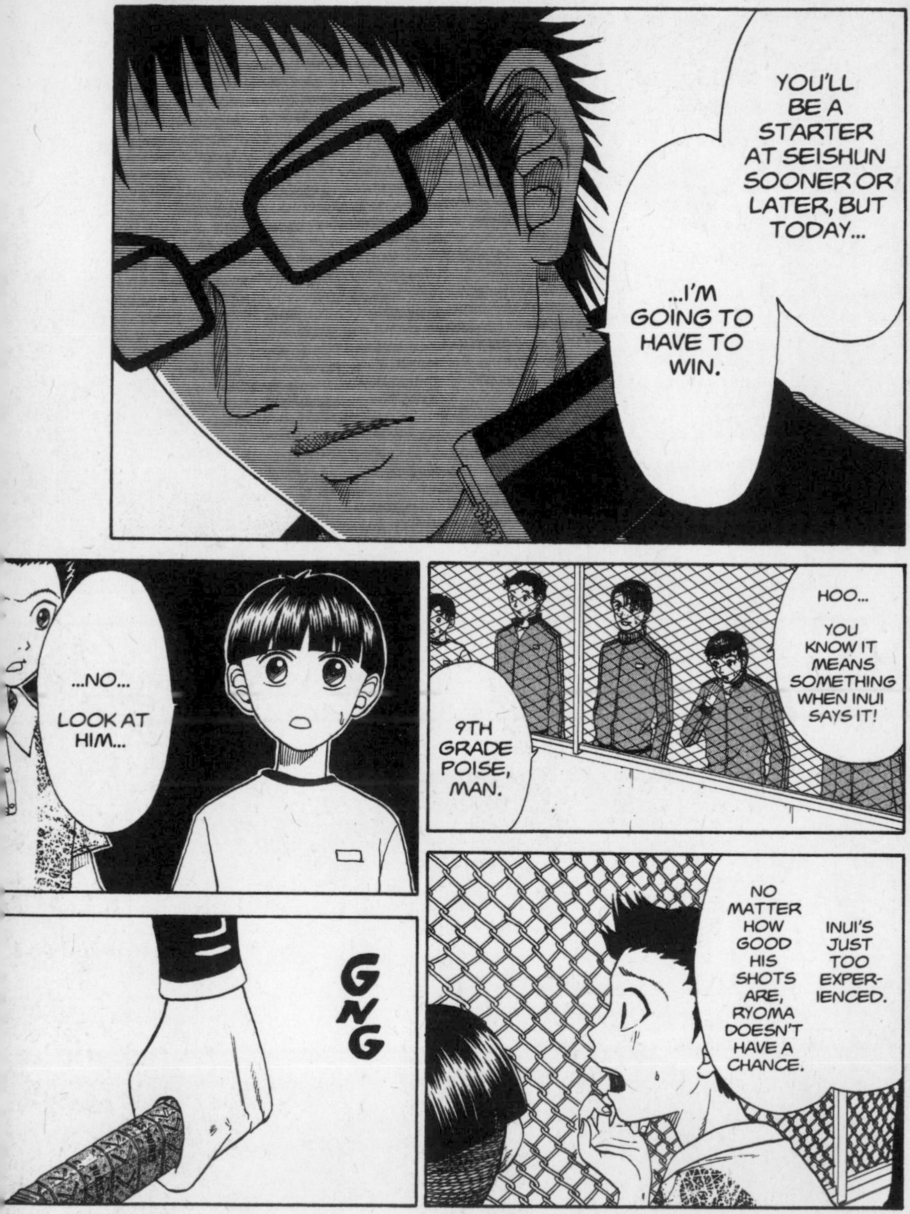
YOU'LL BE A STARTER AT SEISHUN SOONER OR LATER, BUT TODAY...
...I'M GOING TO HAVE TO WIN.
HOO... YOU KNOW IT MEANS SOMETHING WHEN INUI SAYS IT!
9TH GRADE POISE, MAN.
...NO... LOOK AT HIM...
INUI'S JUST TOO EXPER-IENCED.
NO MATTER HOW GOOD HIS SHOTS ARE, RYOMA DOESN'T HAVE A CHANCE.
GNG

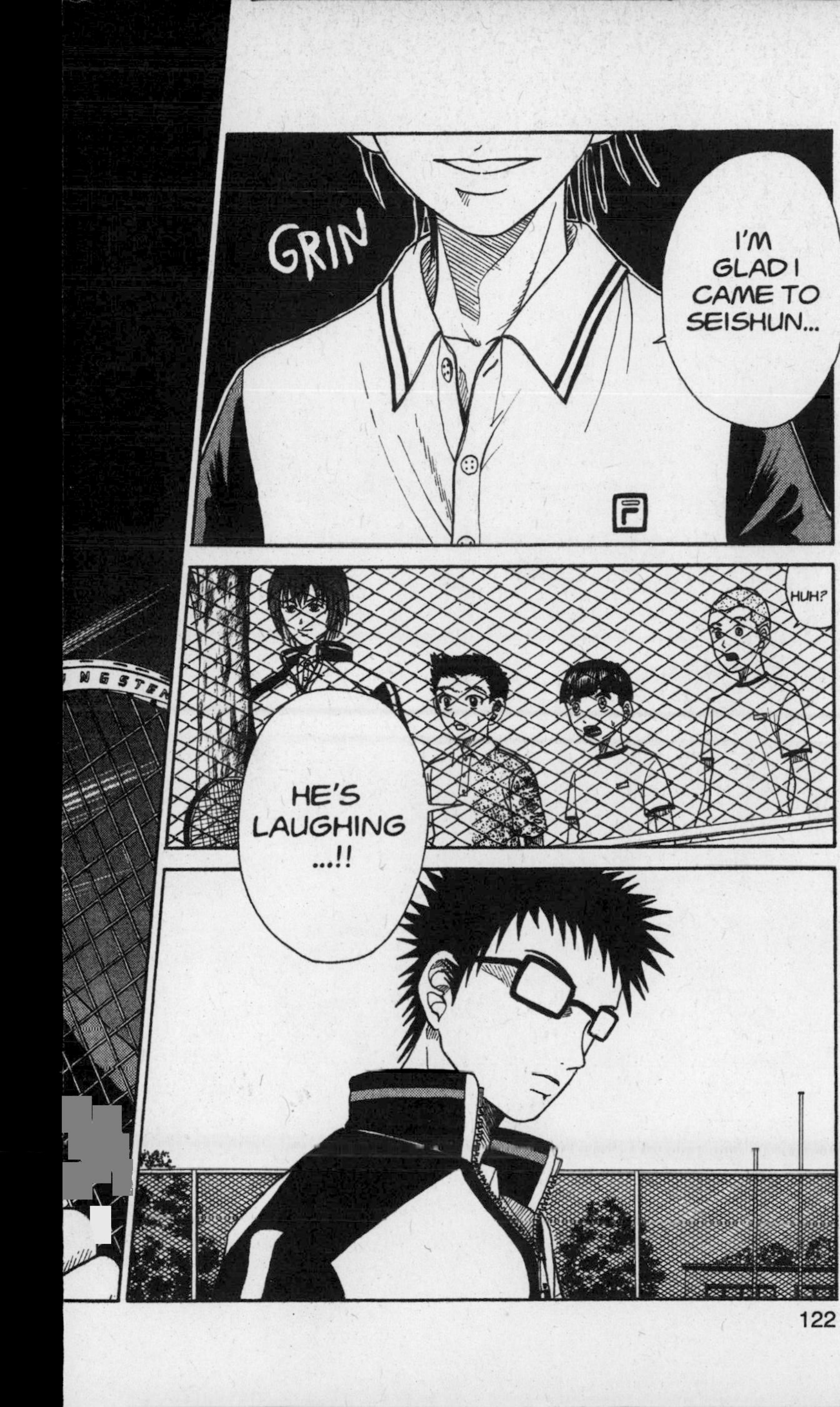
I'M GLAD I CAME TO SEISHUN...
GRIN
HUH?
HE'S LAUGHING ...!!

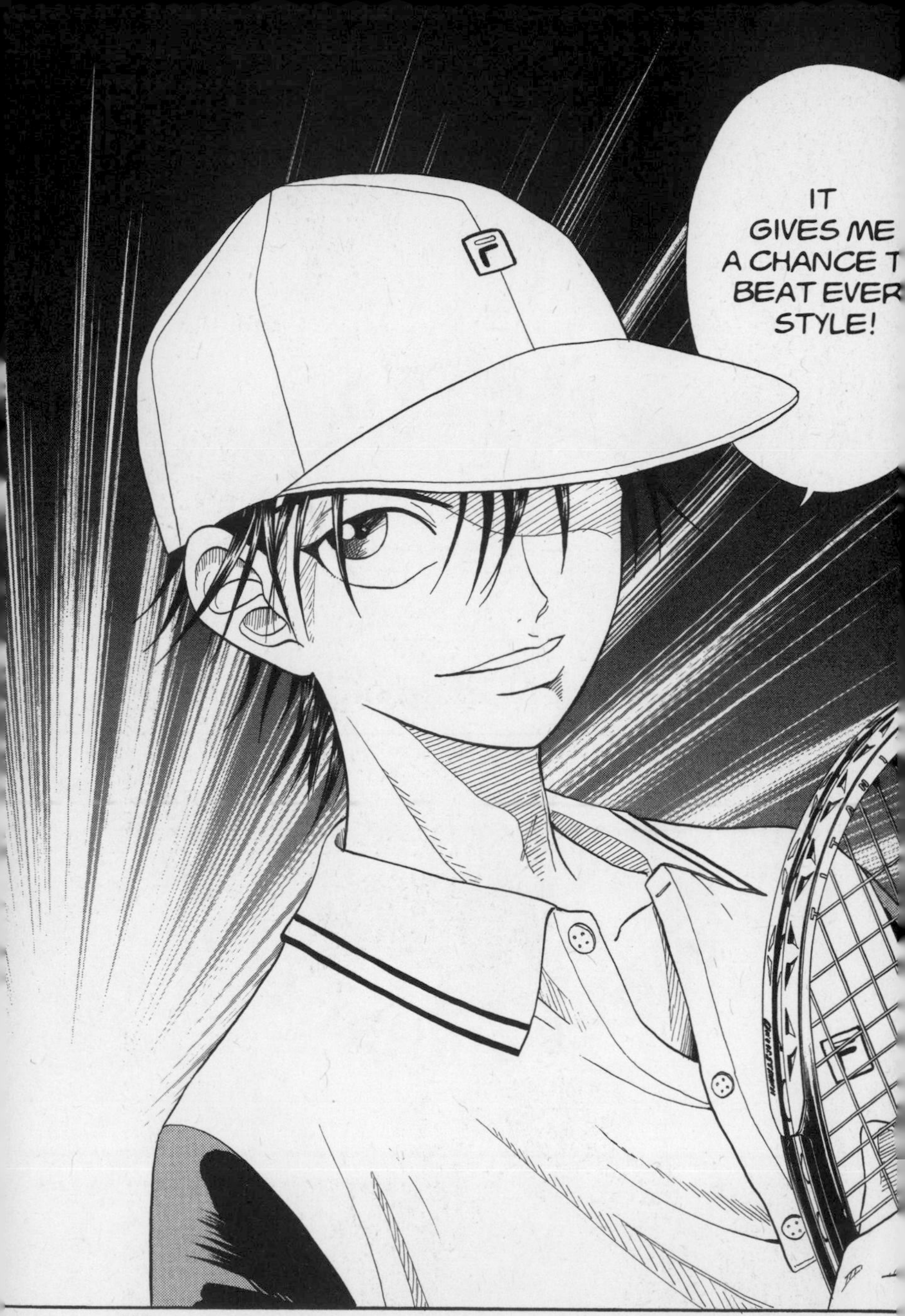
IT GIVES ME A CHANCE T BEAT EVER STYLE!

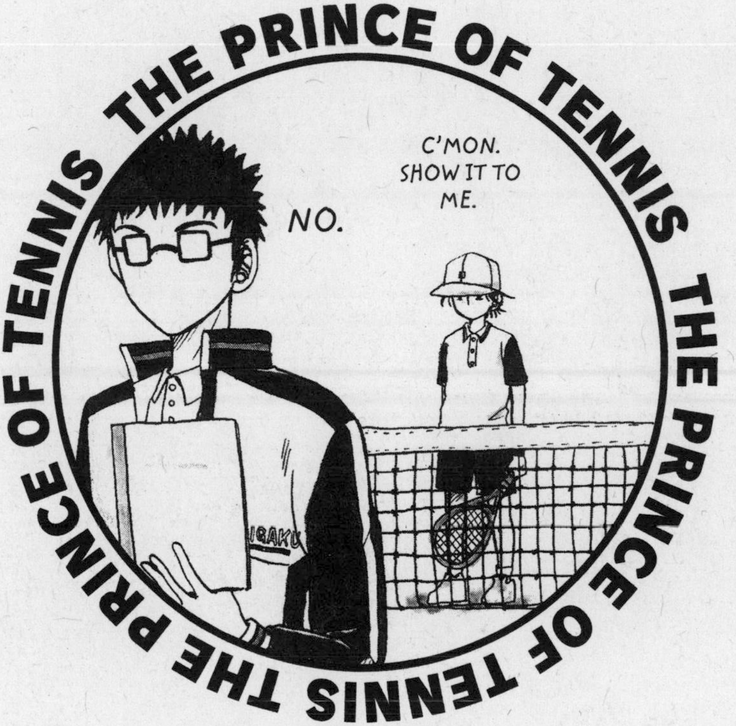
THE PRINCE OF TENNIS THE PRINCE OF TENNIS THE PRINCE OF TENNIS
C'MON. SHOW IT TO ME.
NO.

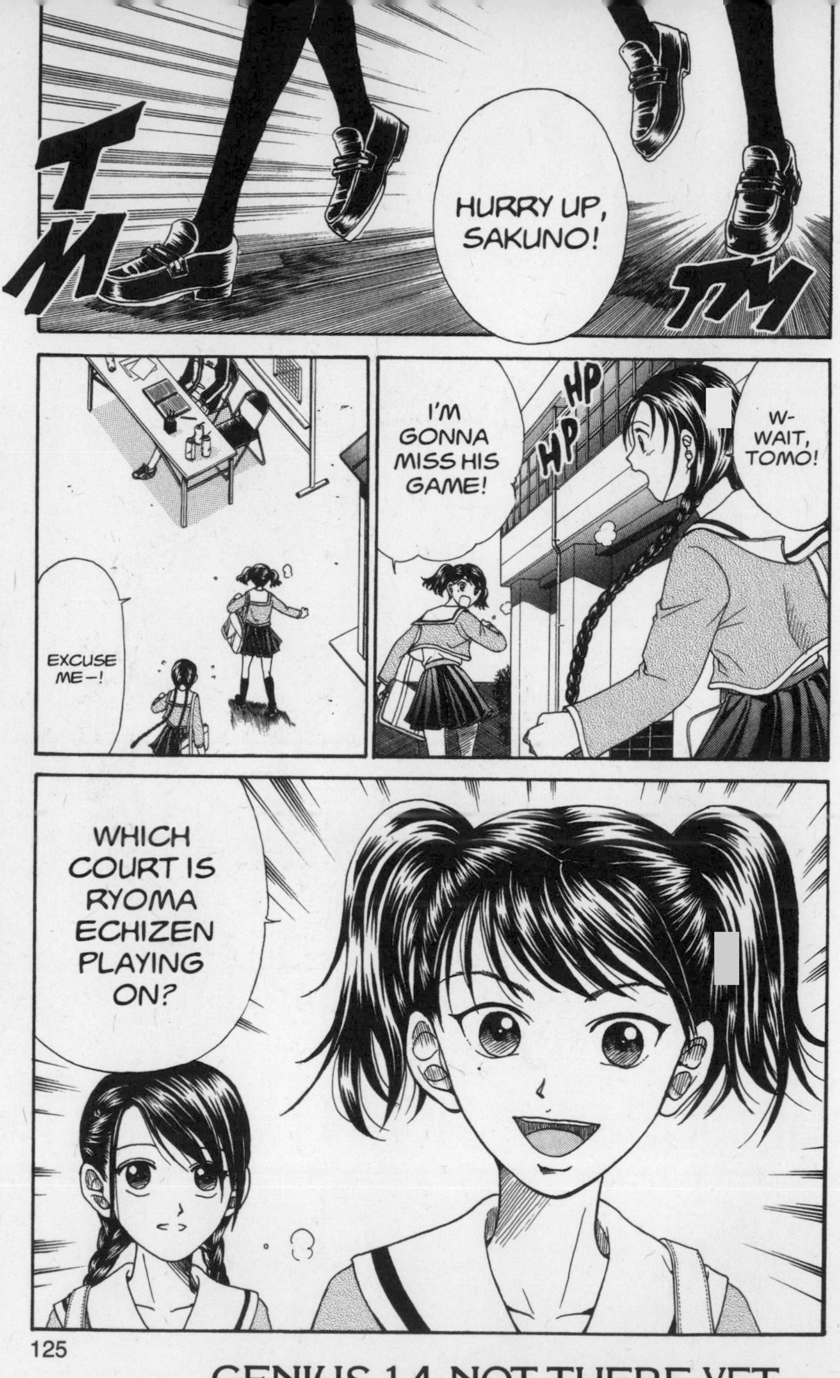
TM
HURRY UP, SAKUNO!
TM
W-WAIT, TOMO!
HP HP
I'M GONNA MISS HIS GAME!
EXCUSE ME—!
WHICH COURT IS RYOMA ECHIZEN PLAYING ON?

GENIUS 14 NOT THERE YET

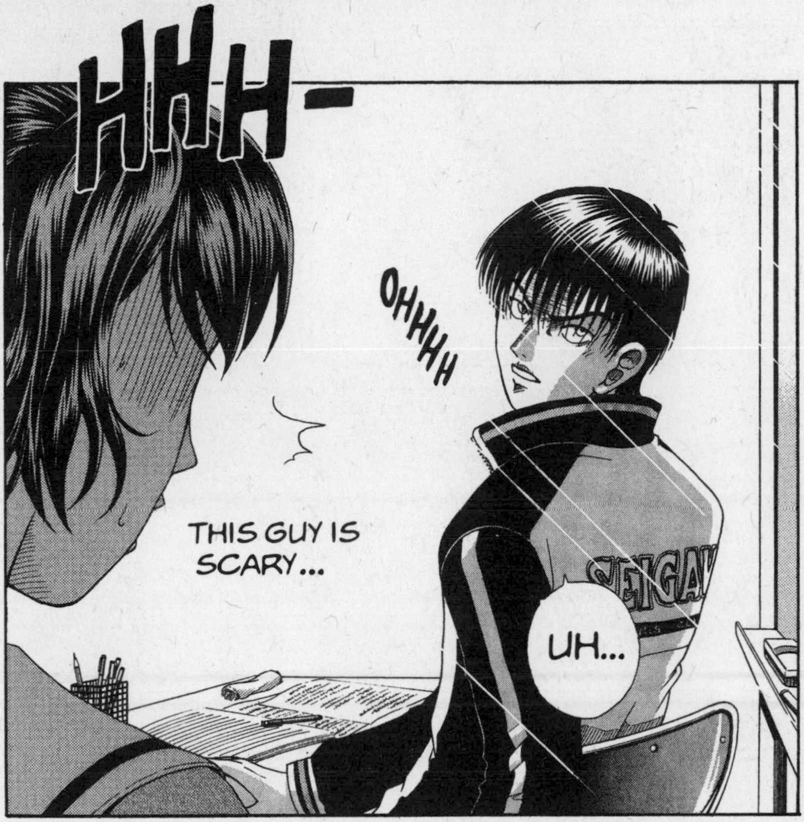
OHHHH
HHH-
UH...
THIS GUY IS SCARY...

GENIUS 14 NOT THERE YET

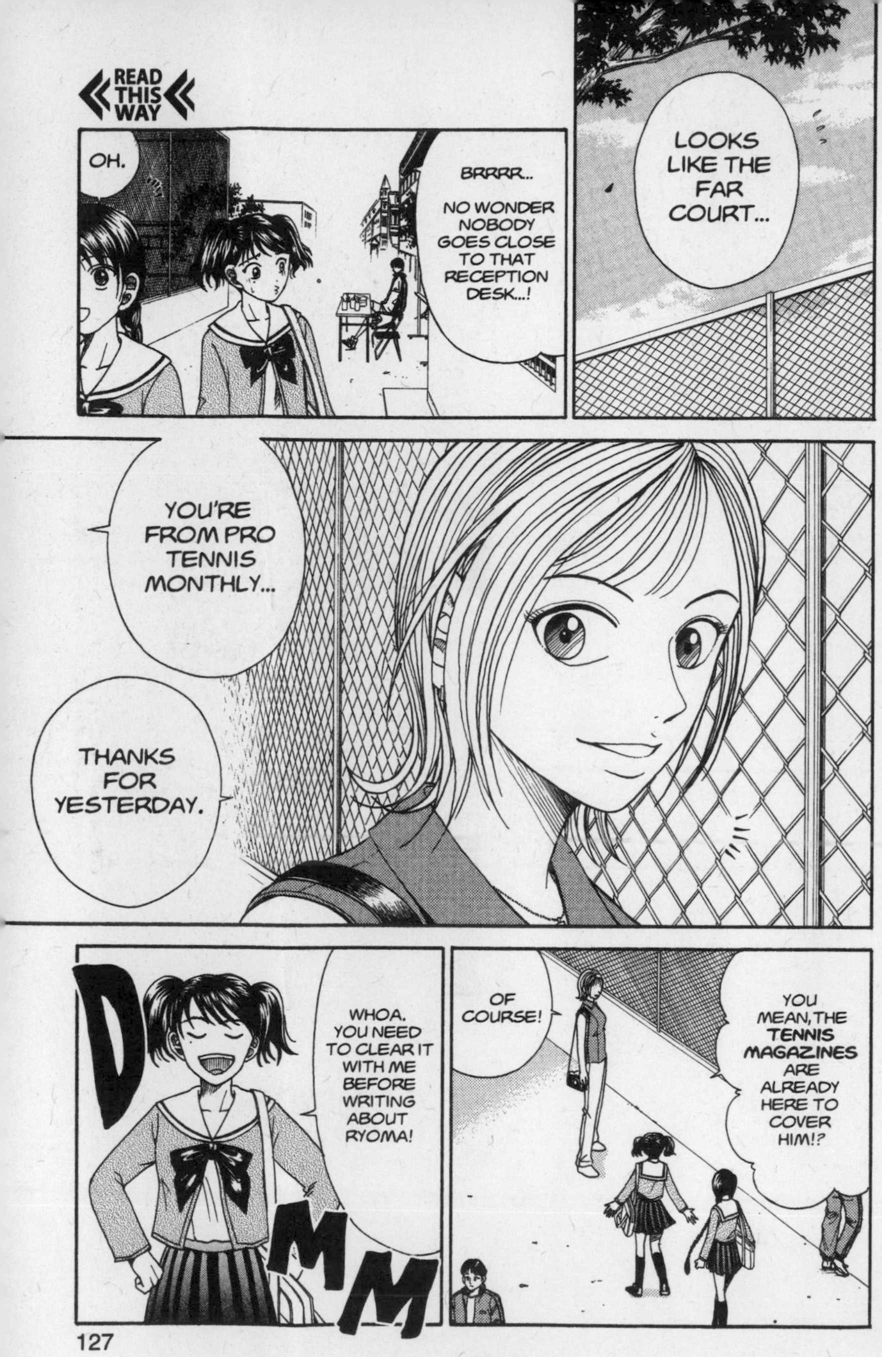
READ THIS WAY
LOOKS LIKE THE FAR COURT...
BRRRR.. NO WONDER NOBODY GOES CLOSE TO THAT RECEPTION DESK...!
OH.
YOU'RE FROM PRO TENNIS MONTHLY...
THANKS FOR YESTERDAY.
YOU MEAN, THE **TENNIS MAGAZINES** ARE ALREADY HERE TO COVER HIM!?
OF COURSE!
WHOA. YOU NEED TO CLEAR IT WITH ME BEFORE WRITING ABOUT RYOMA!
DMM

READ THIS WAY

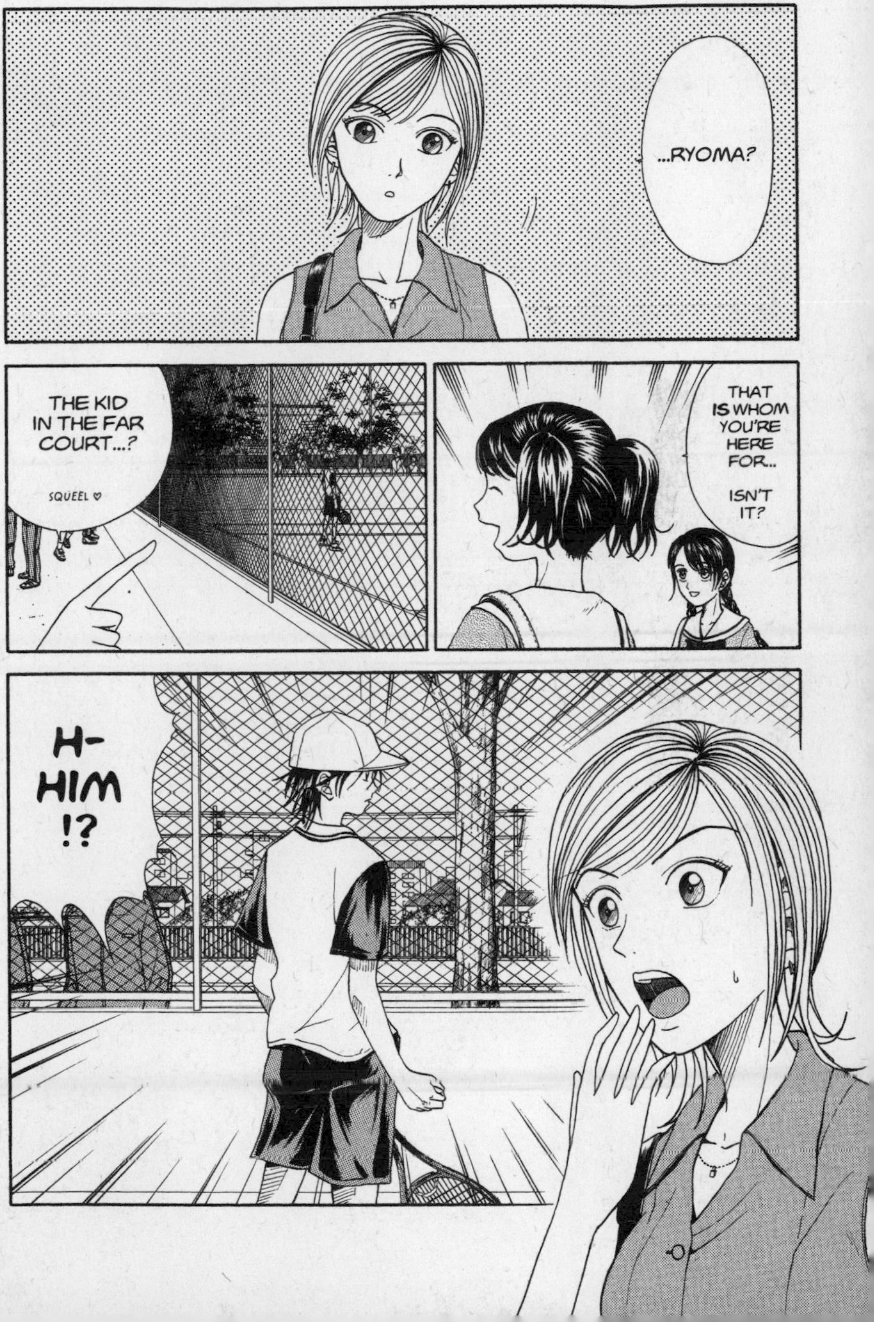
...RYOMA?
THAT IS WHOM YOU'RE HERE FOR... ISN'T IT?
THE KID IN THE FAR COURT...?
SQUEEL ♡
H-HIM !?

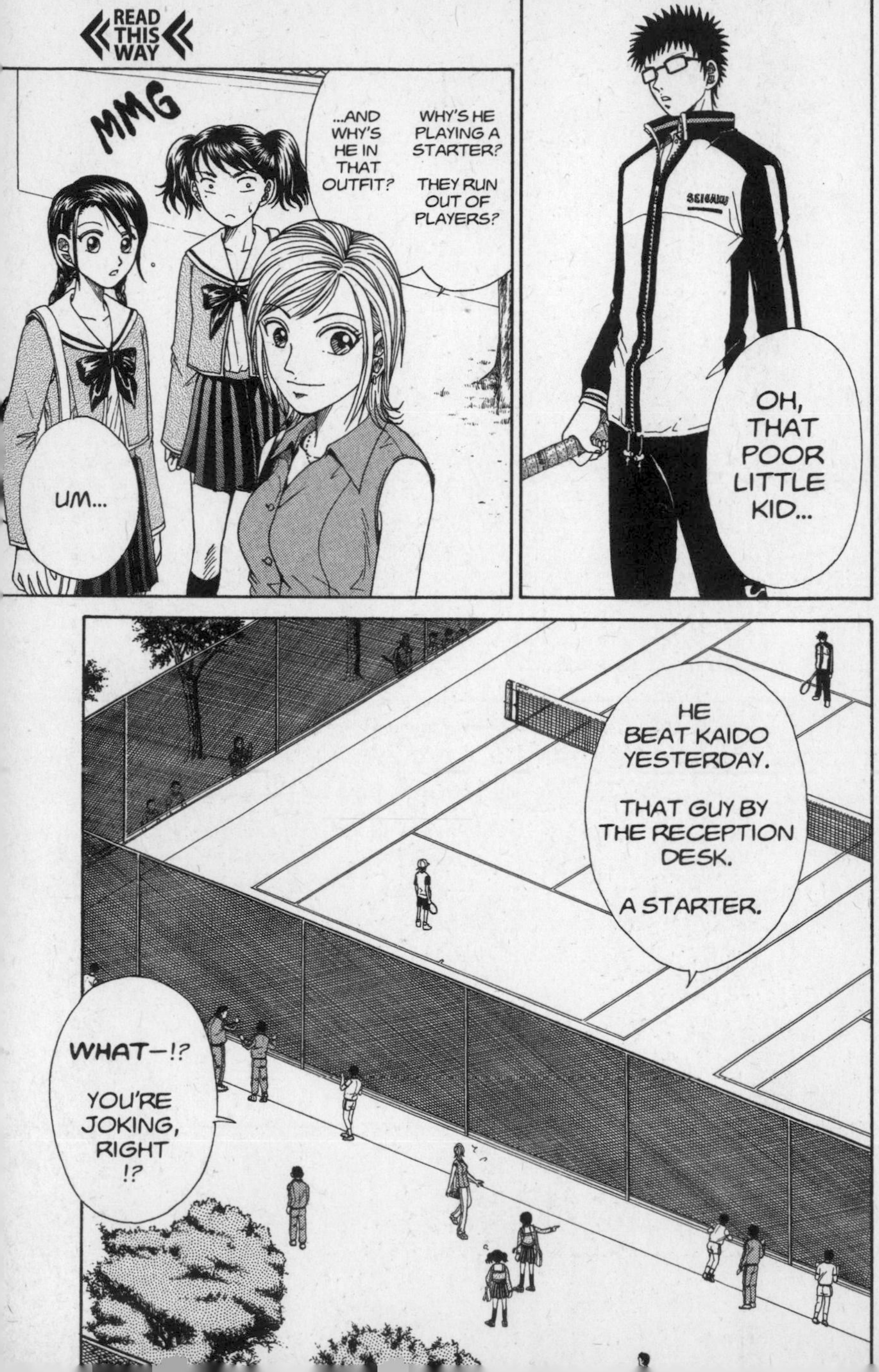
READ THIS WAY
OH, THAT POOR LITTLE KID...
WHY'S HE PLAYING A STARTER? THEY RUN OUT OF PLAYERS?
...AND WHY'S HE IN THAT OUTFIT?
MMG
UM...
HE BEAT KAIDO YESTERDAY. THAT GUY BY THE RECEPTION DESK. A STARTER.
WHAT—!? YOU'RE JOKING, RIGHT!?

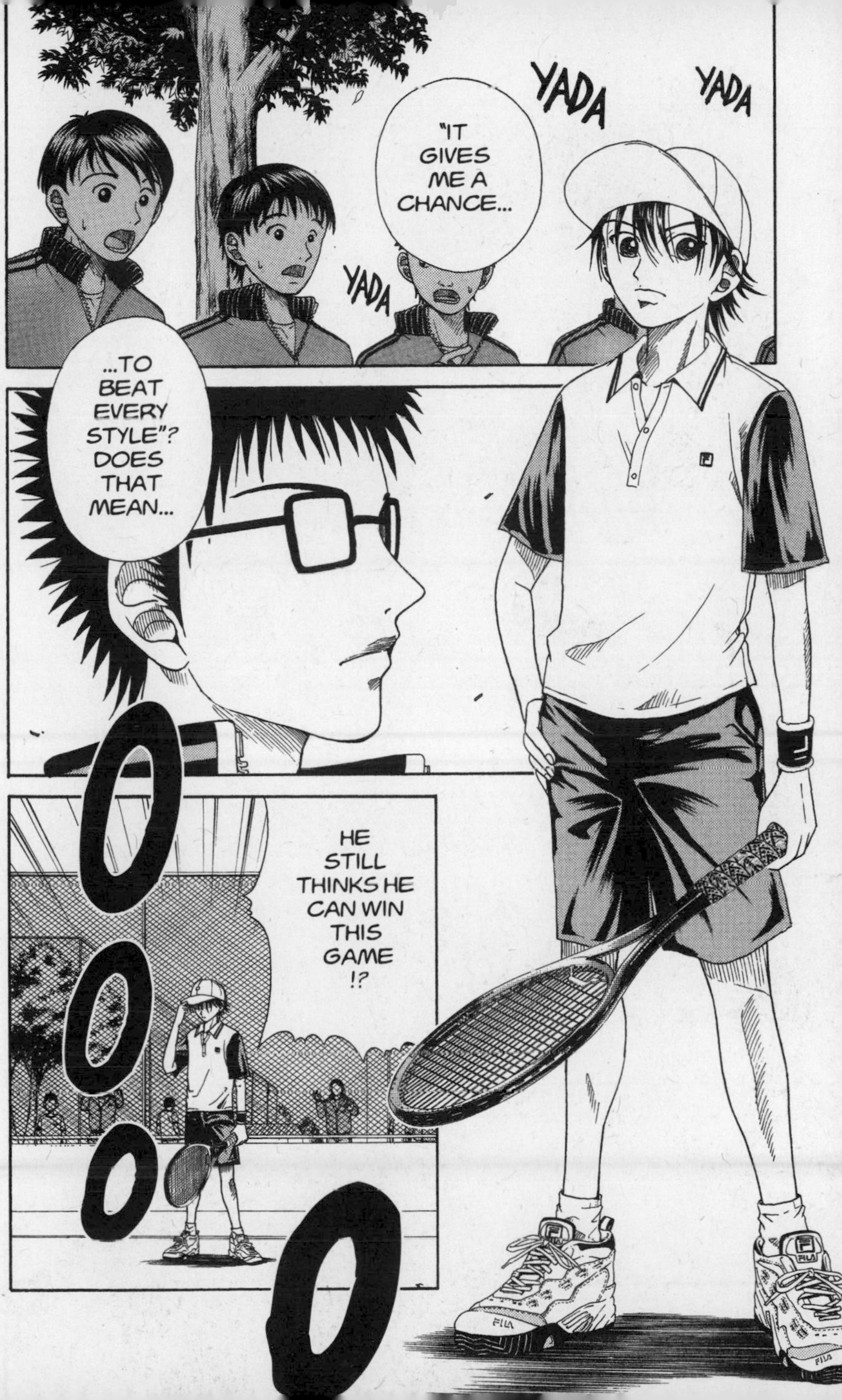
YADA
YADA
"IT GIVES ME A CHANCE...
YADA
...TO BEAT EVERY STYLE"? DOES THAT MEAN...
HE STILL THINKS HE CAN WIN THIS GAME !?

READ THIS WAY

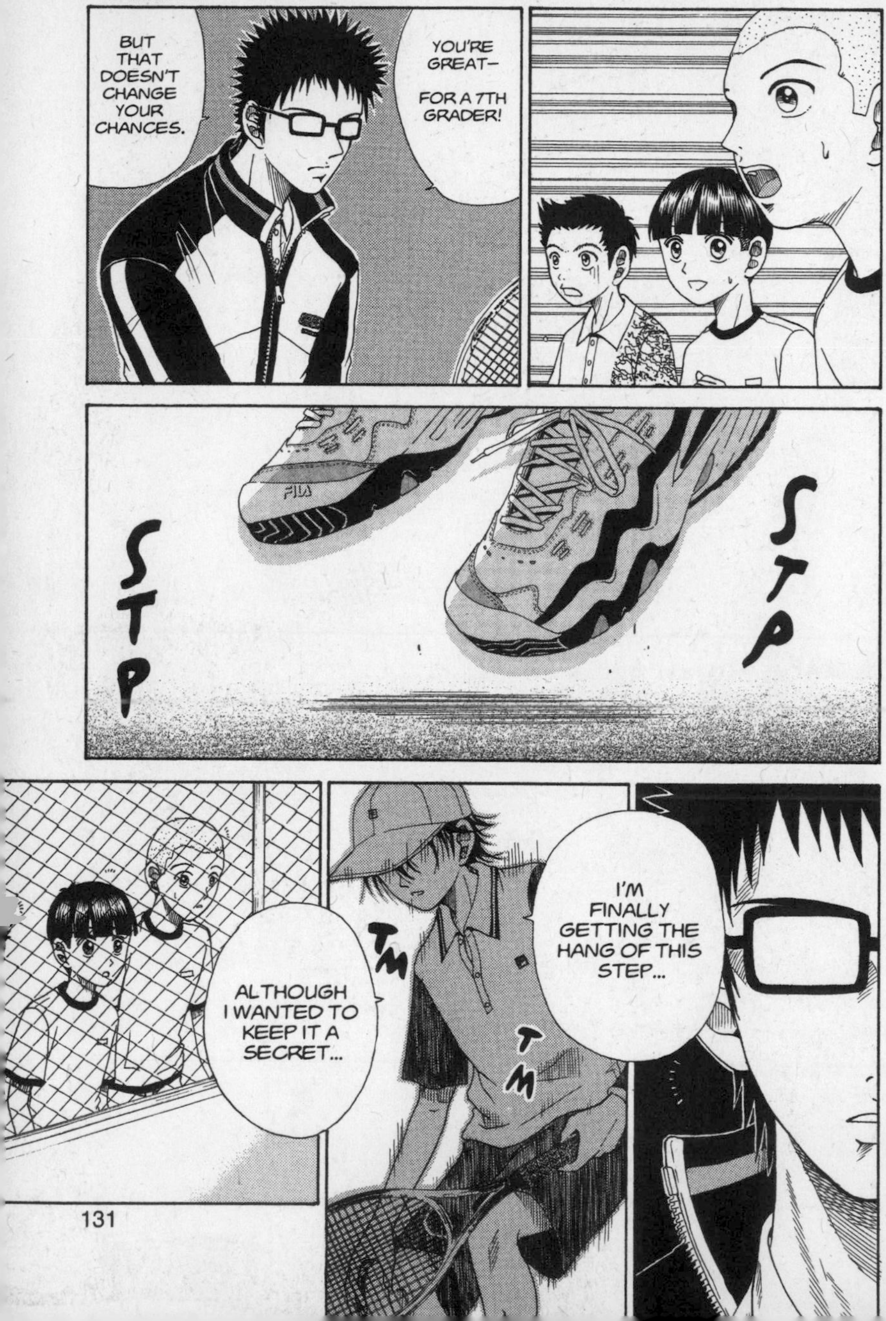

YOU'RE GREAT— FOR A 7TH GRADER!
BUT THAT DOESN'T CHANGE YOUR CHANCES.
STP
STP
TM
TM
I'M FINALLY GETTING THE HANG OF THIS STEP...
ALTHOUGH I WANTED TO KEEP IT A SECRET...

READ THIS WAY

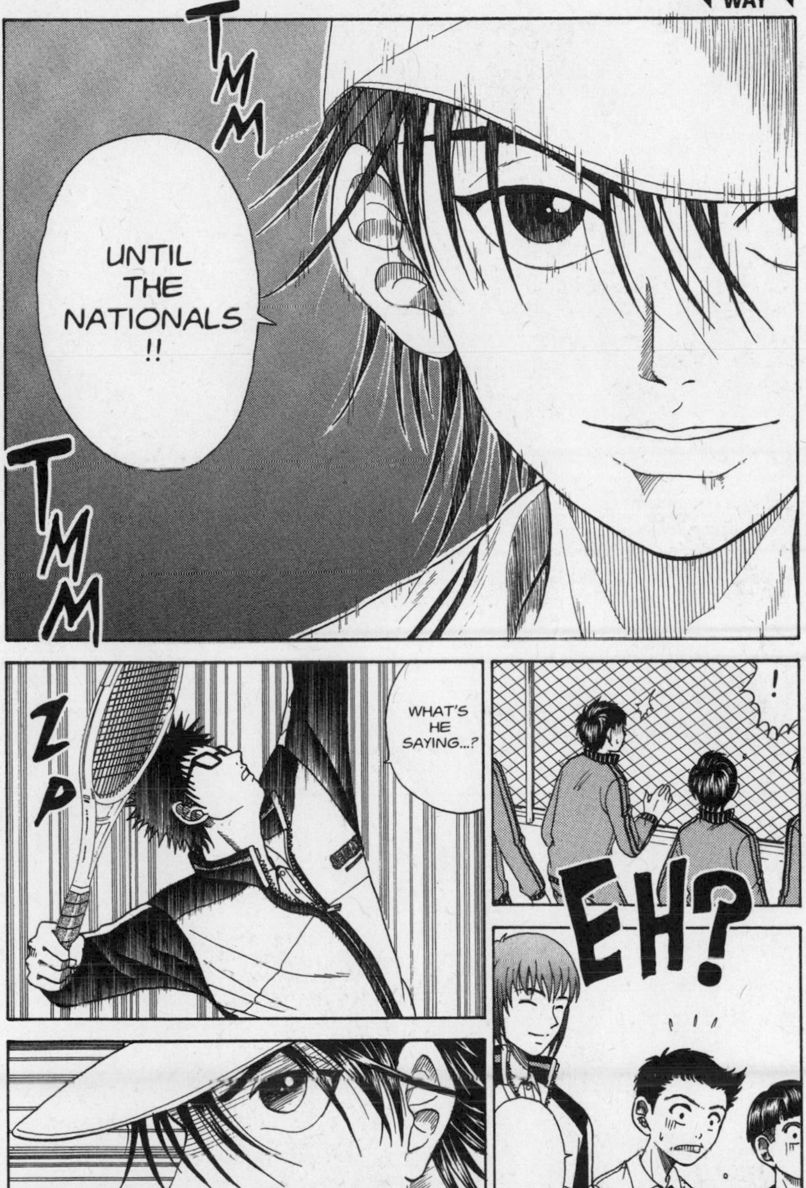
TMM
UNTIL THE NATIONALS !!
TMM
!
WHAT'S HE SAYING...?
ZP
EH?

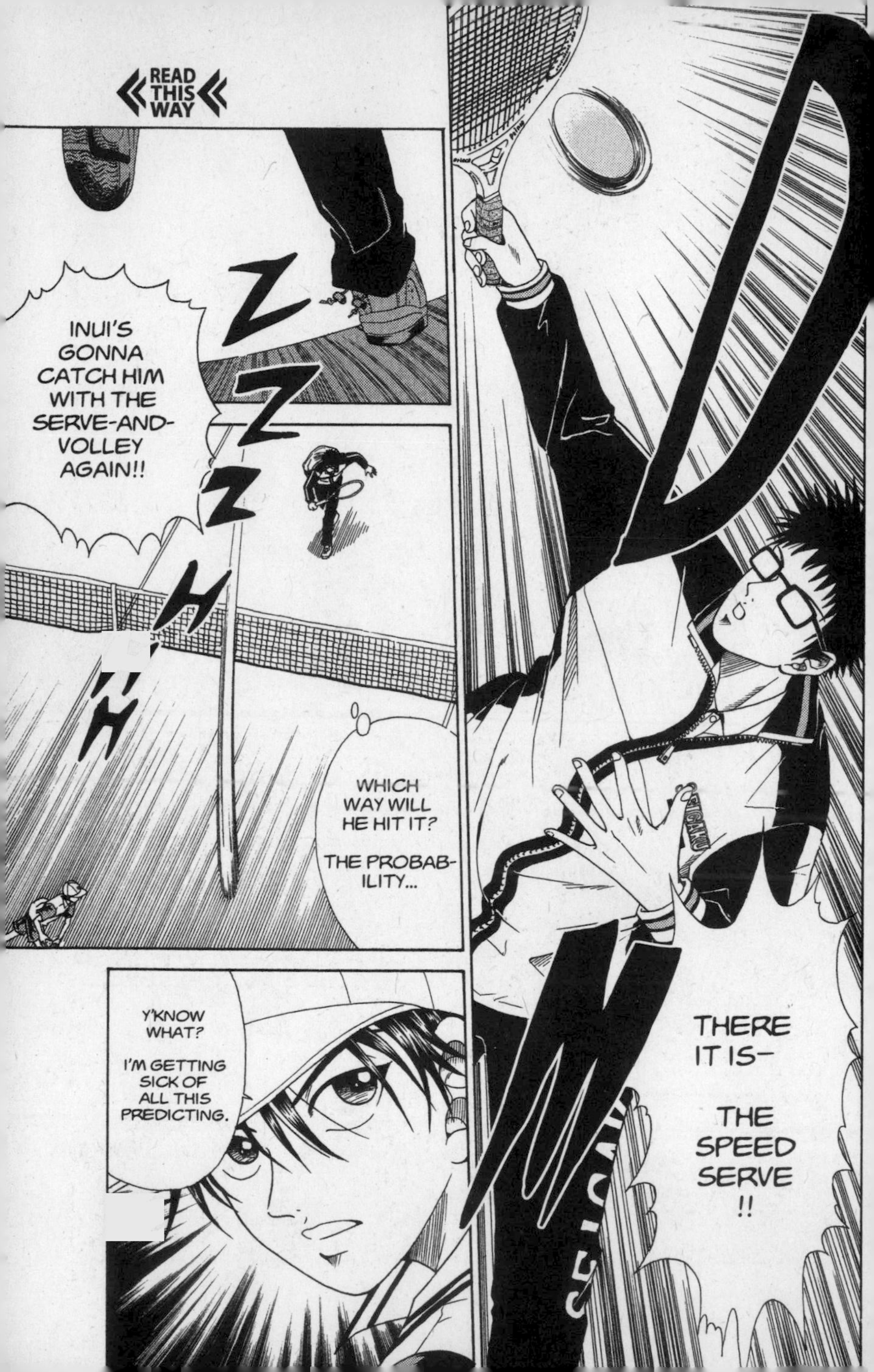
READ THIS WAY
THERE IT IS—
THE SPEED SERVE!!
ZZZHHH
INUI'S GONNA CATCH HIM WITH THE SERVE-AND-VOLLEY AGAIN!!
WHICH WAY WILL HE HIT IT?
THE PROBAB-ILITY...
Y'KNOW WHAT?
I'M GETTING SICK OF ALL THIS PREDICTING.

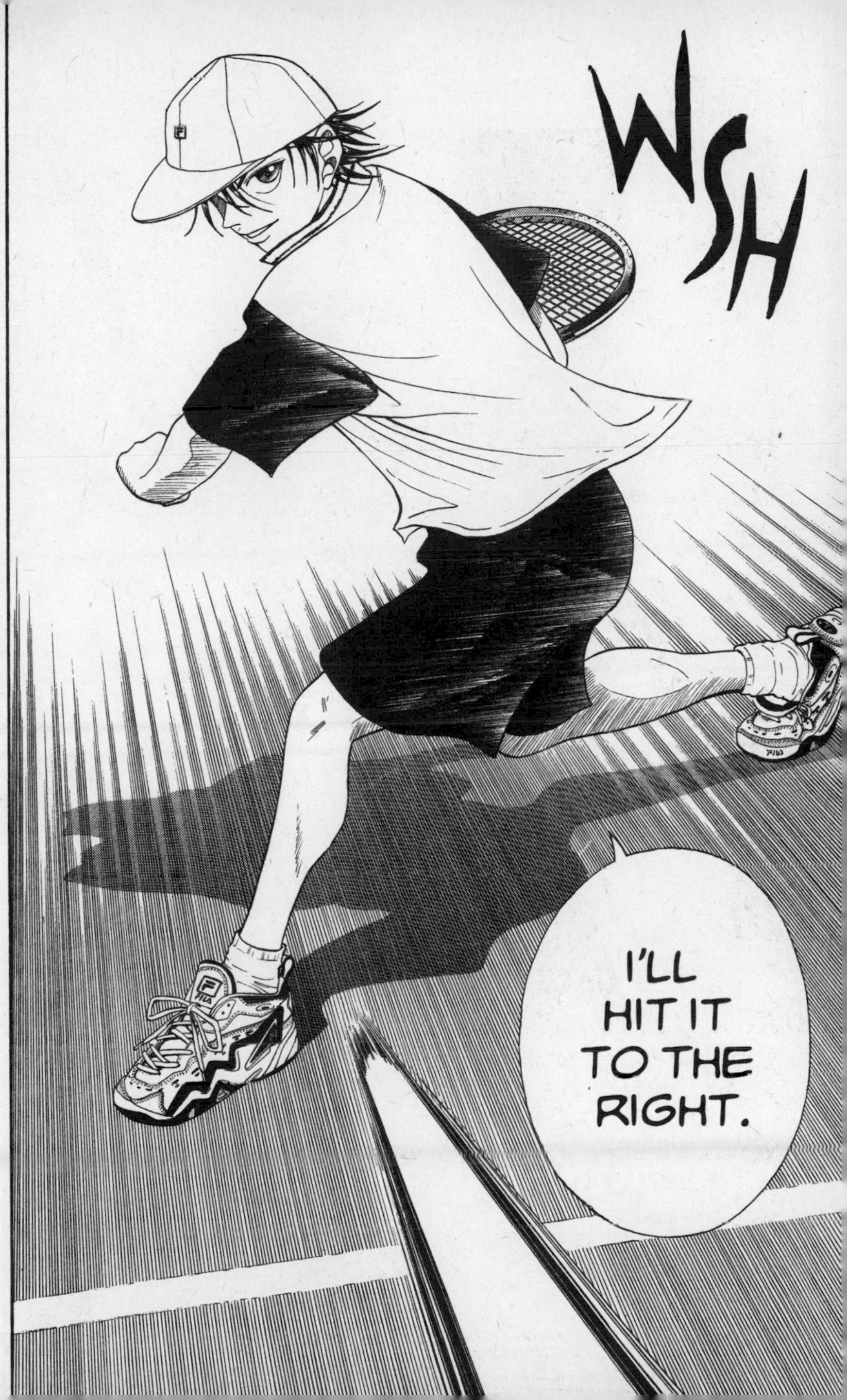
WSH
I'LL HIT IT TO THE RIGHT.

READ THIS WAY

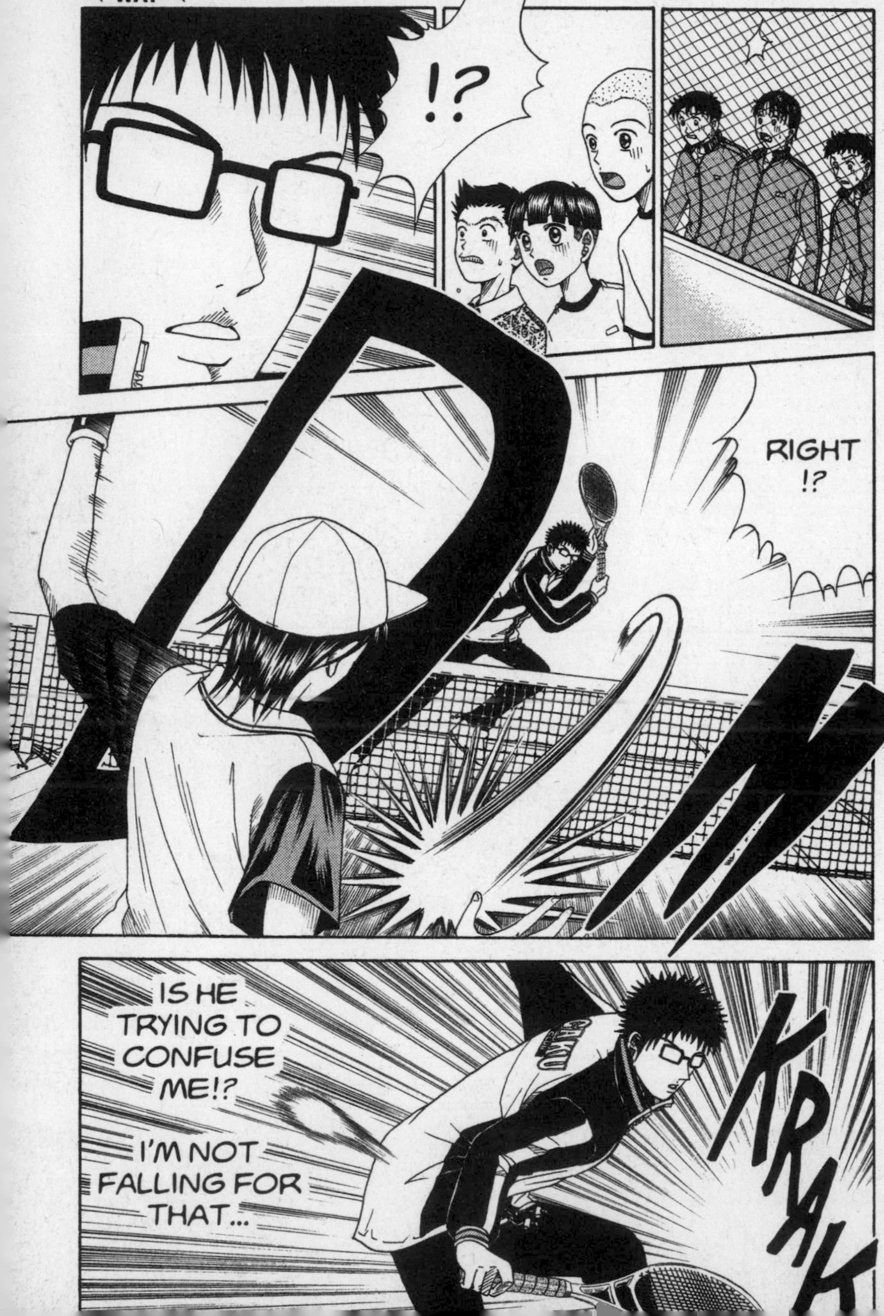
!?
RIGHT !?
IS HE TRYING TO CONFUSE ME!?
I'M NOT FALLING FOR THAT...
KRAK

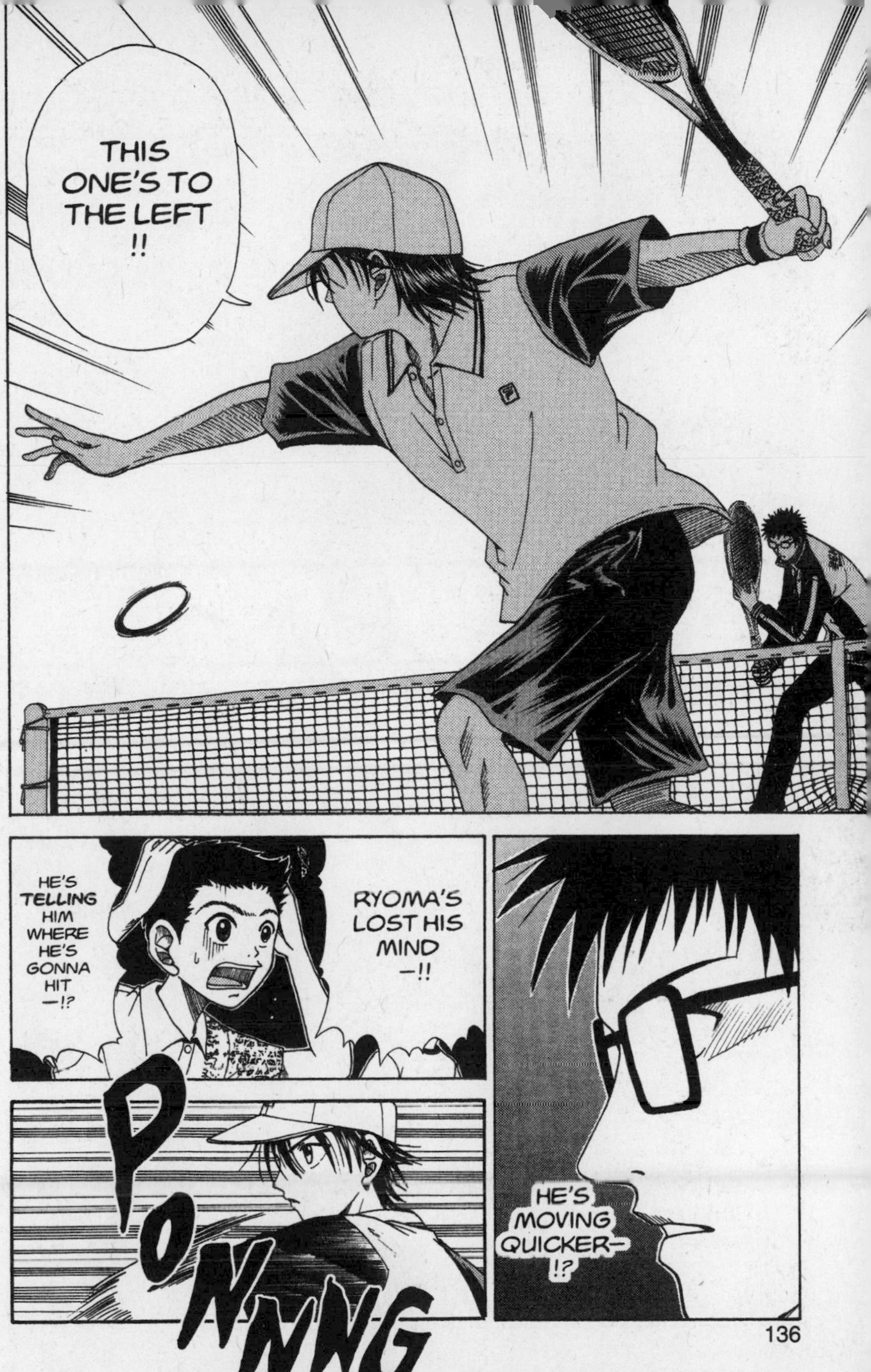
THIS ONE'S TO THE LEFT !!
HE'S MOVING QUICKER— !?
RYOMA'S LOST HIS MIND —!!
HE'S TELLING HIM WHERE HE'S GONNA HIT —!?
PONNNG

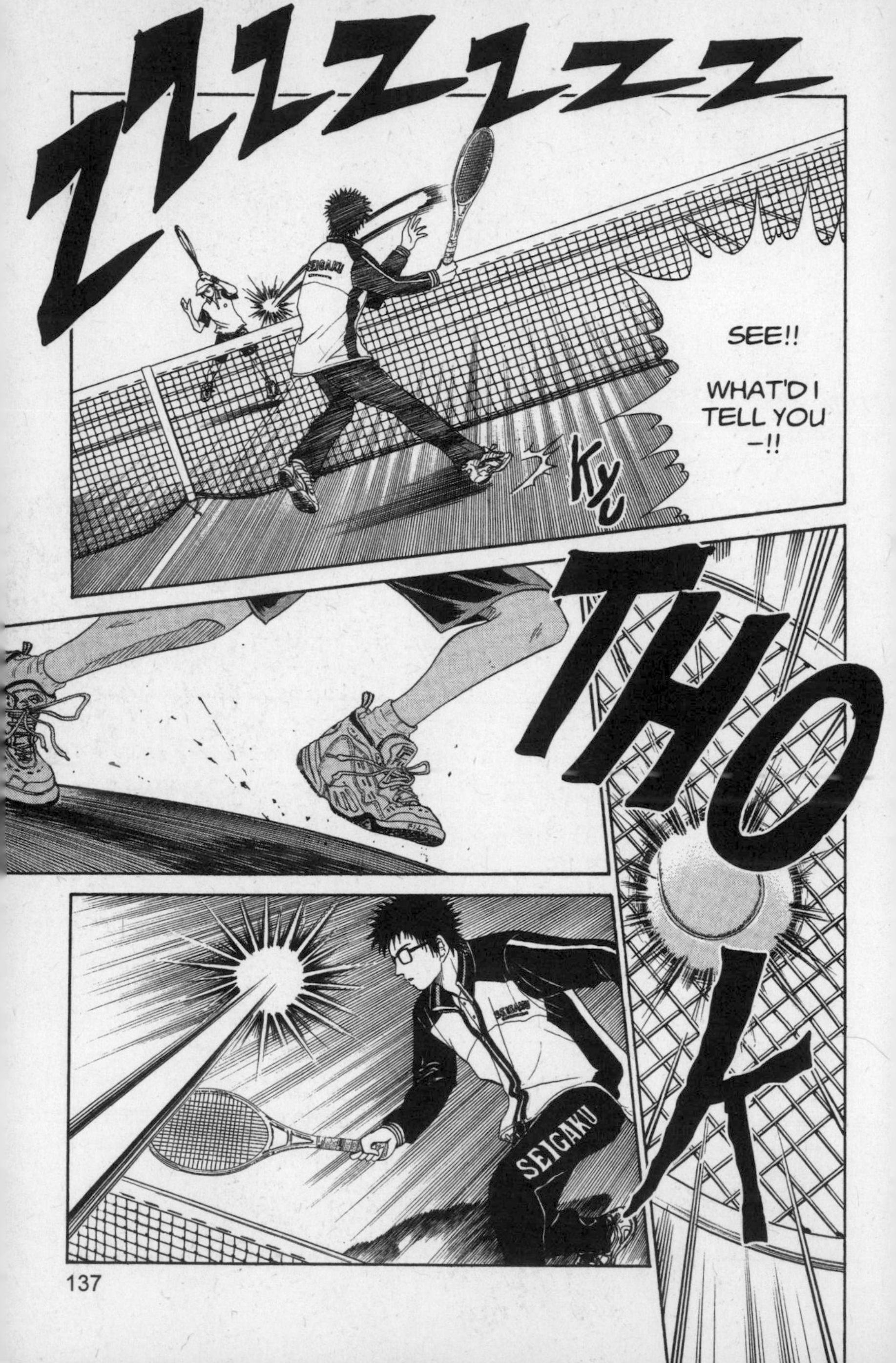
SEE!!
WHAT'D I TELL YOU —!!
KYU
ZZZZZZZZ
THOK
SEIGAKU

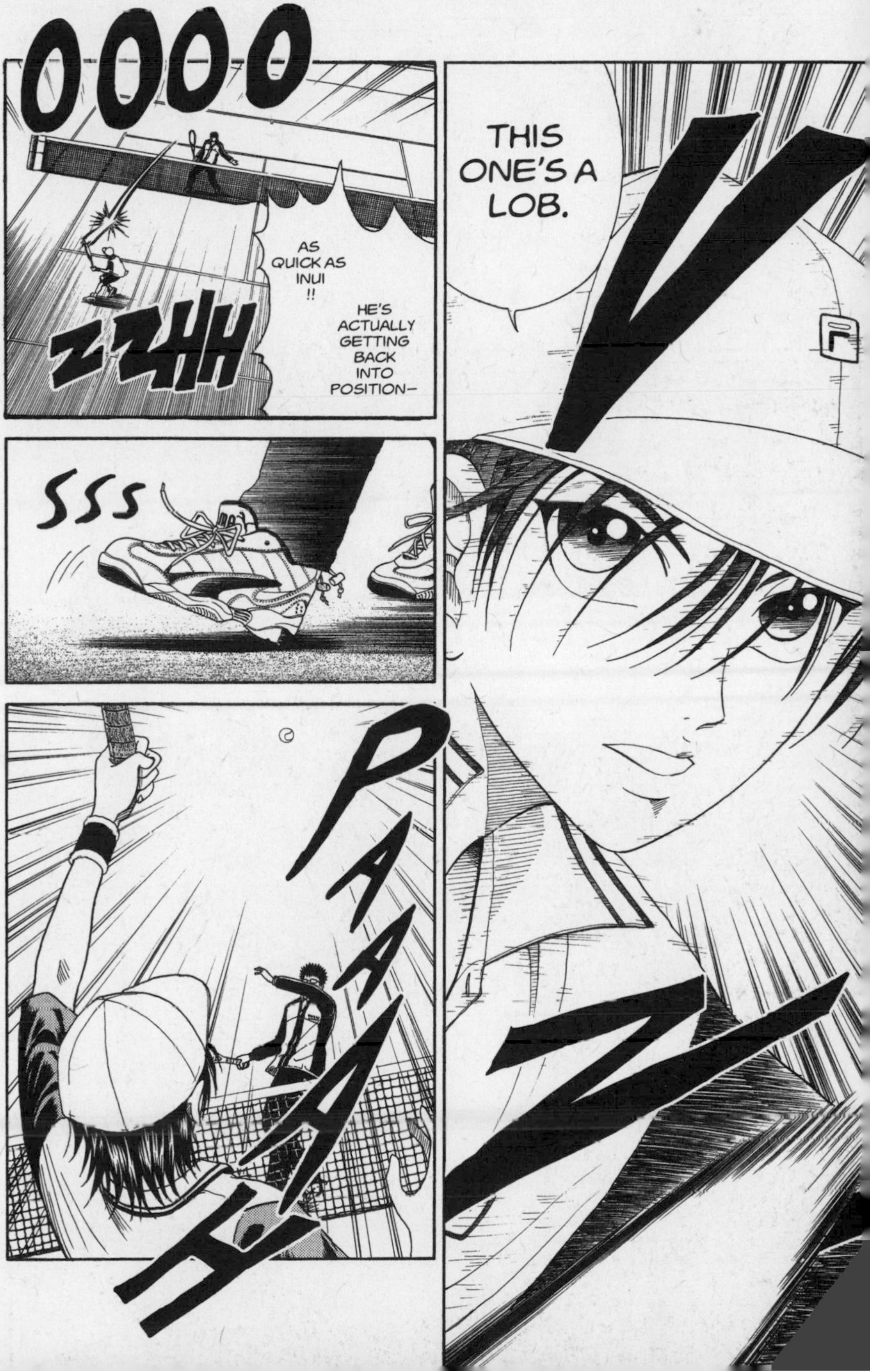
THIS ONE'S A LOB.
OOOO
AS QUICK AS INUI !!
HE'S ACTUALLY GETTING BACK INTO POSITION—
ZZHH
SSS
PAAAAH

READ THIS WAY

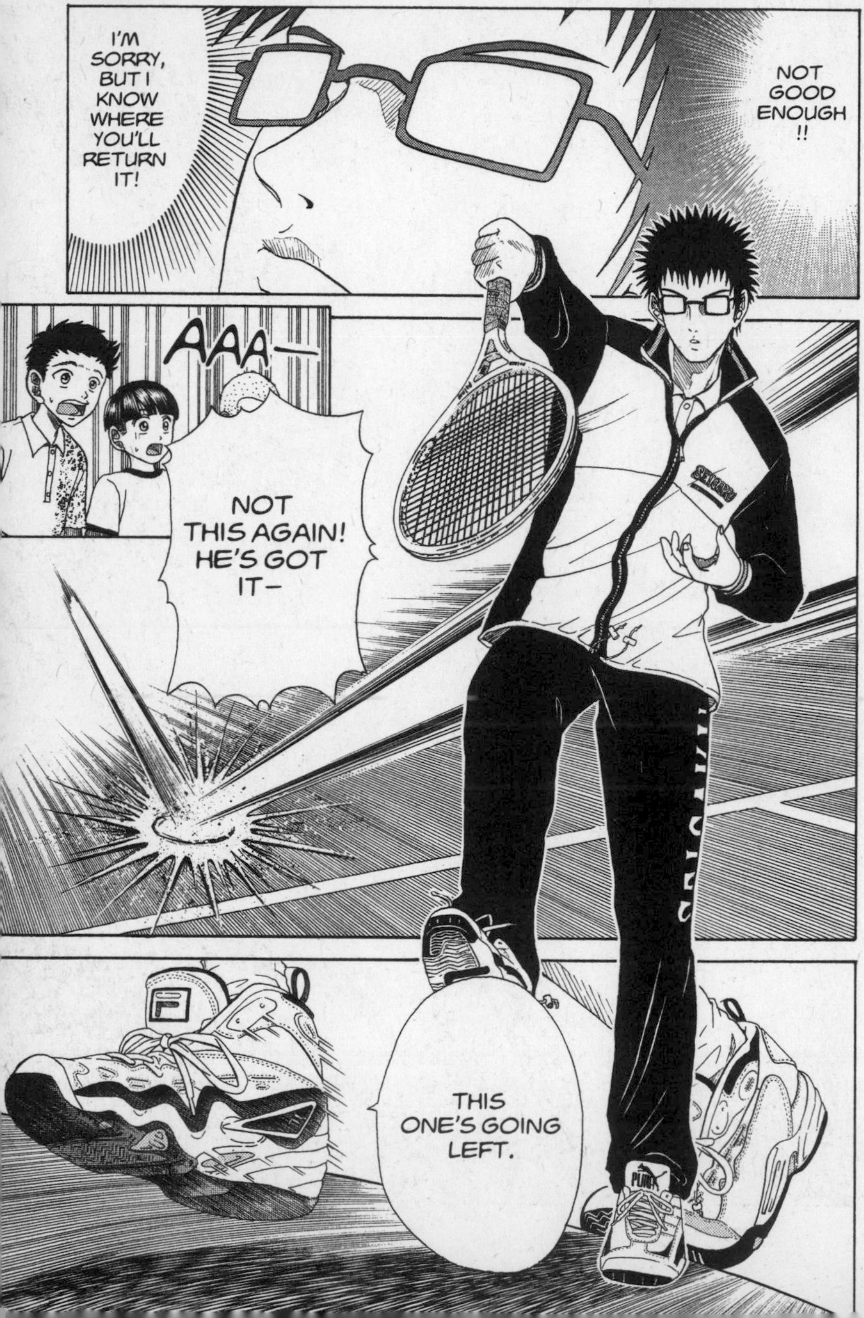
NOT GOOD ENOUGH !!
I'M SORRY, BUT I KNOW WHERE YOU'LL RETURN IT!
AAA—
NOT THIS AGAIN! HE'S GOT IT—
THIS ONE'S GOING LEFT.

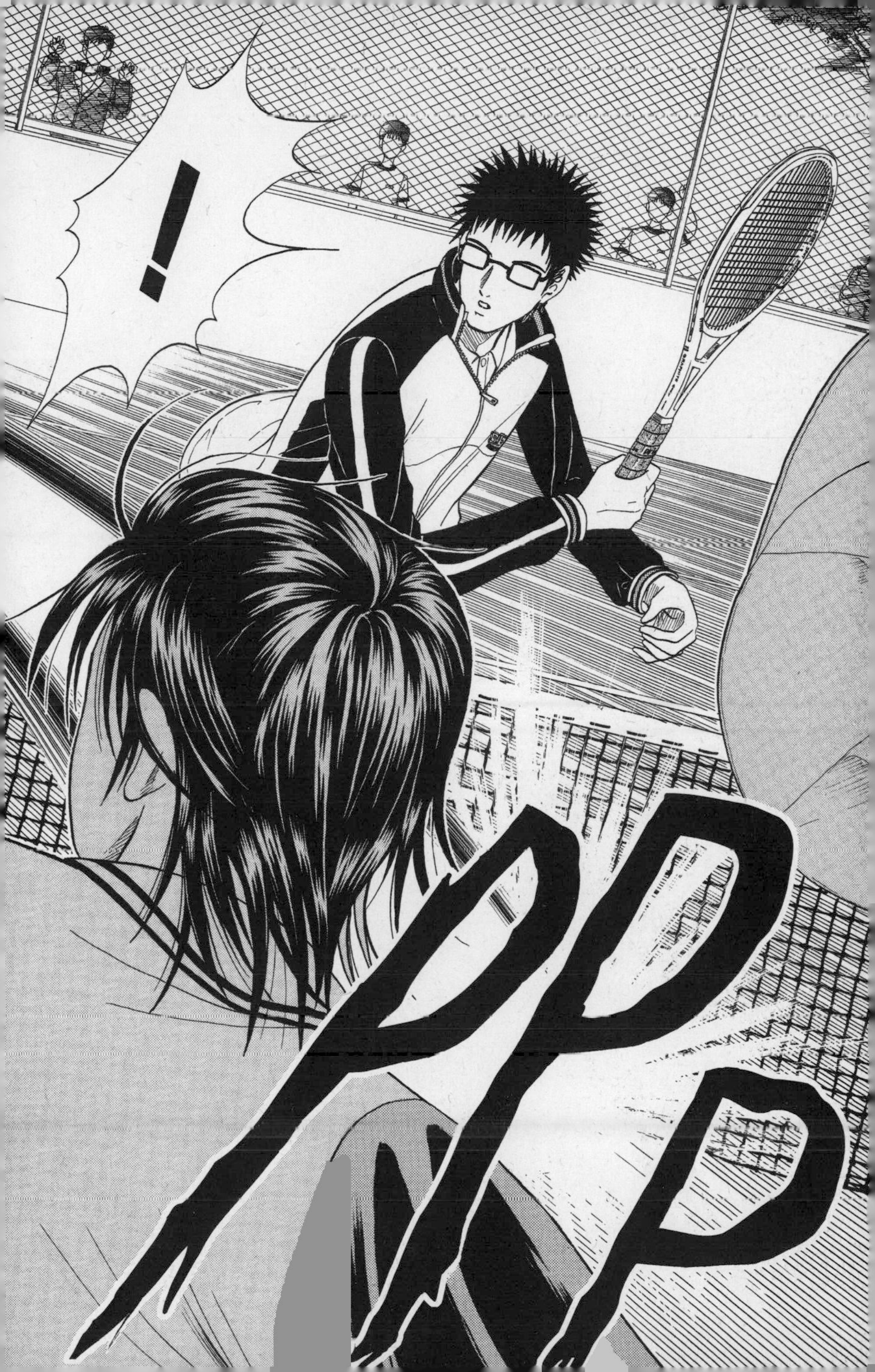
!

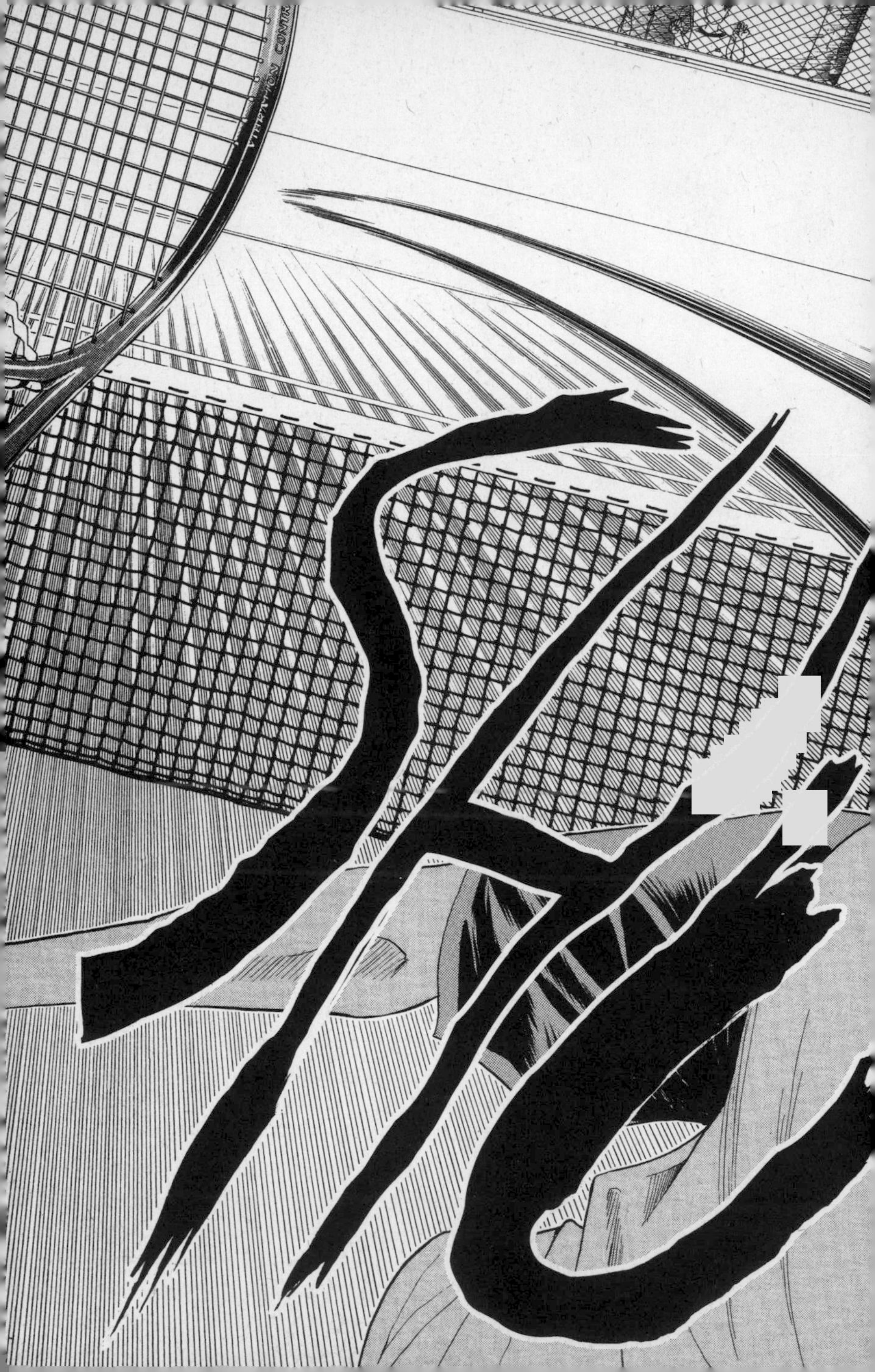

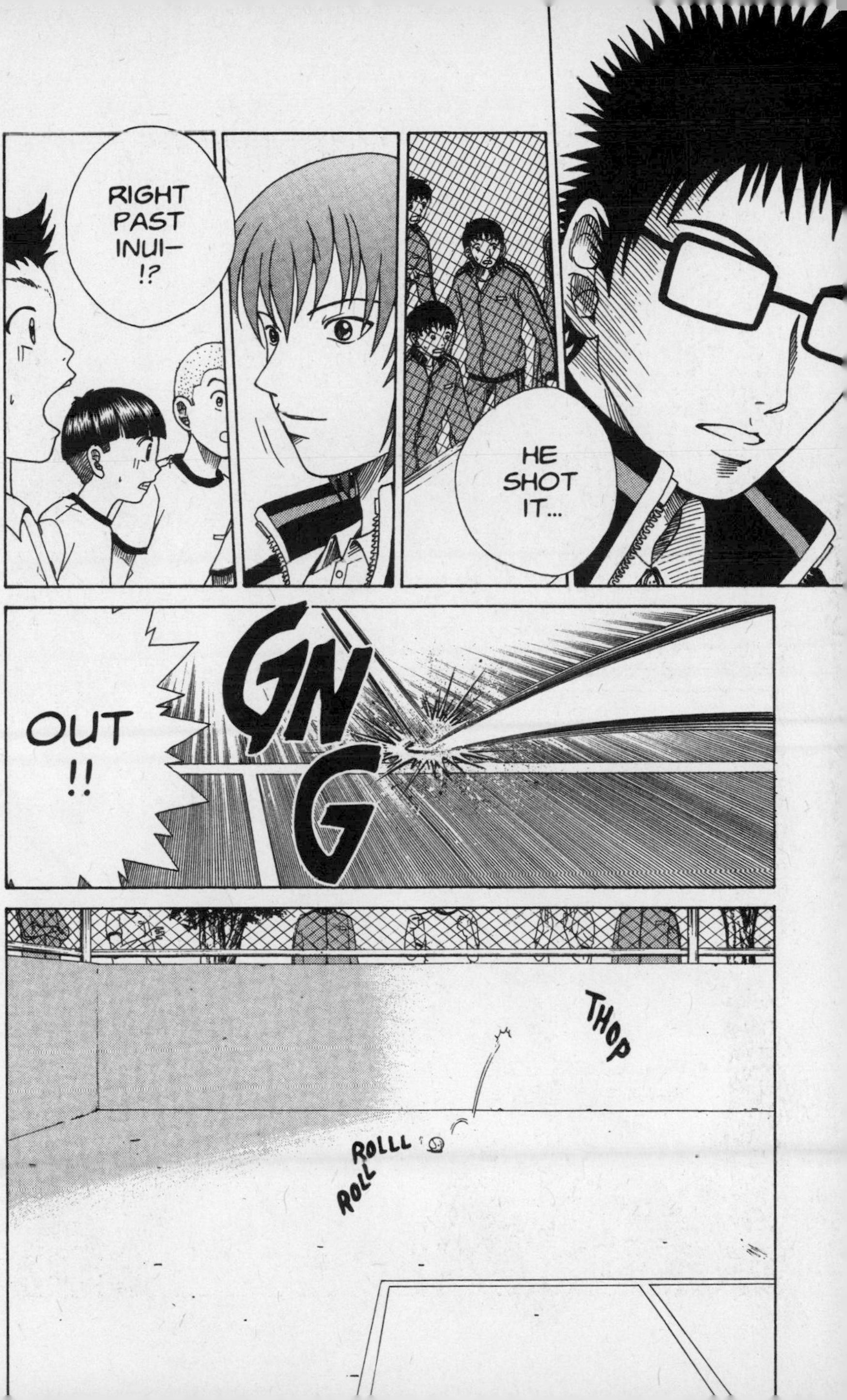
HE SHOT IT...
RIGHT PAST INUI—!?
GNG
OUT !!
THOP
ROLLL
ROLL

READ THIS WAY

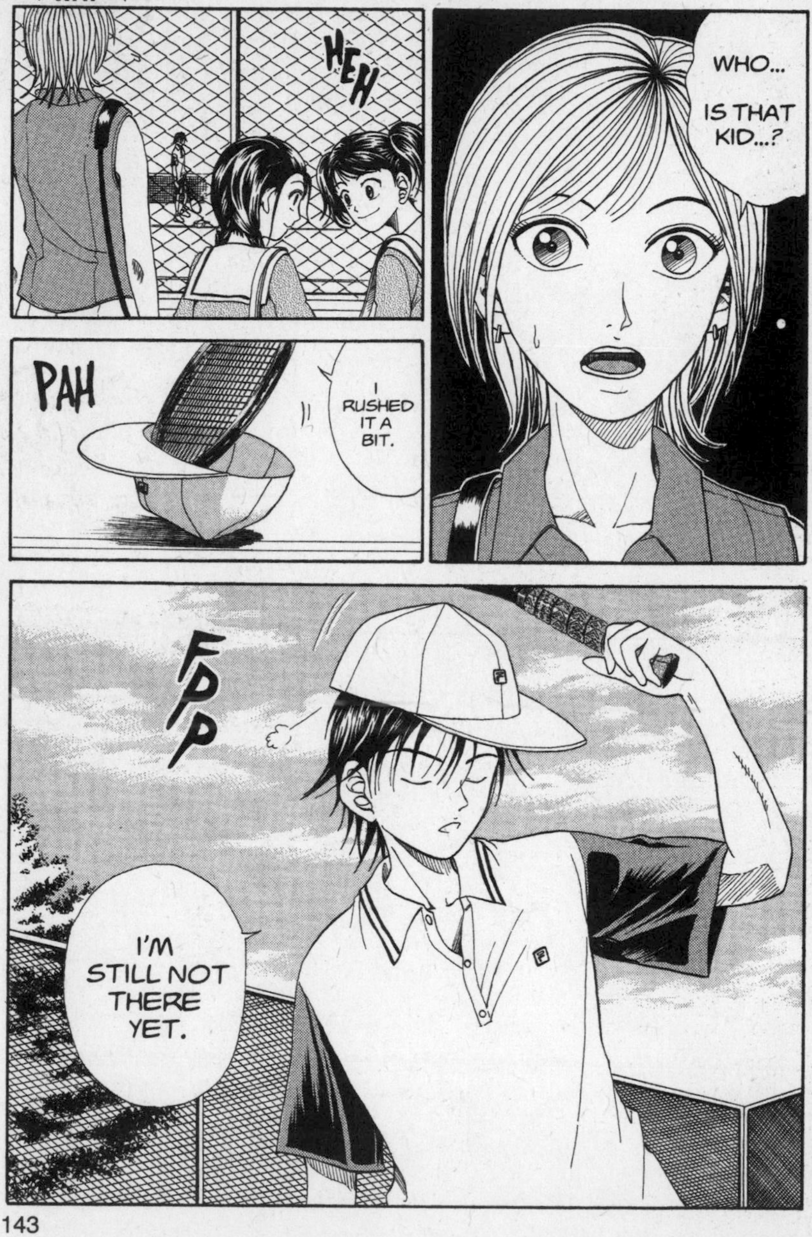
WHO...
IS THAT KID...?
HEH
I RUSHED IT A BIT.
PAH
FPP
I'M STILL NOT THERE YET.

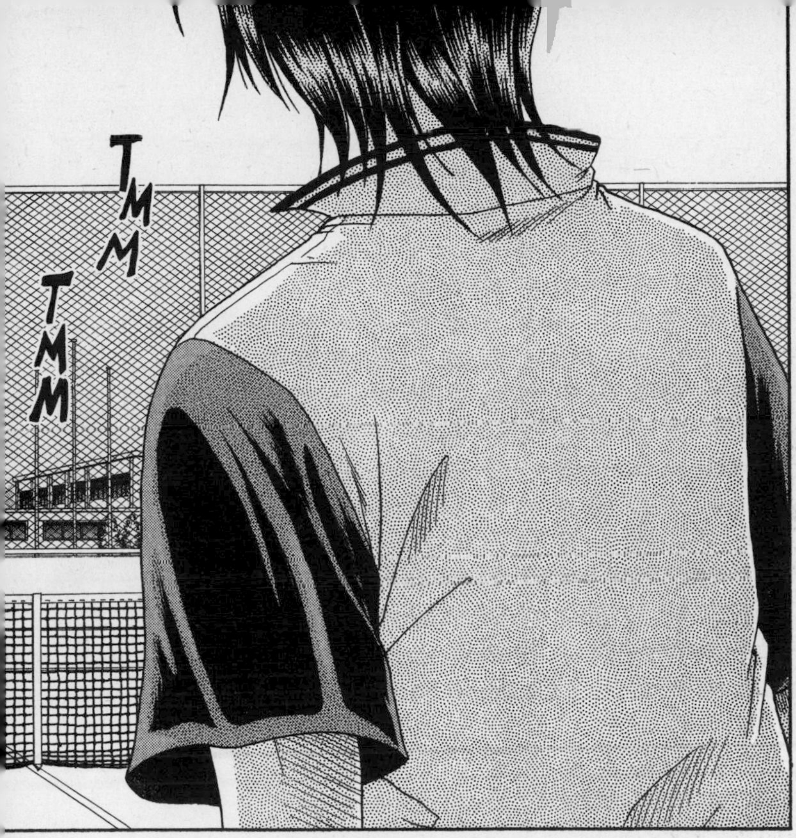
TMM
TMM

GENIUS 15

HALF A STEP

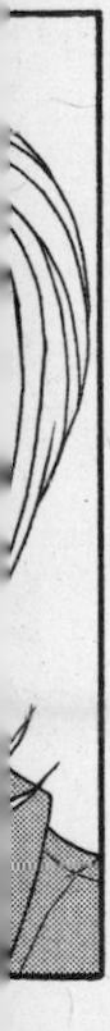

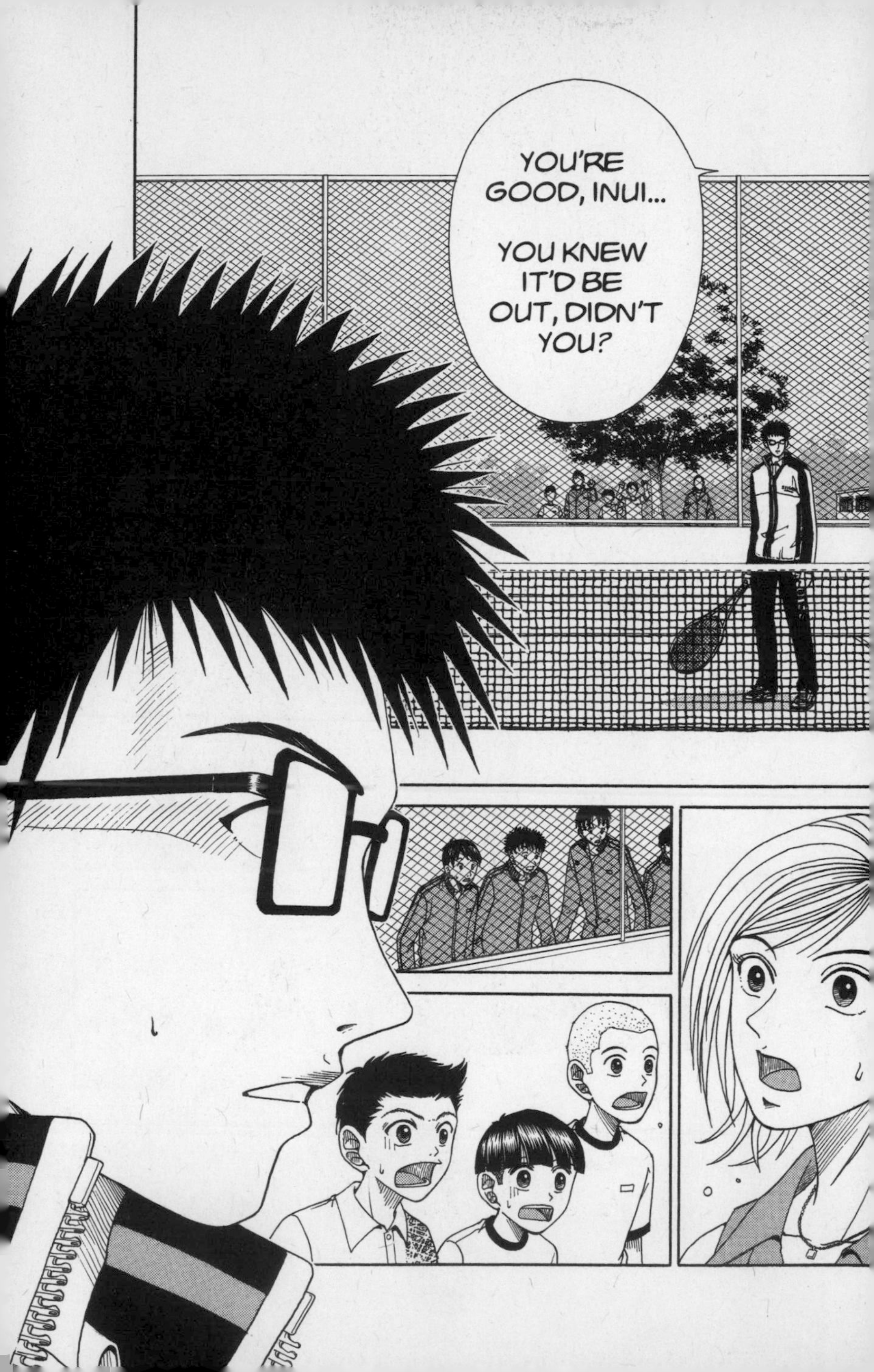
YOU'RE GOOD, INUI...
YOU KNEW IT'D BE OUT, DIDN'T YOU?

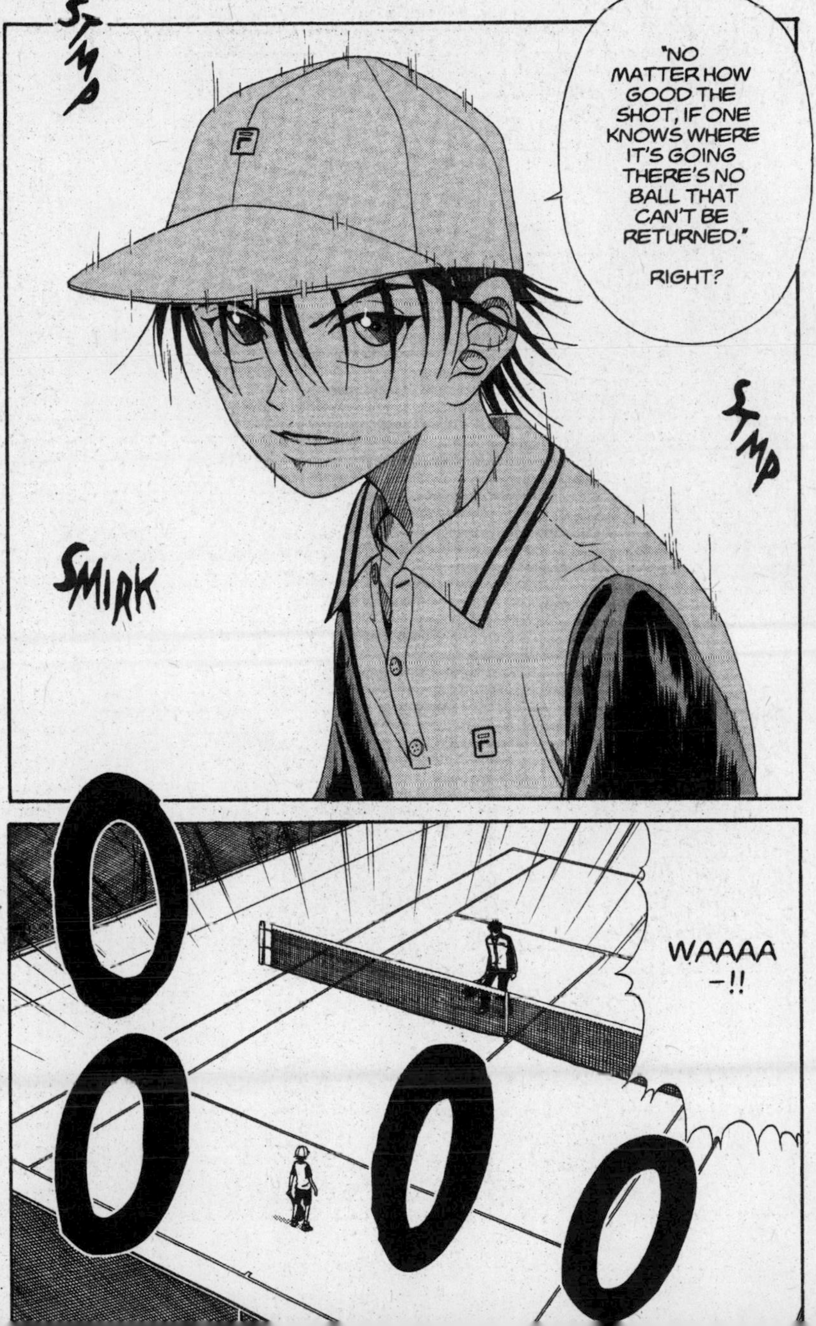
"NO MATTER HOW GOOD THE SHOT, IF ONE KNOWS WHERE IT'S GOING THERE'S NO BALL THAT CAN'T BE RETURNED."
RIGHT?
STMP
STMP
SMIRK
WAAAA —!!
OOOO

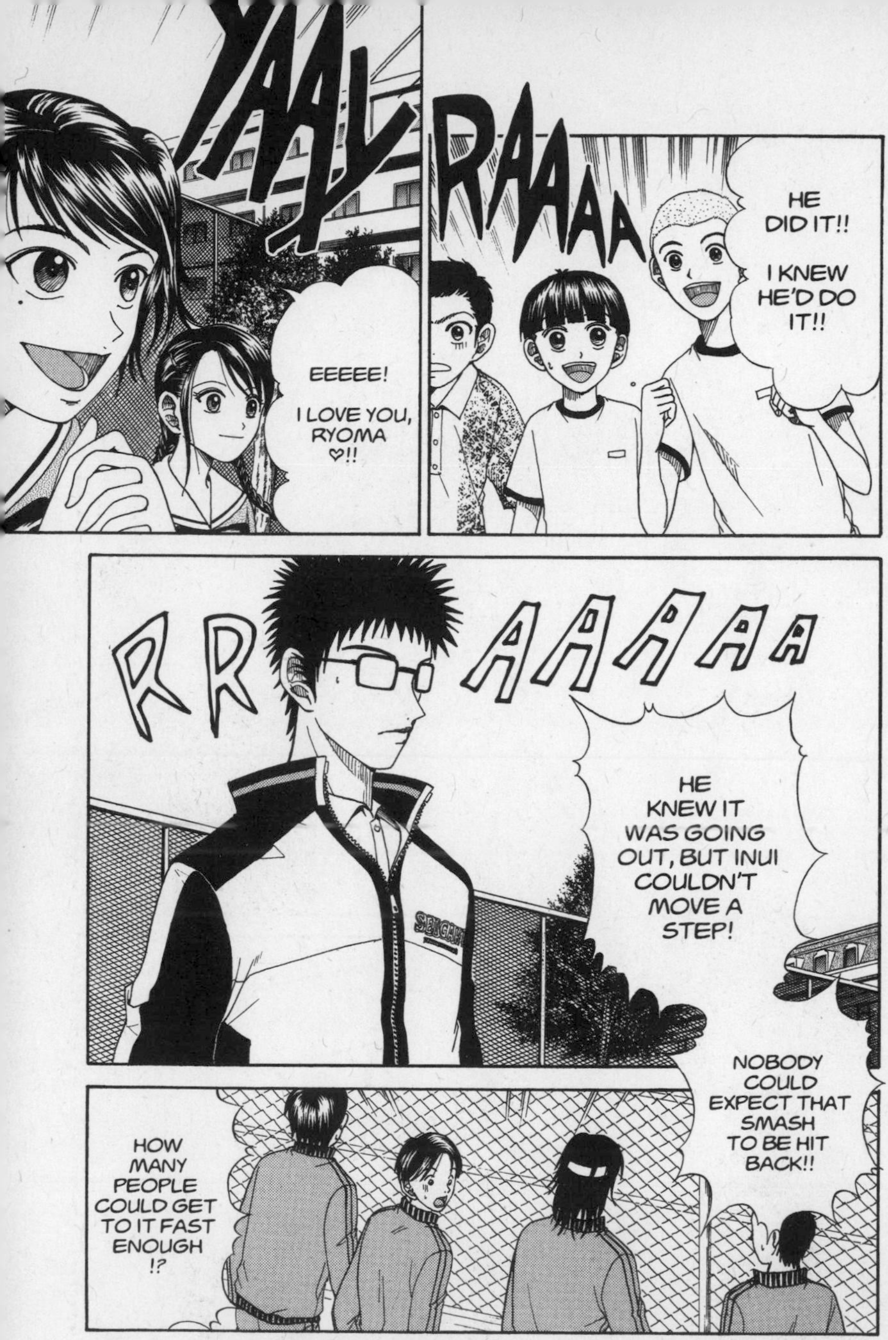
RAAAA
HE DID IT!! I KNEW HE'D DO IT!!
YAAAY
EEEEE! I LOVE YOU, RYOMA ♡!!
RRAAAAA
HE KNEW IT WAS GOING OUT, BUT INUI COULDN'T MOVE A STEP!
NOBODY COULD EXPECT THAT SMASH TO BE HIT BACK!!
HOW MANY PEOPLE COULD GET TO IT FAST ENOUGH !?

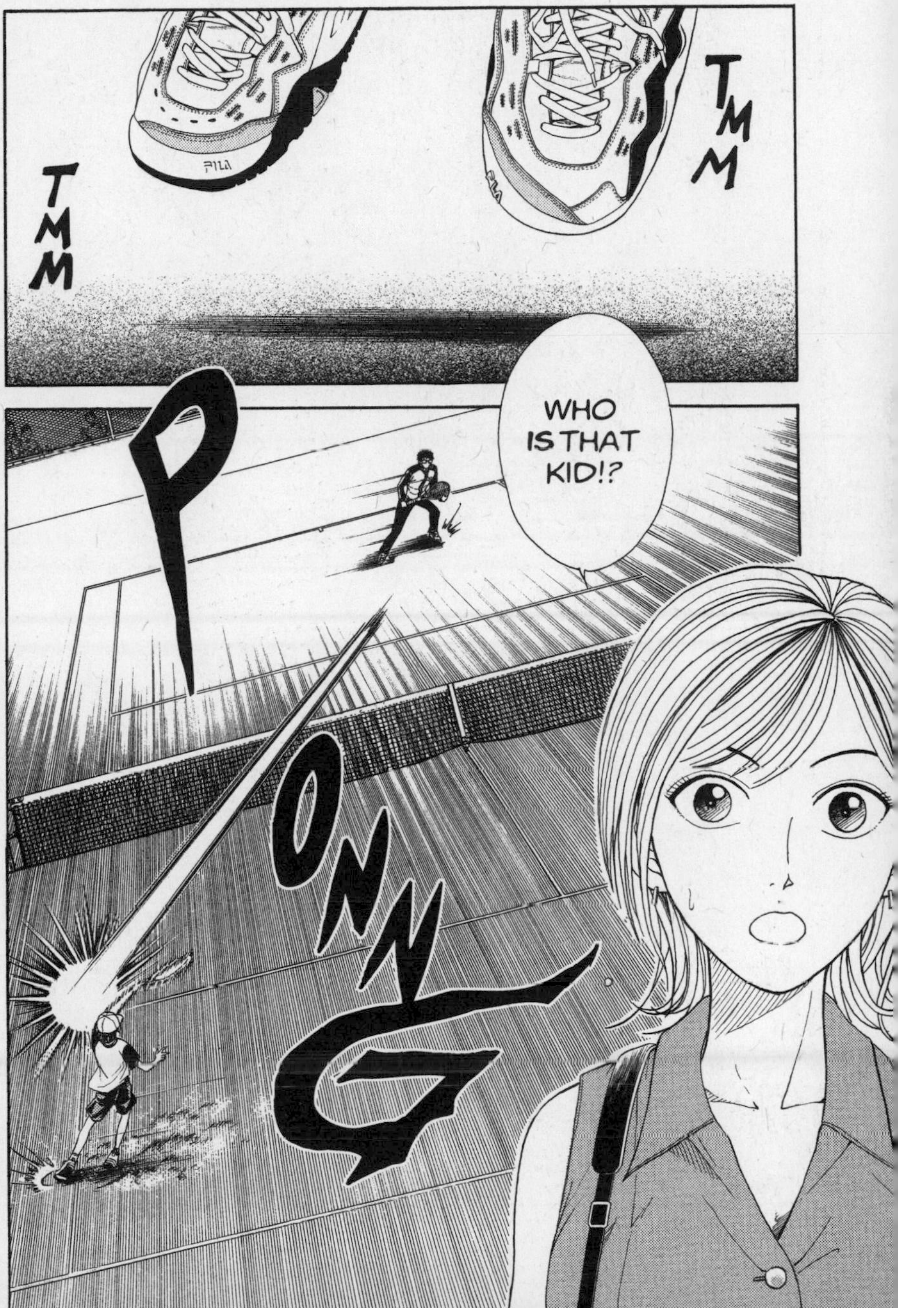
TMM
TMM
FILA
WHO IS THAT KID!?
PONNG

READ THIS WAY

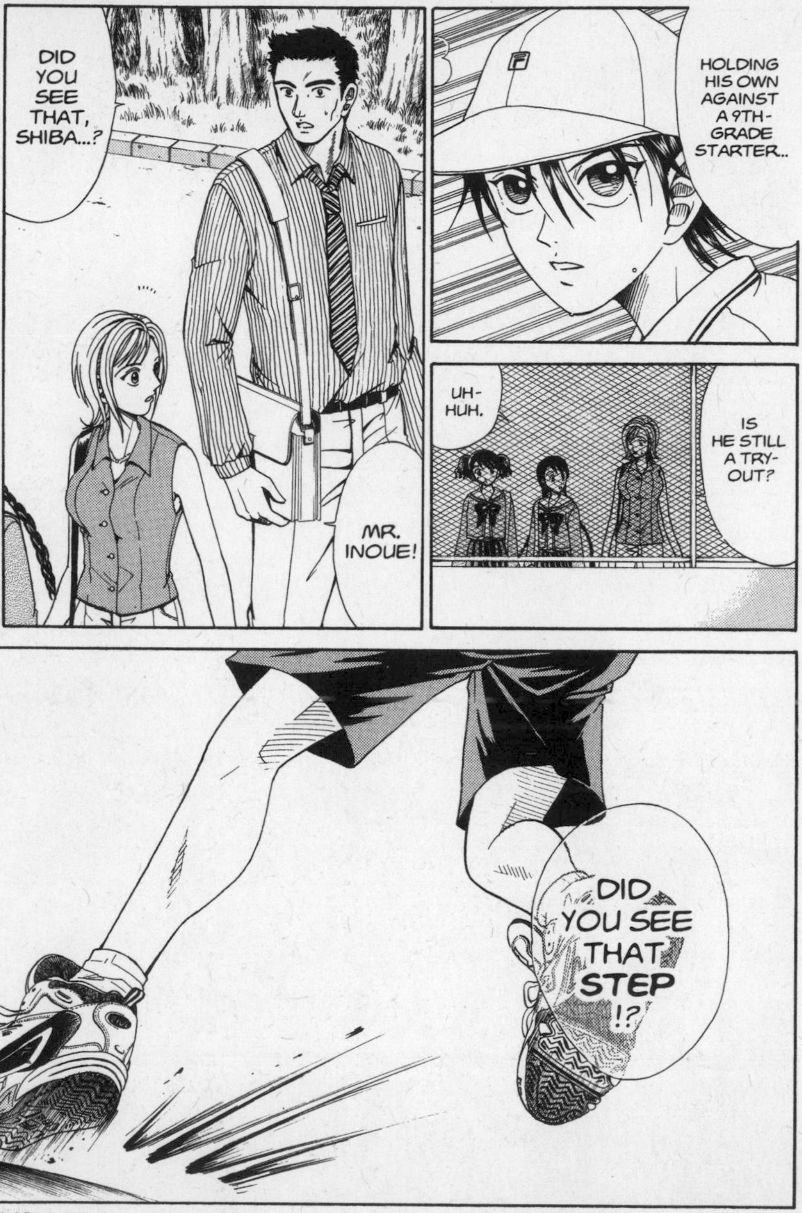

HOLDING HIS OWN AGAINST A 9TH-GRADE STARTER...
IS HE STILL A TRY-OUT?
UH-HUH.
DID YOU SEE THAT, SHIBA...?
MR. INOUE!
DID YOU SEE THAT STEP!?

READ THIS WAY

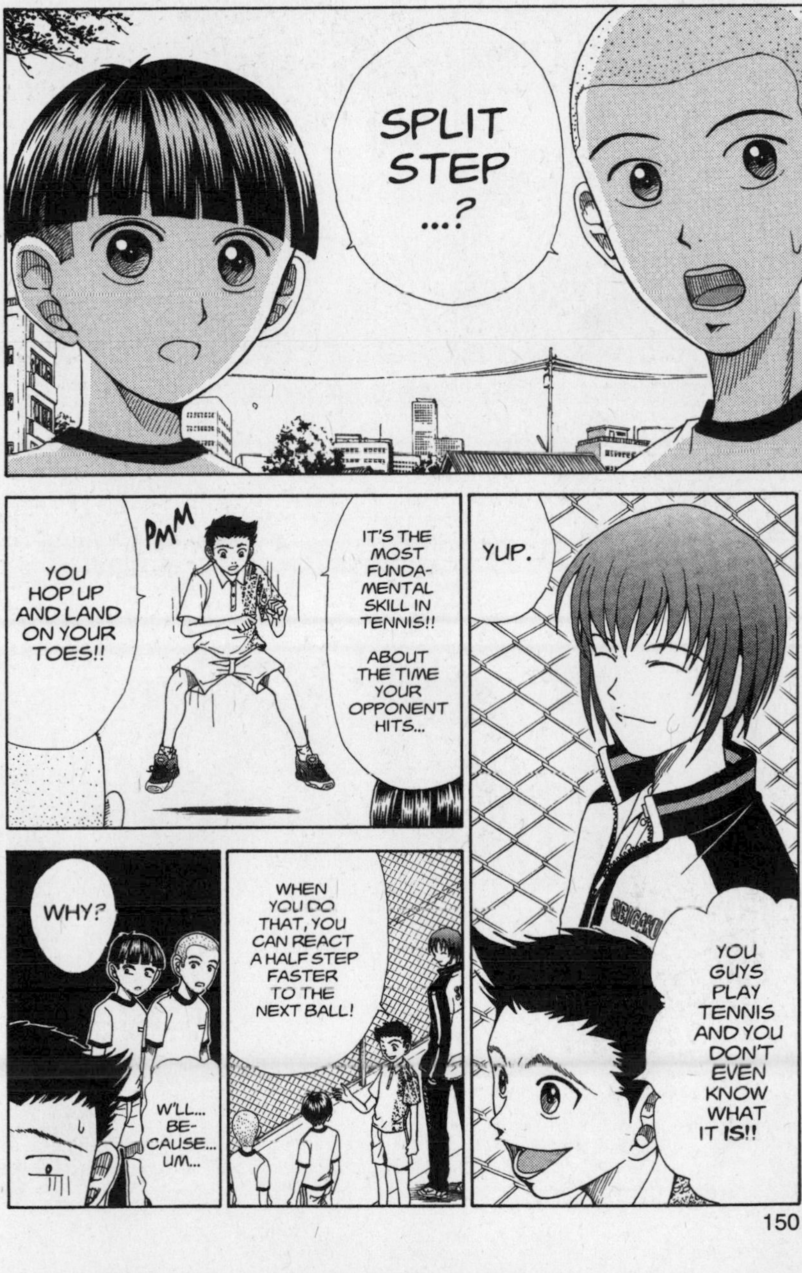
SPLIT STEP ...?
YUP.
IT'S THE MOST FUNDA-MENTAL SKILL IN TENNIS!!
ABOUT THE TIME YOUR OPPONENT HITS...
PMM
YOU HOP UP AND LAND ON YOUR TOES!!
YOU GUYS PLAY TENNIS AND YOU DON'T EVEN KNOW WHAT IT IS!!
WHEN YOU DO THAT, YOU CAN REACT A HALF STEP FASTER TO THE NEXT BALL!
WHY?
W'LL... BE-CAUSE... UM...

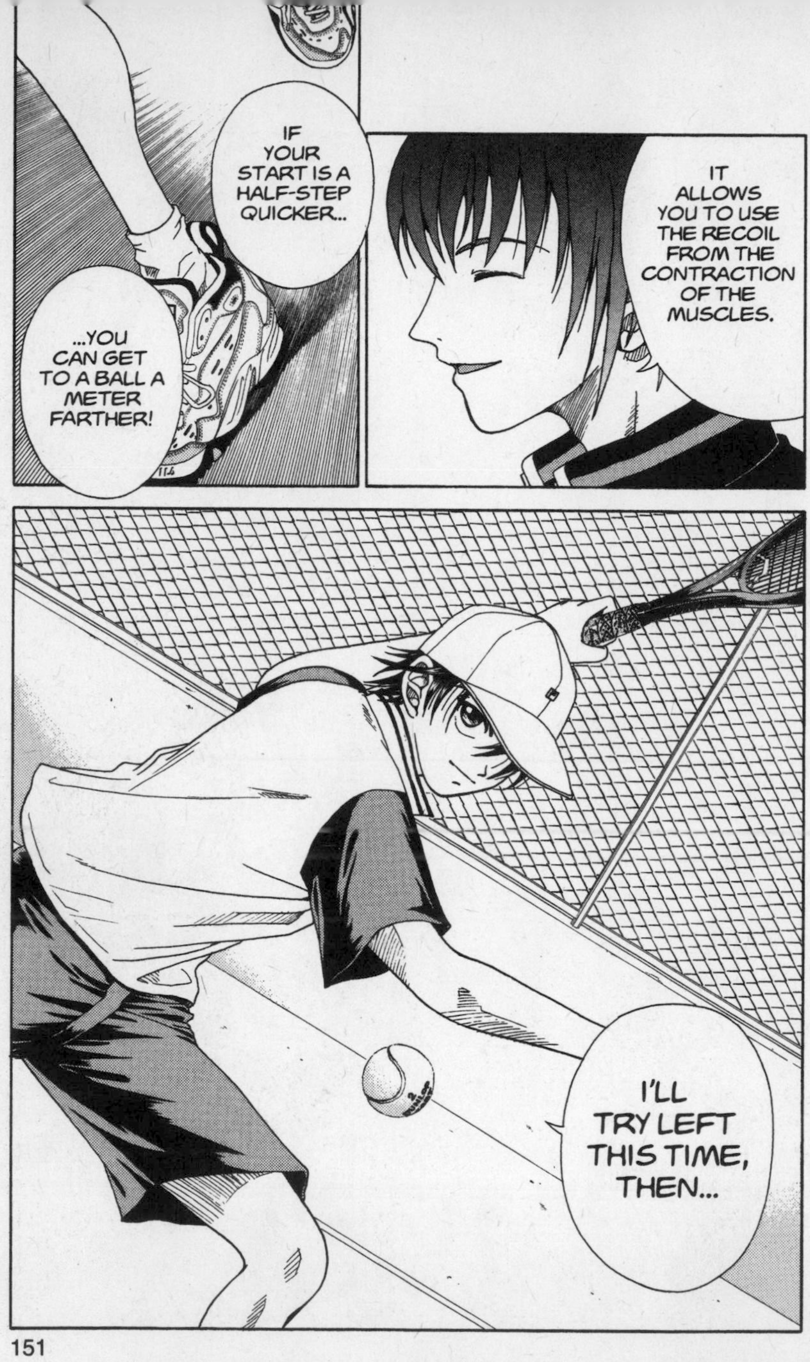
IT ALLOWS YOU TO USE THE RECOIL FROM THE CONTRACTION OF THE MUSCLES.
IF YOUR START IS A HALF-STEP QUICKER...
...YOU CAN GET TO A BALL A METER FARTHER!
I'LL TRY LEFT THIS TIME, THEN...

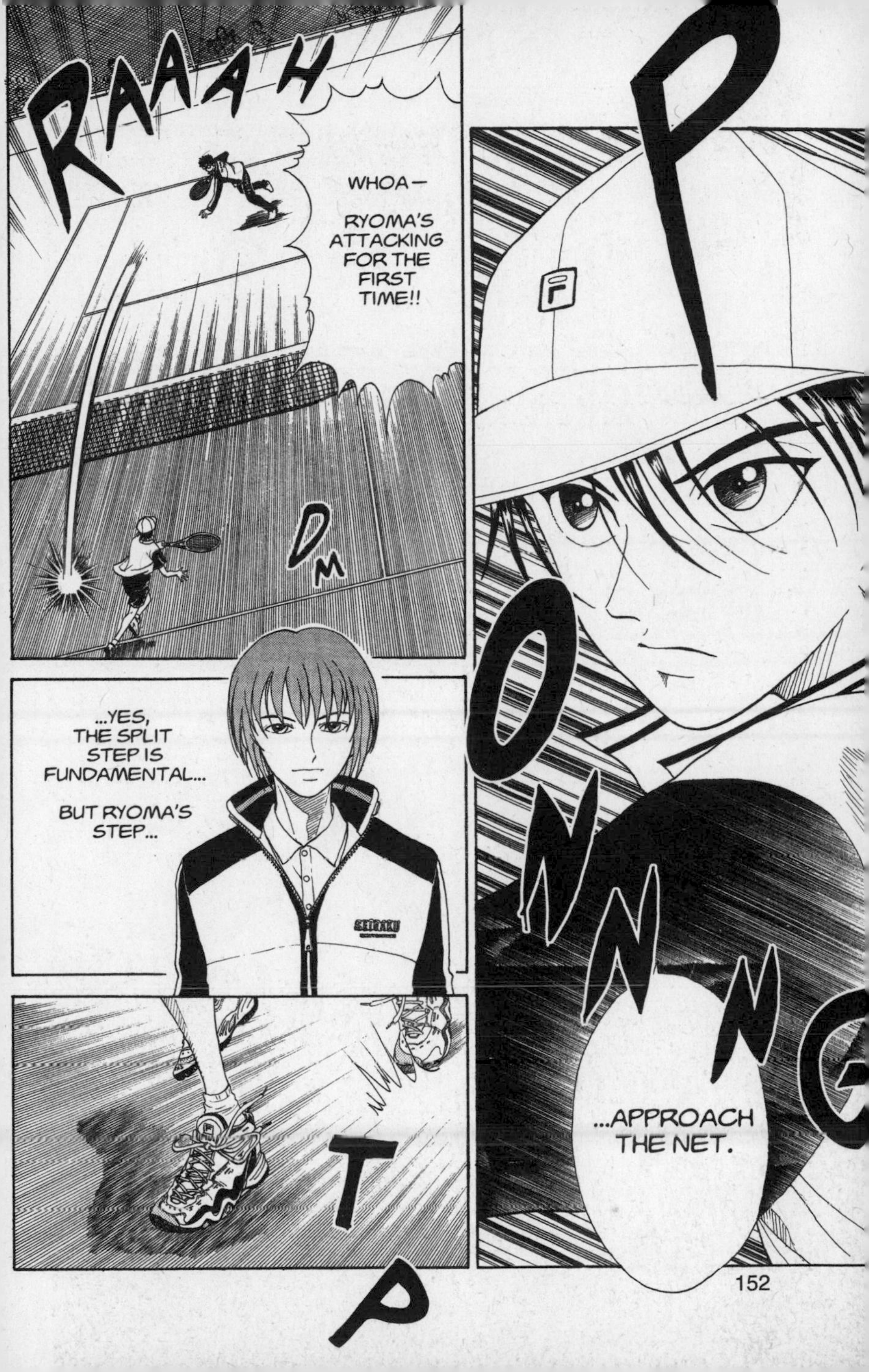
RAAAH
WHOA—
RYOMA'S ATTACKING FOR THE FIRST TIME!!
DM
...YES, THE SPLIT STEP IS FUNDAMENTAL...
BUT RYOMA'S STEP...
TP
PONNNG
...APPROACH THE NET.

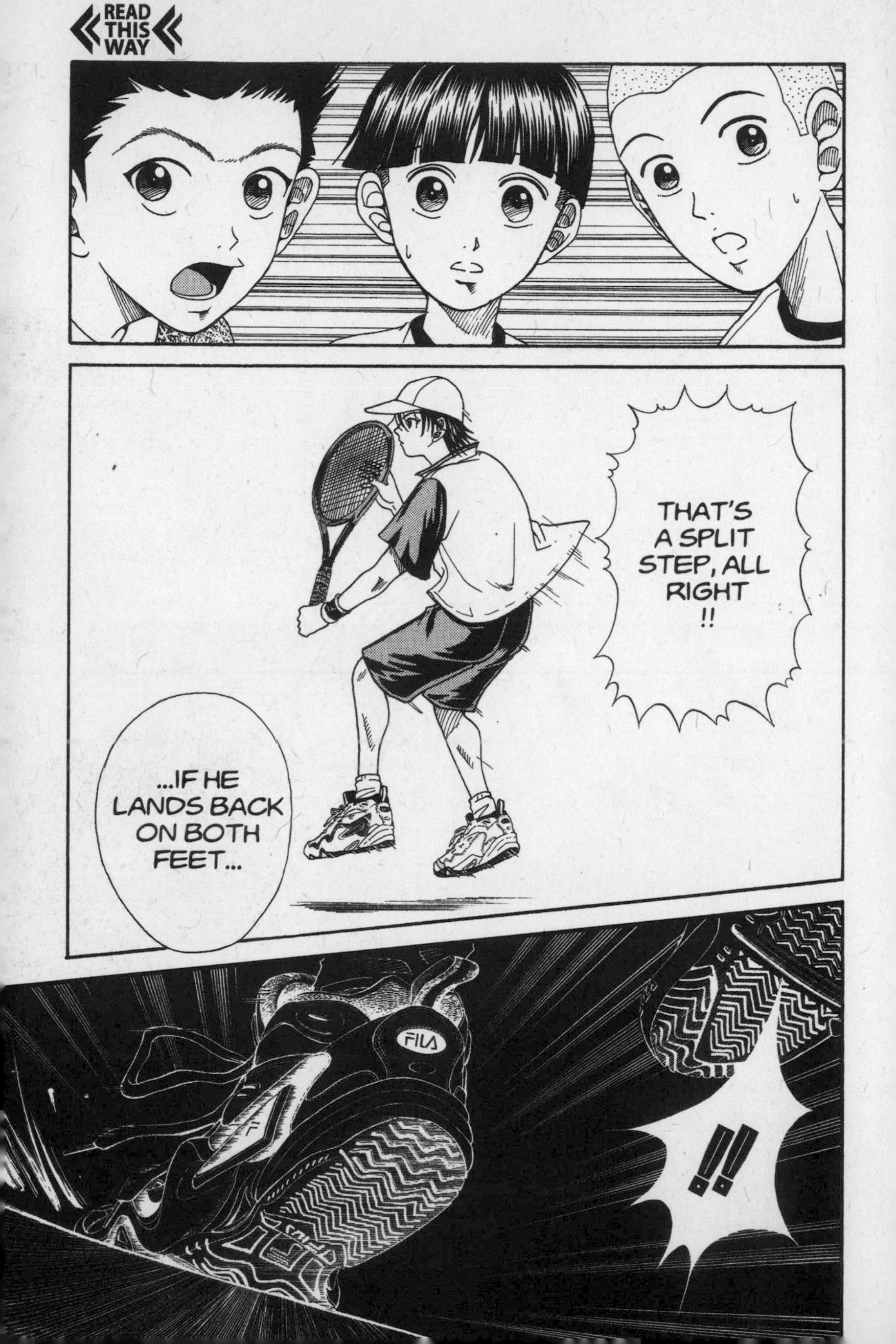
READ THIS WAY
THAT'S A SPLIT STEP, ALL RIGHT !!
...IF HE LANDS BACK ON BOTH FEET...
FILA
!!

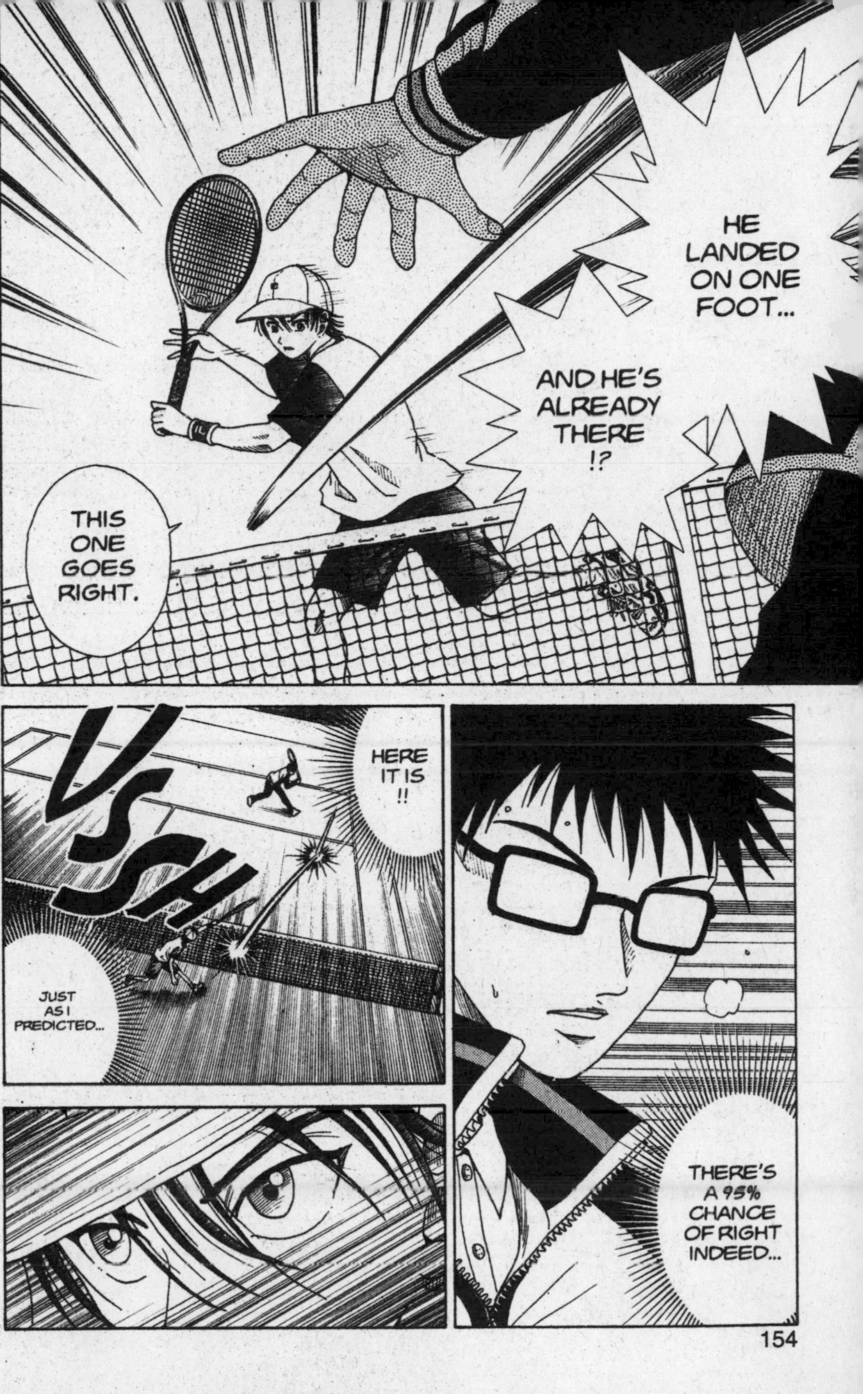
HE LANDED ON ONE FOOT...
AND HE'S ALREADY THERE !?
THIS ONE GOES RIGHT.
THERE'S A 95% CHANCE OF RIGHT INDEED...
HERE IT IS !!
VSH
JUST AS I PREDICTED...

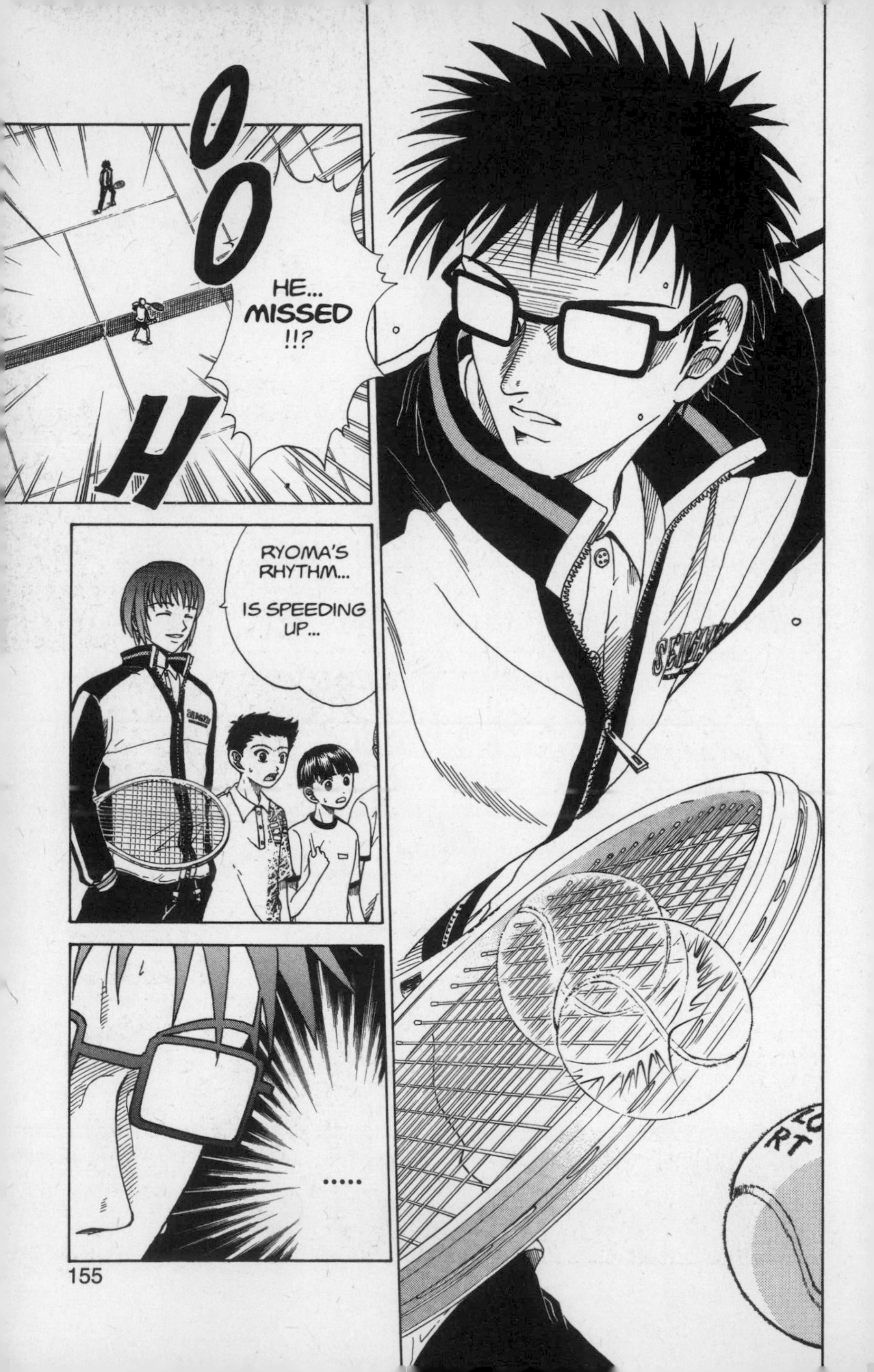
OOOH
HE... MISSED !!?
RYOMA'S RHYTHM...
IS SPEEDING UP...
.....

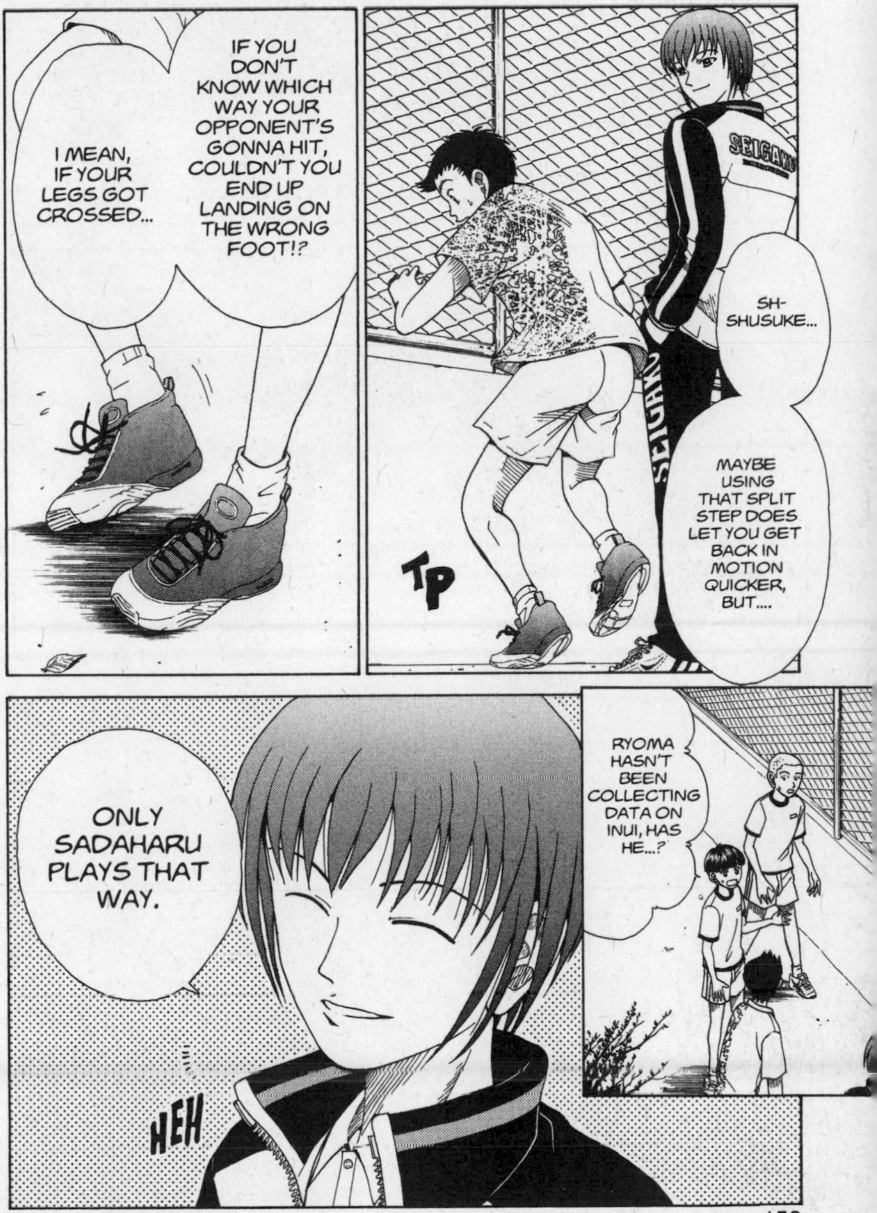
SH-SHUSUKE...
MAYBE USING THAT SPLIT STEP DOES LET YOU GET BACK IN MOTION QUICKER, BUT....
TP
IF YOU DON'T KNOW WHICH WAY YOUR OPPONENT'S GONNA HIT, COULDN'T YOU END UP LANDING ON THE WRONG FOOT!?
I MEAN, IF YOUR LEGS GOT CROSSED...
RYOMA HASN'T BEEN COLLECTING DATA ON INUI, HAS HE...?
ONLY SADAHARU PLAYS THAT WAY.
HEH

READ THIS WAY

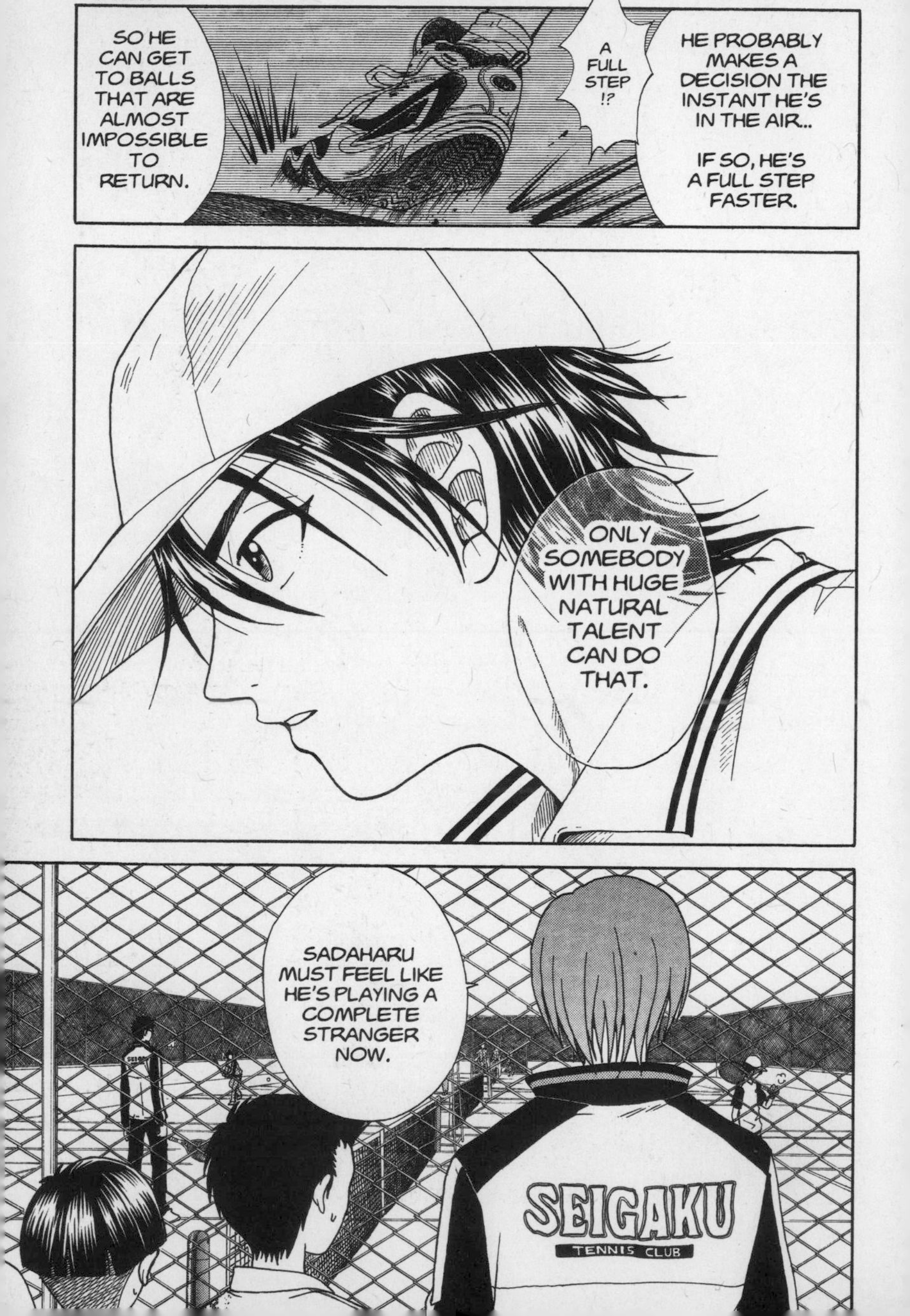

HE PROBABLY MAKES A DECISION THE INSTANT HE'S IN THE AIR...
IF SO, HE'S A FULL STEP FASTER.
A FULL STEP !?
SO HE CAN GET TO BALLS THAT ARE ALMOST IMPOSSIBLE TO RETURN.
ONLY SOMEBODY WITH HUGE NATURAL TALENT CAN DO THAT.
SADAHARU MUST FEEL LIKE HE'S PLAYING A COMPLETE STRANGER NOW.
SEIGAKU
TENNIS CLUB

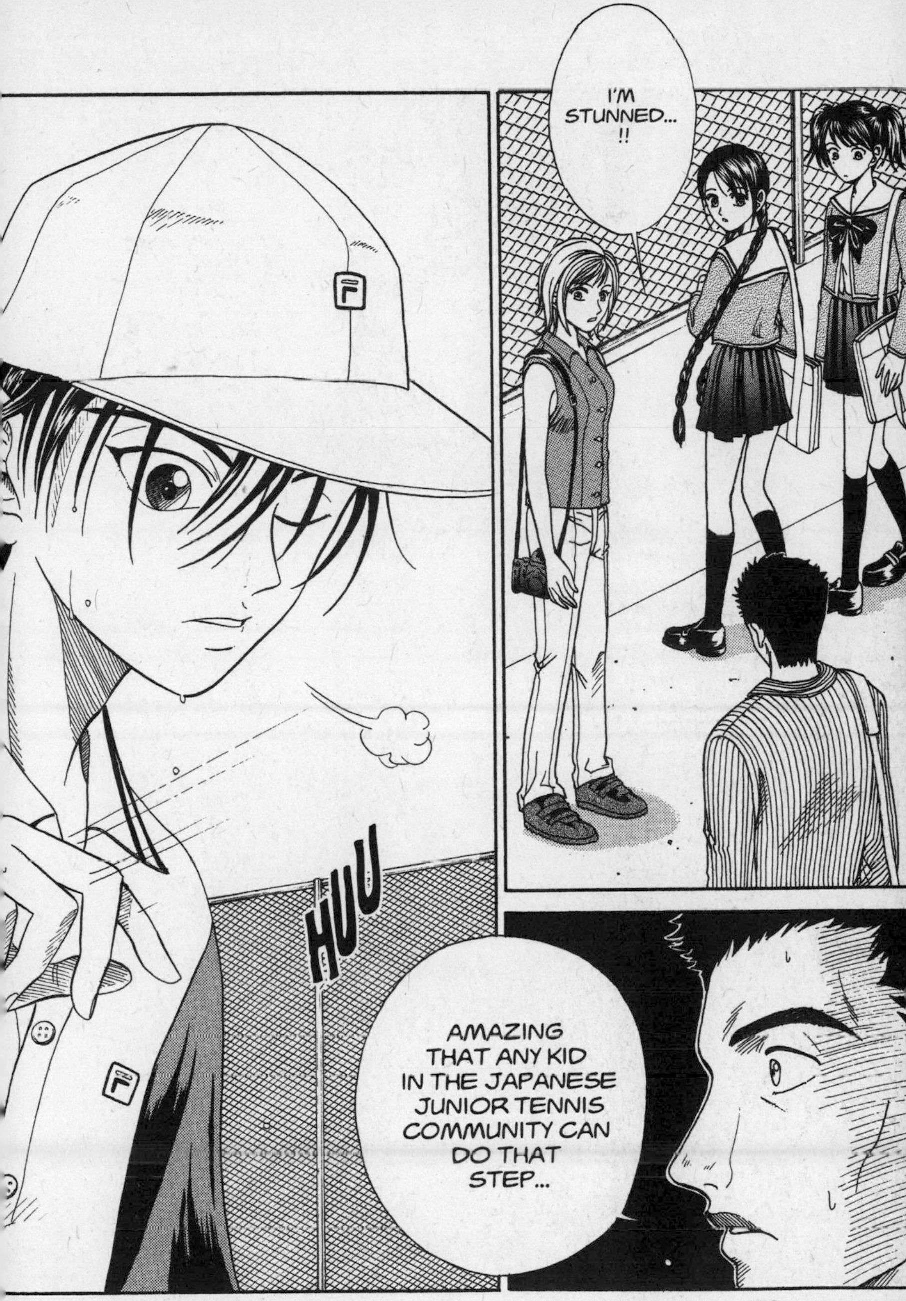
I'M STUNNED... !!
AMAZING THAT ANY KID IN THE JAPANESE JUNIOR TENNIS COMMUNITY CAN DO THAT STEP...
HUU

READ THIS WAY

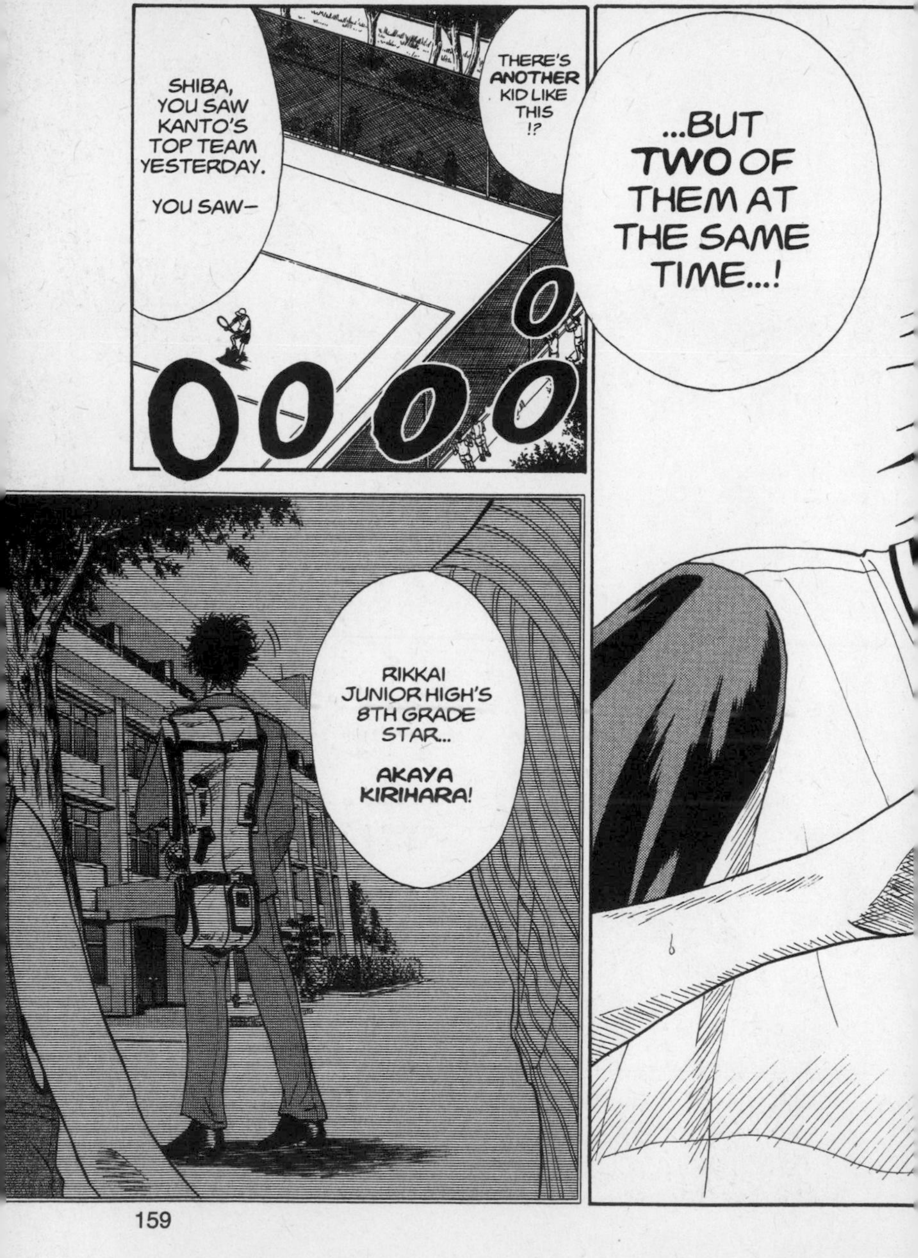
...BUT TWO OF THEM AT THE SAME TIME...!
THERE'S ANOTHER KID LIKE THIS !?
SHIBA, YOU SAW KANTO'S TOP TEAM YESTERDAY.
YOU SAW—
RIKKAI JUNIOR HIGH'S 8TH GRADE STAR...
AKAYA KIRIHARA!

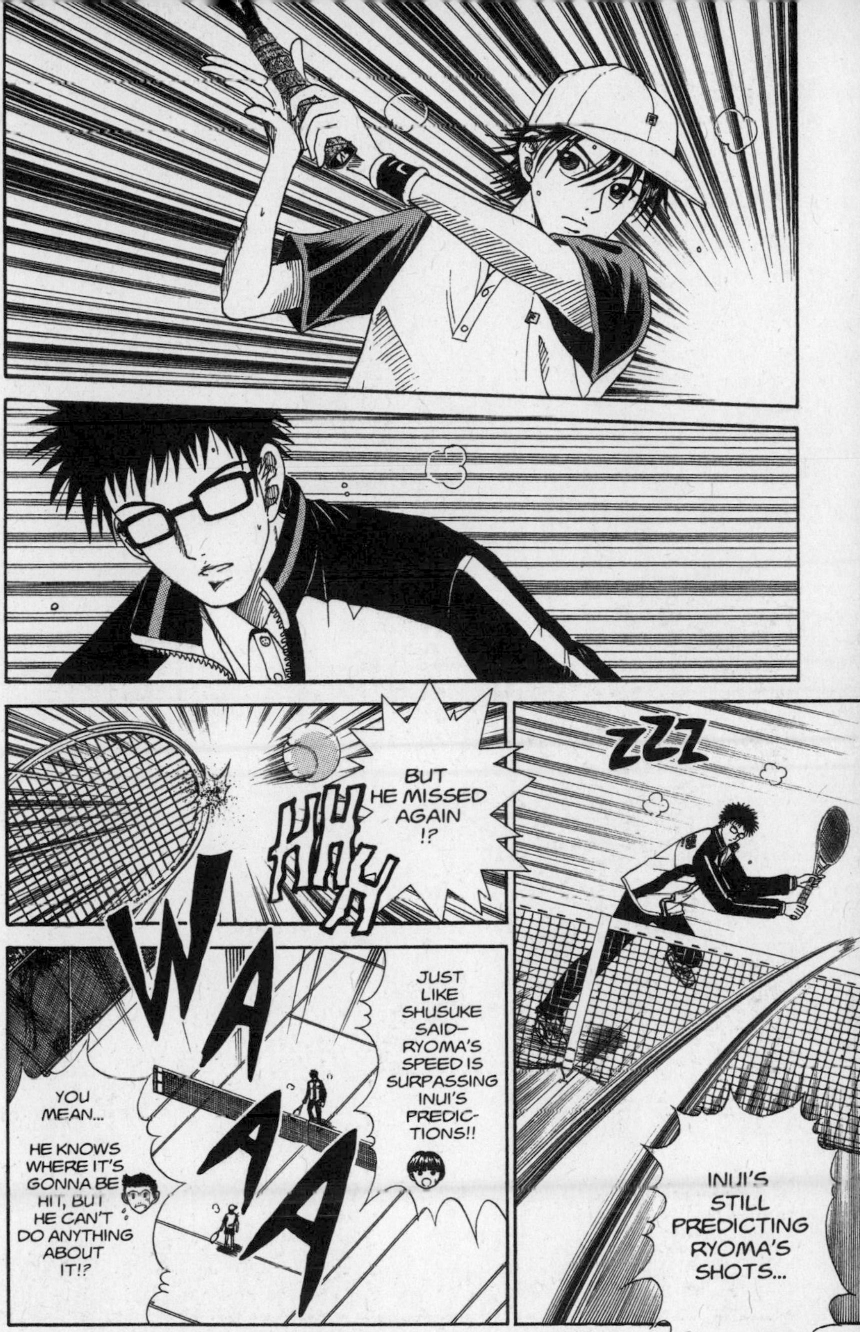
ZZZ
INUI'S STILL PREDICTING RYOMA'S SHOTS...
BUT HE MISSED AGAIN !?
WAAAHHH
JUST LIKE SHUSUKE SAID-RYOMA'S SPEED IS SURPASSING INUI'S PREDICTIONS!!
YOU MEAN...
HE KNOWS WHERE IT'S GONNA BE HIT, BUT HE CAN'T DO ANYTHING ABOUT IT!?

READ THIS WAY

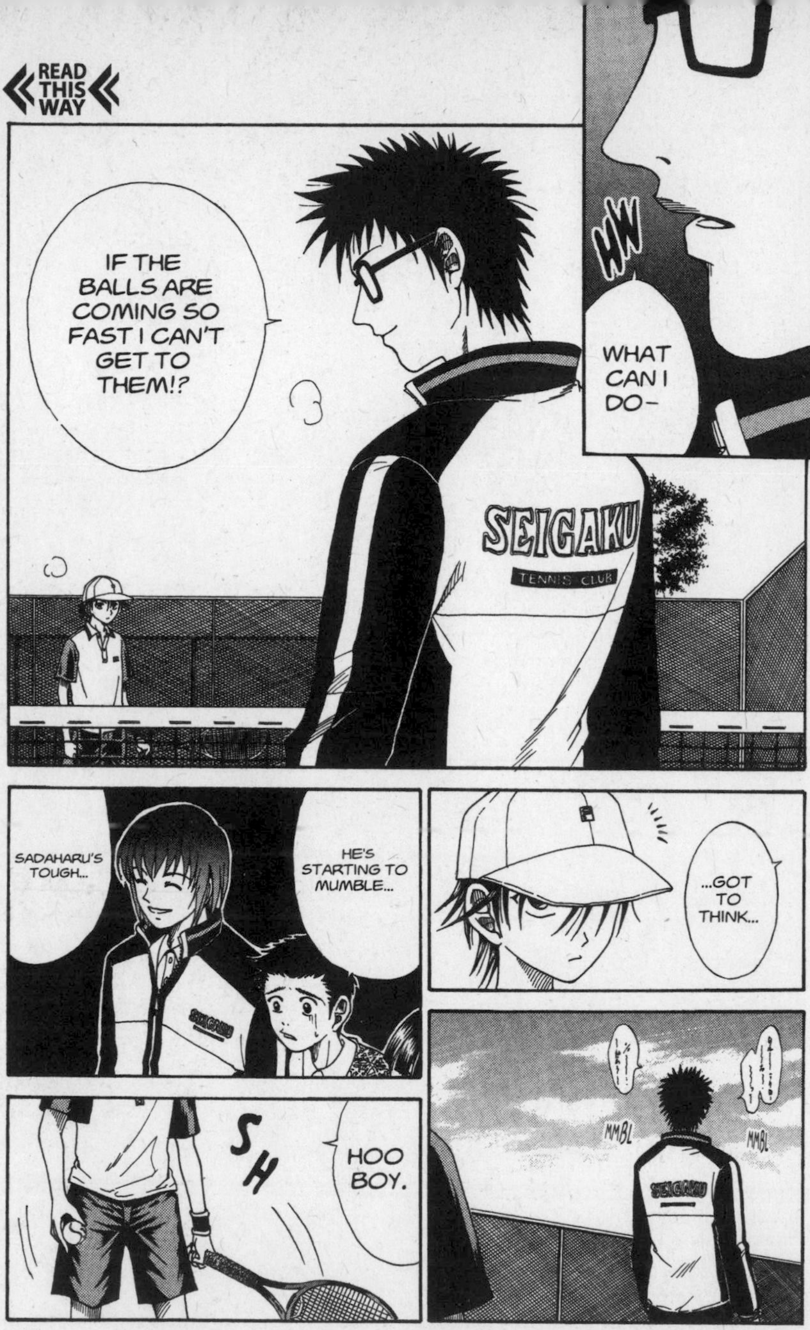
HW
WHAT CAN I DO–
IF THE BALLS ARE COMING SO FAST I CAN'T GET TO THEM!?
SEIGAKU
TENNIS CLUB
...GOT TO THINK...
HE'S STARTING TO MUMBLE...
SADAHARU'S TOUGH...
MMBL
MMBL
HOO BOY.
SH

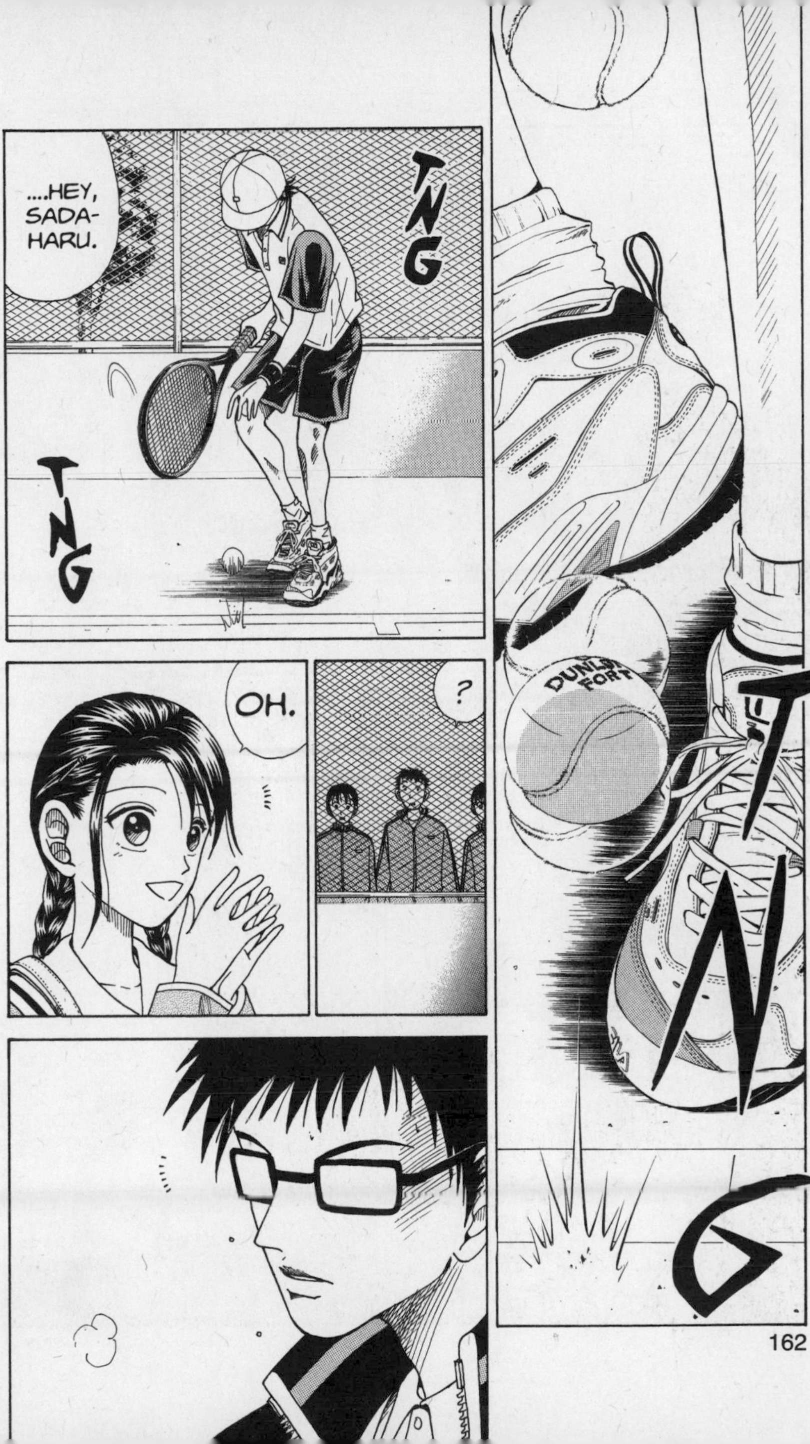
TNG
TNG
....HEY, SADA-HARU.
TNG
?
OH.

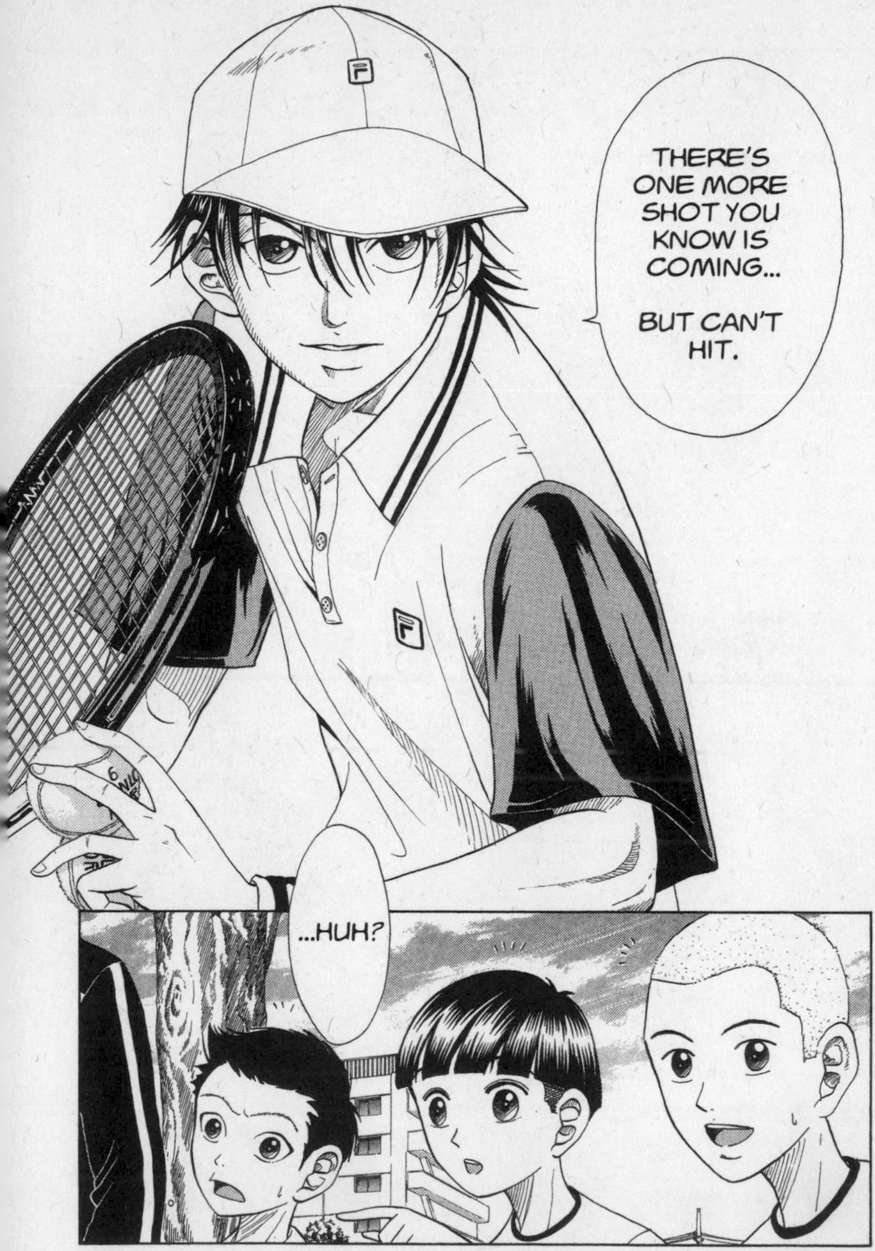
THERE'S ONE MORE SHOT YOU KNOW IS COMING...
BUT CAN'T HIT.
...HUH?

GENIUS 16

ARROGANT ROOKIE

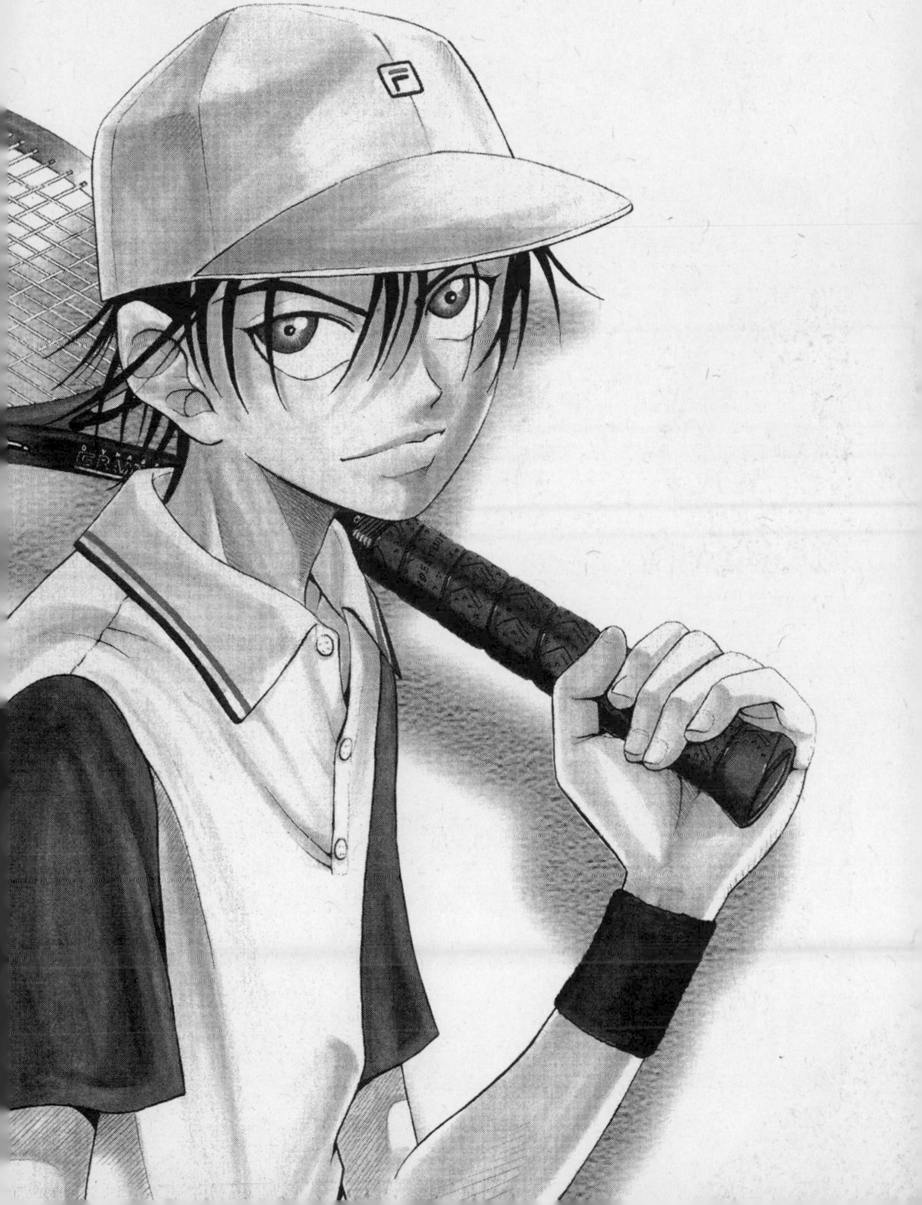

READ THIS WAY

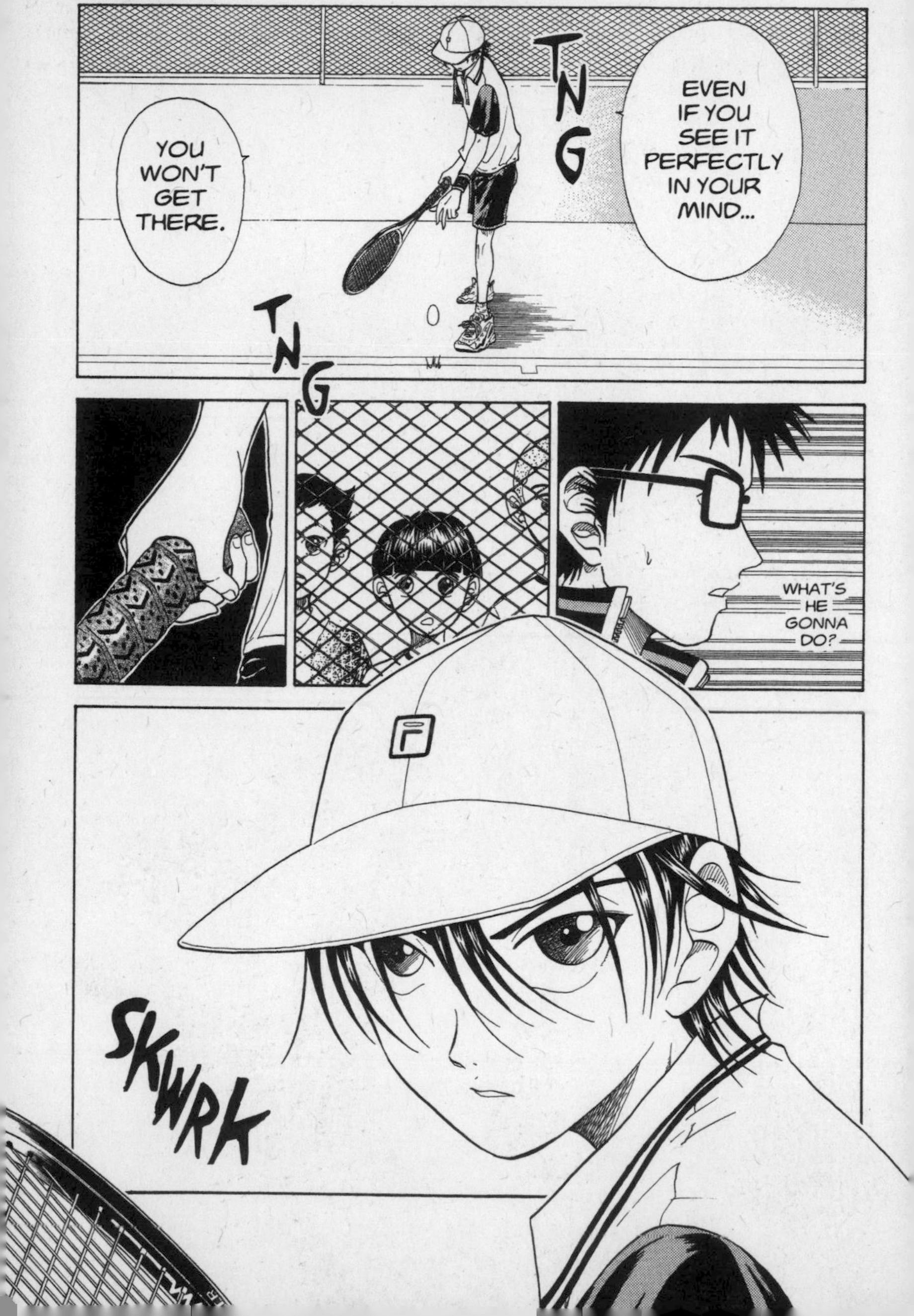
EVEN IF YOU SEE IT PERFECTLY IN YOUR MIND...
TNG
YOU WON'T GET THERE.
TNG
WHAT'S HE GONNA DO?
SKWRK

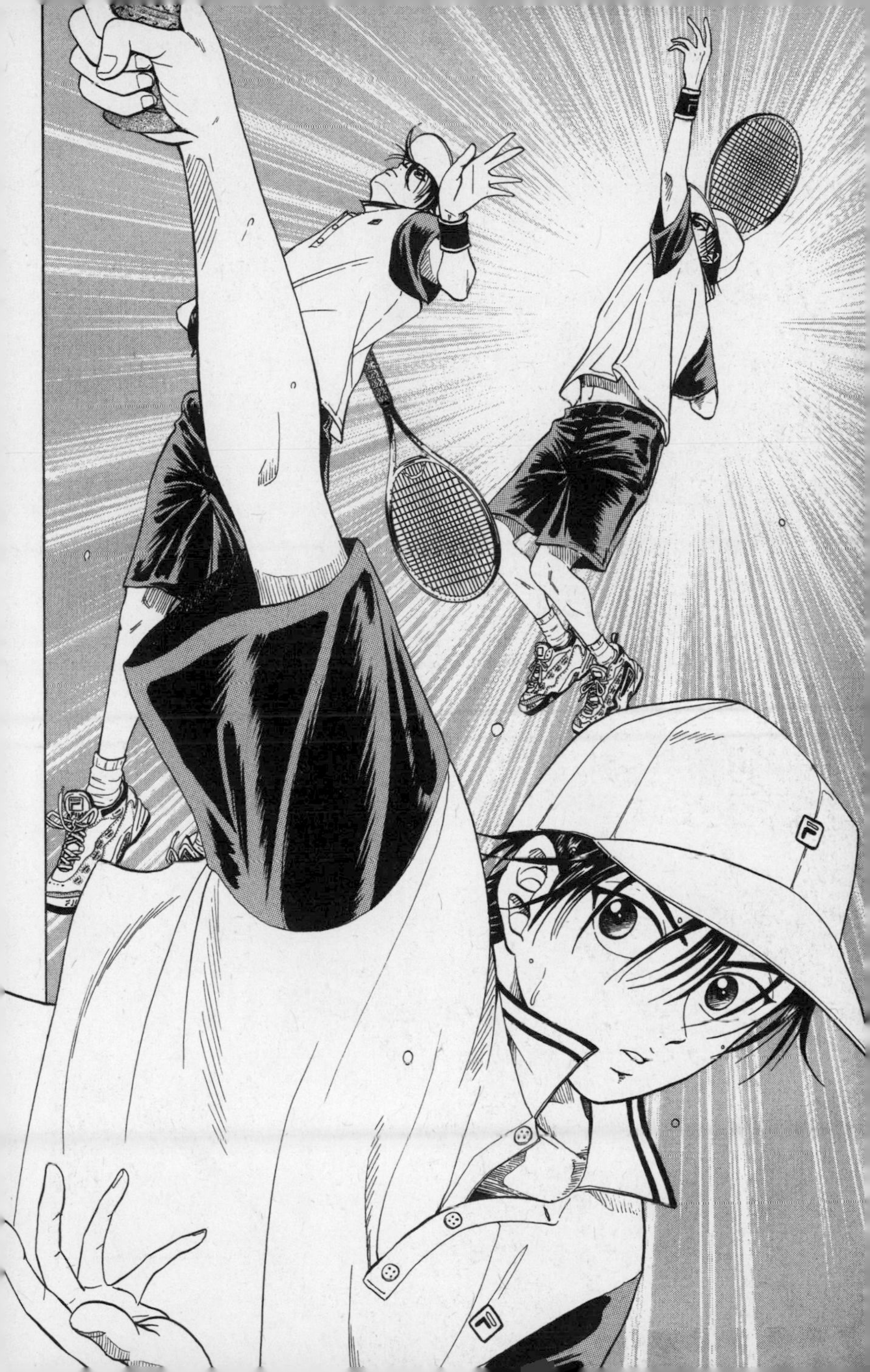

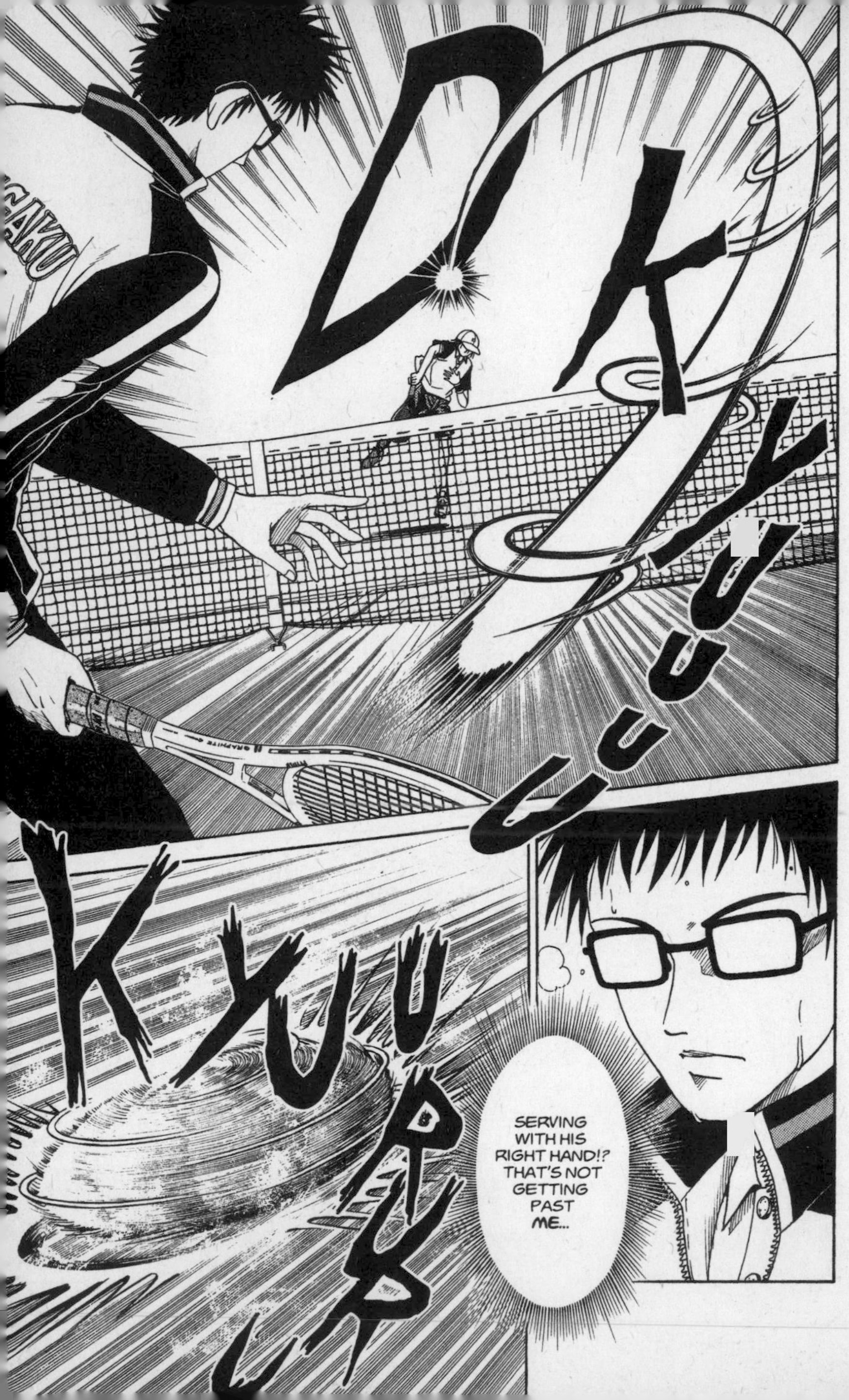
DKYUUUU
KYUU
SERVING WITH HIS RIGHT HAND!? THAT'S NOT GETTING PAST ME...

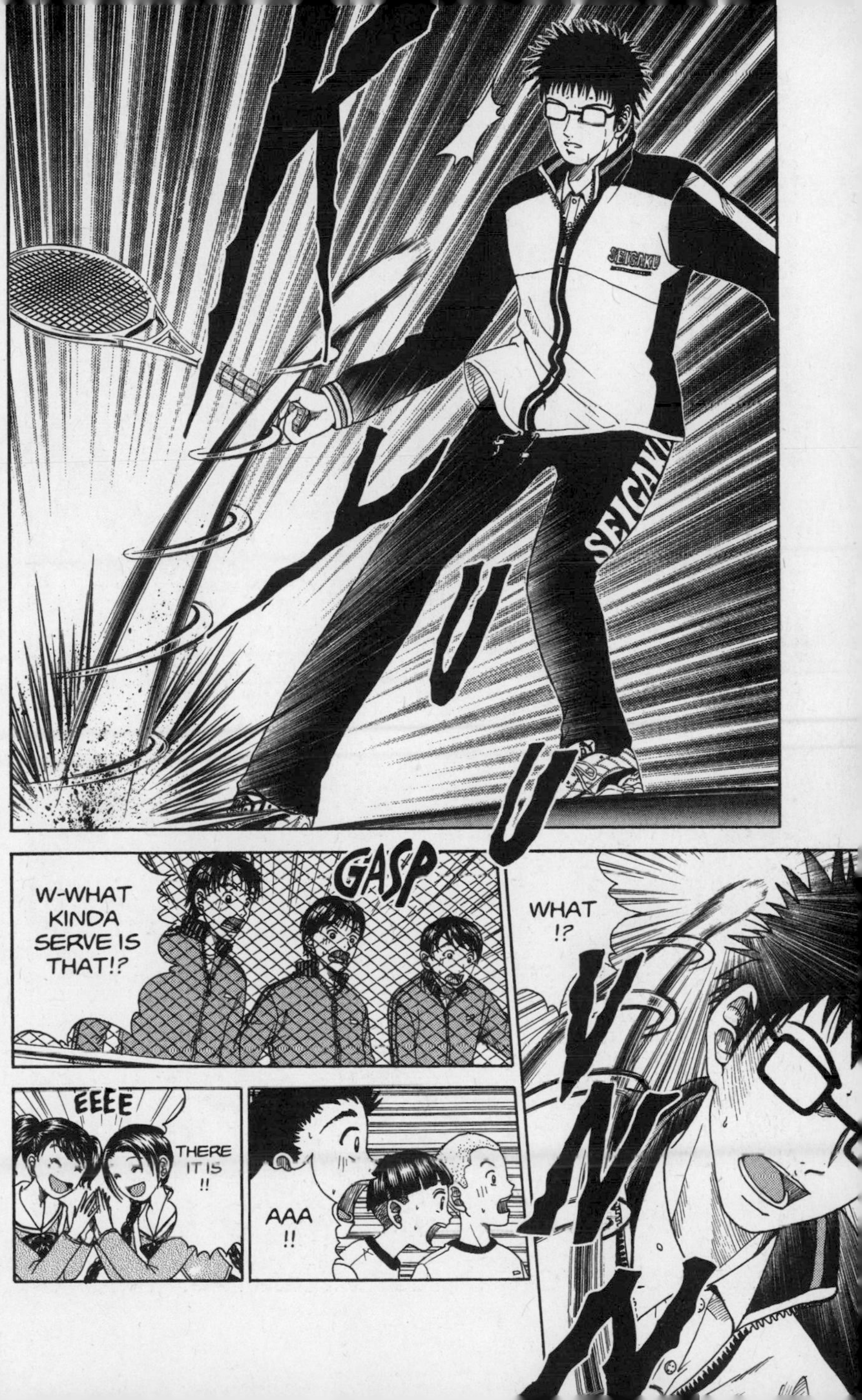
SEIGAKU
WHAT !?
GASP
W-WHAT KINDA SERVE IS THAT!?
AAA !!
EEEE
THERE IT IS !!

READ THIS WAY

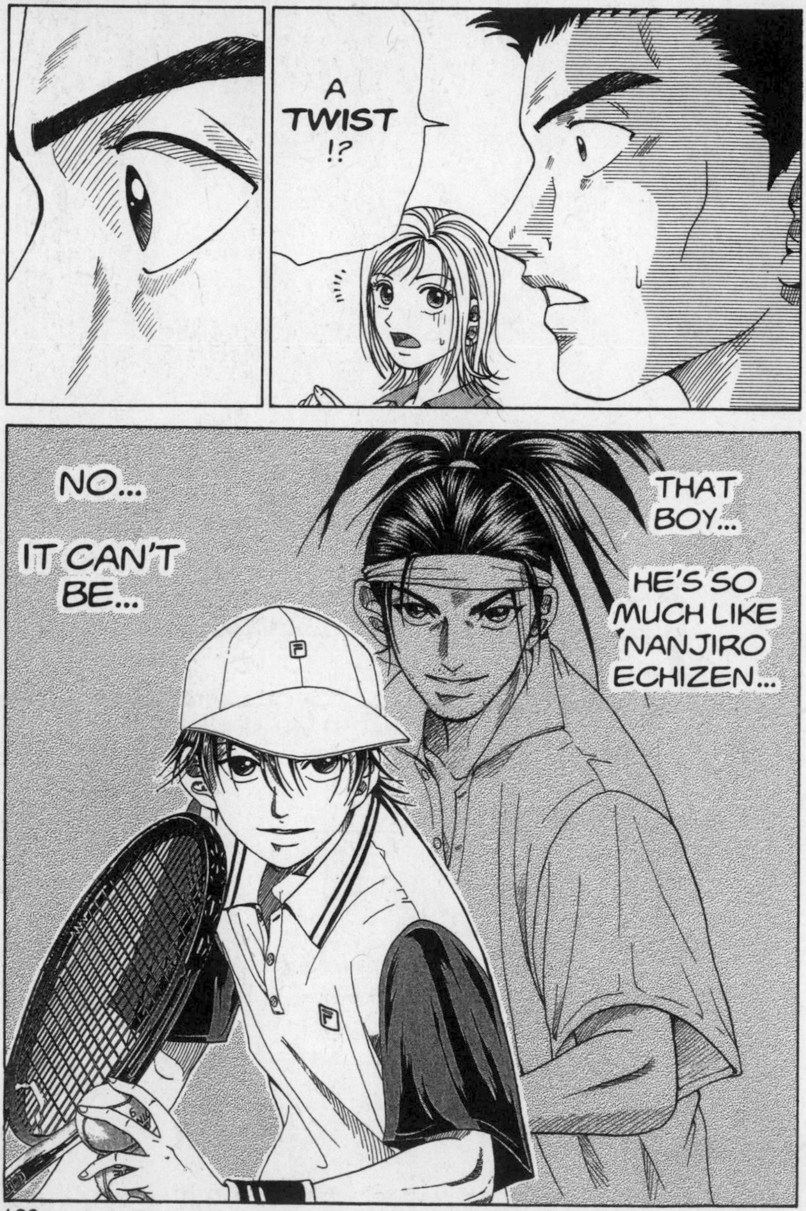
A TWIST !?
THAT BOY...
HE'S SO MUCH LIKE NANJIRO ECHIZEN...
NO...
IT CAN'T BE...

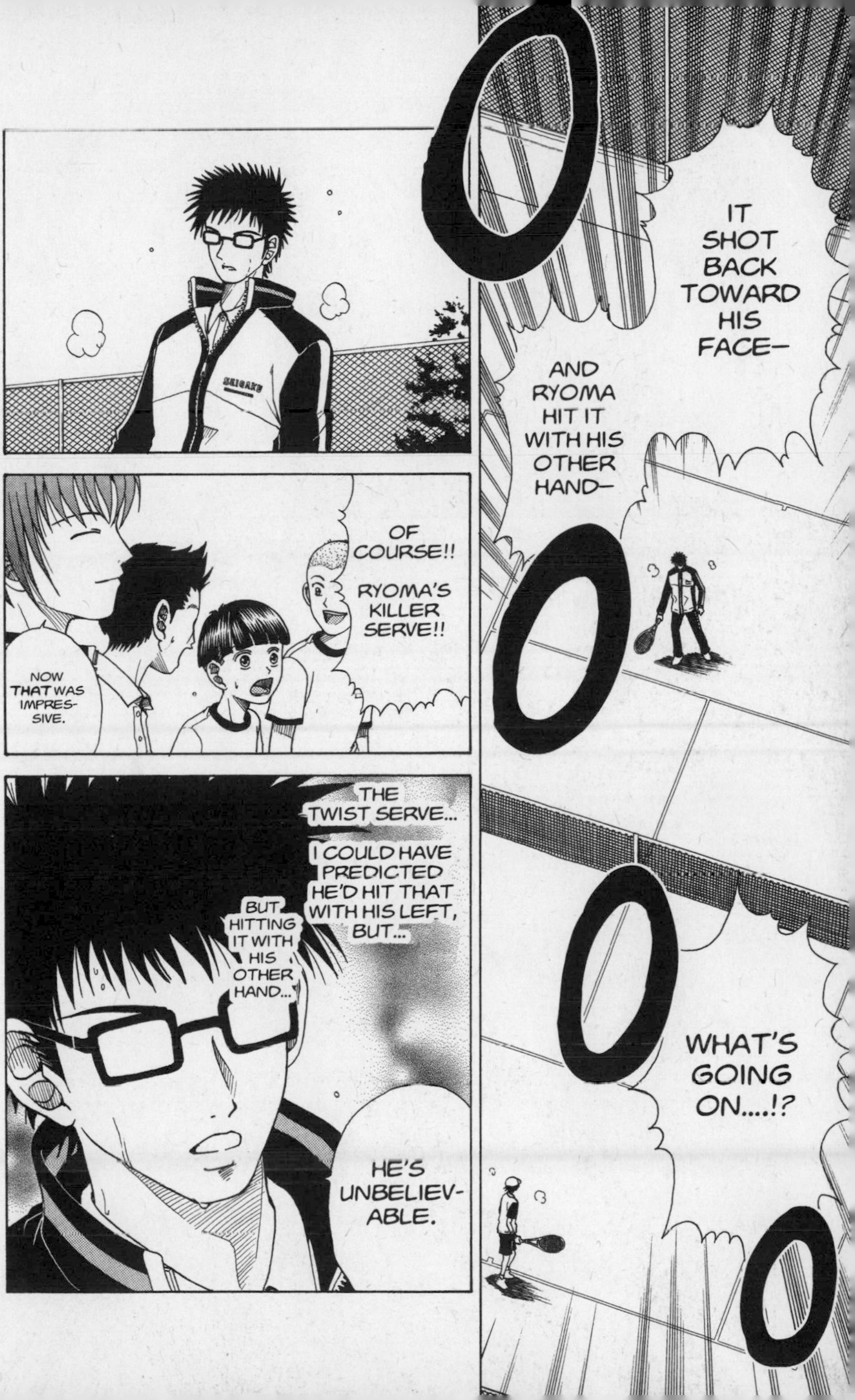
IT SHOT BACK TOWARD HIS FACE—
AND RYOMA HIT IT WITH HIS OTHER HAND—
WHAT'S GOING ON....!?
OF COURSE!!
RYOMA'S KILLER SERVE!!
NOW THAT WAS IMPRES-SIVE.
THE TWIST SERVE...
I COULD HAVE PREDICTED HE'D HIT THAT WITH HIS LEFT, BUT...
BUT HITTING IT WITH HIS OTHER HAND...
HE'S UNBELIEV-ABLE.

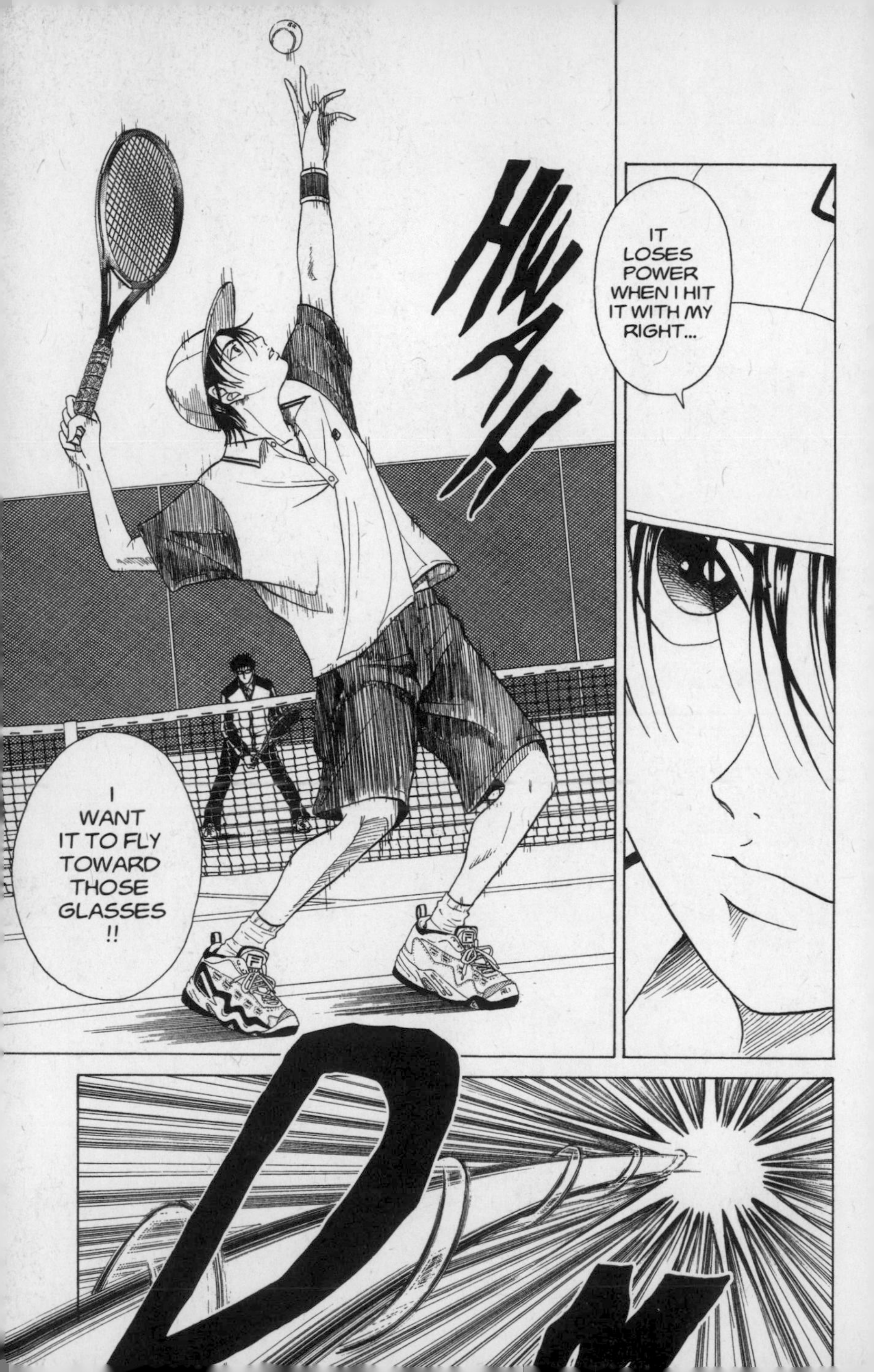
IT LOSES POWER WHEN I HIT IT WITH MY RIGHT...
HWAAH
I WANT IT TO FLY TOWARD THOSE GLASSES !!

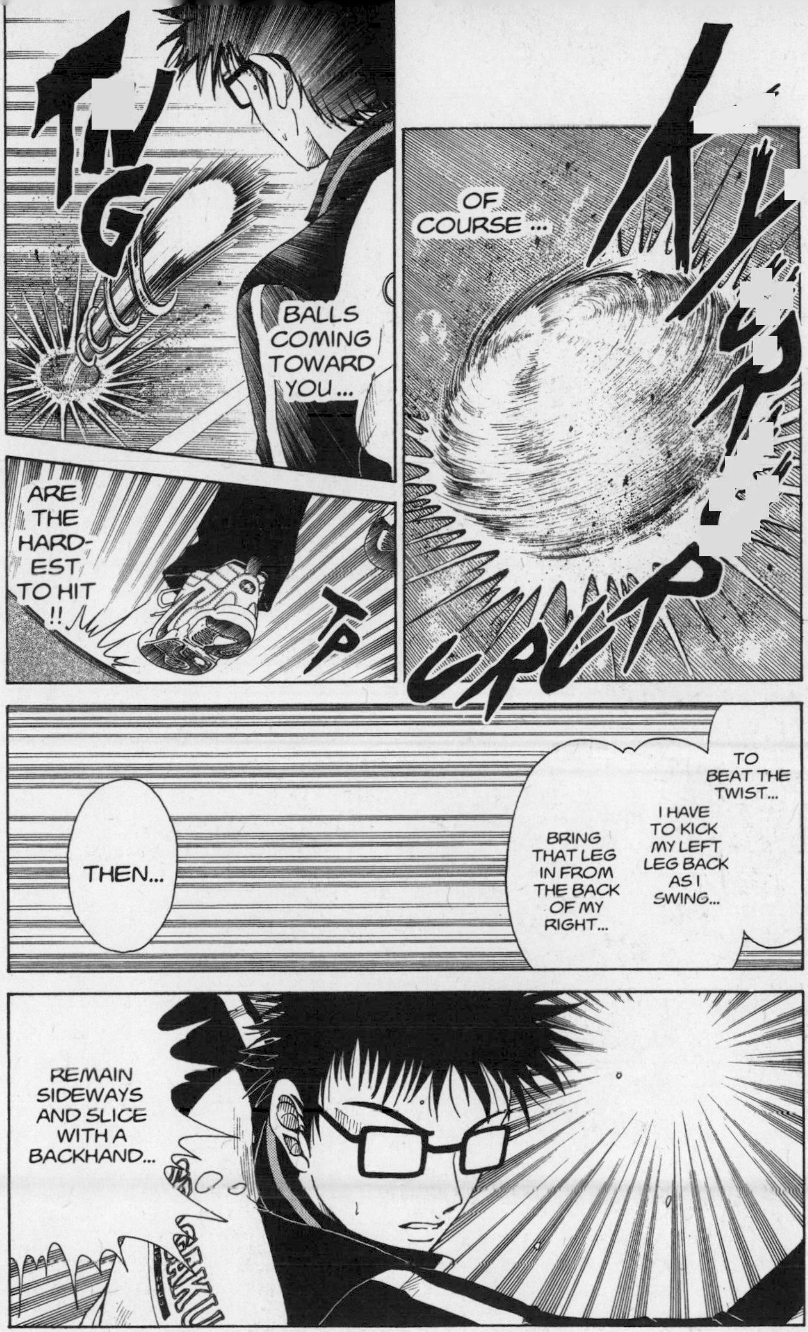
OF COURSE ...
BALLS COMING TOWARD YOU ...
ARE THE HARD-EST TO HIT !!
TP
TO BEAT THE TWIST...
I HAVE TO KICK MY LEFT LEG BACK AS I SWING...
BRING THAT LEG IN FROM THE BACK OF MY RIGHT...
THEN...
REMAIN SIDEWAYS AND SLICE WITH A BACKHAND...

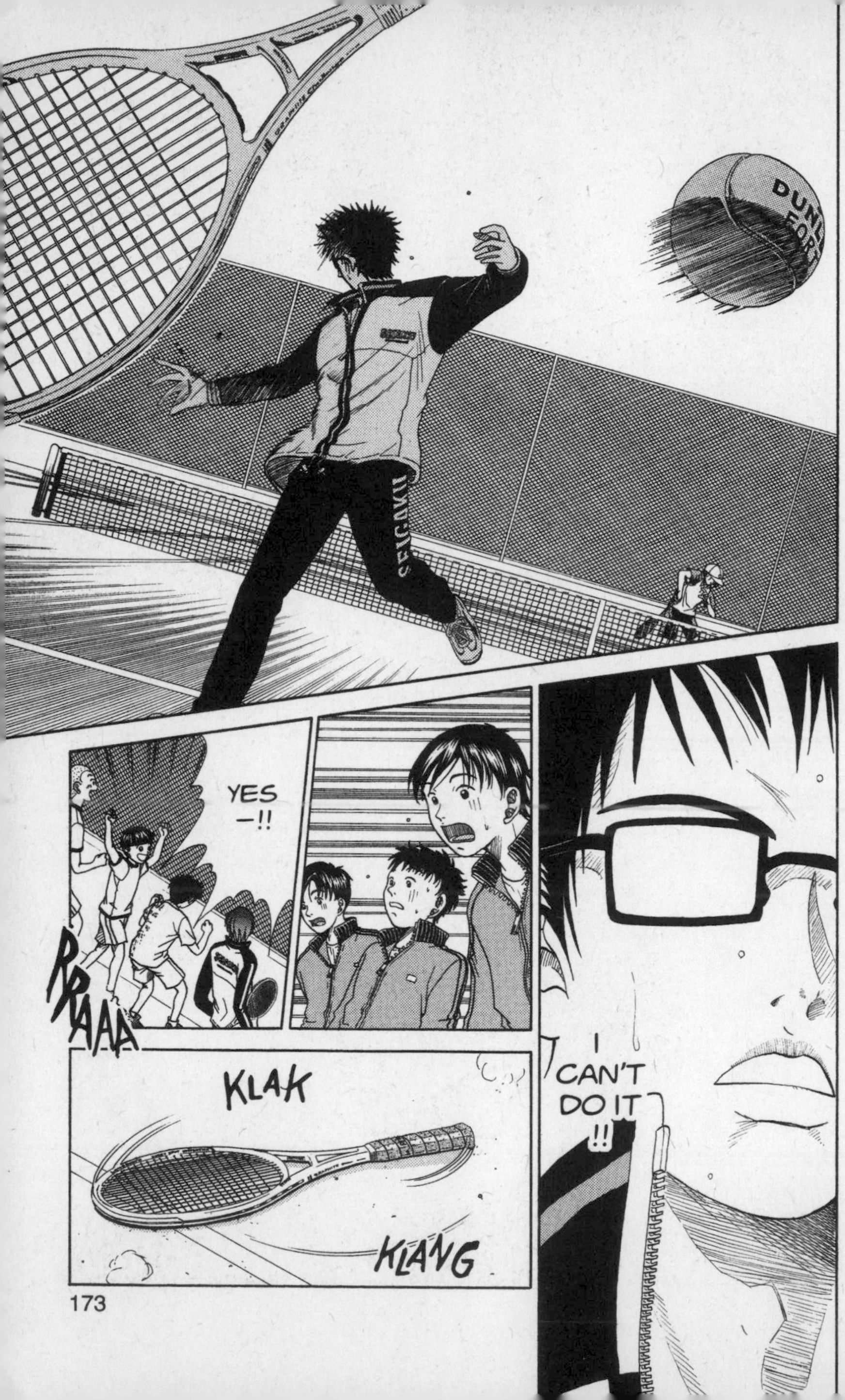
I CAN'T DO IT!!
YES—!!
RRAAAA
KLAK
KLANG

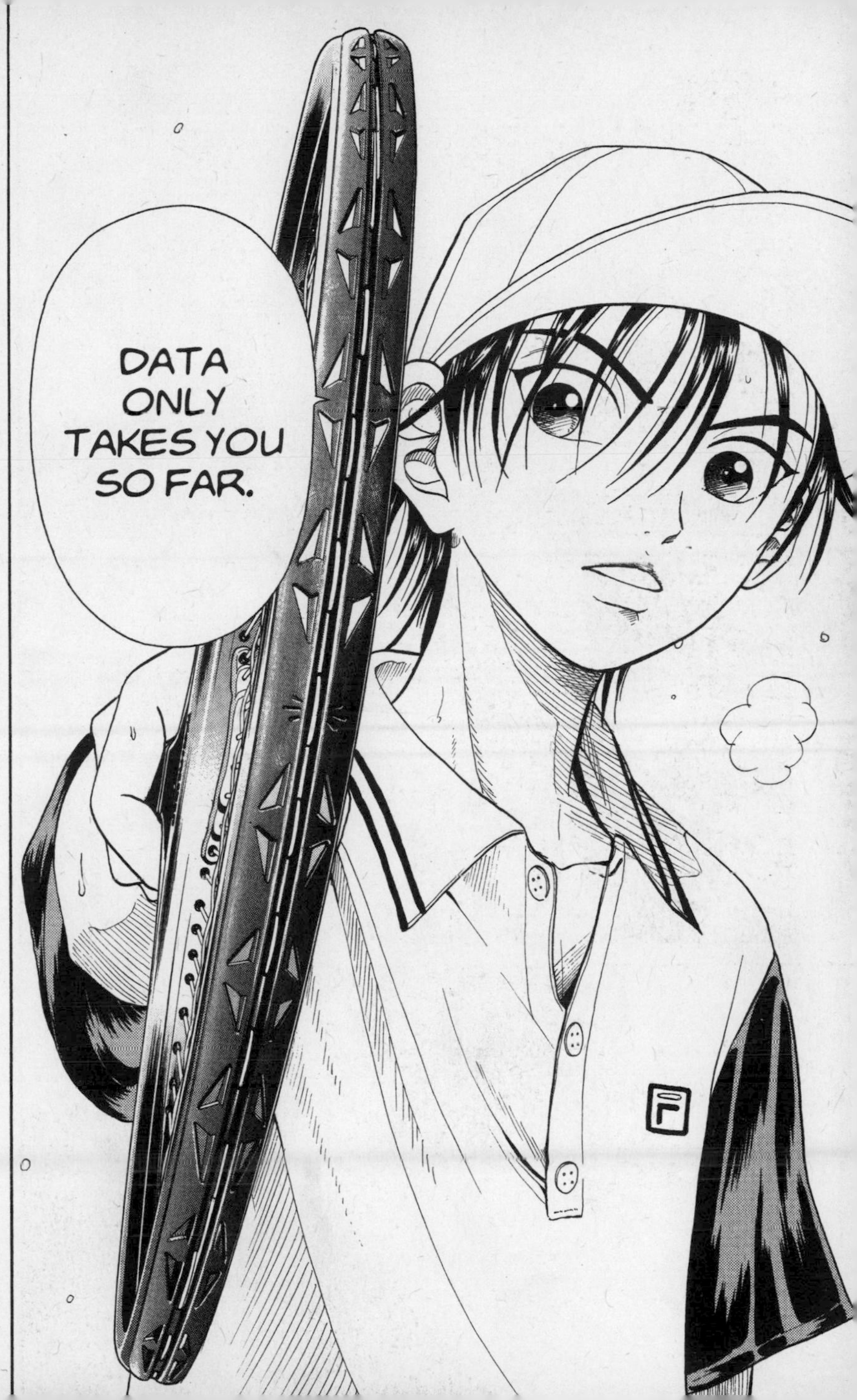
DATA ONLY TAKES YOU SO FAR.

READ THIS WAY

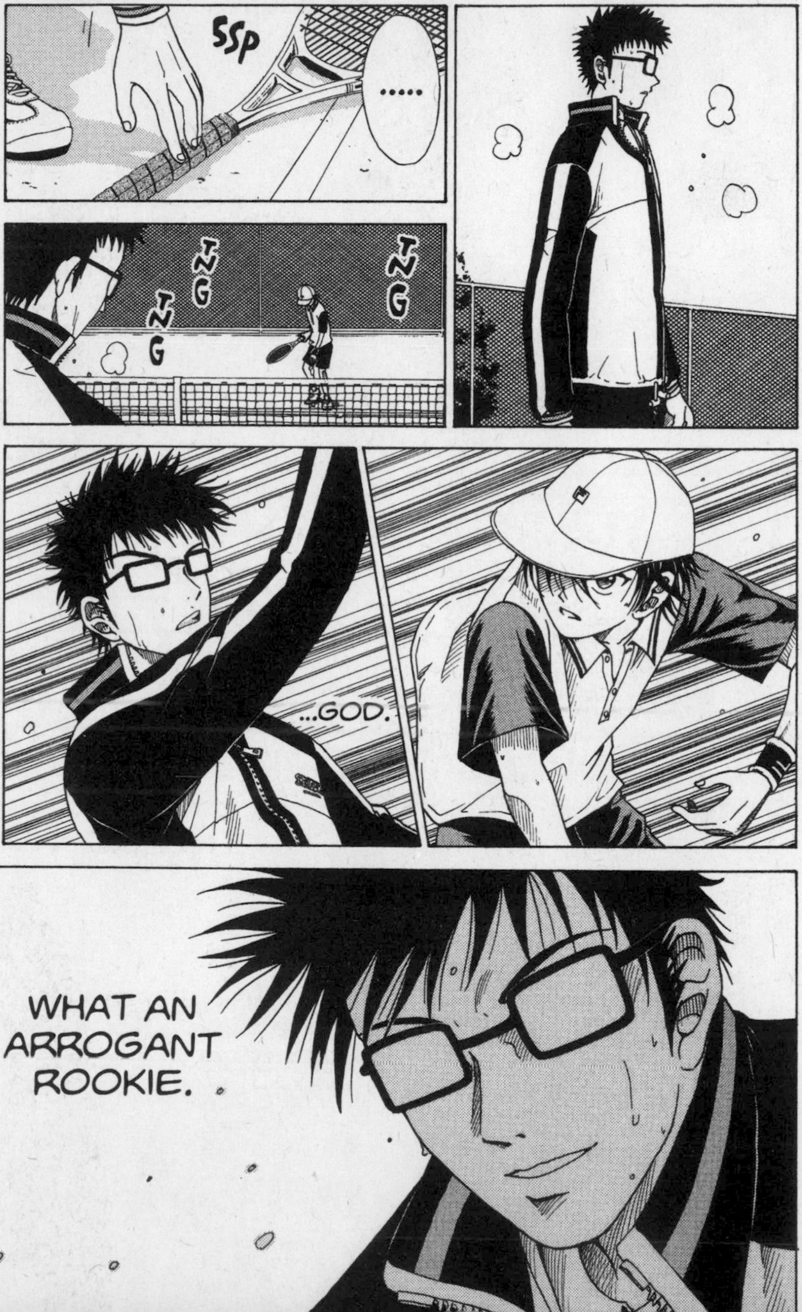
SSP
......
TNG
TNG
TNG
...GOD.
WHAT AN ARROGANT ROOKIE.

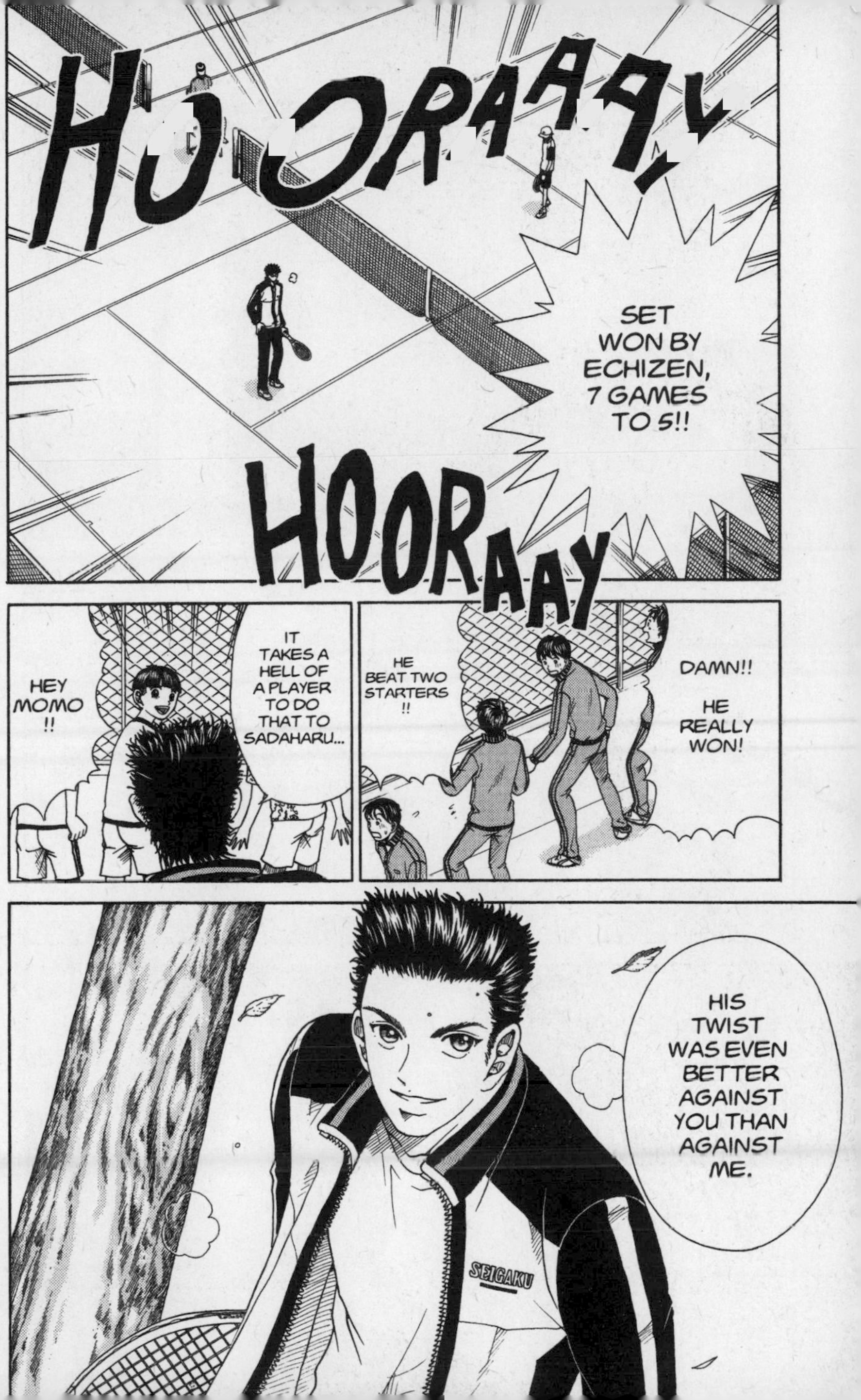
HOORAAAY
SET WON BY ECHIZEN, 7 GAMES TO 5!!
HOORAAY
DAMN!!
HE REALLY WON!
HE BEAT TWO STARTERS!!
IT TAKES A HELL OF A PLAYER TO DO THAT TO SADAHARU...
HEY MOMO!!
HIS TWIST WAS EVEN BETTER AGAINST YOU THAN AGAINST ME.
SEIGAKU

READ THIS WAY

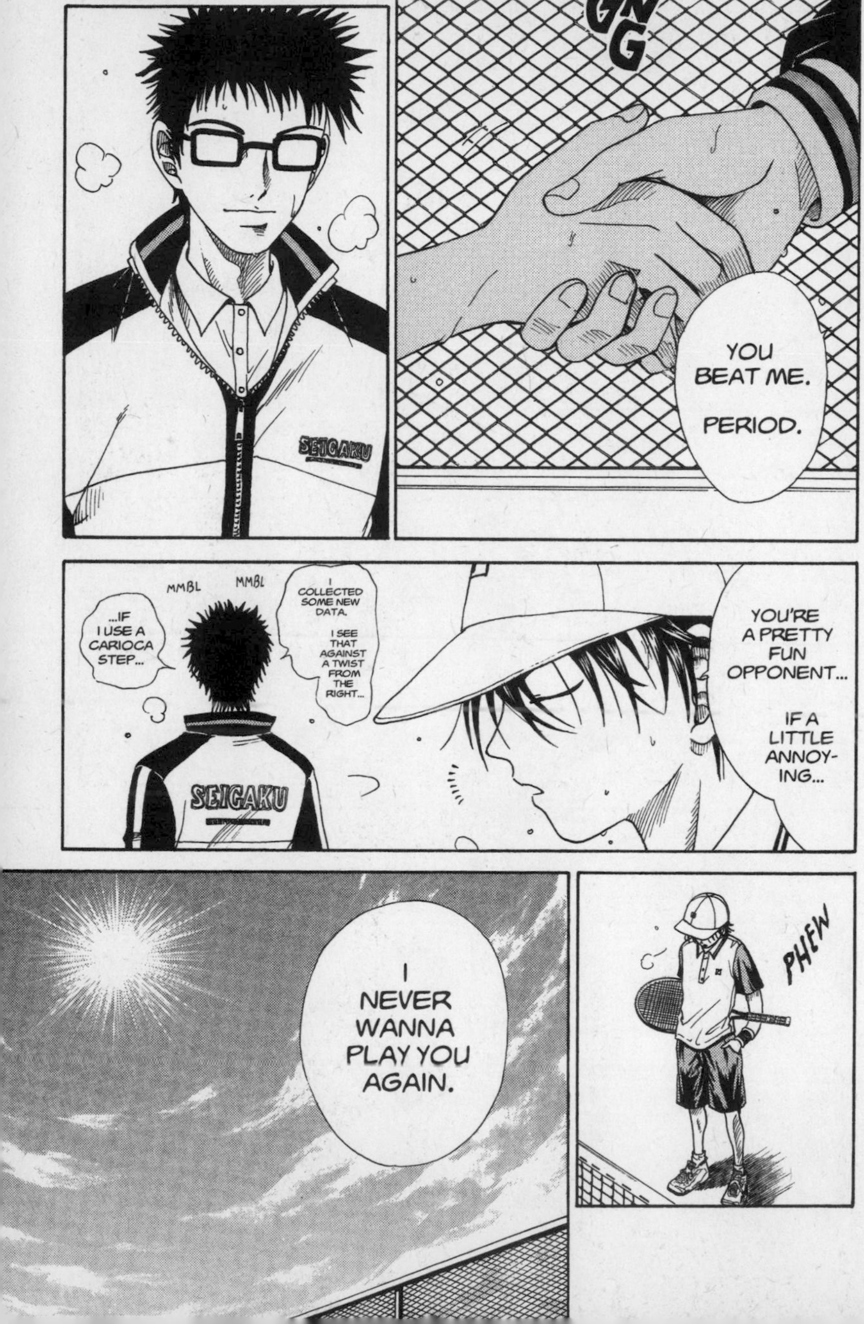
GNG
YOU BEAT ME.
PERIOD.
YOU'RE A PRETTY FUN OPPONENT...
IF A LITTLE ANNOY-ING...
I COLLECTED SOME NEW DATA.
I SEE THAT AGAINST A TWIST FROM THE RIGHT...
MMBL MMBL
...IF I USE A CARIOCA STEP...
PHEW
I NEVER WANNA PLAY YOU AGAIN.

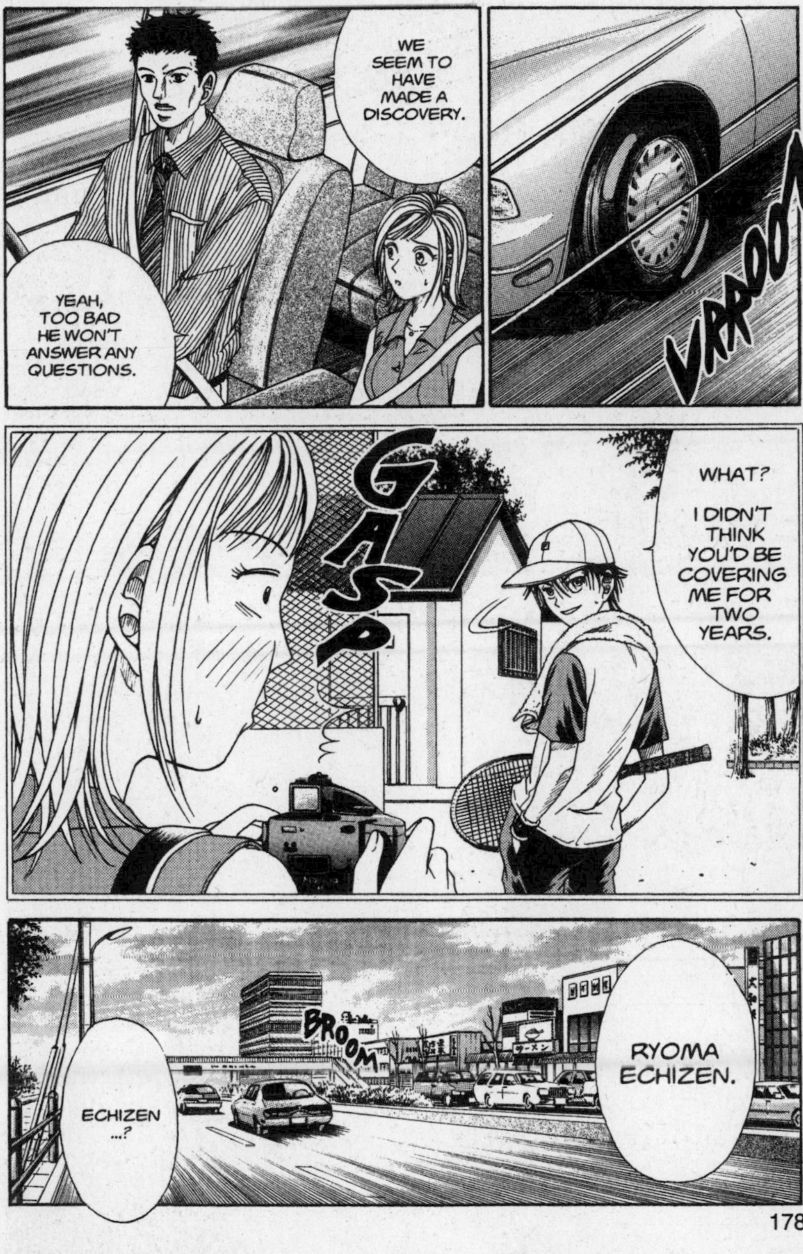
VRROOM
WE SEEM TO HAVE MADE A DISCOVERY.
YEAH, TOO BAD HE WON'T ANSWER ANY QUESTIONS.
WHAT? I DIDN'T THINK YOU'D BE COVERING ME FOR TWO YEARS.
GASP
RYOMA ECHIZEN.
BROOM
ECHIZEN ...?

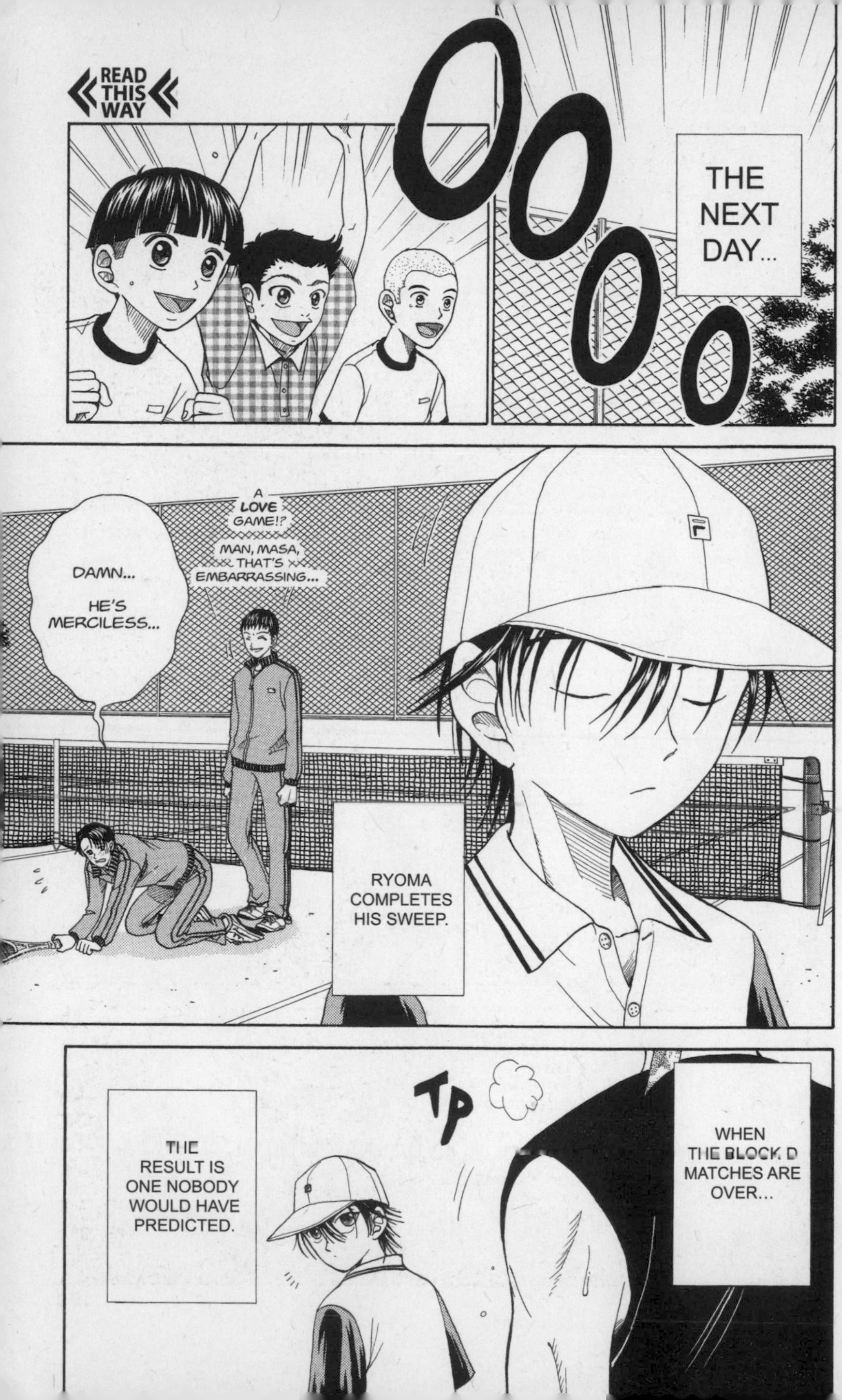
READ THIS WAY
THE NEXT DAY...
OOOOO
A LOVE GAME!?
MAN, MASA, THAT'S EMBARRASSING...
DAMN... HE'S MERCILESS...
RYOMA COMPLETES HIS SWEEP.
WHEN THE BLOCK D MATCHES ARE OVER...
TP
THE RESULT IS ONE NOBODY WOULD HAVE PREDICTED.

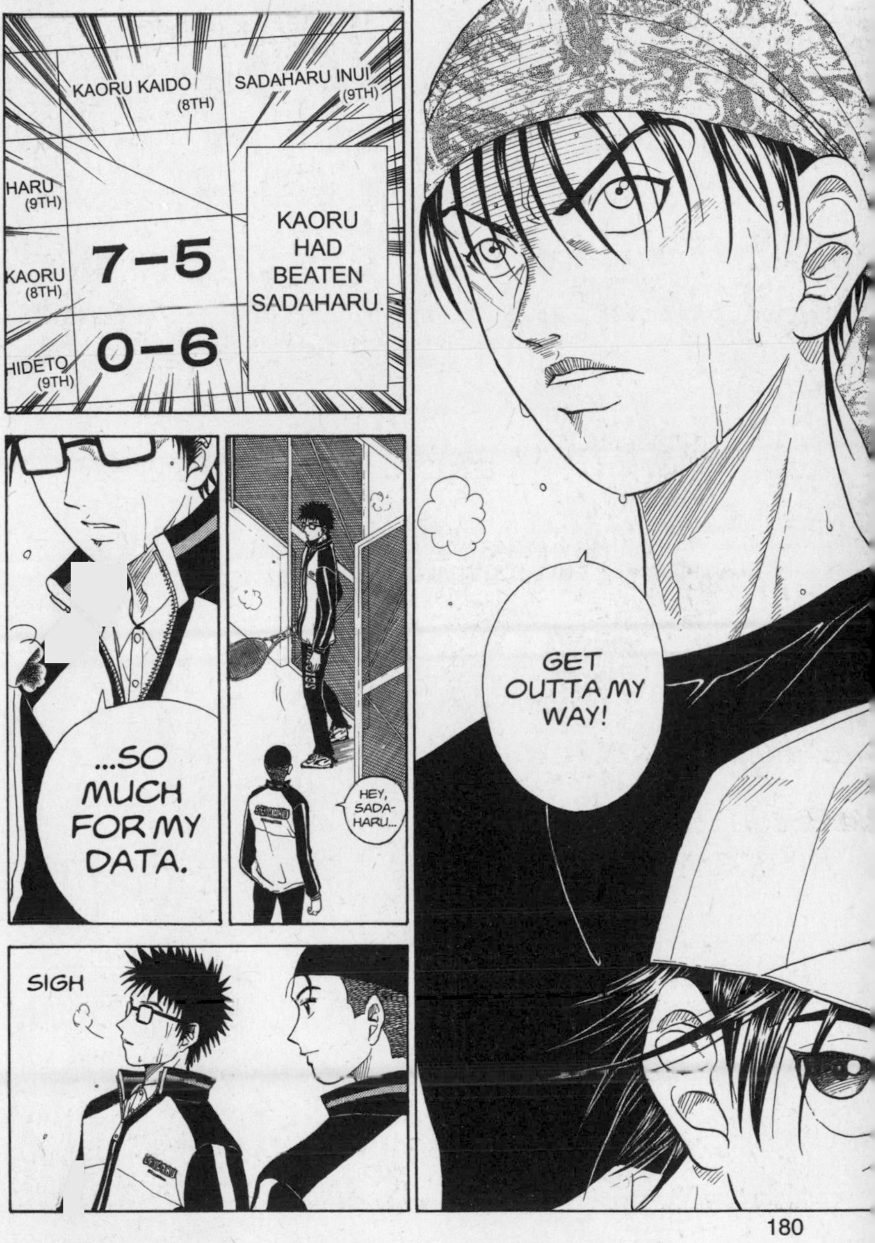
GET OUTTA MY WAY!
SADAHARU INUI (9TH)
KAORU KAIDO (8TH)
KAORU HAD BEATEN SADAHARU.
HARU (9TH)
7–5
KAORU (8TH)
0–6
HIDETO (9TH)
HEY, SADA-HARU...
...SO MUCH FOR MY DATA.
SIGH

READ THIS WAY

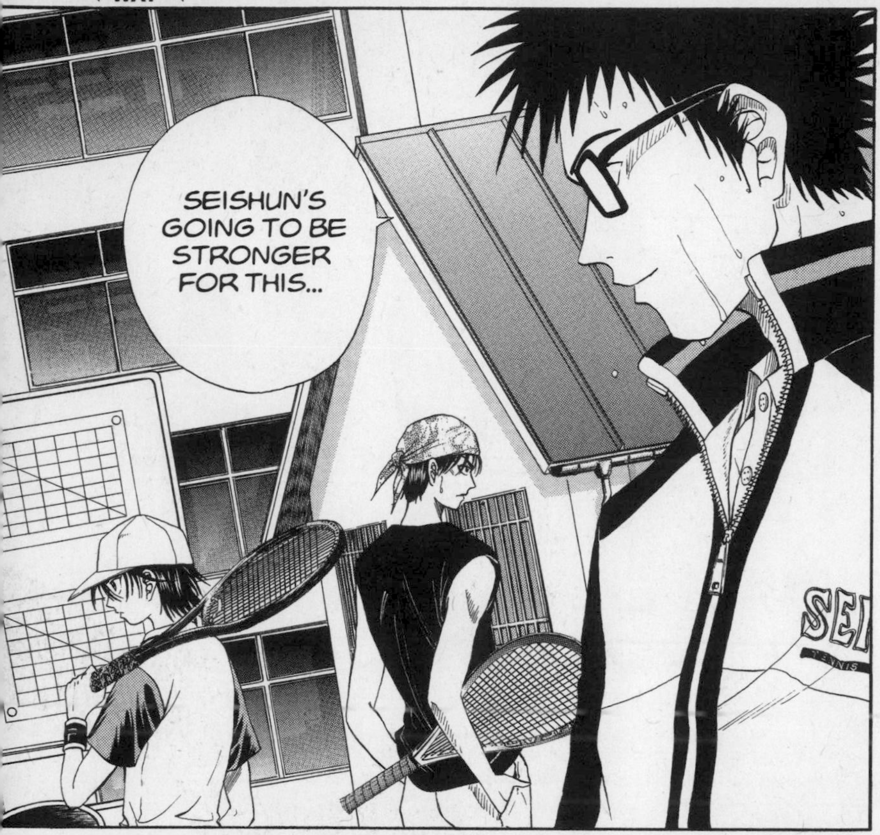
SEISHUN'S GOING TO BE STRONGER FOR THIS...

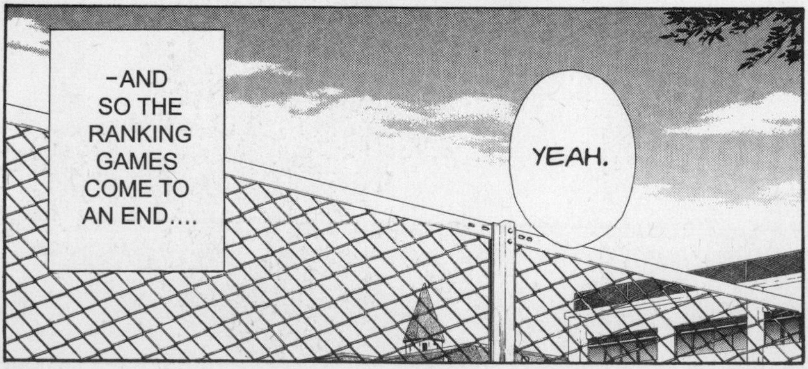
YEAH.
-AND SO THE RANKING GAMES COME TO AN END....

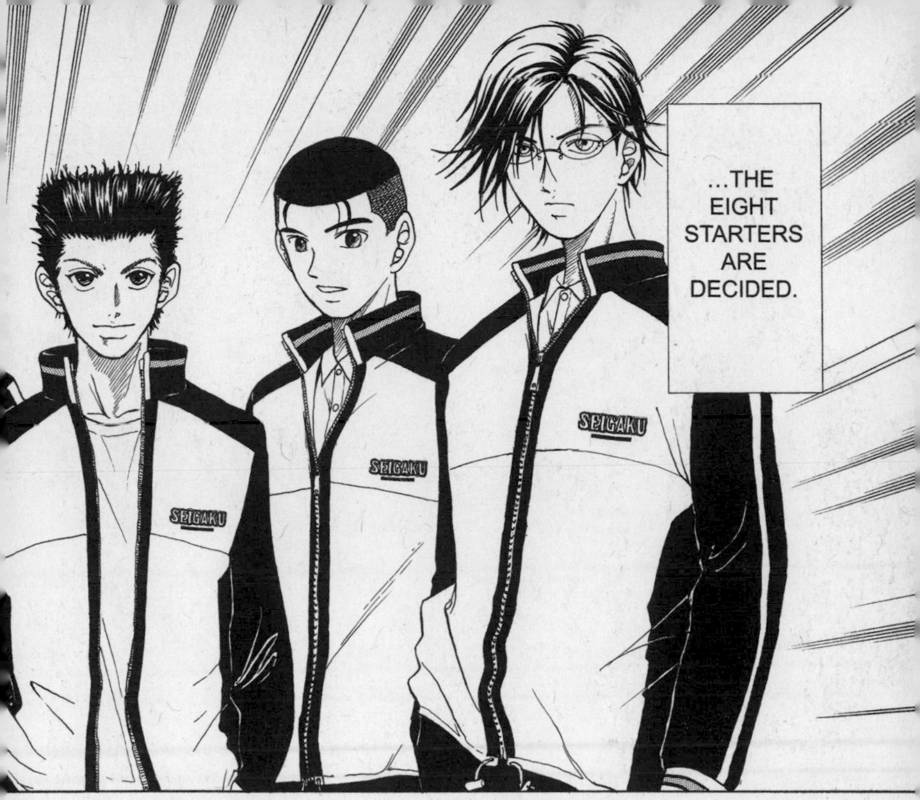
...THE EIGHT STARTERS ARE DECIDED.

SHUICHIRO OISHI (9TH)

KUNIMITSU TEZUKA (9TH)

ESHI MOMOSHIRO (8TH)

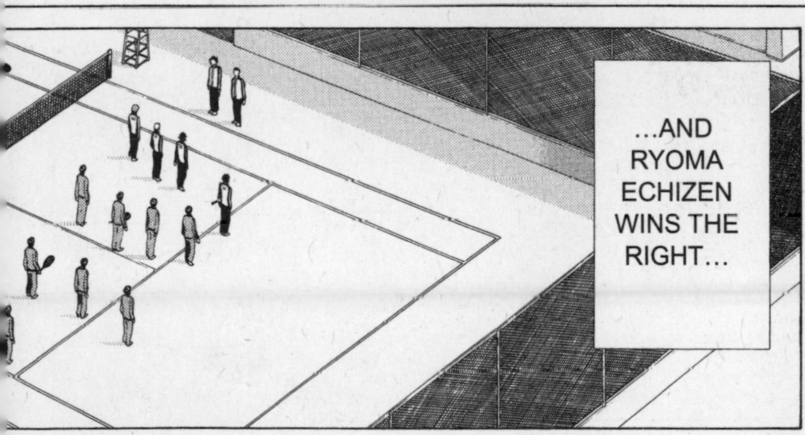
...AND RYOMA ECHIZEN WINS THE RIGHT...

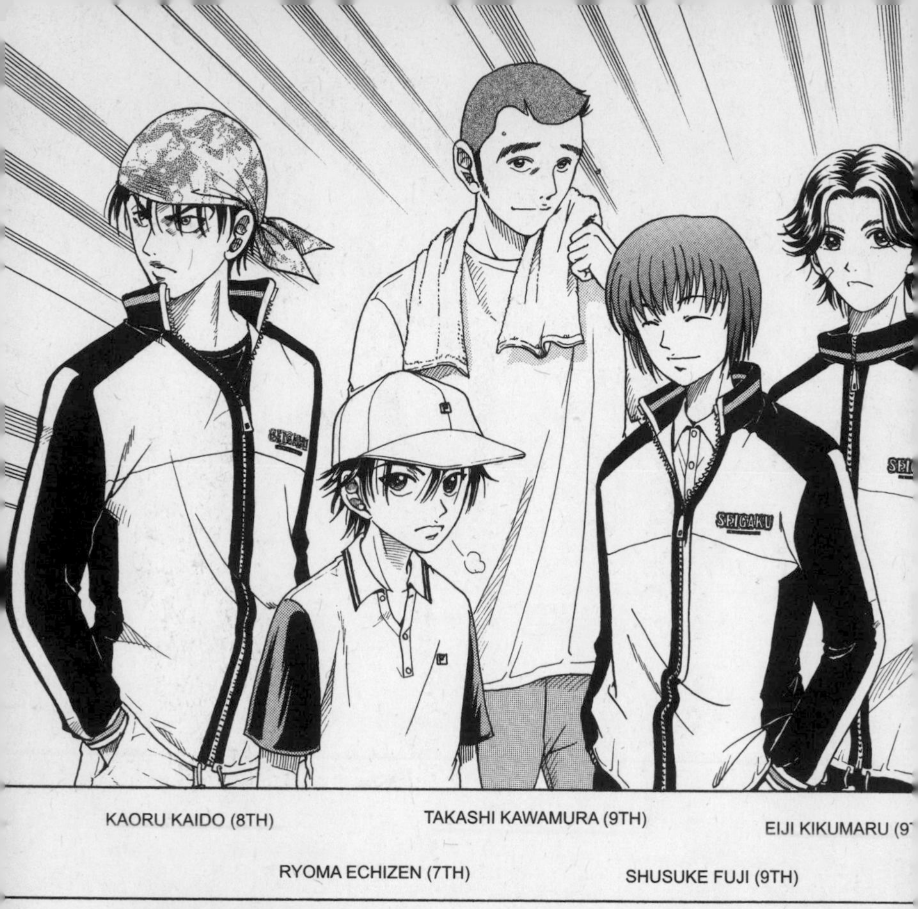
EIJI KIKUMARU (9
SHUSUKE FUJI (9TH)
TAKASHI KAWAMURA (9TH)
RYOMA ECHIZEN (7TH)
KAORU KAIDO (8TH)

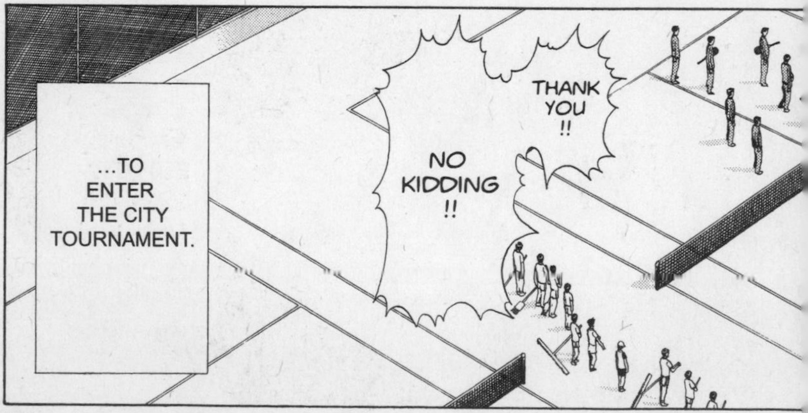
THANK YOU !!
NO KIDDING !!
...TO ENTER THE CITY TOURNAMENT.

TO BE CONTINUED IN VOL. 3

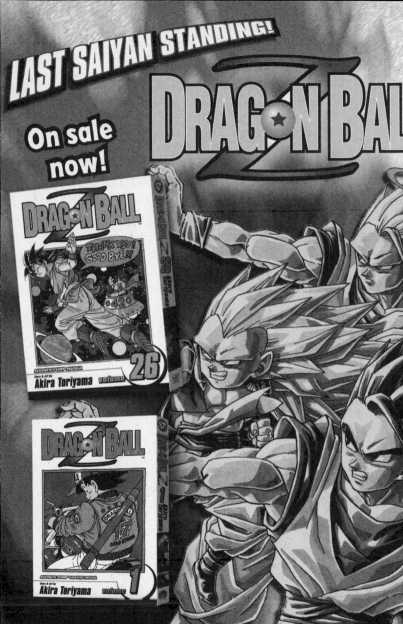

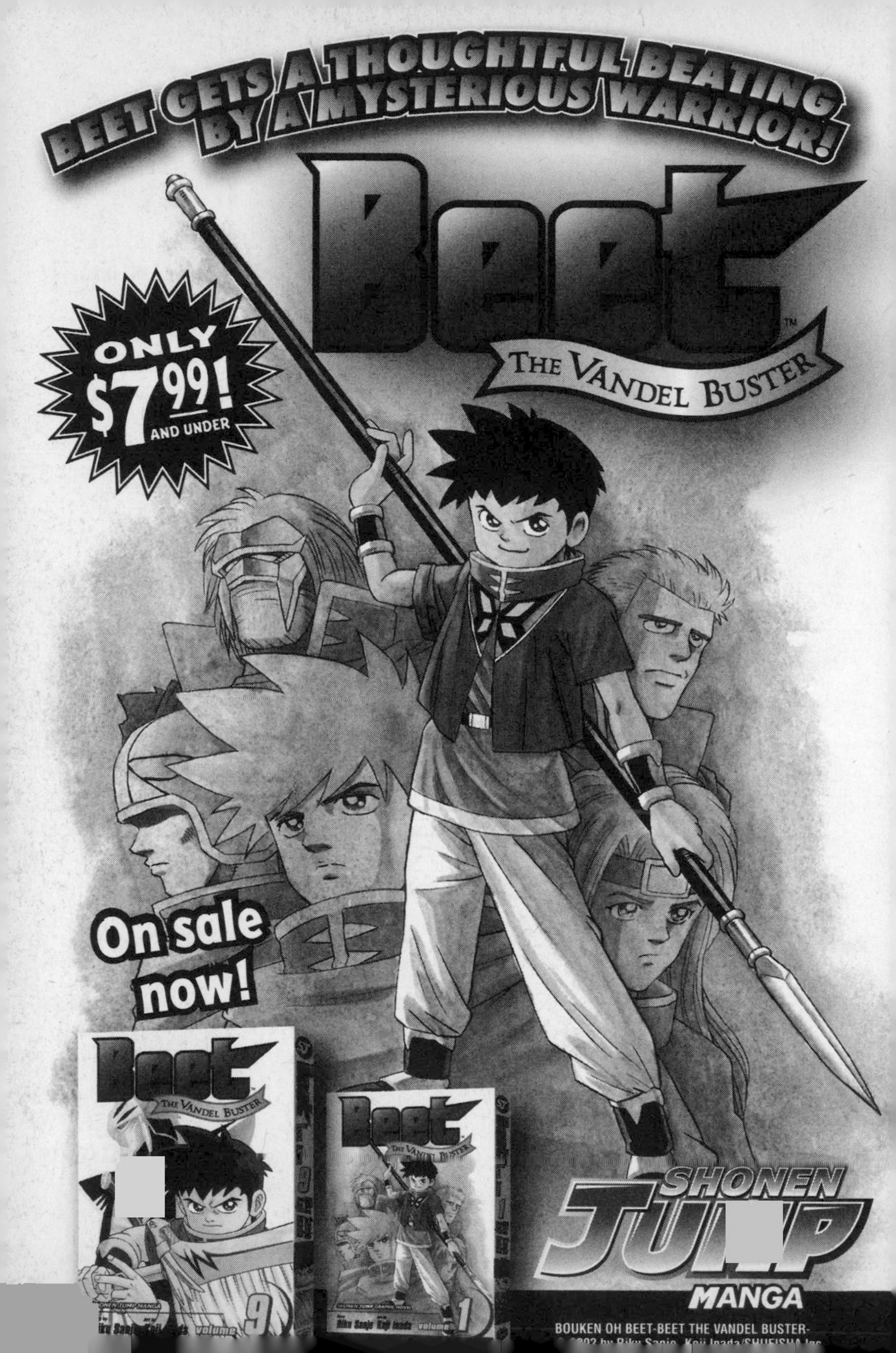

BEET GETS A THOUGHTFUL BEATING BY A MYSTERIOUS WARRIOR!
Beet™ THE VANDEL BUSTER
ONLY $7.99! AND UNDER
On sale now!
SHONEN JUMP MANGA
BOUKEN OH BEET-BEET THE VANDEL BUSTER-

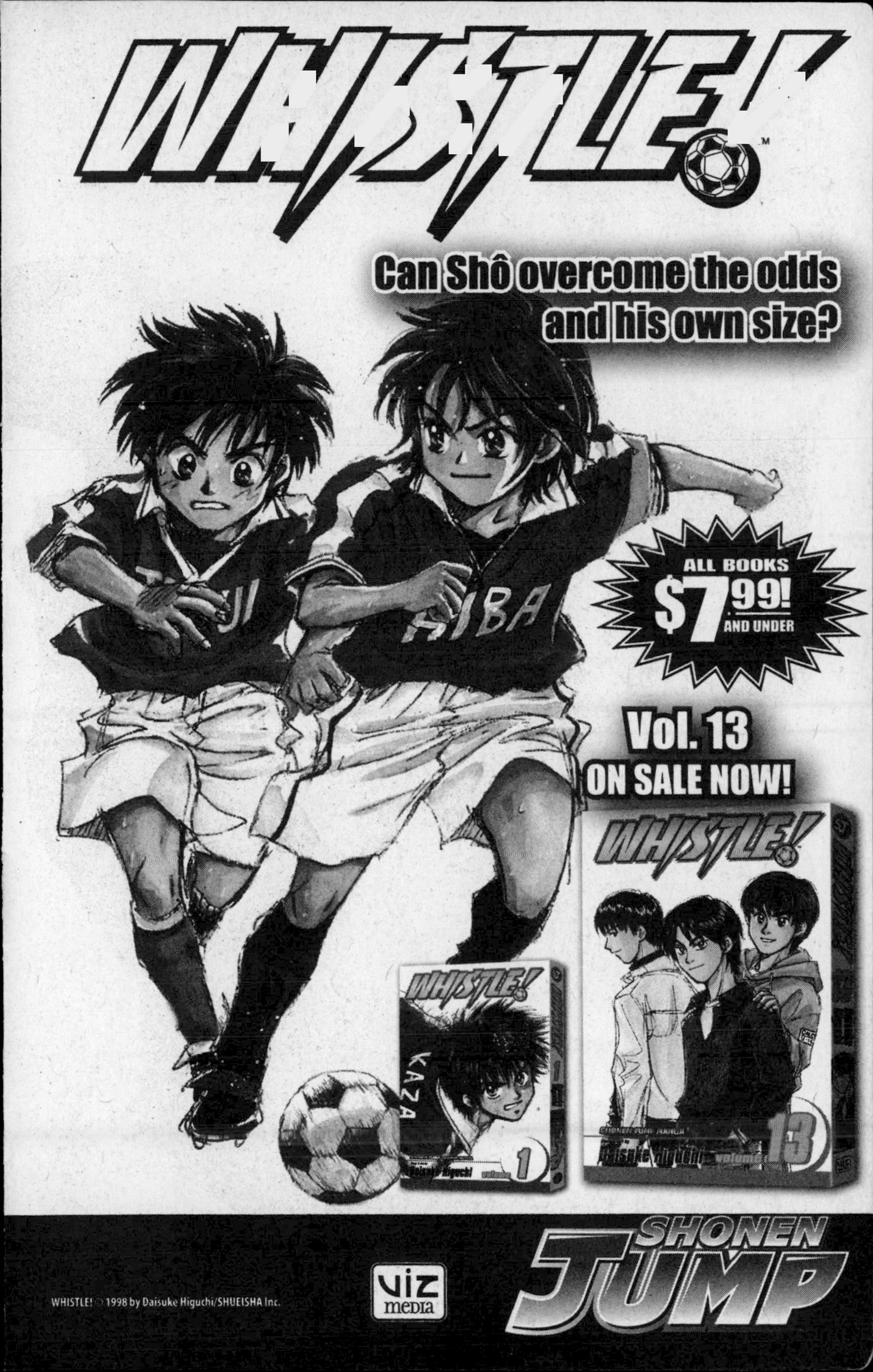
WHISTLE!™
Can Shô overcome the odds and his own size?
ALL BOOKS $7.99! AND UNDER
Vol. 13 ON SALE NOW!
WHISTLE!
WHISTLE!
Daisuke Higuchi volume 1
Daisuke Higuchi volume 13
SHONEN JUMP
viz media
WHISTLE! © 1998 by Daisuke Higuchi/SHUEISHA Inc.

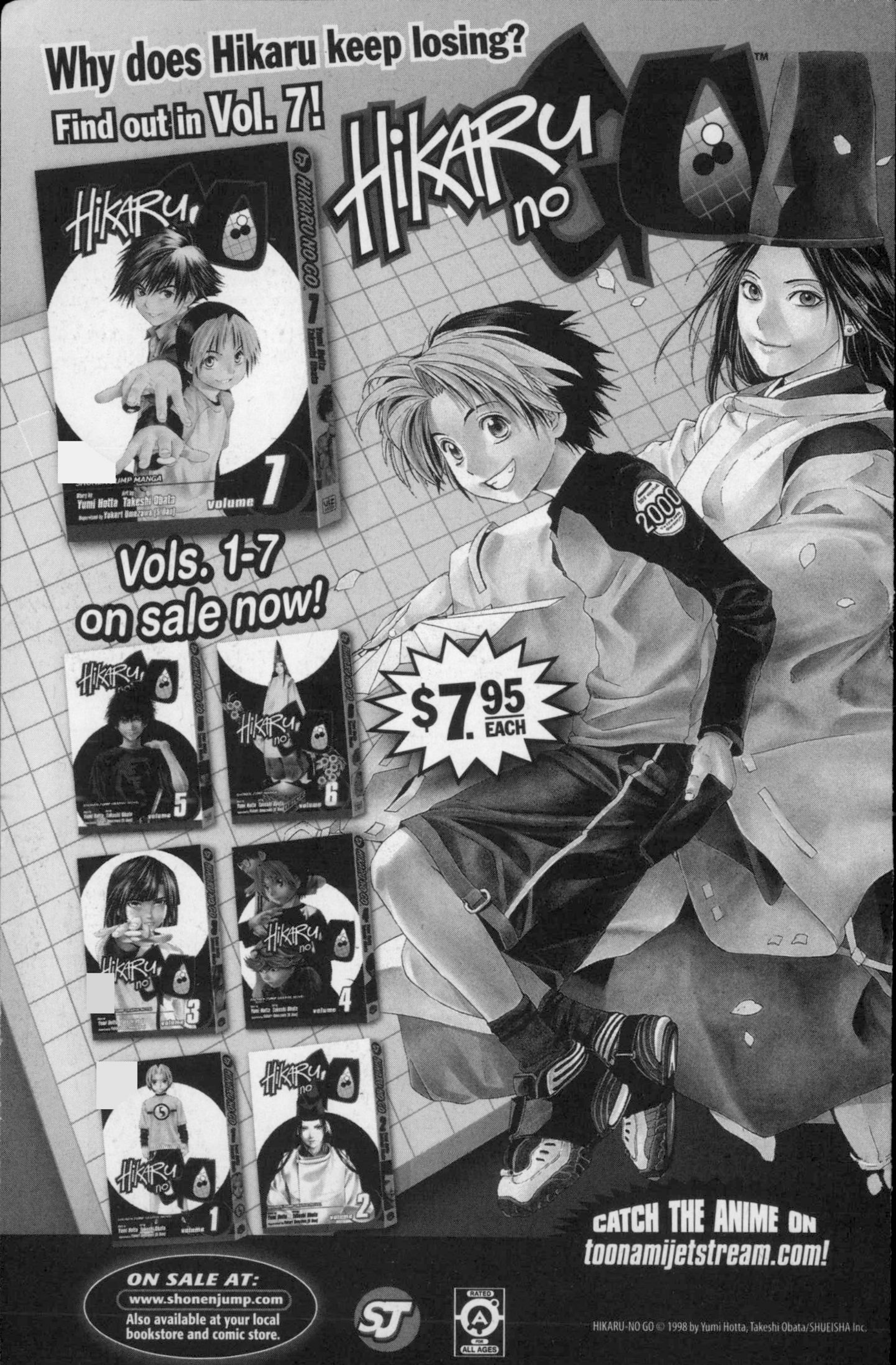

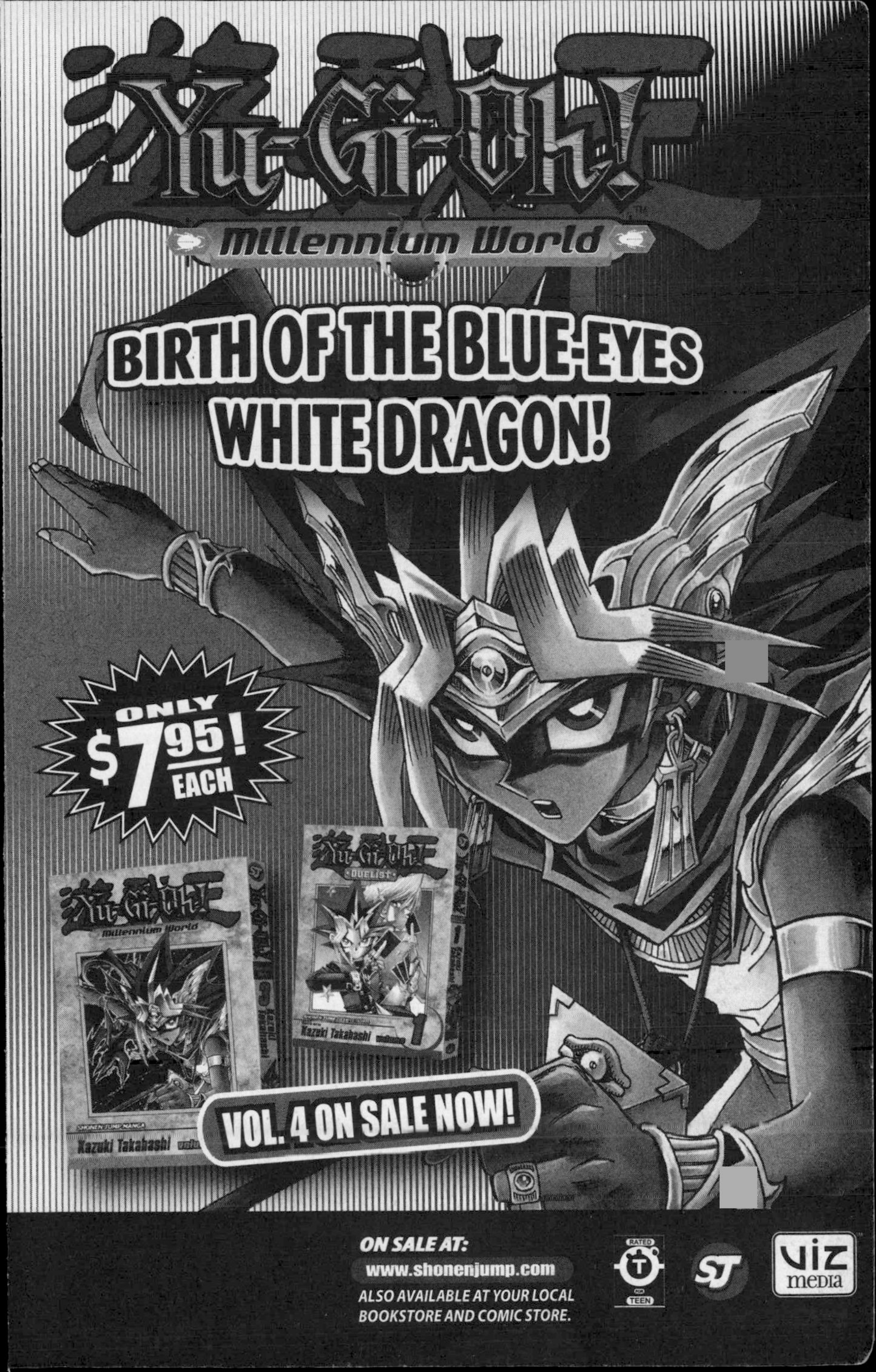

YU-GI-OH!
Millennium World
BIRTH OF THE BLUE-EYES WHITE DRAGON!
ONLY $7.95! EACH
VOL. 4 ON SALE NOW!
Kazuki Takahashi
ON SALE AT:
www.shonenjump.com
ALSO AVAILABLE AT YOUR LOCAL BOOKSTORE AND COMIC STORE.
RATED T TEEN
SJ
viz media

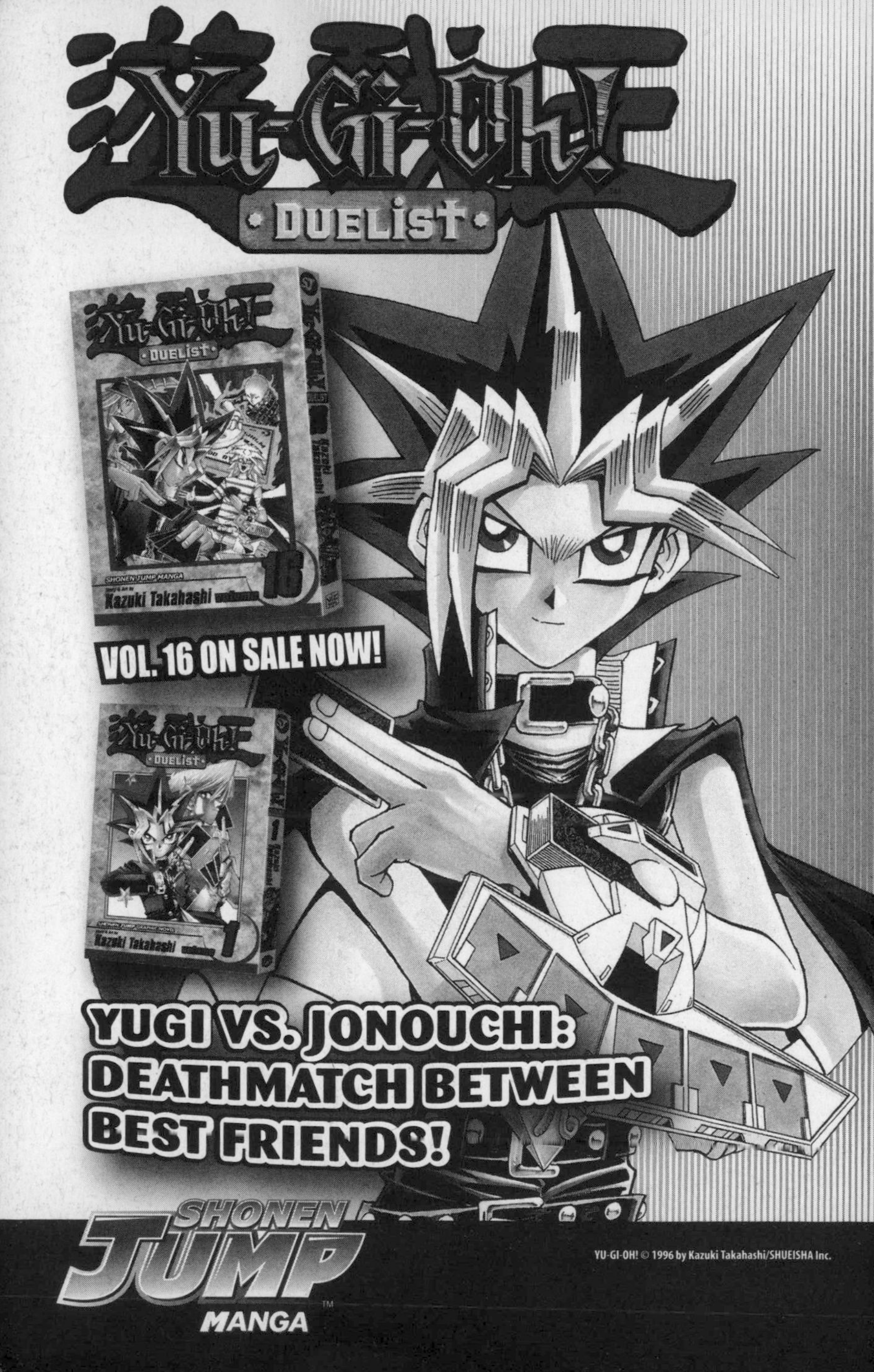
YU-GI-OH!
DUELIST
VOL. 16 ON SALE NOW!
YUGI VS. JONOUCHI: DEATHMATCH BETWEEN BEST FRIENDS!
SHONEN JUMP MANGA
YU-GI-OH! © 1996 by Kazuki Takahashi/SHUEISHA Inc.

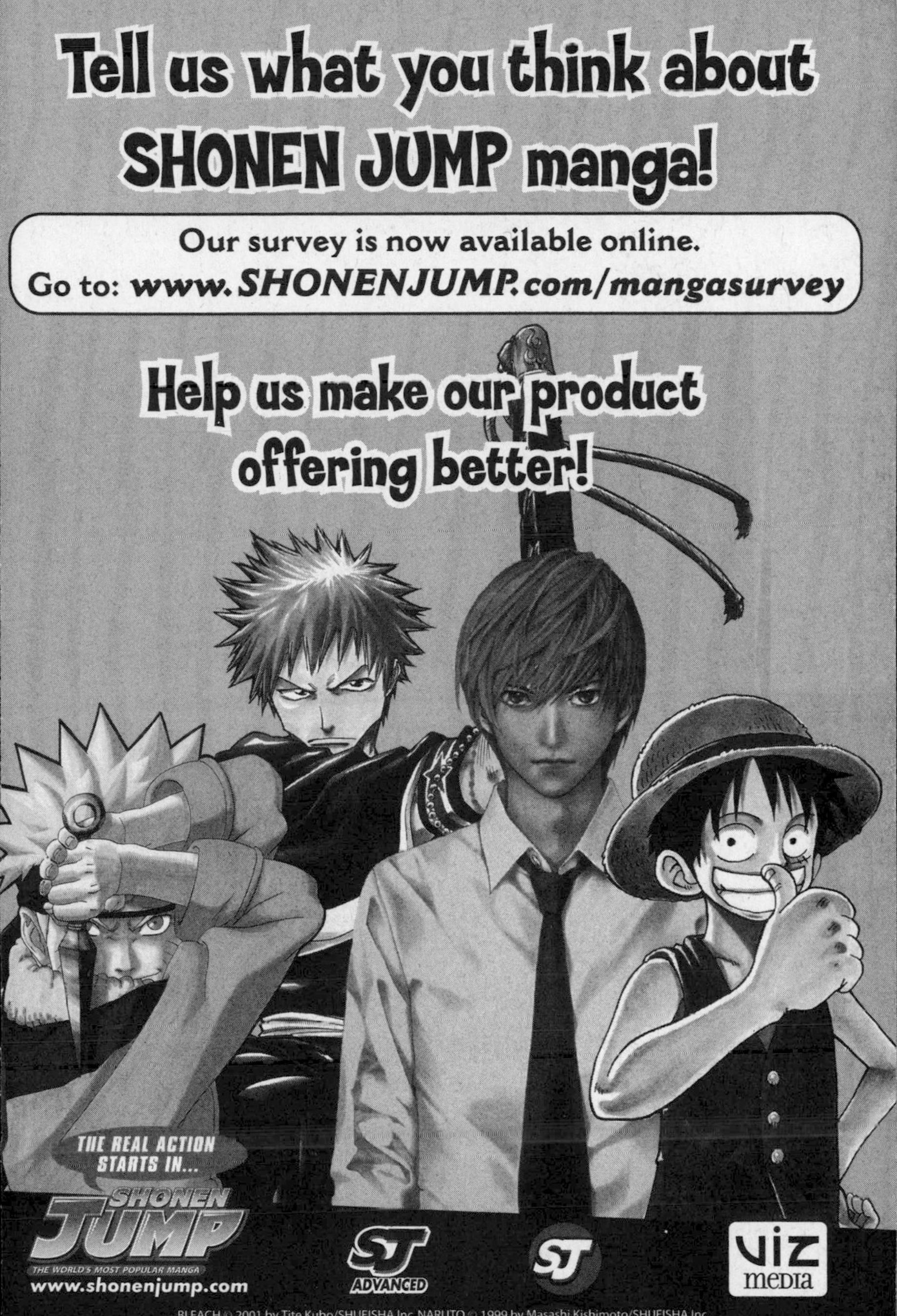
Tell us what you think about SHONEN JUMP manga!
Our survey is now available online.
Go to: www.SHONENJUMP.com/mangasurvey
Help us make our product offering better!
THE REAL ACTION STARTS IN...
SHONEN JUMP
THE WORLD'S MOST POPULAR MANGA
www.shonenjump.com
SJ ADVANCED
SJ
VIZ media

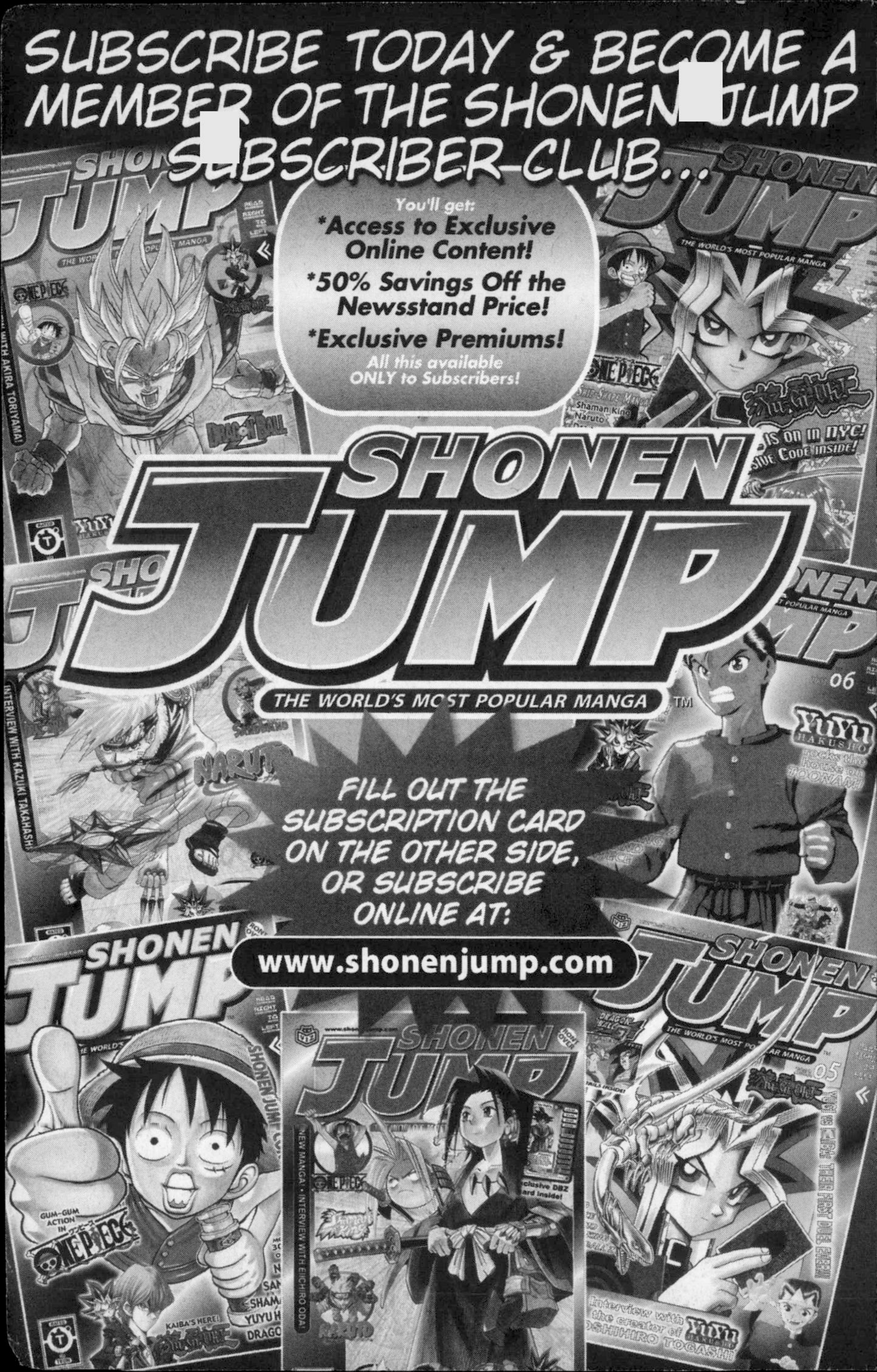
SUBSCRIBE TODAY & BECOME A MEMBER OF THE SHONEN JUMP SUBSCRIBER CLUB...
You'll get:
*Access to Exclusive Online Content!
*50% Savings Off the Newsstand Price!
*Exclusive Premiums!
All this available ONLY to Subscribers!
SHONEN JUMP
THE WORLD'S MOST POPULAR MANGA™
FILL OUT THE SUBSCRIPTION CARD ON THE OTHER SIDE, OR SUBSCRIBE ONLINE AT:
www.shonenjump.com